Lecture Notes in Artificial Intellig

Edited by R. Goebel, J. Siekmann, and W. Wal

Subseries of Lecture Notes in Computer Science

Stefano Carpin   Itsuki Noda
Enrico Pagello   Monica Reggiani
Oskar von Stryk (Eds.)

Simulation, Modeling, and Programming for Autonomous Robots

First International Conference, SIMPAR 2008
Venice, Italy, November 3-7, 2008
Proceedings

 Springer

Series Editors

Randy Goebel, University of Alberta, Edmonton, Canada
Jörg Siekmann, University of Saarland, Saarbrücken, Germany
Wolfgang Wahlster, DFKI and University of Saarland, Saarbrücken, Germany

Volume Editors

Stefano Carpin
University of California–Merced, Merced, CA, USA
E-mail: scarpin@ucmerced.edu

Itsuki Noda
AIST, Information Technology Research Institute, Tsukuba, Japan
E-mail: i.noda@aist.go.jp

Enrico Pagello
University of Padua, Padova, Italy
E-mail: epv@dei.unipd.it

Monica Reggiani
University of Padua, Vicenza, Italy
E-mail: monica.reggiani@unipd.it

Oskar von Stryk
Technische Universität Darmstadt, Darmstadt, Germany
E-mail: stryk@sim.tu-darmstadt.de

Library of Congress Control Number: 2008937919

CR Subject Classification (1998): I.2.9-11, I.2.6, I.6, F.1.1-2, K.4.3, H.5

LNCS Sublibrary: SL 7 – Artificial Intelligence

ISSN   0302-9743
ISBN-10   3-540-89075-0 Springer Berlin Heidelberg New York
ISBN-13   978-3-540-89075-1 Springer Berlin Heidelberg New York

Springer is a part of Springer Science+Business Media

springer.com

© Springer-Verlag Berlin Heidelberg 2008

Typesetting: Camera-ready by author, data conversion by Scientific Publishing Services, Chennai, India
Printed on acid-free paper   SPIN: 12561513   06/3180   5 4 3 2 1 0

Preface

The First International Conference on Simulation, Modeling, and Programming for Autonomous Robots (SIMPAR 2008) was held during November 3-6, 2008, in Venice, at Telecom Future Center, with a special session held in Padua, in the Archivio Antico of the university.

The SIMPAR Conference was promoted to offer to a selected number of researchers the possibility to discuss, in a highly stimulating atmosphere, how to identify and solve the key issues necessary to ease the development of robot software, and boost a smooth shifting of results from simulation to real applications.

Novel robotics applications driven by society and industry call for the development of systems of ever-increasing complexity. Systems with sliding autonomy, humanoid robots, distributed robots, and mobile sensor networks are just a few examples of this exciting area. But unfortunately, steady improvements in robot hardware have not been matched by corresponding advancements in robot software. Besides fundamental open problems still waiting for sound answers, the lack of broadly accepted and reusable development tools, libraries, standards, and algorithms is one of the main technological obstacles towards the efficient development of this new generation of robotics applications.

Hence, simulation environments able to replicate a robot's sensing and motion abilities and their interaction with the physical world are playing an essential role in reducing the development time and cost of large-scale autonomous systems. Notwithstanding, their use is still regarded by many as suspicious. Seamless migration of code from general-purpose simulators to real-world systems is still a rare circumstance, due to the complexity of robot, world, sensors, and actuators modeling. The above challenges drive the quest for next-generation development methods in robotics. We are convinced that SIMPAR has succeeded in giving a first answer to this search, and it can be followed by proper scientific and engineering actions in the near future.

This book collects 29 papers that were presented orally in Venice, selected among a total of 42 that were submitted to the main single-track conference. Seven papers address methodologies and environments of robot simulation, 11 refer to methodologies about autonomous robot programming and middleware, and 11 describe applications and case studies. Each submitted paper received at least two reviews by the members of a carefully selected international Program Committee.

In addition, to enlarge the scientific attention towards particularly challenging environments, six workshops were offered: The Universe of RoboCup Simulators; Standards and Common Platforms for Robotics; Omnidirectional Robot Vision; Mini and Micro UAV for Security and Surveillance; Brain–Computer Interface; and Teaching with Robotics. Papers presented at these workshops were collected in a CD-ROM edited separately, by Emanuele Menegatti. A Tutorial on USARSim/MOAST was kindly offered by Stephen Balakirsky from the National Institute of Standards and Technology. Two invited talks were also given in Venice at the opening, by Herman Bruyninckx and Yoshi Nakamura, while Hiroshi Ishiguro and Giulio Sandini gave invited talks in Padua, at a special session organized on New Perspectives on Humanoids Research.

We want to gratefully thank Telecom Future Center for offering such a beautiful ancient location, in the heart of the city of Venice. We also express our gratitude to the Program Committee members and all other supporters, organizers, and volunteers who contributed in making SIMPAR possible. Without their effort, it would not have been possible to run SIMPAR!

November 2008

Stefano Carpin
Itsuki Noda
Enrico Pagello
Monica Reggiani
Oskar von Stryk

Organization

Executive Committee

General Chair	Enrico Pagello (University of Padua, Italy)
International Program Co-chairs	
America	Stefano Carpin (University of California, Merced, USA)
Asia	Itsuki Noda (AIST, Japan)
Europe	Oskar von Stryk (Technische Universität Darmstadt, Germany)
Local Chair	Monica Reggiani (University of Padua, Italy)
Workshop Chair	Emanuele Menegatti (University of Padua, Italy)
Tutorial Chair	Antonio Cisternino (University of Pisa, Italy)
Award Chair	Paolo Fiorini (University of Verona, Italy)

Steering Committee

Hans-Dieter Burkhard	Humboldt University, Berlin, Germany
Maria Gini	University of Minnesota at Minneapolis, USA
Tamio Arai	The University of Tokyo, Japan

Program Committee

America

Steve Balakirsky	NIST, USA
Joseph Fernando	Microsoft Research, USA
Andrew Howard	Jet Propulsion Laboratory, USA
Mike Lewis	University of Pittsburgh, USA
Michael Quinlan	University of Texas at Austin, USA
Luis Sentis	Stanford University, USA
Bill Smart	Washington University in St. Louis, USA
Richard Vaughan	Simon Fraser University, Canada

Asia

Noriaki Ando	AIST, Japan
Joschka Boedecker	Osaka University, Japan
XiaoPing Chen	University of Science and Technology of China
Hyungsuck Cho	KAIST, Korea
Takayuki Kanda	ATR Intelligent Robotics & Communication Labs, Japan

Mohammed Jarrah	American University of Sharjah, UAE
Alexei Makarenko	Australian Centre for Field Robotics, USYD, Australia
Takashi Minato	Osaka University, Japan
Oliver Obst	CSIRO, Sydney, Australia
Jun Ota	University of Tokyo, Japan
Masaki Takahashi	Keio University, Japan
Ryuichi Ueda	The University of Tokyo, Japan
Changjiu Zhou	Singapore Polytechnic

Europe

Rachid Alami	LAAS/CNRS, France
Davide Brugali	University of Bergamo, Italy
Sven Behnke	University of Bonn, Germany
Berthold Baeuml	DLR/Institute of Robotics and Mechatronics, Germany
Andreas Birk	Jacobs University Bremen, Germany
Antonio Chella	University of Palermo, Italy
Alessandro Farinelli	University of Southampton, UK
Giuseppina Gini	Politecnico di Milano, Italy
Frans Groen	University of Amsterdam, The Netherlands
Martin Huelse	University of Wales, UK
Luca Iocchi	University of Rome "La Sapienza", Italy
Alexander Kleiner	Albert-Ludwigs-Universität Freiburg, Germany
Gerhard Kraetzschmar	FH Bonn-Rhein-Sieg, Germany
Pedro Lima	Lisbon Technical University, Portugal
Olivier Michel	Cyberbotics, Switzerland
Rezia Molfino	University of Genoa, Italy
Mohan Sridharan	University of Birmingham, UK
Antonio Sgorbissa	University of Genoa, Italy

Additional Reviewers

F. Dalla Libera	N. Greggio	M. Sridharan
C. Dornhege	B. MacDonald	K. Tatsuno
J. Gaspar	M. Sartori	T. Tsubouchi
V. Gazi	Z. Song	

Sponsoring Institutions

Telecom Italia, Italy
Department of Information Engineering, University of Padua, Italy
Istituto di Ingegneria Biomedica del CNR, Padua, Italy
University of Padua, Italy

Table of Contents

Programming

Applications

Simulation, Modeling and Programming for Autonomous Robots: The Open Source Perspective

Herman Bruyninckx

Katholieke Universiteit Leuven
Department of Mechanical Engineering
Celestijnenlaan 300B
B3001 Leuven
Belgium
http://people.mech.kuleuven.be/~bruyninc
http://www.mech.kuleuven.be/robotics/acm/

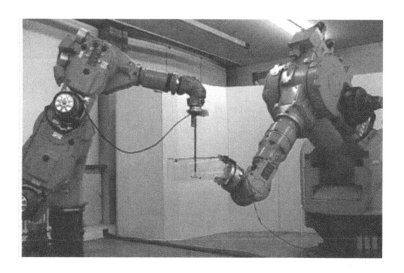

Dr. Bruyninckx has been active in open source robot control software development since the year 2000, and has created the Orocos project that targets (realtime) simulation and control of complex robot systems. In this talk, he will present a broad vision on which software components exist, or have still to be developed, in open source, in order to reach an all-encompassing, powerful and vertically integrated software stack that supports all possible aspects of advanced robotics research and development. The talk gives an overview of current and future projects that work towards these goals, and of the difficult problem of having these projects work towards a common set of long-term objectives. The presentation also indentifies several practical, technical, legal and commercial hurdles, to be taken by participants (both academic and industrial) that are part of the current open source ecosystems, or that are interested in becoming part of such ecosystem.

S. Carpin et al. (Eds.): SIMPAR 2008, LNAI 5325, p. 1, 2008.

Studies on Humanlike Robots – Humanoid, Android and Geminoid

Hiroshi Ishiguro

Department of Adaptive Machine Systems, Osaka University
ATR Intelligent Robotics and Communication Laboratories
JST ERATO ASADA Synergistic Intelligence System Project
ishiguro@ams.eng.osaka-u.ac.jp
http://www.ed.ams.eng.osaka-u.ac.jp

Why are we attracted to humanoids and androids? The answer is simple. We, humans, always anthropomorphize targets of interaction. In other words, we find a human itself in the humanoid. This is the reason why I am studying on humanoids and androids.

I have encountered the uncanny valley problem when I have developed the child android. Then, I have developed the female androids for compensating the problem and studied on human likeness represented with the robot in both of Robotics and Cognitive Science. However, a more serious problem is that the android could not naturally talk with people because of lack of the perfect AI. Therefore, I have developed the geminoid that is a tele-operated android connected through the Internet and studied on human-like presence.

Recently, I am focusing on the complicated mechanism of the humanlike robots and origin of the social intelligence that appears among humans and robots. This talk will introduce the series of the humanlike robot studies and discusses the fundamental issues.

S. Carpin et al. (Eds.): SIMPAR 2008, LNAI 5325, p. 2, 2008.
© Springer-Verlag Berlin Heidelberg 2008

Modeling, Understanding, and Interacting with Humans

Yoshihiko Nakamura

University of Tokyo
Department of Mechano-Informatics and
Information and Robotics Technology Research Initiative
nakamura@ynl.t.u-tokyo.ac.jp
http://www.ynl.t.u-tokyo.ac.jp

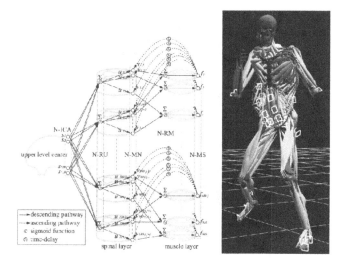

Machines and robots extend their frequency and quality of interaction with humans. Tools invented by humans have shown evolution in the history. One may find a similar genealogical tree of tools to the evolution of life. Machines that interact with humans based on understanding humans are in a sense the ultimate tools for humans. The advance of computational algorithms and modeling technology in robotics encourages us making a challenge pursuing such machines. My talk will highlight and introduce our recent research results on emulating somatosensory sensation of humans, semiotics of human whole-body motion patterns, and using them for machines interacting with humans.

S. Carpin et al. (Eds.): SIMPAR 2008, LNAI 5325, p. 3, 2008.
© Springer-Verlag Berlin Heidelberg 2008

Humanoids, Brain and Cognitive Sciences

Giulio Sandini

Department of Robotics, Brain and Cognitive Sciences
Italian Institute of Technology and
LIRA-Lab, University of Genoa

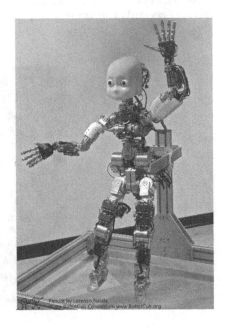

In the talk I will discuss how research on humanoid robots, cognition and brain sciences can be seen as parts of a multidisciplinary, coordinated effort aimed at advancing knowledge on the foundation of human intelligence and at developing new, human-centered technologies. The rationale stems from the observation that developing human-like intelligence in artificial systems with human-like morphology (humanoids) requires to address the same questions cognitive neuroscientists are asking through experimental investigations. Conversely understanding human intelligence from all its multifaceted perspective can take advantage of the realistic simulation allowed by the physical implementation of hardware models. Within this framework I will present results of projects ongoing at the Department of Robotics, Brain and Cognitive Sciences of IIT in the areas of humanoid cognition, robotic rehabilitation and motor learning, multimodal sensory integration and brain machine interface.

S. Carpin et al. (Eds.): SIMPAR 2008, LNAI 5325, p. 4, 2008.
© Springer-Verlag Berlin Heidelberg 2008

XPERSim: A Simulator for Robot Learning by Experimentation*

Iman Awaad[1] and Beatriz León[2]

[1] Bonn-Rhein-Sieg University of Applied Science
Grantham-Allee 20, 53757 Sankt Augustin, Germany
`iman.awaad@fh-bonn-rhein-sieg.de`
[2] Universitat Jaume I, Castellon de la Plana, Spain
`beatriz.leon@smail.inf.fh-bonn-rhein-sieg.de`

Abstract. In this paper, we present XPERSim, a 3D simulator built on top of open source components that enables users to quickly and easily construct an accurate and photo-realistic simulation for robots of arbitrary morphology and their environments. While many existing robot simulators provide a good dynamics simulation, they often lack the high quality visualization that is now possible with general-purpose hardware. XPERSim achieves such visualization by using the Object-Oriented Graphics Rendering Engine 3D (Ogre) engine to render the simulation whose dynamics are calculated using the Open Dynamics Engine (ODE). Through XPERSim's integration into a component-based software integration framework used for robotic learning by experimentation, XPERSIF, and the use of the scene-oriented nature of the Ogre engine, the simulation is distributed to numerous users that include researchers and robotic components, thus enabling simultaneous, quasi-realtime observation of the multiple-camera simulations.

1 Introduction

Robot simulators are widely used in the robotics field for different purposes. They have mainly been used to design and test new robot models as well as to develop the necessary software for running the robots, such as controllers or behaviors. The simulation of multi-robot teams, for example, is a vital tool in fields such as RoboCup [1], where the setting up of a whole team of robots is a time-consuming task. The simulation can be run for as long as is needed and is not limited by physical constraints such as battery life. In this way, simulation also contributes to speeding up the pace of research. Where multi-robot teams

---

* The work described in this article has been partially funded by the European Commission's Sixth Framework Programme under contract no. 029427 as part of the Specific Targeted Research Project XPERO ("Robotic Learning by Experimentation"). The authors thank Keyan Zahedi, Ronny Hartanto, Karl-Heinz Sylla and Paul Plöger for their guidance and the researchers in the XPERO project for their feedback and support.The authors gratefully acknowledge the reviewers' comments.

S. Carpin et al. (Eds.): SIMPAR 2008, LNAI 5325, pp. 5–16, 2008.

are concerned, a simulator that allows the testing of team behaviours is ideal. A 2D simulator is often sufficient for this purpose. The field of evolutionary robotics also relies heavily on simulation, as the time spans used for such purposes are generally very long. In this special case, a fast simulation is the highest priority.

The quality of a simulation is largely dependent on the physics engine which calculates the dynamics of the simulation, and the rendering engine which is used to visualize it. The results of the physics simulation are highly dependent on the accuracy of the models which are provided by the user. There are many physics engines available with varying quality and cost. Similarly, a wide variety of 3D rendering engines also exist. The game industry has helped to advance the quality of these engines to its current limits; to the point where open-source engines that provide this exceptionally high-quality visualization are now available.

In the above-mentioned cases, the visualization of the simulation is used by the researcher to observe the behavior of the robots and is not available to the simulated robots themselves, e.g. for their vision processes (as is the case in the XPERO project, which deals with robot learning by experimentation and for which XPERSim was developed). Within the project, the simulation is used by both the researchers and the robot itself. For the robot to function as expected, its perception of its environment should be as realistic as possible, both dynamically and visually. The dynamics of its environment must use accurate models of friction, mass, forces, rigid body collisions, and so on. The dynamics have to allow for an accurate simulation of the manipulation process itself. Realistic visualization of this interaction with its environment is vital for the observation and the perception processes. The robots use a variety of vision techniques and mechanisms such as focus of attention and novelty detection which allow them to autonomously find objects to experiment with. In order for these techniques to be tested and used in a simulated environment, it is necessary that the visualization be as realistic as possible. The use of lighting, shadows, textures and the ability to simulate optical aberrations contribute to this realism and help to ensure that the same algorithms which are streamlined in simulation may be used in real world scenarios.

XPERSim provides a realistic and accurate physics simulation that is also visually realistic at a reasonable computational cost. It achieves high quality visualization by using the Ogre 3D engine [2] to render the simulation whose dynamics are calculated using ODE [3]. In this paper we describe our simulation of the the Khepera [4] robot and the XPERO environment in which it functions as created using XPERSim. We will first give a brief overview of 3D robot simulators. We will introduce the architecture of XPERSim and the contents of the packages. We then discuss the advantages of using the Ogre 3D engine and the ODE physics library as well as the challenges and results of integrating these technologies before presenting the methods used to distribute the simulation to multiple users simultaneously in a quasi-realtime manner. The results are then presented. Finally, we conclude with a discussion of the work.

2   Related Work

There are numerous 3D robot simulators available, such as Gazebo [5], USARSim [6] and Webots [7]. Many use ODE for their dynamics simulation. ODE is a free, open-source, high-performance library for simulating rigid body dynamics. It is stable, mature and platform-independent with an easy to use C/C++ application programming interface (API). It has advanced joint types and integrated collision detection with friction. ODE's major drawback is that of the quality of rendering done through the DRAWSTUFF library that comes with it. It should be noted that the DRAWSTUFF library is provided by the authors of ODE for debugging purposes and is not meant to be used for a simulation. In this section we briefly survey a number of 3D robot simulators.

Gazebo is part of the Player/Stage project, one of the leading tools in the robotics field. It comes with a large library of sensors and models of existing robots. These can be controlled by either the Player server or by controllers provided by the user. To create one's own robot requires code-based modeling of the robot in C [5]. Gazebo's dynamics simulation is based on the ODE library.

Webots [7] from Cyberbotics is a commercial simulator capable of simulating many kinds of mobile robots. Features include a complete library of sensors and actuators, the ability to program the robots in C, C++, Java or third party software and the use of the ODE library for physics simulation. It also comes with models of some commercially available robots. In addition, there is a robot and world editor that enables the user to create the environment and the robot from the libraries mentioned above.

USARSim is a high fidelity simulation of urban search and rescue robots and environments intended as a research tool for the study of human-robot inter-action (HRI) and multirobot coordination [6]. It uses the Unreal game engine for the dynamics simulation and the visualization. The physics engine used by Unreal is the Karma engine. During the assessment phase of existing simulators, it was the case that USARSim and the Karma engine did not allow actuated entities to manipulate other actuated entities (e.g. a robot manipulator would not be able to grasp a door handle). This was later enabled in [8]. The Unreal engine is much more than a rendering engine. It includes not only the physics and rendering engines, but also sound, networking, AI and even voice support. These features, while extremely useful to game developers, would be excessive if all that is required are rendering and physics engines, as is the case with XPER-Sim. The choice to use the Ogre rendering engine, as opposed to other rendering engines such as CrystalSpace 3D, was based on the feature set, documentation, support and the learning curve needed to get projects up and running. Ogre consistently came out on top in these areas. A detailed comparison of Ogre and CrystalSpace is found in [9].

The simulator which is closest to the one described here is presented in [10]. It uses the Ogre engine for visualization and the PhysX SDK for the dynamics. It is built to support human-controlled avatars to enable HRI and collaboration studies. The similarity between XPERSim and this simulator extends beyond the use of a the same rendering engine. It is the only other robot simulator, to our knowledge, that allows experiments which include users participating from geographically remote locations. To enable this distribution of their simulation, the Torque Networking Library was used. A major difference between this simulator and XPERSim is in the roles of the clients and servers which vary considerably.

3 Approach

To solve the problem of ODE's limited-quality visualization, the Ogre 3D engine was chosen to perform the rendering. Ogre is a free, open source 3D engine written in C++, which is designed to make it easier and more intuitive for developers to produce applications using hardware-accelerated 3D graphics. In addition to the usual feature set found in many other rendering engines, it provides advanced features which are not present in APIs such as OpenGL [10]. It is important to note that Ogre is not a complete simulation engine. It performs many tasks, but most of them are related to 3D computer graphics. It does not, for example, provide physics, sound, networking, GUIs or artificial intelligence. There are, however, other libraries from which one can choose to perform these tasks. This separation provides developers with the flexibility to make the choices on which packages to use in order to fulfill their requirements which in turn enables them to keep it simple.

The core concept of Ogre is the "scene". Within this scene, the "root" object is the entry point to the Ogre system [2]. It maintains pointers to all objects in the system, such as scene and resource managers. These give access to individual entities within a scene. Each entity is attached to a "scene node". The root object also contains a method that is in charge of looping to render continuously. A "scene-graph" (a collection of nodes in a graph or tree structure) is created at the beginning of a simulation and is maintained throughout. Each frame, this graph is traversed and the entities rendered, thus producing the simulation. With each iteration of the simulation loop, the position as well as the orientation of the entities to be simulated is retrieved from ODE and rendered using Ogre.

XPERSim has a client-server architecture where the client controls the robot in the simulation which is running on the server-side. The client can be a console running on Windows or any other platform. The server can be interfaced with a client in the form of an AI program or a planner which would then control the robot. The current version of XPERSim implements the Khepera robot.

3.1 Implementation

XPERSim provides a library of model components, written in C++, that are useful for robot simulation. Its modular architecture also allows for maximum code reuse and makes it open for expansion. Any simulation requires a robot and the environment on which it will act. The contents of the simulation are thus categorized as being either part of the environment or part of the robot.

Setting up the environment requires only very basic knowledge of ODE as a wrapper encapsulates the ODE function calls necessary for the creation of the entities. The same function call stores away information that will be used by Ogre to render the entities into description arrays. Such information includes the specific mesh to be used to visualize the object and its parenthood. This information is then retrieved later on to create the scene-graph that Ogre will use to render these entities and update them every frame. Joints, while critical to the physics of the environment (e.g. used to hold together entities - they do not need to be controlled), it is not desirable to have them rendered or updated as you would a robot's actuators. As such, they are not considered entities and are not saved within any description array.

The robot differs from the environment in that it contains actuators and sensors in addition to rigid bodies and non-actuated joints. These need their own descriptions to facilitate retrieving sensor values and sending commands to the actuators. Two packages have been created specifically for sensors and actuators. In addition, the method of communication with each embodiment will differ. For this reason, each Robot contains its own communicate function.

3.2   Actuators and Sensors

The ACTUATOR package contains a number of actuators, namely a differential drive, the Khepera arm and the gripper have been implemented. The arm, for example, has been implemented using a hinge joint that connects the arm to its turret. The joint is parameterized to enable the arm to be moved as per the specifications of the Khepera. The two grippers are then connected to the arm via slider joints. Additional joints can be easily added.

The SENSOR package currently implements a number of sensors, such as the IR proximity sensor, light barrier sensor, touch sensor, wheel encoder and the camera. The light barrier and touch sensors are simulated using the IR sensor implementation.

The IR sensors have been implemented using five rays, all with the same start position. This implementation was provided by [11]. One ray lies in the exact orientation given. Two of the remaining rays are directed at orientations that take into consideration a spread angle on the x-axis, while the remaining two rays take into consideration the spread angle in the y-axis. In this way, a cone is created that more accurately emulates an IR sensor's field. The spread angles are parameters that the user is able to set, as is the length of the ray which is set to the sensitivity of the IR sensor being simulated. This is an advantage over other simulators, which use only one ray for an IR sensor. This method of modeling the sensor with five rays also allows a more realistic sensor model to be created. The real sensor detects a distant object, if a close object penetrates the cone less than halfway. If one of the other rays is activated, a weighted sum could be used to calculate the distance instead of the minimum value [11]. By varying the spread-angles of the rays, the sensor model can be changed to reflect a real sensor whose values have been obtained, or to simulate noise. By gradually changing the parameters, a transition can be made from the idealistic simulated world to the real world.

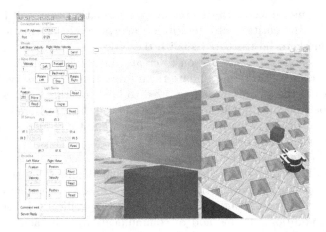

Fig. 1. A screenshot of the XPERSim window running alongside the console

The XPERSim window contains two viewports, each displaying the view from a specific camera (see Fig. 1). The "overhead" camera is displayed on the right while the left half of the window displays the "first-person" camera attached to the robot. Ogre allows the user to add as many viewports as is needed and as many cameras. This feature can be used to easily simulate stereo-vision. While the rendering is done in all the viewports, XPERSim currently allows the user to move the "overhead" camera only. It is possible to save and retrieve rendered frames to and from a file. This means that it is also possible to apply vision algorithms to these frames, or transmit them over a network to users. A perception module with basic vision algorithms was implemented for the Logging version of XPERSim which allowed the frames to be analyzed in an off-line manner. The process of saving a file to disk is however a costly process as the image must first be flushed from the GPU (Graphics Processing Unit).

The communication framework enables the simulation running on the server-side to communicate with a client-side console over TCP/IP. It is robot-specific. For this reason, the communication for the Khepera robot is included within the class implementing it.

4   Distributing the Simulation

This section details the efforts made to distribute the simulated images for tele-observation. Although the implementation is specific to the XPERSim simulator, the same approach could conceptually be used for other simulators. XPERSim has been integrated into the XPERSIF framework [12], a component-based software integration framework which was specified, defined, developed, implemented and tested by the authors. The framework and architecture comprise loosely-coupled, autonomous components that offer services through their well-defined interfaces and form a service-oriented architecture. The Ice [13] middleware is used in the communication layer. The framework enables components (running in a distributed setting) that are responsible for such tasks as the design of experiments, planning, robot control, motivation, machine learning and of course feature extraction and vision to be integrated into an architecture for learning by experimentation. This integration of XPERSim into XPERSIF enables the simulation of an experiment and the testing and streamlining of the components mentioned above, thus providing a tool-driven validation process.

While tele-operation and tele-observation of the simulation were previously implemented, the solution for tele-observation was provided with a focus on fulfilling a use case for data generation which provided traces for the machine learning tools. These traces included the simulated image which was requested and transmitted through a synchronous Remote Procedure Call (RPC). While this requirement was met, the solution did not enable a frame-by-frame viewing of the simulation. The specification of new use-cases specified the need for the architecture to supply quasi-real time observation of the simulated image. The implementation of the solution is presented in this section.

A number of issues precluded the use of the same method for true real time tele-observation of the experiment. One is the presence of a bottleneck in obtaining the rendered image from the GPU to the CPU which makes the process of simply obtaining the image a time-consuming affair. Another issue is the transmission of the image itself takes time.

It should be noted that these issues made infeasible the real time or quasi-real time tele-observation of the experiment by even one single client. In order to facilitate scalability, bottlenecks must be avoided.

The solution presented here, which bypasses this bottleneck, uses a proven methodology (implemented in multi-player games for over a decade) which involves moving the rendering of images from the server-side to the client-side by sending out a subset of the scene information to ensure that all clients are operating synchronously [14], thus drastically reducing the amount of data being transmitted. This is facilitated due to the scene-oriented nature of the XPERSim simulation. As mentioned previously, the Ogre 3D rendering engine simplifies the processing of objects or groups of objects by using scene-graphs (a graph of nodes) to represent hierarchies. If a parent node is translated or rotated, this transformation is applied to the child scene nodes as well.

The latency resulting from the distributed nature of the application is ameliorated by sending the node information from the simulator while the client is rendering the previous one – i.e. the server does not wait for the client to request the image but sends it continuously once it has subscribed. The method described above to distribute a simulation to multiple clients is implemented here by decoupling the physics and graphics engines of XPERSim to create an XPERSim Server (calculating dynamics) and a TeleSimView client (rendering the nodes at their new positions). The XPERSim Server sends out the positions and orientations of all scene-nodes to the clients that simply transform the specified nodes to the specified positions and orientations and in so doing produce the same scene in an efficient and real time manner. In this refactored

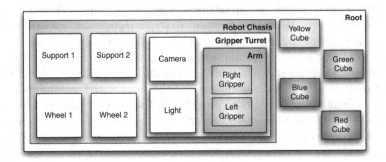

Fig. 2. An example setup for a simulation with 15 nodes (4 cubes, and the Khepera robot). With optimization, only the shaded nodes (8) would need to be published.

implementation of the XPERSim simulator, no distinction is being made between parent nodes and child nodes. It is recommended however that this distinction be made as it would reduce the number of nodes whose data needs to be transmitted (transmit parent nodes only and nodes which can be moved separately from the hierarchy – a gripper for example which, despite being a member of the robot node, may be moved on its own). This can be seen in Fig. 2. The implementation details are described below.

4.1   XPERSim Server

As mentioned above, the XPERSim Server is now solely responsible for calculating the dynamics of the simulation and for their distribution. The separation of the two engines was straightforward due to the modular structure of the simulator. Previously, every rendered frame would step the simulation by 0.05 seconds (5 x 0.01 seconds). With this link to the rendering of a frame gone, the speed at which the simulation proceeded was much faster. Various methods for transmitting the node information were evaluated.

During the start-up of the simulation and the creation of the ODE bodies, the information pertaining to the Ogre-scene is accumulated. This information is stored in a container structure that is requested by the CAMERA subcomponents as they are the image providers (Fig. 3). The XPERSim server continuously sends out node positions and orientations in absolute coordinates (i.e. the same node information is sent to all CAMERA subcomponents). As the robot's camera is attached to it, it will automatically be moved when the robot does. If a pan/tilt camera is used, then its position and orientation could be sent out as a node.

In an effort to further reduce network latency, a one-way invocation is used to send the new frame. This can in fact be quite expensive when many such small messages need to be sent. This is because the run time taps into the OS kernel for each message and because each of these messages is sent out with its own message header [13]. To ameliorate this problem, batched one-way invocations are used. This allows the Ice run time to buffer these small messages until the XPERSim Server explicitly flushes them.

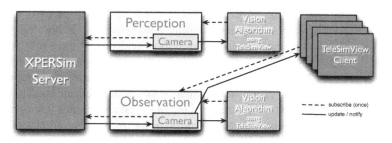

Fig. 3. An overview of the system showing the XPERSim Server sending node updates to the camera subcomponents within XPERSIF. They in turn act as image providers to the various TeleSimView clients which have subscribed to receive the updates.

Originally, it was envisioned that the parametrization of XPERSim would be done through an XML file. This would allow the client to send the setup for a new experiment without necessitating the recompilation of XPERSim. The limited number of scenarios and the low frequency at which these scenarios are changed dispenses with the need for the XML parametrization and makes it equally efficient to choose precompiled setups.

4.2 TeleSimView Client

The TeleSimView client is used to visualize the simulated scene. With the same node information, the view from both cameras is rendered. The subscription to receive the node information is made with the XPERSIF components: PERCEPTION (robot camera) or OBSERVATION (overhead camera). This provides clients with the flexibility to choose the cameras they wish to subscribe to.

A two-way invocation to the PERCEPTION (or OBSERVATION) component fetches the scene which will be created and subsequently updated. The creation of the scene involves the creation and attaching of nodes, their positioning and the creation of such basic scene items as the plane, lights, and sky. Once this has been done, the client uses operations found within the interfaces which are extended by the PERCEPTION and OBSERVATION components in order to subscribe as an image-observer. As soon as this is done, the images will be transmitted to it from the relevant CAMERA subcomponent (as seen in Fig. 3).

The TeleSimView client only requires Ogre (and its dependencies). Ogre has always been available for all platforms. The source for a project running under Windows could not previously be compiled and used on other platforms however due to the use of Windows-specific libraries handling events and key input. With the release of Ogre version 1.4.6 (a.k.a. 'Eihort'), this problem is now solved with the use of the Object-oriented Input System (OIS) platform.

5   Results

The XPERO project has provided XPERSim with an invaluable testing ground. XPERSim has proven to be highly useful and effective in speeding up the pace of research. This has been made even more evident within the distributed research environment. XPERSim has been successfully used to aid the human researcher in developing and evaluating concepts as well as providing test data [15] by using the initial Logging version of XPERSim and subsequent versions following its integration via XPERSIF. A perception module has been developed as proof of concept that allows basic vision algorithms to be performed on the simulated scene. The Client Console (used with the Logging version) enables tele-operation of the simulated robot using the same commands that are sent to the physical robot. In this way, any user with code to control a Khepera can use this code in XPERSim. Simultaneous multiple camera simulation of the rendered scene is possible at high frame rates. A library of components that can be parametrized by the user has been created. This library includes a number of commonly-used sensors and actuators.

Due to the modular architecture of the simulator, it should be possible to easily simulate multiple robots by making minor additions to the structure of XPERSim. The number of simultaneous camera simulations is limited by the maximum resolution of the screen if real-sized viewports are required for the "first-person" cameras. The frame-rate is mainly affected by the number of objects within a scene and the number of triangles in the mesh used to visualize it. A slowdown in the frame-rate usually occurs when many hundreds of nodes are being visualized. There are many optimizations that can be made within Ogre to help in situations where these numbers are very large. Many are available to download from the Ogre website. A potential bottleneck exists in flushing the buffer in the graphics card to save the rendered image. If this is done often, for example for logging purposes, the simulation speed slows down. This is in fact a focus of graphics-cards manufacturers who are currently establishing two-way communication to the GPU in order to ease this process.

Distribution of the simulation through its integration via the XPERSIF architecture was successfully achieved. The scalability of the implementation described above was evaluated by measuring the impact on the quality of the simulation by varying the number of subscribers to the tele-observation service. This detailed scientific evaluation validated the use of a batched one-way invocation for distributing the image. Table 1 shows the measurements made when one, three, five and then ten clients are subscribed to the service. All experiments were repeated three times, measuring the time it took for 60 frames to

Table 1. The time in seconds between receiving two subsequent images (15 nodes) using the batched one-way invocation method. Optimizing the process by sending only parent and actuated nodes out (as described in section 4) in this scenario would result in a total of only 8 nodes needing to be published and processed for updating.

Trial	1 client	3 clients	5 clients	10 clients
1	0.0039 s	0.0039 s	0.0219 s	0.0227 s
2	0.0023 s	0.0172 s	0.0128 s	0.0352 s
3	0.0075 s	0.0036 s	0.0120 s	0.0448 s
Mean	0.0046 s	0.0082 s	0.0156 s	0.0342 s

be delivered to the TeleSimView client. It is worth noting that the size of the image to be rendered is inconsequential. As nodes are being sent and not an image, it is the number of nodes within a scene that impacts the time and not the image size. For the test case above, 15 nodes were transmitted (representing the Khepera robot and four cubes). Using this information, the scene may be rendered from the viewpoint of any number of cameras.

6   Discussion

The system presented here has been used successfully, not only in the initial stages of the project in allowing the researchers to pursue multiple scenarios simultaneously to develop and evaluate concepts, but also in the later stages by providing vital traces used for the machine learning process. The initial results [15] from the XPERO project support the original assertion that simulation has indeed enhanced the speed of research within the project.

As robotic vision techniques become more and more sophisticated, any simulation of a robot using these techniques must be as visually realistic as possible. Given that the technology which enables this is freely available, there is no barrier to robot simulators taking advantage of these technologies. In addition, given that robotics is very much a multi-disciplinary field. and that the benefits of cooperation across these field boundaries are great, tools that facilitate such cooperation are a necessity. In this context, the distribution of a simulation to researchers (and their tools) is a valuable feature to have.

XPERSim has the advantages of providing a more realistic camera simulation at over 30 fps and a library of available model components that are useful for robot simulation and include realistic sensor models. It is modular, extensible, easy to use and understand and provides logging functionality. It enables distributed work without the need for a physical robot and enables easy replicability.

We have addressed the problem of tele-observation by decoupling the physics and rendering components within the simulator in a manner that optimizes computational power and harnesses the power of node-oriented scene-graphs, and thus reduced network latency. We have produced a simulation with accurate physics and high quality graphics that can be used with great ease and without the use of special hardware.

The extension of the library to include more robot models, sensors and actuators is a top priority on our agenda. One which is facilitated by the use of the Ogre 3D engine and ODE as base components in our simulator's architecture since many models for these engines already exist within the robotics community. The current version of the simulator runs on both Windows and Linux platforms. A port to the Mac platform is well underway. Upgrading the Ogre engine to the new release will enable cross-platform compatibility of the same source code. Enabling simulated robots to be controlled though the Player API [16] is another goal as this would make available the libraries within (e.g. landmark tracking and probabilistic localization). Additional optimizations which would further reduce the number of nodes being sent out (see section 4) will also be tested.

References

1. The RoboCup Federation, http://robocup.org
2. The Ogre Team: Ogre Manual v1.2.0 (Dagon) (2006)
3. Smith, R.: Open Dynamics Engine (2006)
4. Mondada, F., Franzi, E., Ienne, P.: Mobile robot miniaturization: A tool for investigation in control algorithms. In: Proceedings of the Third International Symposium on Experimental Robotics, pp. 501–513. Springer, Berlin (1993)
5. Koenig, N., Howard, A.: Design and use paradigms for gazebo, an open-source multi-robot simulator. In: IEEE/RSJ International Conference on Intelligent Robots and Systems, pp. 2149–2154 (2004)
6. Wang, J.: USARSim: A Game-based Simulation of the NIST Reference Arenas (2006)
7. Cyberbotics Ltd.: Webots User Guide. release 5.1.7 edn. (2006)
8. Zaratti, M., Fratarcangeli, M., Iocchi, L.: A 3d simulator of multiple legged robots based on usarsim. In: RoboCup Syposium 2006 (2006)
9. Crystal Space or Ogre 3D, http://www.arcanoria.com/CS-Ogre.php
10. Faust, J., Simon, C., Smart, W.D.: A video game-based mobile robot simulation environment. In: IEEE/RSJ International Conference on Intelligent Robots and Systems, pp. 3749–3754 (2006)
11. Ghazi-Zahedi, K.: Self-regulating neurons: A real-time learning algorithm for recurrent neural networks. PhD thesis, University of Osnabrueck (to appear, 2008)
12. Awaad, I., Hartanto, R., Leon, B., Plöger, P.: A software system for robotic learning by experimentation. In: Carpin, S., Noda, I., Pagello, E., Reggiani, M., von Stryk, O. (eds.) SIMPAR 2008. LNCS (LNAI), vol. 5325, pp. 99–110. Springer, Heidelberg (2008)
13. Henning, M., Spruiell, M.: Distributed Programming with Ice. ZeroC Inc. Revision 3.2 edn. (2007)
14. Funkhouser, T.: Ring: A client-server system for multiuser virtual environments. In: Proceedings of the SIGGRAPH Symposium on Interactive 3D Graphics, ACM SIGGRAPH, pp. 85–92 (1995)
15. Bratko, I.: Initial experiments in robot discovery in xpero. In: International Conference on Robotics and Automation Workshop on Concept Learning for Embodied Agents (2007)
16. Gerkey, B., Vaughan, R.T., Howard, A.: The player/stage project: Tools for multi-robot and distributed sensor systems. In: Proceedings of International Conference on Automation and Robotics, pp. 317–323 (2003)

From Simulated to Real Scenarios: A Framework for Multi-UAVs

Andrea Cesetti, Adriano Mancini, Emanuele Frontoni, Primo Zingaretti, and Sauro Longhi

Universitá Politecnica delle Marche, DIIGA, Ancona, Italy
{cesetti,mancini,frontoni,zinga}@diiga.univpm.it,
sauro.longhi@univpm.it

Abstract. In this paper a framework for simulation of Unmanned Aerial Vehicles (UAVs), oriented to rotary wings aerial vehicles, is presented. It allows UAV simulations for stand-alone agents or multi-agents exchanging data in cooperative scenarios. The framework, based on modularity and stratification in different specialized layers, allows an easy switching from simulated to real environments, thus reducing testing and debugging times. CAD modelling supports the framework mainly with respect to extraction of geometrical parameters and virtualization. Useful applications of the framework include pilot training, testing and validation of UAVs control strategies, especially in an educational context, and simulation of complex missions.

Keywords: modelling framework for robots and environments, testing and validation of robot control software, simulated sensors and actuators, UAV.

1 Introduction

Nowadays mobile robotics is going through a period of constant growth, producing tangible results in both scientific and commercial areas. However there is a significant difference between the results achieved with ground vehicles and aircrafts. *Unmanned Aerial Vehicles* (UAVs) represent a challenging research field due, on one hand, to the complexity of systems and operating environment and on the other hand to the variety of tasks they can perform. The range of aerial vehicles is ample (blimps, gliders, kites, planes, helicopters, etc.) and each one has a particularity that makes the difference in a mathematical description of physical phenomena.

Mathematical models are really complex because an aerodynamic description has to be taken into account and dynamics is also influenced by turbulence from rotors and wind. Small-scale helicopters probably represent the most difficult systems to model because of the complex nature of their dynamics. At the same time their unique manoeuvrability capabilities (including hovering, vertical take-off and landing) and multiple flight modes make them able to perform various tasks, such as surveillance, search and rescue, photogrammetry and mapping.

In many cases, complex missions can be carried out by fleets of cooperating autonomous and heterogeneous vehicles, hence interaction, cooperation and

S. Carpin et al. (Eds.): SIMPAR 2008, LNAI 5325, pp. 17–28, 2008.

supervision become the main problems. UAV application development is closely linked to the possibility of exploiting all benefits of simulation: modularity, repeatability and low cost. The risks produced from a direct use of real aircrafts are obvious. The only alternative to a powerful simulation framework could be the supervision of an expert pilot, but this solution is often quite difficult to practise. The complexity correlated to today challenges in terms of missions and tasks sets up the necessity of simulating, debugging and testing. Simulation activities are essential for testing and validation of control strategies because different methodological approaches can be easily implemented and evaluated to reduce developing times [1].

To allow an easy transfer of results from simulated to real applications is important to design a modular structure in which dedicated modules can be substituted with real devices.

In the case of ground robots a lot of simulation and test frameworks have been developed [2,3]. Player/Stage/Gazebo is actually one of the most complete framework owing to advanced features like the emulation of 2D-3D environments, the simulation of sensors (LRF, sonar,...) and the integration with commercial robotic platforms (i.e., MobileRobots, Segway...) [3]. Other simulation environments are Carmen [4], Microsoft Robotics Studio [5] and USARsim (for RoboCup) [6]; these are taking the attention of scientific community for the full integration with a lot of commercial platforms. For the UAV branch of robotics the state of the art is a bit different.

In this paper a framework for simulation and testing, oriented to rotary wings aerial vehicles, is presented. The framework allows the simulation of UAVs (as stand-alone agent or exchanging data for cooperation) owing to a *Ground Control Station* (GCS) that supervises the tasks of each agent involved in the mission. The control of a single agent can be switched between the GCS and a human pilot using a joystick. The framework, based on modularity and stratification in different specialized layers, allows an easy switching from simulated to real environments, thus reducing testing and debugging times. CAD modelling supports the framework mainly with respect to extraction of geometrical parameters and virtualization. Useful applications of the framework include pilot training, testing and validation of UAVs control strategies, especially in an educational context, and simulation of complex missions.

The paper is organized as follows: next session introduces our framework. The use of a UAV CAD modelling for parameter extraction and simulation aids is proposed in Section III; the modelling activity is contextualized to the Bergen Twin Observer Helicopter. In Section IV, a test case involving two helicopters in a leader-follower mission is presented. Section V presents a methodology to validate the proposed framework. In Section VI conclusions and future works are outlined.

2   Framework

Robotic systems are inherently multi-disciplinary and for such applications software aspects are of prime importance. Even a single robot application generally implies the use of external hardware and sensors having each their own control system and has de facto a distributed architecture. Several research has been devoted to build simulation frameworks of distributed systems. Two different approaches have been considered when identifying requirements for a framework. The first approach takes into account the functionality of typical applications that would be performed with the framework itself, whereas the second one considers the needs of potential users. From this analysis we derived the following requirement list for our framework: integration of different robotic systems, concurrent control of several robots, platform independent GUI, shared control between several users, easy integration of user's algorithms, flexibility (Distribution, Modularity, Configurability, Portability, Scalability, Maintainability), performance and efficiency. It is obvious that some requirements conflict with each other: performance and efficiency for instance have to be traded with flexibility.

Looking at the simulator panorama, game engines and flight simulators are the only available frameworks to simulate UAVs. Also most of them are developed for planes and not for helicopter. Game engines (like FlightSimulator [7] or FMS [8]) are optimal for visualization, while flight simulators (like JSBSim, YASim and UUIU [9]) are characterized by a high-fidelity mathematical model, but they are lacking in visualization. A good but expensive exception is the RotorLib developed and commercialized by RTDynamics [10]; in the helicopter context, frameworks with good performances are almost absents [11]. The framework here proposed aims at overtaking this lack. In Fig.1 a graphical abstraction with the main layers of the developed simulator is shown. The stratification of the framework permits to identify five different modules as Supervision, Communication, Dynamics, Agent, User Interaction.

An interface for sockets allows the data exchange between GCS and agents in the case of simulated agents, while the communication makes use of a dedicated long-range radio modem if a real vehicle (e.g., helicopter) is used [12].

All the modules are implemented in Matlab/Simulink; the main motivation of this choice is the reduced complexity for code development and costs of commercial products. In particular, the end-user of the framework can easily integrate his

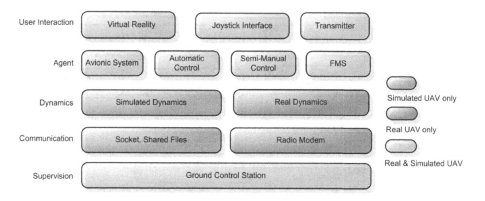

Fig. 1. Structure of the framework for UAV simulation

code for developing and testing an algorithm, e.g., for obstacle avoidance, without the necessity of re-compiling other activities. An additional motivation for the adoption of Matlab is the capability to interface the AeroSim toolbox released by Unmanned Dynamics [13]. The AeroSim Blockset is a Matlab/Simulink block library that provides components for rapid development of nonlinear 6-DOF aircraft dynamic models. In addition to aircraft dynamics the blockset also includes environment models such as standard atmosphere, background wind, turbulence, and earth models (geoid reference, gravity and magnetic field). These blocks can be added to the basic framework to increase the realism of simulation.

2.1   Agent Structure

In a simulated or real case, the structure of an agent in the context of Unmanned Aerial Vehicles is based on a complex interaction of different specialized modules. In the real case, the *Flight Management System* (FMS) is implemented as real-time code running on high performance architectures; in the simulation environment, FMS is a complex set of S-functions to reduce the simulation complexity.

However, in both cases FMS has a series of basic packages as: Communication Module, Queue of Tasks, Guidance Module, Fast Path Re-planner, Attitude and Pose Estimator, Auto and/or Semi-Manual Pilot, Obstacle Avoidance, Fault Diagnosis Identification and Isolation (see Fig.2).

Tasks like take-off, landing, point to point or waypoint navigation are currently available in the developed framework.

FMS exchanges data continuously with GCS for telemetry and task assignments/supervision. Its *Communication Module* makes use of sockets or functions to interface the radio modem.

References about position are generated by the *Guidance Module*, which decides step by step what references should be passed to the controllers (auto-pilot). This module takes into account the actual position of the agent with respect to the local inertial frame and the goal to reach.

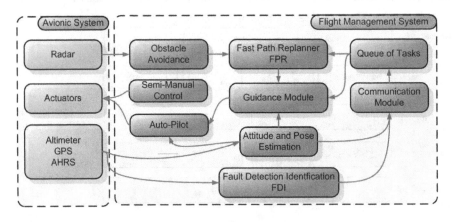

Fig. 2. The Avionic and Flight Management Systems

The *Fast Path Replanner* (FPR) provides a real-time re-calculation of path according to information provided by the *Obstacle Avoidance* package. FPR provides also for correcting the path if external disturbances (e.g., wind) generate a high error in position.

The *Attitude and Position Estimator*, using the inertial data obtained by the *Attitude Heading Reference System* (AHRS) and the *Inertial Navigation System* (INS) calculates the position and attitude of the vehicle; inertial strapdown equations are currently implemented and solved [14]. The *Auto and/or Semi-Manual Pilot* is the core of vehicle's control. The user can control a set of axes by a joystick/transmitter interface. This feature is especially suitable in the field of photogrammetry, where the user concentrates only on forward and/or lateral movements, while the control of altitude and heading (heading lock) is performed by inline controllers. The adopted philosophy tries to emulate the training process of a novel-pilot, who usually controls directly only a limited set of vehicle's axes, while the teacher supervises the activities.

Controllers can be easily updated or modified by changing their code; no additional activities are required. Controllers can be simple PID or PID with gain scheduling and fuzzy logic. Feedback linearization is available in the framework, with some tricks to increase its robustness: computational cost is a major drawback of this technique. Other control techniques, e.g., based on H_∞ can be included.

The *Obstacle Avoidance* module tries to avoid obstacles owing to information obtained by the avionic system, e.g., by radar and Laser Range Finder (LRF) sensors; actually, a set of modules (based on fuzzy logic) are available in the framework to improve the safety of vehicles during navigation.

The *Avionic System*, in the case of simulated or real vehicles, is formed by actuators and sensors. Actuators are usually analog or digital servos in reduced-scale helicopters; a second order model to represent the servos dynamics is adopted in simulated environments. Sensors provide information for a large set of aspects as navigation, obstacle avoidance, mapping and other. Using a radar sensor new tasks become feasible, as flight/operate at a given altitude or avoid an unexpected obstacle. In fact, the *Radar Altimeter* provides the altitude above the ground level, calculated as the difference between height above the sea level and ground elevation (Digital Elevation Model maps); geometric corrections, due to pitch and roll angles, are then applied. Noise is added to make the simulation more realistic; failure occurrences are also simulated. Simulated sensors as IMU and AHRS are also available in the framework; in this case an error model of each sensor is implemented (misalignment, temperature drift, non-linearity and bias).

In a similar way, to emulate the Global Position System (GPS), the geographic coordinates of the aircraft are computed from the knowledge of data about a starting point; noise is then added to match the performance of a common GPS receiver able to apply EGNOS corrections.

An analysis of main differences between the real and simulated case is presented in Table 1; this table summarizes an analysis of main differences between real and simulated case.

Table 1. Many elements (features) are shared between real and simulated scenario. The main difference concerns the Communication and Avionic System.

ASPECT	SIMULATED SCENARIO	REAL SCENARIO
Supervision	Similar	Similar
Communication	Socket	Radio Modem
Dynamics	Blade element, Actuator Disk	Real Phenomena
FMS	Similar (different control laws)	Similar
Avionic System	Simulated Sensors & Actuators	Real HW
User Interaction	Similar	Real streaming video

The switch from virtual to real world and vice versa is relatively easy; mainly FMS is the module that requires different set-up especially for the automatic control (control laws of each servo installed on the real helicopter).

2.2   Helicopter Dynamics Simulation

The framework is actually provided with a helicopter mathematical model. Employing the principles of modularity and standardization, the complete model is broken down into smaller parts that share information and interact among themselves, as shown in Fig.3. In particular, we identified four subsystems describing actuator dynamics, rotary wing dynamics, force and moment generation processes and rigid body dynamics [15].

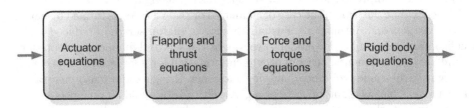

Fig. 3. Helicopter dynamics

2.3   Ground Control Station

The Ground Control Station has a lot of capabilities among which telemetry data acquisition and data logger for post flight analysis; in the cooperative context GCS is responsible for mission and task allocation/supervision. Data are collected and sent using the communication layer. A GUI was developed to obtain a visual feedback of a single agent, all agents, mission status, telemetry. A screenshot of the developed GCS is shown in Fig.4. User can control the mission of each agent choosing the vehicles; the main panels allow to monitor in real-time the agent status owing to the Attitude Direction Indicator (ADI); information as global position (GPS coordinate), status of embedded electronics-batteries, fuel consumption are currently shown in the GUI. An interesting feature of GUI is

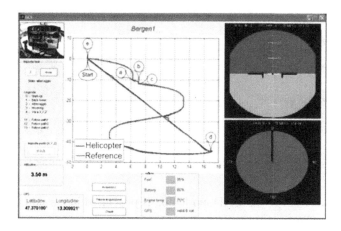

Fig. 4. A screenshot of developed GCS' GUI

the capability to control directly a set of vehicle's axes using a joystick interface; in this case the interaction between human and machines (remote controlled vehicles) allows to control the vehicles taking into account the information provided by ADI indicators. In a simulation context, joystick is interfaced using the Virtual Reality Toolbox (described below).

2.4   Virtual Reality and World Representation

A synthetic rendering of world and agents is one of the basic module; as mentioned in the introduction section, market offers a series of different complex systems to virtualize world and agents. The choice adopted in the proposed framework is to integrate the Matlab Virtual Reality Toolbox. A VRML model of world (environment) and agents (aerial vehicles) can be easily controlled in a Simulink diagram. Students are often familiar with the Matworks software. The mission area is represented as a digital grid map or Digital Elevation Model (DEM). A set of different world scenarios is available in the developed framework. Scenarios are generated considering the DEM of mission area. DEM maps represent the mission area (real or simulated) as a grid map; a critical parameter is the cell resolution. The resolution of available maps is usually 10m in the case of real scenarios. This value is too high in critical mission where an accurate localization is required. The GUI allows to edit/create a new DEM to overtake this limitation; data are obtained by exploration of mission area.

Virtual Reality Toolbox is used to present in soft real-time the state of each vehicle involved in the mission. A VRML world can be customized in terms of textures, position of camera(s) (attached to vehicle or fixed), light(s). The above mentioned toolbox is also used to interface a joystick; this kind of device allows a manual control of the helicopter (user can select the set of axes that wants to control). This features is really useful for novel pilot(s) during the training phases. A 3D model of Bergen Twin Observer Helicopter was developed; a more

Fig. 5. An example of scenario where two UAVs are performing a mission

detailed introduction to 3D CAD modelling is presented in Section 3. In Fig.5 a basic virtual scenario is presented.

Currently, work is focused on the adoption of other virtual reality environments inspired to flight simulators games as FlightGear [16] and Microsoft Flight Simulator [7].

3   CAD Modelling

CAD modelling plays an essential role, supporting the framework mainly with respect to mathematical model parameterization and virtual reality rendering.

Blocks describing the helicopter simulated dynamics need a set of geometrical and inertial parameters such as inertia matrix, mass, distances between Centre Of Gravity (COG) and force attacking points, rotors geometry and leverage gains.

Fig. 6. A view of the CAD model of Bergen Twin Observer; the transparencies allow to see hidden parts, e.g., avionic box and fuel

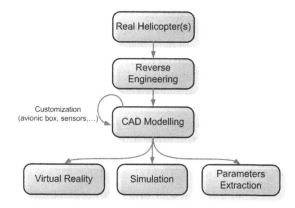

Fig. 7. Diagram of Reverse engineering process

Providing the model with the real parameters of a specific helicopter makes really useful the simulations, allowing an effective shift of results to real applications.

Because some data are time-variant, due to fuel consumption, not trivial to be determined, and should be re-calculated at every change of mass disposal like a new device installation, a detailed 3D CAD model helps to solve the problem, allowing to simply extract all information needed.

Performing an accurate reverse engineering process on a RC mini helicopter a model implementation was carried out. The Bergen Twin Observer available at our laboratory, designed in Solid Edge environment, is presented in Fig.6.

Solid Edge represents a standard in 3D mechanical modelling. It is a powerful feature-based CAD software, quite simple to use and available in a cheap academic license. It allows an accurate and rapid design of the system and its geometric and inertial characterization. The model can be exported to specific software, saved in VRML format or merely used for a rendering process. In Fig.7 the whole procedure is shown.

The obtained digital model can be mostly used to evaluate the effect of customization (e.g. addition of payloads, sensors) by simply extracting geometrical and inertial parameters after any structural or set up variation. It is also functional to visualize the agent in a Virtual Reality environment, allowing a pleasant and more significant representation of the simulation results.

4   Test Case: A Leader-Follower Mission

In this section, a simulation using the presented framework is reported. This simulation presents two Bergen Twin Observer helicopters involved in a "leader-follower mission" [17,18]. Leader-follower mission belongs to the problem of *coalition formation* inspired by the motion of bevies; the main objective of coalition formation is the clustering of a series of agents to reach a target or to cooperate, extending the capabilities of each agent ("union is strength") [19,20].

Simulated sensors adopted are AHRS, GPS and Radar. The helicopters are linked to GCS using sockets for data exchange. Each helicopter has five servos (digital and analog) and one main engine (piston engine). The simulation time of reported simulations is strongly close to the real time (simulation is a bit slowly in particular conditions and the lag depends on the complexity of controllers). The GCS and the two instances of helicopters run on three PCs connected by an Ethernet link.

Leader starts the mission (a simple circular path) and follower tends to maintain a fixed distance minimizing the error in terms of the following expression.

$$P\left(s\right) = \left[x\left(s\right) y\left(s\right) z\left(s\right)\right]^{T} \left\|P_f\left(s_f\right) - P_l\left(s_l - k\right)\right\|^2 < \varepsilon k, \varepsilon \in \mathbb{R}$$

where subscript l and f stand for leader and follower, respectively (see Fig. 8); P is the helicopter position and k the distance between helicopters evaluated along the trajectory.

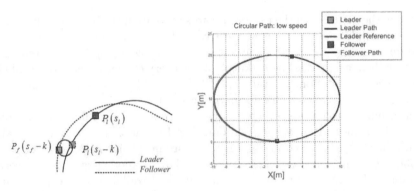

Fig. 8. During the flight, the helicopter-follower maintains a fixed distances to leader

Follower estimates leader trajectory using leader position that is obtained by radar and GCS telemetry. Then, on the base of estimated trajectory, follower tends to track leader trajectory minimizing the error [21]. A graphical representation of simulation is shown in Fig. 8.

5   Validation

According with a principle of modern behaviour-based robotics, an efficient framework should omit internal representations, centering rather on the direct relation between stimulus and action. Hence a quality simulator has to implement accurate models of: robots' geometry and kinematics, sensors, environment and, finally, robot-environment interactions. Since all these components work properly, simulation will provide an adequate model of the process and the results may be shifted to real applications.

This approach to robotics research, however, depends crucially on validation of the models used so that researchers have reasonable assurance that the problems

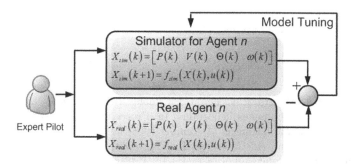

Fig. 9. An approach for fine-tuning of simulation model

they encounter and solutions they devise are representative of actual problems and solutions in robotics rather than simply artifacts of the simulation.

The level of effort devoted to validation has been a distinguishing feature of this work, even if in preliminary stage. Each of its major constituents (robot kinematics, interaction with the environment, sensors and camera video) have been subjected to ongoing validation testing.

A schematic idea for *fine model tuning* is shown in Fig. 9. An expert pilot controls the helicopter performing manoeuvres with a high dynamic content. The actions of pilot are real-time recorded; real and simulated measures of agent state are compared evaluating the goodness of the simulation model; this methodology is inspired by adaptive control systems (e.g, Model Reference Adaptive System).

6 Conclusions and Future Works

In this paper a framework for UAV simulation in cooperative scenarios and testing was presented. The modularity of its architecture permits to update or rewrite a block in a short time; new controllers can be easily tested. This activity does not require re-compiling or deep rearrangement of the code.

Adding or changing the mathematical model, different aerial vehicles can be simulated; actually the research unit is working on simulating a quad-rotor helicopter. This kind of vehicle is versatile and useful for short range missions; due to these characteristics, the quad-rotor is widely used by researchers in the UAV context. Moreover, the proposed approach allows an easy switching from simulated to real environments; this is possible owing to stratification of functions in specialized layers. User interaction, e.g., training of novel-pilots, is supported by GCS, joystick or RC-transmitter interfaces.

Future works will be steered to improve the quality of the VR module for an easy interaction with vehicles without a video streaming feedback. Integration of new kind of aerial vehicles will be the main activity. The adoption/integration of FlightGear or Microsoft Flight Simulator graphical engines will be then investigated. New robust non-linear control techniques to enhance the performance (in terms of energy consumption and Time To Task) of agents will be tested.

At the end of validation phase (introduced in Section V), the simulator will be relesed to scientific community under the GNU license.

References

1. Sanders, C.P., DeBitetto, P.A., Feron, E., Vuong, H.F., Leveson, N.: Hierarchical control of small autonomous helicopters. In: Proceedings of the 37th IEEE Conference on Decision and Control (December 1998)
2. Frontoni, E., Mancini, A., Caponetti, F., Zingaretti, P.: A framework for simulations and tests of mobile robotics tasks. In: Proceedings of 14th Mediterranean Conference on Control and Automation, MED 2006 (2006)
3. Collett, T.H.J., MacDonald, B.A., Gerkey, B.P.: Player 2.0: Toward a practical robot programming framework. In: Australasian Conf. on Robotics and Automation, ACRA 2005 (2005)
4. Carmen robot navigation tool kit (2008), http://carmen.sourceforge.net/
5. Microsoft robotics studio (2008), http://msdn.microsoft.com/robotics/
6. Usarsim (2008), http://sourceforge.net/projects/usarsim/
7. Microsoft fs (2008), http://www.microsoft.com/games/flightsimulatorX/
8. Fms project (2008), http://www.flying-model-simulator.com/
9. Jsbsim home page (2008), http://jsbsim.sourceforge.net/
10. Rotorlib home page (2008), http://www.rtdynamics.com/v1.0/
11. Taamallah, S., de Reus, A.J.C., Boer, J.F.: Development of a rotorcraft mini-uav system demonstrator. In: The 24th Digital Avionics Systems Conference, DASC 2005 (2005)
12. Frontoni, E., Mancini, A., Caponetti, F., Zingaretti, P., Longhi, S.: Prototype uav helicopter working in cooperative environments. In: Proceedings of IEEE/ASME international conference on Advanced intelligent mechatronics, AIM 2007 (2007)
13. Aerosim toolbox (2008), http://www.u-dynamics.com/aerosim/
14. Jetto, L., Longhi, S., Venturini, G.: Development and experimental validation of an adaptive extended kalman filter for the localization of mobile robots. IEEE Trans. on Robotics and Automation 15(2), 219–229 (1999)
15. Koo, T.J., Sastry, S.: Output tracking control design of a helicopter model based on approximate linearization. In: Proceedings of the 37th IEEE Conference on Decision and Control (1998)
16. Flightgear project (2008), http://www.flightgear.org
17. Wang, X., Yadav, V., Balakrishnan, S.N.: Cooperative uav formation flying with obstacle/collision avoidance. IEEE Transactions on Control Systems Technology 15, 672–679 (2007)
18. Lechevin, N., Rabbath, C.A., Sicard, P.: Trajectory tracking of leader-follower formations characterized by constant line-of-sight angles. Automatica 42(12), 2131–2141 (2006)
19. Merino, L., Caballero, F., Martinez de Dios, J.R., Ollero, A.: Cooperative fire detection using unmanned aerial vehicles. In: Proceedings of IEEE International Conference on Robotics and Automation, ICRA 2005 (2005)
20. Beard, R.W., et al.: Decentralized cooperative aerial surveillance using fixed-wing miniature uav. Proceedings of the IEEE 94(7), 1306–1324 (2006)
21. Mahony, R., Hamel, T.: Robust trajectory tracking for a scale model autonomous helicopter. Int. Journal of Robust and Nonlinear Control 14(12), 1035–1059 (2004)

Simulation of Multi-Robot Teams with Flexible Level of Detail

Martin Friedmann, Karen Petersen, and Oskar von Stryk

Technische Universität Darmstadt, Department of Computer Science
Hochschulstr. 10, D-64289 Darmstadt, Germany
{friedmann,petersen,stryk}@sim.tu-darmstadt.de
http://www.sim.tu-darmstadt.de

Abstract. A key methodology for the development of autonomous robots is testing using simulated robot motion and sensing systems. An important issue when simulating teams of heterogeneous autonomous robots is performance versus accuracy. In this paper the multi-robot-simulation framework (MuRoSimF) is presented which allows the flexible and transparent exchange and combination of the algorithms used for the simulation of motion and sensing systems of each individual robot in a scenario with individual level of realism. It has already been used successfully for the simulation of several types of legged and wheeled robots equipped with cameras and laser scanners. In this paper the core functionalities of MuRoSimF are presented. Existing algorithms for simulation of the robots' motions are revised. Newly added features including the execution of the simulation on multi core CPUs and two different algorithms for the simulation of laser scanners are presented. The performance of these features is tested in an urban scenario using wheeled robots.

1 Introduction

The development of control software for teams of autonomous robots is a highly challenging task. Reasons for lack of performance as well as for failure are extremely difficult to analyze by experimental evaluation only, because an autonomous robot usually consists of a highly interacting set of different software and hardware modules. Therefore one of the most valuable tools supporting the development of control software is software in the loop (SIL) testing using simulation of robot hardware under real-time conditions. The benefits of simulation are manifold, including testing of software under repeatable and controllable conditions and unlimited availability (compared to real hardware).

The general requirements on the simulation may differ significantly depending on the scope of the simulation experiment. For example, a high level of detail in robot motion simulation using multi-body dynamics is important for investigation of motion control of robots with high motion dynamics and inertial stabilization like humanoid or flying robots. On the other hand for four-wheeled robots on even ground usually vehicle kinematics models are sufficient to test

S. Carpin et al. (Eds.): SIMPAR 2008, LNAI 5325, pp. 29–40, 2008.
© Springer-Verlag Berlin Heidelberg 2008

team cooperation and kinetical models which would need a larger computational effort are not required. In some cases, even a too realistic robot motion simulation may not be desireable for some tests. E.g., the disturbing effects of a robot's motion like sliding or shaking may overshadow other sources of observed errors.

Similar considerations apply to the simulation of sensors: For testing sensor data processing, it is necessary to have a high fidelity simulation of the sensors, including simulation of possible sources of errors. If higher levels of abstraction within the control software (like behavior control) are under consideration, it may be useful to provide the software with ground truth data from the simulation skipping sensor simulation and processing completely. The latter kind of tests are very difficult to conduct on real robots, as ground truth data usually require additional sensors in the environment and may also suffer from measurement errors. An obvious tradeoff when creating a robot simulation is fidelity vs. real-time performance.

1.1   Requirements for Robot Simulation

As mentioned before, the requirements on the simulation of mobile autonomous robots may differ strongly for different purposes even for the same robot. One way to handle this problem is to use different simulators on different levels of detail and realism. Although often practiced, this approach has the major drawback of multiplying user efforts as well as sources of errors, as each robot has to be modeled for each simulator and each simulator has to be linked to the robot control software for specific tests.

Therefore it is highly desirable to use one simulator enabling different levels of accuracy and realism in robot motion and sensing (sub-)systems. Depending on the requirements, different simulation algorithms for each robot of a team within one scenario should be selectable *at the same time*, e. g., by having a full multi-body system dynamics simulation for one robot and kinematic models for other robots. To achieve this flexibility for the simulation setup, the simulator must provide means to exchange a variety of algorithms with different level of physical detail for the same robot motion or sensor (sub-)system as well as the possibility to flexibly combine these algorithms for different robots in the scene.

A second issue for simulation of large robot teams is real-time-performance: When executing simulations on normal laptop or desktop computers (as in many cases of research and education), CPU power often is a limiting factor for the overall performance of a simulation. As the majority of all new laptop and desktop computers features at least a dual-core CPU, optimal performance of a simulation requires support for multi-threaded execution.

1.2   Existing Robot Simulators

USARSim [1] is an open source simulation which supports several different types of robots (wheeled, legged, tracked robots, submarines, helicopters) and sensors (cameras, different distance sensors, RFID sensors, odometry, sound, motion sensors, etc.). Physics simulation and visualization are based on the game engine *Unreal Engine* by Epic Games [2].

Several simulators rely on the Open Dynamics Engine ODE [3] for physics simulation: Gazebo [4] is the 3D simulator of the player/stage project [5] providing different sensors (cameras, distance sensors, GPS) and several types of robots (wheeled, legged robots, helicopters). SimRobot [6] is a simulator which supports wheeled and legged robots which can be equipped with some sensors, e.g. cameras, distance sensors, and bumpers. Webots [7] is a commercially available simulator that is able to simulate many different types of robots, including wheeled, legged and flying robots. It comes up with many configurable sensors, e.g. cameras, distance sensors, range finders, touch sensors, light sensors, GPS.

Microsoft Robotics Studio [8] is another commercially available simulator. It also supports many different robots and sensors. Physics simulation is done with PhysX by NVIDIA [9], which can be accelerated by using special hardware.

Simbad [10] is an open source simulator written in Java. It supports some different robot models and sensors like cameras, range sensors and bumpers. Dynamics are calculated with a simplified physics engine.

To the authors' knowledge none of these 3D simulators fulfills all requirements stated before. Most of them depend on external physics engines, restricting them to a very specific level of accuracy of the algorithms used for simulation of robot motion dynamics and for the numerical integration of the underlying initial value problems for ordinary differential equations. If no algorithms on different levels of accuracy are available, these effects only can be reached by huge efforts like remodeling parts of the scene on different levels of detail.

Also multi-threading is not available in most of the aforementioned simulations. The *Unreal Engine 3* supports the usage of multiple CPUs, but USARSim is currently based on the *Unreal Engine 2* without multi-threading. PhysX, which is used by the *Unreal Engine 3* and by Microsoft Robotics Studio, supports multi-threading, but it is not stated if Microsoft Robotics Studio makes use of this functionality. ODE, which is used by Gazebo, Webots and SimRobot is not multi-threaded.

In this paper the Multi-Robot-Simulation-Framework (`MuRoSimF`) is presented. It provides a wide variety of simulation algorithms which can be combined to create simulations for autonomous mobile robots on different levels of accuracy. As the data models describing the robot's structure and state are separated from the algorithms used, algorithms can be exchanged transparently. `MuRoSimF` has already been used successfully for the simulation of several mobile autonomous robots (e. g. [11,12]). Recent developments covered in this paper include algorithms for the simulation of laser scanners and the possibility to execute simulations multi-threaded thus improving scalability on multi-core CPUs.

2   Structure of Simulation in `MuRoSimF`

2.1   Data Models

The basic building blocks for the data models of robots and environment are so called *objects*. An object is a container for a set of *properties* which can be constant or variable. Properties can be assigned at runtime to each object.

It is possible to declare a set of properties of different objects to be explicitly equal, so that all properties will share the same space in memory thus avoiding unnecessary copying of data. Due to this feature objects representing sensors can be attached easily to any other object by simply sharing the properties of interest, e. g. the object's position and orientation.

Complex models can be created by joining any number of objects into a so called *compound*. Compounds may have arbitrary internal structures and relations of the single objects.

Robots are special compounds with a tree shaped structure. The basic building blocks for a robot's kinematic structure are the robot's base, forks, fixed translations and rotations (to represent rigid bodies) as well as variable rotations and translations (to represent joints). For the sake of simplicity only binary forks are used.

During model setup the kinematic structure of a robot is created from these basic blocks. To create a robot model a set of helper functions is provided. These functions allow creation of the tree in a depth-first manner as well as adding constant properties to each part of the tree. Currently models are programmed directly in C++. Readers to load models created with external 3D modeling tools can be added to MuRoSimF. As the rendering of shapes is based on textured meshes, this will also improve the quality of the simulation's visualization.

2.2   Algorithms

To make the simulation do something, simulation algorithms are needed. Algorithms are classes which can be connected during simulation setup to the data models of a simulation. When an algorithm is connected to an object, the algorithm can add additional variable properties dynamically to the object. Due to this feature, objects only store variable properties required or calculated by the algorithms in use.

Externally implemented simulation algorithms can be used within MuRoSimF based simulations by creating a new algorithm class which will connect to the required properties of the model. This approach is less efficient than implementing algorithms using the tools provided by MuRoSimF as all required properties need to be copied between the external algorithm and the rest of the simulation.

2.3   Controllers

Controllers are special algorithms which may change and read variable properties of an object due to external requests. They are used to interface the simulation to external control software, thus enabling software in the loop testing. Controllers can interface to data stream oriented connections like serial ports or TCP-sockets. As controllers may connect to any property of a simulated robot, new controllers for arbitrary external control software can be added to MuRoSimF.

Several generic controllers for setting joint values and reading sensors are provided. For more complex control tasks a controller is provided which can execute arbitrary control algorithms loadable from a dynamic link library.

2.4   Execution of Simulations

After setup of the models and algorithms of a simulation, the simulation can be executed. To do this, all algorithms are registered at a scheduler which will execute each algorithm at an arbitrary rate, thus allowing algorithms with different purposes to be run at different speeds (e. g. high rates for robot dynamics and lower rates for camera simulation). The execution rate can be chosen individually for each algorithm and each robot, enabling fine tuning of the performance and accuracy of the simulation.

As the structures required for the exchange of data between the algorithms in use are created during simulation setup, it is not possible to exchange algorithms at runtime.

The set of algorithms registered at the scheduler can be structured in two ways. Sequences of algorithms which have to be executed always in the same order and at the same rate can be added as one item to the scheduler. It is possible to execute a set of such sequences in parallel threats. Parallel execution can be controlled in several ways: It is possible to spawn an individual threat for each sequence, thus exploiting the maximum number of cores on a CPU present, but it is also possible to limit the number of parallel threads, e. g. if part of the CPU time has to be saved for other purposes.

3   Motion Simulation

MuRoSimF provides several modules for robot motion simulation, differing in levels of accuracy, complexity and generality. The modules can be divided into two major groups: robot-specific algorithms and general algorithms.

3.1   Robot Specific Algorithms

Two robot specific algorithms are currently provided for kinematic motion simulation for biped robots and for vehicles with differential drive. Both algorithms make strong assumptions limiting the motion possibilities as well as the accuracy of the simulation. Nevertheless these algorithms have been used successfully when investigating the high level behavior for homogeneous (e. g. [13]) and heterogeneous (e. g. [12]) teams of robots. Another merit of these algorithms is the low complexity. It is possible to simulate many robots in real time on a standard computer.

Kinematic biped simulation. The kinematic simulation for biped robots is based on the assumption, that the robot places its feet on a plane and that always at least one foot touches this plane. Using this assumption the robot's motion is simulated by calculating the direct kinematics of the robot while keeping one foot fixed to the ground. Whenever a contradiction occurs (e.g. one foot penetrating the ground plane), the standing foot is swapped. A feature of this algorithm is the fact, that the simulated humanoid robot does not suffer from effects like shaking, sliding or falling over which is helpful for certain SIL tests.

Differential Drive. Motion of vehicles with differential drive is simulated under similar assumptions: Both wheels always touch the ground plane. In this case the angular and linear velocity of the vehicle's base can be calculated from the velocity of the wheels.

3.2   General Algorithms

The algorithms presented in this section do not make any assumptions on the robot's structure.

Point Model. The point model is the most simple motion simulation algorithm available in MuRoSimF. Only motion of the robot's base is considered (and controlled) externally. If necessary (e. g. when investigating control of articulated external sensors), direct kinematics relative to the robot's base can be calculated to give the position and orientation of the robot's parts. This algorithm can be used when investigating large scale scenarios considering problems like team communication or coordination.

Simplified Dynamics Simulation. The simplified dynamics simulation makes no assumption on the robot's kinematic structure. Unlike the algorithms presented before, the following algorithm considers the dynamics of a robot system. To allow for real-time simulation of teams of robots, this algorithm simplifies the simulated robot to a single body with center of gravity (CoG) and inertia tensor changing due to the motion of the robots joints. All internal motions of the robot are calculated by direct kinematics. Motions of the robot relative to the environment are calculated by summing up any external forces and torques (e. g. caused by friction, collision or gravity) at the current CoG and calculating the resulting linear and angular accelerations of the CoG. The algorithm does not consider the forces generated by the servo motors of the robot's joints. Instead it assumes that the motors are moving at a given rate or acceleration. Further the algorithm neglects any effects caused by relative motions of the parts of the robot like Coriolis forces. Even though these simplifications limit the use of this algorithm when studying whole body motions of a robot, the algorithm has been used successfully for several types of wheeled, biped and quadruped robots.

As the algorithm requires the external forces experienced by the robot, detecting and handling of collisions are essential. Detection of collisions is currently based on primitive shapes (box, sphere, cylinder, plane) assigned to the bodies of the robots. To avoid intersecting each body of each robot with each other body in the scene, a hierarchy of bounding volumes is used (see [11]). As collision-detection and -handling are modules separated from the motion simulation, they can be substituted by other algorithms, e. g. by collision detection using meshes.

3.3   Discussion

The algorithms presented in this section differ in complexity, realism and generality. Depending on the requirements of a given simulation setting an appropriate algorithm can be chosen allowing to set up an adequate simulation.

Due to the modular design of `MuRoSimF` any other algorithm like full multi-body system dynamics simulation can be added easily and be exchanged transparently for existing models.

4   Sensor Simulation

Simulation of sensors is performed by algorithms which are connected to the respective object representing the sensor under consideration. These algorithms may need further information to simulate the sensor (e. g. rendering information for the scene in case of camera simulation). In the following subsections the capabilities of `MuRoSimF` for simulation of internal sensors and cameras already presented in [11,13] are revised. After this the newly developed algorithms for simulation of laser scanners are discussed in detail.

Internal Sensors. Simulation of internal sensors like joint encoders, gyroscopes or acceleration sensors is based on respective physical values calculated by the simulation. Sensor errors like noise, saturation or limited resolution of AD converters can be simulated in a post processing step.

Camera. The camera simulation uses the OpenGL based visualization module of `MuRoSimF` which is also used for generating the main view. The scene is rendered from the camera's point of view, later it is possible to apply blur using a Gaussian filter or distortion like it is caused by a lens.

Laser Scanner. `MuRoSimF` provides two different approaches for simulating distance sensors like laser scanners. One approach is using the z-Buffer information generated during OpenGL based 3D rendering. The other approach is calculating intersections of rays with the objects present in the simulation. The approaches vary in terms of performance and usability, depending on the configuration of the laser scanner (2D/3D, resolution) and the structure of the scene (number of static and dynamic objects and their distance to the sensor).

Using the z-buffer to simulate a laser scanner is similar to the camera simulation up to the point, that the complete scene is rendered from the point of view of the laser scanner. As only the depth-information is processed, it suffices to render the geometry data of all objects omitting lighting, color or texture information thus improving performance. The depth-information is read back after rendering and can be used to calculate the orthogonal distance of the depicted objects from the viewing plane. Considering the direction of the rays, this information can be used to calculate the length of the rays (see Fig. 1).

Within the standard pinhole model used by OpenGL rendering the view rays are distributed uniformly on the projection plane yielding a non-uniform angular distribution of the rays (cf. Fig. 1). For a scan of $2n + 1$ rays of the range $[-\alpha_{max} \ldots \alpha_{max}]$, the i-th ray from the center has the direction

$$\tilde{\alpha}_i = \arctan\left(\frac{i}{n} \cdot \tan(\alpha_{max})\right).$$

Fig. 1. Left: Distribution of the rays and measured distance in z-buffer. Middle: Vehicle with 3D laser scanner, augmented with visualization of the scan. Right: Depth-image read from the z-Buffer.

As most real laser scanners have a uniform angular distribution, a mapping of the distances calculated from the z-buffer to the rays of the simulated scanner must be performed. This can be done by using interpolation, optionally preceded by supersampling (that is, rendering at a higher resolution than desired).

As the pinhole projection is limited to aperture angles below 180 deg, the opening angle for the simulated laser scanner is limited. Due to the non-uniform distribution of the angles it should be well below this limit. Simulation of laser scanners with a wider angular range can be done using multiple rendering passes with different viewing directions.

Simulating a laser scanner by calculating ray intersections may use an arbitrary number of rays with any distribution. To speed up the calculation, a hierarchy of bounding volumes is used. The same hierarchy already is used for collision detection (see [13]), so it imposes no extra overhead on the simulation. The calculation is further sped up exploiting local coherence: If a ray intersects an object, it is likely, that a neighboring ray will also intersect this object, so that the search space can be limited further.

To integrate simulated laser scanners with a control application a controller-algorithm (see Sect. 2.3) can be attached to the simulated laser scanner. This controller is used to handle communication with any external application. A special controller has been developed implementing the SCIP2.0 (see [14]) protocol of the widely used Hokuyo URG04LX laser scanner. Using this controller, applications can be connected transparently to the real or the simulated device.

5   Results

5.1   Applications

MuRoSimF has been used to create several simulations for a wide range of robots differing in mode of locomotion as well as simulated sensors. Due to the easy recombination of the existing algorithms simulations *adequate* for a given purpose, e. g. by choosing appropriate algorithms for motion or sensor simulation can be created easily.

Simulation of biped robots has been used successfully for testing several modules of the control software including image processing, world modeling, behavior

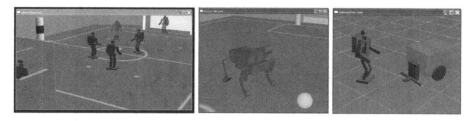

Fig. 2. Left: Simulation of a team of humanoid soccer playing robots. Middle: Simulation of a newly developed quadruped robot. Right: Simulation of a heterogeneous team of autonomous robots.

control and motion generation. Beyond biped robots `MuRoSimF`-based simulations have been used for several purposes including development of a quadruped robot and research in the field of cooperation for heterogeneous teams of autonomous robots (see, e.g., Fig. 2 and [12,15]).

Most recently a simulation for a newly developed small four-wheeled autonomous offroad vehicle equipped with a laser scanner has been created. This simulation is used to evaluate high level behavior and sensor processing for control applications for single vehicles as well as teams of vehicles (cf. Figs. 3, 4). The simulation consists of model data for the environment and for each simulated vehicle. Each vehicle is modeled as a compound object, including a laser scanner object. Motion simulation is based on the simplified dynamics algorithm presented in Sect. 3.2. The laser scanner can be simulated with either algorithm described in Sect. 4.

5.2   Performance of Simulation

The performance of the simulation has been measured for the simulation of four-wheeled vehicles in a simplified urban scenario described above. Measurements were taken on two laptop computers (cf. Table 1) equipped with a single resp. dual core CPU.

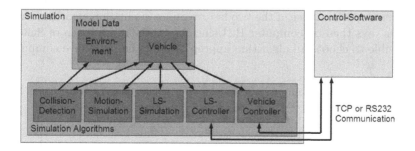

Fig. 3. Structure of the simulation: Vehicle data, motion and laser scanner (LS) simulation and the controllers can be duplicated to simulate more than one vehicle. Arrows indicate direction of data flow.

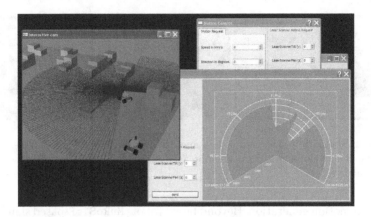

Fig. 4. Simulation of the vehicle (left) connected to a `RoboFrame`-based control application (right). The visualization of the simulation is augmented with the readings from the vehicle's laser scanner.

The performance of the motion simulation was measured with disabled laser scanners. Only the collision detection and the dynamics modules (both running at 1000 fps) and the controllers were active in this test. Using one core of the CPU of computer A up to 20 vehicles could be simulated in real time. Using both cores (parallelizing only dynamics simulation, but not collision detection), up to 30 vehicles could be measured. On computer B (single core CPU) up to 19 vehicles could be simulated in real time.

The performance of the laser scanner simulation has been measured for several setups of laser scanners in 2D and 3D configurations (see Table 2). During these measurements the motion simulation was running single threaded at 1000 fps. An interesting result of the measurements is the fact, that simulation of scanners with many rays is more efficient using the z-buffer method while calculation of ray intersections is more efficient for scanners with very view rays.

Another result from these measurements is, that the performance of the single simulation algorithms strongly differs by the hardware used. On computer A the break even in performance of the two laser-scanner-simulation algorithms was at much less rays then on computer B. Using the modular approach of `MuRoSimF` it is possible to choose an algorithm appropriate for the respective computer.

Table 1. Computers used for performance measurements

	Computer A	Computer B
CPU	Intel Centrino Duo (dual core)	Intel Pentium M (single core)
Speed	1.67 GHz	1.86 GHz
RAM	1 GByte	1 GByte
Graphics-chipset	Intel 945GM express	ATI Mobility Radeon X700

Table 2. Measurement of real-time performance of laser scanner simulation

Method	Resolution	Scanner FPS	Vehicles on Computer A	Computer B
z-buffer	10×1	10	7	12
	100×1	10	7	10
	100×10	10	5	6
	100×100	10	2	5
ray-intersection	10×1	10	9	16
	100×1	10	5	10
	100×10	10	2	2

6   Conclusions and Outlook

In this paper `MuRoSimF`, a framework capable of creating 3D simulations for teams of autonomous mobile robots with different modes of locomotion (wheeled, biped, quadruped) and different sensors has been presented. To the authors' best knowledge it has the unique feature of enabling a very flexible selection of simulation methods and algorithms for motion and sensing (sub-)systems with different levels of realism for different robots in the same scene. Specifically, a newly developed simulation for teams of wheeled vehicles has been presented and evaluated in this paper.

Several improvements of the earlier developments described in [11,13] have been achieved: The high performance of `MuRoSimF` when simulating legged robots could be transfered to wheeled robots. Two new algorithms for the simulation of laser scanners were added to the framework. They can be exchanged transparently allowing to choose the algorithm appropriate for a given simulation task. It is planned to enhance these algorithms by considering distortions of the scan caused by the robot's motion.

First steps were taken to enable the distribution of the simulation to multiple CPUs. Even though currently only the algorithms used for motion simulation can be parallelized, by using a dual core CPU the number of vehicles simulated in real-time could be increased by 50%. The next step in improving the simulation's performance will be the development and integration of collision-detection algorithms which can be executed in parallel threads.

To provide more realistic simulations, it is planned to validate motion- and sensor-simulation algorithms by comparing performace of simulated and real devices and improving model data. One possible way to do this is the iterative approach presented in [16] to determine the motor data of a robot motion dynamics model.

Even though `MuRoSimF` is not open source, the source code is available upon request for research and educational purposes (see www.dribblers.de/murosimf).

Acknowledgment. Parts of this research have been supported by the German Research Foundation (DFG) within the Research Training Group 1362 "Cooperative, adaptive and responsive monitoring in mixed mode environments".

References

1. Carpin, S., Lewis, M., Wang, J., Balakirsky, S., Scrapper, C.: USARSim: a robot simulator for research and education. In: Proc. of the 2007 IEEE Intl. Conf. on Robotics and Automation (ICRA) (2007)
2. Epic Games, Unreal engine (2007), http://www.epicgames.com
3. Smith, R.: ODE - Open Dynamics Engine (2007), http://www.ode.org
4. Koenig, N., Howard, A.: Gazebo - 3D multiple robot simulator with dynamics (2003), http://playerstage.sourceforge.net/gazebo/gazebo.html
5. Gerkey, B.P., Vaughan, R.T., Howard, A.: The Player/Stage project: Tools for multi-robot and distributed sensor systems. In: Intl. Conf. on Advanced Robotics (ICAR), Coimbra, Portugal, 30 June - 3 July 2003, pp. 317–323 (2003)
6. Laue, T., Spiess, K., Röfer, T.: SimRobot - a general physical robot simulator and its application in RoboCup. In: Bredenfeld, A., et al. (eds.) RoboCup 2005. LNCS (LNAI), vol. 4020, pp. 173–183. Springer, Heidelberg (2006)
7. Michel, O.: Cyberbotics ltd. - webots(tm): Professional mobile robot simulation. Intl. Journal of Advanced Robotic Systems 1(1), 39–42 (2004)
8. Microsoft Robotics Studio (2007), http://msdn.microsoft.com/robotics/
9. AGEIA PhysX website (2007), http://www.ageia.com/physx/
10. Hugues, L., Bredeche, N.: Simbad: an autonomous robot simulation package for education and research. In: Proceedings of The Ninth International Conference on the Simulation of Adaptive Behavior (SAB 2006), Rome, Italy (2006)
11. Friedmann, M., Petersen, K., von Stryk, O.: Tailored real-time simulation for teams of humanoid robots. In: Visser, U., Ribeiro, F., Ohashi, T., Dellaert, F. (eds.) RoboCup 2007: Robot Soccer World Cup XI. Lecture Notes in CS/AI, vol. 5001, pp. 425–432. Springer, Heidelberg (2008)
12. Kiener, J., von Stryk, O.: Cooperation of heterogeneous, autonomous robots: A case study of humanoid and wheeled robots. In: Proc. IEEE/RSJ International Conference on Intelligent Robots and Systems (IROS), San Diego, CA, USA, October 29 - November 2, 2007, pp. 959–964 (2007)
13. Friedmann, M., Petersen, K., von Stryk, O.: Adequate motion simulation and collision detection for soccer playing humanoid robots. In: Proc. 2nd Workshop on Humanoid Soccer Robots at the 2007 IEEE-RAS Int. Conf. on Humanoid Robots, Pittsburgh, PA, USA, November 29 - December 1 (2007)
14. Kawata, H., Ohya, A., Yuta, S.: Development of ultra-small lightweight optical range sensor system. In: Proc. IEEE/RSJ International Conference on Intelligent Robots and Systems (IROS) (2005)
15. Friedmann, M., Petters, S., Risler, M., Sakamoto, H., Thomas, D., von Stryk, O.: A new, open and modular platform for research in autonomous four-legged robots. In: Berns, K., Luksch, T. (eds.) Autonome Mobile Systeme 2007, Informatik aktuell, Kaiserslautern, October 18 - 19, 2007, pp. 254–260. Springer, Heidelberg (2007)
16. Stelzer, M., Hardt, M., von Stryk, O.: Efficient dynamic modeling, numerical optimal control and experimental results for various gaits of a quadruped robot. In: CLAWAR 2003: 6th International Conference on Climbing and Walking Robots, Catania, Italy, September 17-19, 2003, pp. 601–608 (2003)

MM-ulator: Towards a Common Evaluation Platform for Mixed Mode Environments

Matthias Kropff, Christian Reinl, Kim Listmann, Karen Petersen,
Katayon Radkhah, Faisal Karim Shaikh, Arthur Herzog, Armin Strobel,
Daniel Jacobi, and Oskar von Stryk*

Technische Universität Darmstadt, Research Training Group "Cooperative, Adaptive
and Responsive Monitoring in Mixed Mode Environments", 64289 Darmstadt,
Germany
http://www.gkmm.tu-darmstadt.de

Abstract. We investigate the interaction of mobile robots, relying on information provided by heterogeneous sensor nodes, to accomplish a mission. Cooperative, adaptive and responsive monitoring in Mixed-Mode Environments (MMEs) raises the need for multi-disciplinary research initiatives. To date, such research initiatives are limited since each discipline focusses on its domain specific simulation or testbed environment. Existing evaluation environments do not respect the interdependencies occurring in MMEs. As a consequence, holistic validation for development, debugging, and performance analysis requires an evaluation tool incorporating multi-disciplinary demands. In the context of MMEs, we discuss existing solutions and highlight the synergetic benefits of a common evaluation tool. Based on this analysis we present the concept of the *MM-ulator*: a novel architecture for an evaluation tool incorporating the necessary diversity for multi-agent hard-/software-in-the-loop simulation in a modular and scalable way.

1 Introduction

Mixed Mode Environments cover the range from static and structured to highly dynamic and unstructured environments and consist of a myriad of networked nodes including sensors, robots and possibly humans-in-the-loop. Further, MMEs are characterized by different kinds of heterogeneity with respect to the utilized devices and their capabilities (e.g. communication interfaces, energy resources, sensor data). The scenarios addressed within MMEs may vary from monitoring and surveillance tasks, using heterogeneous sensors, to the coordination of autonomous vehicles. Accomplishing these tasks requires knowledge from four main domains: (1) robotics and control, (2) communication, (3) sensing, and (4) dependable middleware.

---

* This research has been supported by the German Research Foundation (DFG) within the Research Training Group 1362 "Cooperative, adaptive and responsive monitoring in mixed mode environments".

S. Carpin et al. (Eds.): SIMPAR 2008, LNAI 5325, pp. 41–52, 2008.

In order to respect the multi-disciplinary issues, a common tool is needed to examine the various problems and mutual dependencies. Throughout the last years, the design of such simulation environments has been of significant interest, particularly to the RoboCup community [3]. To the best of our knowledge, however, there exists no evaluation tool covering the diversity of the above named fields. Thus, a concept introducing a holistic validation tool respecting the interdisciplinarity and heterogeneity in MMEs is developed. In the remaining of the paper, we will refer to this concept as the *MM-ulator*.

The paper is organized as follows: Next, we highlight the benefits of a common evaluation tool and define the necessary requirements. In Section 3 we survey relevant simulation tools and discuss their applicability to relevant scenarios. The proposed architecture of the *MM-ulator* is presented in Section 4.

2   Benefits and Challenges of a Common Evaluation Platform

For the purpose of validation and performance analysis, three well known evaluation methodologies can be applied: (1) analytical modeling, (2) simulation, and (3) real experiments. Since analytical modeling is rather impractical and real experiments are expensive and time consuming, a valuable approach is to use simulation. But as only real experiments provide realistic results, they cannot be neglected in general. Hence, validation techniques giving the opportunity to incorporate real systems, would be beneficial. To this end, we focus on *emulation*, a hybrid validation technique combining simulation and real-world experiments, including the known elements of software- and hardware-in-the-loop tests. Figure 1 highlights the conceptual differences to pure simulation.

Relying on the emulation approach, the developer does not have to cope with simulation time semantics, and the integration of existing sensor and robot hardware to a certain degree is facilitated. This turns emulation into a suitable tool for controlled prototype testing and debugging. Figure 1 also indicates that the

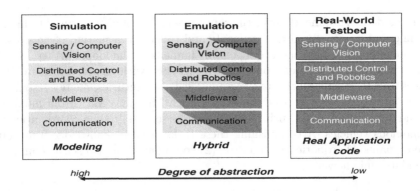

Fig. 1. Emulation as hybrid approach of simulation and real-world experiments

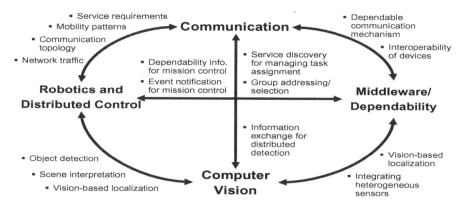

Fig. 2. Multi-disciplinary knowledge

degree of abstraction depends merely on the modeled building block: Since only minor parts need to be modeled in detail, the degree of abstraction for the middleware and communication module is low, whereas the sensing and control module require a moderate degree of abstraction.

2.1 Benefits of Validation by Using Multi-disciplinary Knowledge

The synergetic benefits of tightly coupled multi-disciplinary knowledge is shown in Figure 2. The interconnecting arrows indicate the potential decrease in the level of abstraction regarding the shown dependencies, enabling more realistic results. To have a more thorough understanding of the highlighted challenges, let us consider an explosion in a chemical plant and a subsequent spread of fire, evolving into a toxic environment, inaccessible to human operators. In order to support the rescue operations, a team of robots starts exploring the environment. Fundamental tasks are building a map of the environment, locating victims and marking safe exit pathways or unreachable areas.

In the following, we will point out some sparsely tackled research questions from the perspective of cooperative control and mobile communicating, as well as sensing and middleware.

Benefits for Mobile Communicating Teams of Vehicles and Nodes: In order to use heterogeneous autonomous mobile sensing platforms such as robots within MMEs, it is crucial to combine their control and coordination oriented communication. It has been shown that the information flow among the robots influences the stability of their coordinated movement [10]. Due to this mutual coupling, the communication properties of the environment and the robots need to be respected when applicable control algorithms are being designed. These properties include reflections, fading effects, communication range and packet losses. On the one hand, these effects have a significant impact, e.g. on close loop stability for cooperative control. On the other hand, distributed control may change the network topology, improving routing efficiency or covering a wider area while remaining connected. This combination is obviously bidirectional and very important with respect to cooperative control of robotic groups.

Typically, field data is provided by sensors. Cooperative data gathering based on aggregated information is closely related to the positions of the robots and viewing angles of their sensors. Thus, the verification of hypotheses in scene interpretation and object detection can be significantly improved by connecting the algorithms to the motion control of robots. Realistic simulated sensor outputs, e.g. including noise, will show the reliability of control algorithms in non-ideal situations and will give rise to increase the robustness of the applied methods. Furthermore, visual servoing [8], dynamic acquisition of navigational data, and distributed cooperative mapping strategies are other representative topics. They incorporate fundamental issues from sensing and motion control, such as the amount of necessary information exchange between multiple unmanned vehicles, mission control, or stability of coordination of partially autonomous robots.

Benefits for Sensing and Middleware: In the exemplified scenario, robots will have to discover services offered by sensor nodes in radio proximity and therefore, help to re-establish a reliable and efficient communication infrastructure. This smart behavior still imposes several research challenges on communication and middleware concepts. Self-description and self-profiling mechanisms are needed to spontaneously migrate devices into the networked environment, regardless of the given sensor manufacturer or interface. Middleware simplifies the interconnections between sensing, communication, and distributed control. A formal specification of interfaces for these parts leads to an increase of the interoperability of different devices. One challenge is to specify a common representation, to allow hardware independent robot task assignment, actuator control, interpretation of pre-processed sensor data, and robot capability description.

Dependability supporting approaches like multi-path routing require the specification of constraints, which can be provided by the middleware if appropriate interfaces are defined. Finally, several questions in the communication domain are closely linked to information provided by a well-defined middleware concept. For instance, approaches like efficient semantic addressing and routing of sensing and actuation data require certain self-description functionalities on the communication level.

Even by this brief discussion on upcoming research challenges, a fundamental question arises: How will multi-disciplinary performance metrics look like? We believe that having a holistic evaluation tool, available solutions for MME problems can be regarded from new perspectives. For instance, as migrating wireless network constraints into robot control, new metrics like coordination stability will emerge.

To our knowledge, these cross-sectional issues are not supported by any of the existing simulation environments. Based on this analysis we propose the requirements, which are fundamental for such a holistic evaluation tool.

2.2 Basic Requirements

The simulation and emulation of a real physical world requires a flexible approach. A modular architecture is necessary to facilitate scalability and adjustable degrees of abstraction. Furthermore, the *MM-ulator* needs to provide realistic fault and security models as well as efficient analysis and visualization of gathered data. Dependability aspects provide different faults and threat models which can also be considered in the *MM-ulator*.

Modeling Node Properties: Robots, unmanned vehicles, sensors, actuators, and main servers require heterogeneous 3D models. Besides, the locomotion properties, kinematics and motion dynamics of robots and vehicles are essential to be modeled. Sensor readings, e.g., for laser scanners, cameras, or contact sensors must be considered with an adjustable accuracy. Specific resources like processing power (e.g., for on-board image processing), memory, communication capabilities, energy consumption, and sensing devices with different levels of accuracy have to be modeled properly and comprehensively.

Modeling Physical Environment Properties: The physical environment splits up in static and dynamic properties. The static part consists of a realistic 3D model of the environment, including obstacles, buildings, surface properties, and various objects of interest as well as physical effects like gravity. The dynamic parts of the physical environment include basic radio frequency propagation models for identifying communication links and specific scenario settings like mobility patterns of victims and rescue teams, chemical and physical concentrations (e.g., radioactivity), diffusion process of (toxic) gas, or the spread of fire. The dynamic parts need to be modeled thoroughly. Also interactions with the environment by the nodes, e.g., the distribution of RFID tags, robot driven installment of sensor nodes need to be incorporated in the model of the physical environment.

3   Related Work

Currently available simulation environments for testing algorithmic approaches for the addressed scenarios are either rooted in the area of 3D robot simulation, Wireless Sensor Networks (WSNs) or in Mobile Ad Hoc Networks (MANETs).

USARSim [6] is a 3D simulator for testing robotic applications, especially for search and rescue scenarios. It is based on the *Unreal Engine* by epic games [1], providing plausible physics simulation and high quality visualization. State information is exchanged with the engine using the scripting language *Unrealscript*. USARSim supports a variety of robot models, including legged, wheeled and tracked vehicles, as well as submarines and helicopters, and additionally provides a wide range of sensor models, including cameras, range, touch or odometry sensors. Based on existing classes and adapted scripts new robots/sensors can be added, respectively. Robot control can either be performed by sending text messages via TCP sockets, or by utilizing wrappers for the middleware Player [7], Pyro [5] or MOAST [4], that are already available in USARSim. In most cases, code that was developed within the simulation will also work on the real robots.

The Multi-Robot-Simulation-Framework (MuRoSimF) [12] (cf. Fig. 5(left)) can be used to create simulations for cooperating teams of heterogeneous robots in dynamic environments. MuRoSimF provides models for different legged and wheeled robots equipped with sensors, like cameras and laser range finders. Its modular structure facilitates to assign different algorithms to each part in the simulation (e.g. motion or sensor simulation for individual robots) and provides the option to be extended by the required inter robot communication mechanism.

Other related robot simulation environments are Webots [24], Gazebo [17], Microsoft Robotics Studio [2] and SimRobot [18]. Common to the named tools is their focus on detailed 3D models of the environment, surfaces, robots and physics simulation, while they predominantly lack of components for modeling wireless multi-hop communication, integration of mediating middleware concepts or the incorporation of dependability models for realistic scenario test-runs.

A second category of simulation environments evolves from the area of Wireless Sensor Networks (cf. Fig. 5(right)). TOSSIM [19] is a simulator for wireless sensor nodes which are running the operating system TinyOS. Its dual mode functionality allows to run TinyOS code in a controlled simulation mode as well as on real sensor hardware. In simulation mode TOSSIM models link connectivity by probabilistic models and provides detailed hardware abstraction effects including ADC and battery models. A similar approach is the cycle-accurate instruction level simulator Avrora [26], which operates on sensor node firmware images and provides simulation of fine grained radio models including detailed models to evaluate the energy efficiency of different protocols. A two tier form of WSN heterogeneity is supported by the EMStar framework [13]. It provides simulation and emulation capabilities for constrained motes, as well as more powerful microservers, and therefore focus on middleware mechanisms to provide interoperability.

The most significant drawback of the presented platforms is that they were intentionally designed for static, resource constrained nodes. This disallows the simultaneous integration of more powerful platforms within this setup.

Mobile nodes possessing higher processing/communication capabilities are addressed in the area of Mobile Ad Hoc Networks. Typical emulation environments strongly focus on the evaluation of routing protocols for Mobile Ad Hoc Networks and are shown in [9,11,14,20,21,22,23,25,27]. However, these approaches address predominantly algorithmic solutions on the network and medium access layer, while mobility and network traffic patterns are predefined in advance of a testrun. As a result, the evaluation of mechanisms for dynamic and cooperative task assignment, motion control under constraints of network connectivity or the interaction of heterogeneous groups of mobile robots are disregarded.

4   Proposed Architecture

The proposed architecture for the *MM-ulator* aims to fulfill two main requirements: (1) reducing the software re-implementation overhead when switching from validation by simulation to a real-world test-run and (2) incorporating real hardware platforms in the evaluation process. To cover a wide range of possible devices, a generic node architecture is proposed that allows to run the same software code either on real embedded systems like robots or sensor hardware, or to instantiate a pure software entity as a virtual node on a common PC platform to increase the scalability of a test-run.

4.1   Inner Node Architecture

The inner node architecture describes the functionalities of the node modules and their interconnecting interfaces. The modularity of the architecture allows to model a variety of heterogeneous devices. For instance, while the algorithms encapsulated in the distributed control module model the task planning component on a mobile robot, they might be absent in case the instantiated node entity represents a static, resource limited node, which only supports basic sensing capabilities. The *Knowledge Database* provides information about the node's communication, processing and memory capabilities. It also comprises the node's sensing and actuating resources and provides information about the node's type of locomotion, allowing to easily configure an autonomous vehicle or a static sensor node. Moreover, the knowledge database provides details about a node's energy source and depletion process during operation.

The *Middleware* module provides standardized interfaces to bridge the intra node communication between the sensors, actuators, distributed control- and communication module. It encapsulates algorithms and protocols to provide semantic node addressing and basic Publish/Subscribe mechanisms, facilitating efficient group communication among diverse node groups. Furthermore, the middleware architecture comprises mechanisms for idle sleep cycles to model energy saving algorithms for wireless sensors. Based on information from the knowledge database, the middleware module can generate a generic node description, which can be distributed to neighboring nodes to provide and discover remote sensing capabilities and to coordinate actuation capabilities for distributed task planning. Additionally, the middleware module encapsulates mechanisms for controlling data privacy and security issues.

The *Distributed Control* module comprises the algorithms for distributed task planning, coordinated task assignment and mission control. It holds the control logic for robot movements and deduces possible task goals, depending on the predefined mission statement or the scene interpretation based on sensing information. Predefined mission tasks range from fetching simple sensor readings at a specific location to more elaborated tasks such as exploring the environment and finding injured people.

The *Communication* module encompasses higher level algorithms and protocols for wireless ad hoc communication. To provide an heterogeneous emulation

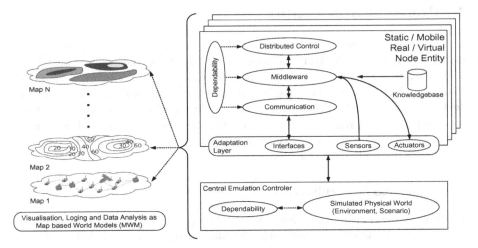

Fig. 3. Architecture of the proposed *MM-ulator*

scenario of virtual and hardware nodes simultaneously, network layer functionalities like routing algorithms, service discovery and interface management mechanisms are modeled consistently on node level. For modeling further wireless network mechanisms like the Medium Access (MAC) layer or topology control algorithms, the communication interface at the adaptation layer provides means to specify packet based scheduling policies and transmit power adjustments, which are used in the centralized emulation controller to determine the resulting packet scheduling and network topology.

The inner node core is enriched by the *Dependability* module, which provides the extra-functional abstraction layer (EFAL) for other modules. The EFAL provides fault modeling and injection of faults to ensure the proper execution of application code in the face of failures. For secure execution of applications, the EFAL provides threat modeling and threat injection mechanisms. The EFAL also enables dependability/security evaluation metrics for comprehensive evaluation and debugging of inner node interactions.

4.2   Inter Node Architecture

The connection of the nodes to the simulated world, the so called *central emulation controller*, is crucial to the architecture presented in Fig. 3. Generally, all node-to-environment and node-to-node interactions are exchanged using this connection. The connection is mainly supported by the adaptation layer on the side of the node and by the simulated physical world on the side of the central emulation controller. The former acts as a filter for the exchanged data such that only the information relevant to this node is incorporated and passed to the inner node modules. The latter defines the world model leading to physically correct information. This world model consists of a 3D model of the environment possessing real physical properties (e.g. friction, gravity). Moreover, communication

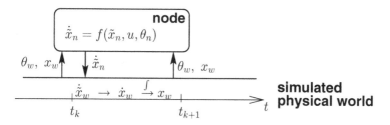

Fig. 4. Information flow between the node and the central emulation controller

links (basic RF propagation) and scenario settings can be respected. Considering our interest in search and rescue operations, the spread of substances/fire needs to be modeled; also an interaction with the environment is necessary. Such architecture leads to the information flow structure shown in Fig. 4.

A state space description of each node is applied which, e.g. for a mobile robot, describes its dynamical motion. At time t_k every node computes its own, desired change of state $\dot{\tilde{x}}_n$ using the node's own state $\tilde{x}_n$, control variable u and the relevant parameters θ_n. The relevant information for each node needs to be filtered out of the world information and adapted according to the properties of the node. As already mentioned, this adaptation is performed by the adaptation layer. This layer can work with real hardware or simulated virtual nodes. In the case of a pure simulation, threat, sensor and actuator models for the virtual node mimic the features of real sensors or actuators, resulting in a versatile structure and enabling realistic simulation.

After the computation of $\dot{\tilde{x}}_n$, each node transmits its desired change of state to the world simulation. Here, the desired changes of state of each node are combined to $\dot{\tilde{x}}_w$, the desired change of state of all nodes. Due to the fact that only local knowledge is available for each node, $\dot{\tilde{x}}_w$ is not necessarily reasonable. Thus, before computing the eventual change of state of each node $\dot{x}_w$, feasibility of $\dot{\tilde{x}}_w$ must be checked. The feasibility study is conducted by physical engines, e.g. PhysX™ by Ageia/nVIDIA or the Open Dynamics Engine ODE. Given an appropriate interpretation of $\dot{\tilde{x}}_w$ due to environmental properties, these engines can compute $\dot{x}_w$, excluding impossible movements this way. Additionally, a dependability interface provides the system with realistic fault/threat models. Similar to the inner node architecture, it investigates which, when and where to inject faults and threats [15] to influence the system behavior.

Dependability can simulate the probability of specific consequences, such as catastrophic failures. As simulation progresses, it is possible to observe 1) how the system evolves, 2) how different failures impact the system, and 3) how well the protocols handle security threats. Provided that some system properties are uncertain, the significance of those uncertainties can be determined. To the authors' knowledge, these dependability models have not been respected in the design of multi-robot system simulators before.

The above described inner node architecture enables real change of state of each node $\dot{x}_w$. A standard integration leads to the new state of all nodes x_w.

Fig. 5. Robot simulation of a wheeled vehicle equipped with a laser scanner exploring an urban area (left). WSN simulation without locomotion properties (right).

Including the possibly altered parameters of the simulation and the environment θ_w, the state x_w is subsequently sent back to each node at time t_{k+1} and the simulation can proceed.

4.3   Visualization and Analysis

In general, efficient tracing, analysis, and visualization of log data is one of the main and important aspects of a simulation. Since spatial correlation is common in MMEs, the *MM-ulator* visualization abstractly presents the regions of interest instead of single sensor values. Maps are a natural way to describe the physical real world as well as the network world. The *MM-ulator* provides a Map-based World Model (MWM) [16] consisting of a stack of maps of relevant attributes (e.g., fault/threat map, connectivity map, residual energy map) (cf. Fig. 3).

The MWM abstracts different levels in *MM-ulator* such as communication issues and supports arbitrary applications. It allows efficient event detection, prediction and querying the network. The analysis based on MWM provides efficient mechanisms for predictive monitoring, proactive MME reconfiguration, enhancement of MME functionality, dependability and security.

4.4   First Implementation Steps

The screenshot outlined in the left part of Fig. 5 shows our search and rescue benchmark scenario in the MuRoSimF-based simulation [12] environment. Although, MuRoSimF with its origin in robot simulation provides detailed information on the physical environment and on the control/task states during the exploration phase, the aspects of wireless communication for robot interaction and remote sensor reading is not fully supported yet.

The right part of the figure shows the simulation of a homogeneous, static wireless sensor network (e.g. by using [19]) incorporating detailed protocol performance depending on sensor coverage and network connectivity for reliable event reporting. Based on the design proposed in 4.1 - 4.3 it is possible to integrate the communication characteristics of wireless multi-hop networks to MuRoSimF's dynamic environment models, providing more realistic radio propagation models as well as scenario dependent packet flows.

5   Conclusion

A novel architecture for a simulation environment has been proposed for emulation and validation of fundamental research topics from the diverse fields involved in using heterogeneous networks of sensors and mobile robots in mixed mode environments. Motivated by various benefits of such a tool, a modular architecture has been presented to meet the different requirements and levels of realism in simulation. The architecture itself is comprised of a central emulation controller acting as the physical world and independent modules, incorporating the node specific characteristics, that are connected to this physical world emulation. Resulting in a highly scalable approach, this architecture respects issues that have not been considered before and is designed such that every node instance may either be simulated or real hardware equipment.

Future work will primarily deal with the implementation of this architecture as a stand-alone simulation tool extending existing simulators.

Acknowledgements. The authors thank Johannes Meyer, Paul Schnitzspan, Mykhaylo Andriluka, Martin Friedmann, and Abdelmajid Khelil for helpful discussions.

References

1. Epic games, unreal engine (2007), http://www.epicgames.com
2. Microsoft Robotics Studio (2007), http://msdn.microsoft.com/robotics/
3. Balakirsky, S., Scrapper, C., Carpin, S., Lewis, M.: USARSim: providing a framework for multi-robot performance evaluation. In: Proceedings of PerMIS (2006)
4. Balakirsky, S., Scrapper, C., Messina, E.: Mobility open architecture simulation and tools environment. In: Proc. of the Intl. Conf. on Integration of Knowledge Intensive Multi-Agent Systems (2005)
5. Blank, D.S., Kumar, D., Meeden, L., Yanco, H.: Pyro: A python-based versatile programming environment for teaching robotics. Journal of Educational Resources in Computing (JERIC) (2004)
6. Carpin, S., Lewis, M., Wang, J., Balakirsky, S., Scrapper, C.: USARSim: a robot simulator for research and education. In: Proc. of the 2007 IEEE Intl. Conf. on Robotics and Automation (2007)
7. Collett, T.H.J., MacDonald, B.A., Gerkey, B.: Player 2.0: Toward a practical robot programming framework. In: Proc. of the Australasian Conf. on Robotics and Automation (2005)
8. Cowan, N., Lopes, G., Koditschek, D.: Rigid body visual servoing using navigation functions. In: Proc. of the 39th IEEE Conf. on Decision and Control (2000)
9. Engel, M., Freisleben, B., Smith, M., Hanemann, S.: Wireless Ad-Hoc Network Emulation Using Microkernel-Based Virtual Linux Systems. In: Proc. of 5th EUROSIM Congress on Modeling and Simulation, pp. 198–203 (2004)
10. Fax, J.A., Murray, R.M.: Information flow and cooperative control of vehicle formations. IEEE Trans. on Automatic Control 49(9), 1465–1476 (2004)
11. Flynn, J., Tewari, H., O'Mahony, D.: JEmu: A Real Time Emulation System for Mobile Ad Hoc Networks. In: Proc. of the SCS Conf. on Communication Networks and Distributed Systems Modeling and Simulation, pp. 115–120 (2002)

12. Friedmann, M., Petersen, K., von Stryk, O.: Adequate motion simulation and collision detection for soccer playing humanoid robots. In: Proc. 2nd Workshop on Humanoid Soccer Robots at the 2007 IEEE-RAS Intl. Conf. on Humanoid Robots (2007)

13. Girod, L., Stathopoulos, T., Ramanathan, N., Elson, J., Estrin, D., Osterweil, E., Schoellhammer, T.: A system for simulation, emulation, and deployment of heterogeneous sensor networks. In: Proc. of the 1st Intl. Conf. on Embedded Networked Sensor Systems (2004)

14. He, R., Yuan, M., Hu, J., Zhang, H., Kan, Z., Ma, J.: A Real-time Scalable and Dynamical Test System for MANET. In: Proc. of 14th IEEE Conf. on Personal, Indoor and Mobile Radio Communications, pp. 1644–1648 (2003)

15. Johansson, A., Murphy, B., Suri, N.: On the impact of injection triggers for os robustness evaluation. In: The 18th IEEE Intl. Symp. on Software Reliability Engineering (2007)

16. Khelil, A., Shaikh, F.K., Ayari, B., Suri, N.: MWM: A map-based world model for event-driven wireless sensor networks. In: The 2nd ACM International Conference on Autonomic Computing and Communication Systems (AUTONOMICS) (to appear, 2008)

17. Koenig, N., Howard, A.: Gazebo - 3D multiple robot simulator with dynamics (2003), http://playerstage.sourceforge.net/gazebo/gazebo.html

18. Laue, T., Spiess, K., Röfer, T.: SimRobot – A General Physical Robot Simulator and Its Application in RoboCup. In: Bredenfeld, A., et al. (eds.) RoboCup 2005. LNCS (LNAI), vol. 4020, pp. 173–183. Springer, Heidelberg (2006)

19. Levis, P., Lee, N., Welsh, M., Culler, D.: Tossim: accurate and scalable simulation of entire tinyos applications. In: Proc. of the 1st Intl. Conf. on Embedded Networked Sensor Systems, pp. 126–137 (2003)

20. Lin, T., Midkiff, S.F., Park, J.S.: A Dynamic Topology Switch for the Emulation of Wireless Mobile Ad Hoc Networks. In: Proc. of the 27th Annual IEEE Conf. on Local Computer Networks, pp. 791–798 (2002)

21. Mahadevan, P., Rodriguez, A., Becker, D., Vahdat, A.: MobiNet: A Scalable Emulation Infrastructure for Ad hoc and Wireless Networks. In: Proc. of Intl. Workshop on Wireless Traffic Measurements and Modeling, pp. 7–12 (2005)

22. Maier, S., Herrscher, D., Rothermel, K.: On Node Virtualization for Scalable Network Emulation. In: Proc. of Intl. Symp. on Performance Evaluation of Computer and Telecommunication Systems, pp. 917–928 (2005)

23. Matthes, M., Biehl, H., Lauer, M., Drobnik, O.: MASSIVE: An Emulation Environment for Mobile Ad-Hoc Networks. In: Proc. of IEEE 2nd Annual Conf. on Wireless On-demand Network Systems and Services, pp. 54–59 (2005)

24. Michel, O.: Cyberbotics ltd. - webots(tm): Professional mobile robot simulation. Intl. Journal of Advanced Robotic Systems 1(1), 39–42 (2004)

25. Puzar, M., Plagemann, T.: NEMAN: A Network Emulator for Mobile Ad-Hoc Networks. In: Proc. of 8th Intl. Conf. on Telecommunications (2005)

26. Titzer, B.L., Lee, D., Palsberg, J.: Avrora: Scalable sensor network simulation with precise timing. In: Proc. of 4th Intl. Conf. on Information Processing in Sensor Networks, Los Angeles (2005)

27. Zheng, P., Ni, L.M.: EMWIN: Emulating a Mobile Wireless Network Using a Wired Network. In: Proc. of 5th ACM Intl. Workshop on Wireless Mobile Multimedia, pp. 64–71 (2002)

A Multi-agent 3D Simulation Environment
for Clothing Industry

Rezia Molfino[1], Enrico Carca[1], Matteo Zoppi[1], Fabio Bonsignorio[1],
Massimo Callegari[2], Andrea Gabrielli[2], and Marco Principi[2]

[1] PMARlab, DIMEC, University of Genova, Italy
[2] Department of Mechanics, Polytechnic University of Marche, Ancona, Italy
{molfino,carca,zoppi}@dimec.unige.it,
{m.callegari,andrea.gabrielli,m.principi}@univpm.it

Abstract. The clothing artefact business is facing relevant restructuring to become able to produce items with enhanced value as for quality reliability, fashion inventiveness and mass customization. The paper presents a multi-agent
simulation environment developed to assess and virtually check the feasibility
and performances of flexible automation solutions that can help the clothing industry to overcome the shift towards knowledge driven organizations. It addresses new options based on distributed intelligence and robotized cooperative
resources including human assisted working.

Keywords: Cloth manufacture, multi-agent simulation, robotics.

1 Introduction

The textile clothing industry characterizes by wit and knowledge driven settings, followed by labour intensive shop lay-outs and, so far, to improve effectiveness, productive break-up is exploited, with advertising and creative firms fed by decentralized
processing sections, to distribute the work according to wages and skills figures. Business success is sought, balancing added value and cost reduction, by productive decen-
tralization aiming at preserving quality critical jobs under direct control.

The evolution coherently moves towards new organizations, based on distributed intelligence to grant products quality monitoring, while enabling flexibility by including functional robotic resources and specialized manufacturing cells as well as new production
schedules assuring return on investment following the lean manufacturing concept [1].

The paper addresses innovation based on the development of a simulation environment
able to reconstruct cloth manufacturing processes including traditional and innovative robotized devices. First, basic organizational requirements are outlined, with reference
methods to establish and assess improvements; then, multi-agent simulation aids are reviewed [2], with explanatory discussion on cloth manufacturing environments. The simulator is purposely referred to the case of quality man jacket production but, thanks to the
modular architecture it can be used for different garments production. The main scope of
the simulator is to offer to users (garment manufacturers) and to system integrators (manufacturing process developers) a mean to assess the value of the adoption of new resources
and new technologies introducing different levels of flexible automation [3].

S. Carpin et al. (Eds.): SIMPAR 2008, LNAI 5325, pp. 53–64, 2008.

2 Cloth Manufacturing Flexibility and Leanness: State of the Art and Trends

Cloth suppliers are increasingly concerned by quick-response policies, ranking at customers driven scopes [4]. These, by the way, presume technological versatility, adaptive resources and process schedules, so that effectiveness is directly related with flexibility issues, to find out better facility lay-outs and production as well as organization and schedules.

In automotive industries, e.g., integration of flexibility and leanness is recognised to be winning opportunity and prospected as Toyota paradigm (to replace Ford paradigm), whenever fast changing product mixes need be processed, to satisfy likes and tastes of diversified buyers. Very little has been done, so far, in that direction by clothes industries; labour centred shops are maintained and performance is accepted to be ranked into non uniform ranges, with quality and price highly dependent on each other. Indeed, dresses manufacture distinguishes several quality ranks, from high-standing articles (in the domain of handicraft), down to cheap offers, with standard attributes whether properly mass produced [5].

Even for mass production, clothes enterprises use loosely connected automation, bringing about flexibility in job schedules and delivery issues by means of operators trained skill and decision ability.

In view of intelligent manufacturing, the area peculiarities bring about to re-think resources and methods, stressing on flexible automation, and process control integration [6]. The simulation techniques promote betterments, by balancing added value investments with transparency of the effects. To such a purpose, a multiple-step procedure should be available, as indicated in Fig. 1.

An intelligent manufacturing solution, on these premises, is more a bet than a challenge, unless the selected lay-out is made to operate with proper production programmer and the strategic, tactical or execution flexibility is turn by turn exploited, with due account of the technological resources versatility [7].

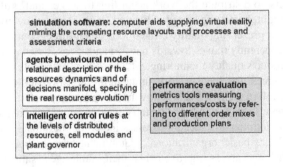

Fig. 1. Tools to assess flexibility effects in manufacture

Computer simulation and testing with virtual set-ups should be used as powerful decision aids, for off- and on-line use to deal with flexibility. The tools are typical issue of the IT, providing: - at the facility *design-development* stage to select the resources and to set-up the layout configurations: resources setting needs comply with enterprise sale policies; agendas are stated for balanced throughput and due time; - at the facility *management-fitting* stage to update the plans and to explore the recovery ability: production schedules are updated by on-process data, to face planned (e.g. itemization) or unpredictable (e.g. failures) discontinuities. In the first stage simulation will provide a precious demonstration tool for new manufacturing concepts to establish comparative enterprise forecasts and to anticipate benefits or drawbacks of the proposed solutions; in the second one simulation will support the plant management also in case of unexpected events on the basis of the embedded reference knowledge.

Simulation codes are, now, standard options, mainly, based on object languages and modular structures. Modularity is useful, to focus the attention on subsets of quantities, while leaving unaffected other parameters, drawn out from the facts to be assessed [8]. The plant effectiveness, actually, depends on a large number of properties and the investigation should distinguish direct from cross-related effects, so that the knowledge frame [5] is step-wise built up to the required level of completeness.

The clothing industry benefits move that way; the 'intelligent factory' concept is observed with caution: technology-driven additions, to a labour-intensive environment, cannot be accepted without fully acknowledging the return on investment. The throughout testing of achievements and drawbacks of virtual plants offers an affordable commitment, making easy to rank competing facilities and/or plans. Multi agent manufacturing model and simulation allow to reproduce accurately the production environment including traditional, robotic and human resources in order to make knowledge based design choices and plant management. A main advantage of multi agent simulation is in the parallel development of the processes with concurrent activities ongoing. Maintenance and upgrading of the simulator including introduction of new classes of agents for new types of resources are easy.

Ergonomic modules can be used for better definition and utilization of the involved human resources.

3   The Reference Environment

The reference environment is high quality cloth manufacturing plants where special attention is devoted to the adoption of new resources developed within the Leapfrog IP project[1]. The process flow is sketched in Fig. 2, where the grey boxes represent the sub-processes for which new resources have been purposely developed and for which the integration in the overall process has to be virtually assessed through the simulator. The main new resources are:

- a grasping robotic system for cut parts unloading from the cut table and delivering to the transport system;
- an intelligent transport system where single part carriers have complete information about the part (order, delivery, specific manufacturing operations..);
- a 3D sewing robotized system and a 2D sewing autonomous device.

[1] Leadership for European Apparel Production From Research along Original Guidelines, FP6-2003-NMP-NI-3, Contract n° 515810-2.

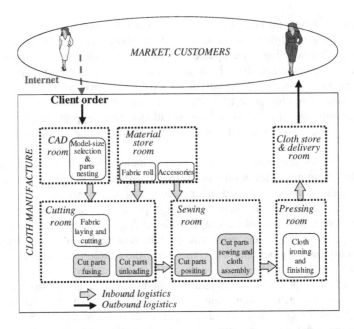

Fig. 2. Sketch of the cloth manufacturing process and foreseen areas of application of new technologies (green boxes)

4 Simulator

The system to be designed is a complex multi-agent non linear manufacturing system where the relation between the design parameters and the constraints cannot be expressed in a closed form [9]. Therefore this is a typical case where the simulation of the various alternative solutions can be an effective design support tool: in this case a DES (Discrete Events Simulation) model[2] of a whole quality cloth manufacturing plant has been implemented and analysed. The specific simulation environment provides both a qualitative (e.g. by means of visual animation) and quantitative (e.g. by means of performance indices) verification of the possible design choices.

In order to assess the technical feasibility and advantage of introducing new robotized resources for fabric manipulation, transport and joining operations, CAE applications have been adopted to test in advance the functionality of the innovative resources and their integration within the overall layout design. To this aims, a 3D physics-based multibody (PBMS) detailed simulator[3] has been developed and integrated with the DES model under a common simulation framework, as shown in Fig. 3: in the PMBS simulation the process execution strategies can be tested against realistic metrics of the production resources and actors, as interactively communicated by DES simulation. Symmetrically, the modifications on the production agents caused by the process are scheduled as events influencing the operative strategy of the whole plant.

---

[2] Based on DELMIA Quest package (by Dassault Systemes).
[3] Based on DELMIA IGRIP package (by Dassault Systemes).

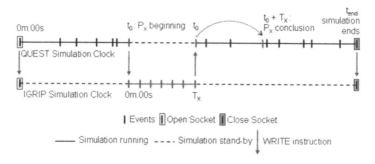

Fig. 3. Interaction between continuous time simulation and discrete event simulation (courtesy Dassault Systemes)

The run-time interfacing of the DES and PBMS models has proven to be very important for the detection of the functionalities that the control architecture must provide to make the innovative production agents cooperate. The results of this integrated approach is a realistic simulation model where the flows of materials is governed by a discrete events logics and the preparation of the list of future events depends by the results of physics based simulation, mainly in terms of the duration of processes and the kind of the produced items. In the following a brief overview of the main objects is given. The process P_X is modeled in the PBMB environment and it is recalled by the discrete events simulation at time t_0 whose master session freezes waiting for PBMB P_X process end. The process duration is T_X. Then the simulation control passes to the DES that restarts the simulation clock from t_0 and updates the list of future events by considering that the items generated by P_X will be available at time $t_0 + T_X$.

4.1 Part Models

Parts are passive entities object of the activities of system resources (agents). Parts are generated by sources, transformed and processed by agents and destroyed by sinks at the end of their lives. Cloth kinds, cut parts, fabric rolls, cloth finishing accessories are the main parts considered in the simulator environment. In our case study we considered formal man jackets and parts are represented in Fig. 4 laying down on a cutting table.

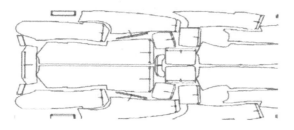

Fig. 4. Man jacket cut parts

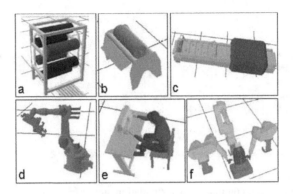

Fig. 5. Icons of the main agent resources

Due to the mass customization and quality clothing production it has been assumed a single layer cutting [10]. The part models include information about geometry and fabric physical properties useful for the PBMS software modules. User defined attributes can be introduced if and when necessary according to the application peculiarities: a meaningful example is the ID that identifies the production batch to which every part belongs to.

4.2 Agent Models

The productive facilities in cloth manufacturing plants have been classified including new purposely developed robotic resources: this led to the definition of the corresponding element classes. Each family of entities is displayed through an easily recognizable 3D mock-up. A survey is hereafter given.

• *FabricRollWareHouse* (Fig.5a). The formal jacket production orders are generated by this entity, which acts as a source of the simulation model. The icon of produced items is a fabric roll. The launch of an order is done in agreement with a Bill of Order, read from an external text file.

• *FeederMachine* (Fig.5b). The attributes of this entity reproduce the functions of the fabric roll spreaders and cloth wrapping.

• *CutTable* (Fig.5c). The fabric rolls entering this machine are destroyed and substituted by the parts that belong to the jacket or, in general, to the cloth to be manufactured. To the CutTable are associated different processes and related logics like: the scanning of the fabric faults, the single-ply cutting, the fusing with application of stiffening agents and labelling for the future recognition of the parts.

• *OperatorLoadingOfInterlining*. This resource models the operator loading of interlining on specific cut parts laying down on the cut table. This agent works in tight cooperation with the CutTable resource.

• *FusingPress* (Fig.5c). It represents the conventional thermal curing of cut parts as well as the pre-shaping of fabric shells by mean of new resources for the application of nano-agents.

• *CutTableUnloading robotic system* (Fig.5d). This resource class stands for the robot work-cell deputed to the picking of the cut parts and their loading on the conveyor.

• *Automatic2DSewing*. The resources of this family are the fixed automation 2D sewing machines for special sewing operations.

• *Manual2DSewing* (Fig.5e). This denomination indicates several agent classes that model the manual sewing stations for particular seams, sleeves or other operations that cannot be profitably automated. At this detail level the only differentiation between manual and automatic stations consists on different failure statistics that represent the workers' daily shifts. The distinction may indeed be useful for to the further sustainability assessment of the work burden to human operators: software solutions for the ergonomic analysis of manual tasks could indeed be integrated on the detailed simulation of these tasks.

• *Robot3DSewing* (Fig.5.f). This resource models the whole 3D robotized sewing cell; it is a new concept cloth assembly system that develops a set of actions like the loading and positioning of parts to be joined, the robotic 3D sewing performing and the unloading of the semi-manufactured items.

• *Transport system*. Different transport systems have been modelled taking into account their specific features. The main transport families are: - AGV and Labour: Mobile storage capacities that are used to model respectively transporters (e.g. fork lifts), automated guided vehicles, cranes, or hand moving of parts; - Conveyor and Power and Free (PnF): one-way continuous parts movement units with a fixed spatial interval between moved parts: they are conceptually identical, but conveyors perform a simple point-to-point, one-way linear transport, while PnF transportation is based on carriers travelling along a complex shape, closed loop track.

4.3 Agent's Behaviours

All elements in the simulator are controlled by built-in behavioural rules, that have a generic scope. The need for controlling the model behaviour at a very detailed level, by providing built-in data structure and methods that are specific for the run-time control and monitoring of any elements, led to write specific behavioural rules, that go beyond the standard ones: the QUEST's Simulation Control Language (SCL) was used, that is a Pascal-like, object based programming language.

These rules may be classified into the following categories:

- routing rules or productive parameters of an agent as a function of the characteristics and state of any other agent or process in execution;
- conditional execution of agents' logics;
- interruptions (e.g. maintenances) or random failures rules;
- unexpected user-driven events management rules.

Each element class has its own procedures that control the behaviour of the agents in the class. Hereafter the main procedures implemented for the innovative robotic agents are introduced with reference to the cut table unloading process, see Fig. 6.

The fabric is unwrapped and cut on each cutting table and the cut parts are loaded with their lining by operators just before entering the fusing. The duration and requirements of all simulated processes were determined in agreement with the indication suggested by an expert industrial partner. At last the processed parts are removed from the cutting table's conveying belt by means of a robotic arm equipped with a grasping device that clamps the fabric parts to the hangers and puts them into the Power and Free based internal logistic system.

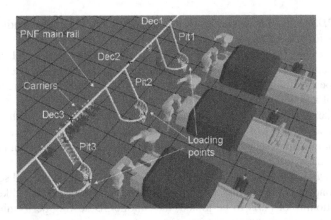

Fig. 6. PnF at cut line exit: empty hangers wait into pits, loaded hangers flow along main rail

All parts coming from the same fabric cloth inherit from it a common univocal ID that allows to recognize and reassemble them in the plant. This ID is coded as a numeric "user attribute". The process starts when all previous parts have been removed from the cutting table. Afterwards a suitable command causes a new fabric cloth to enter the machine and its ID is retrieved. The cutting process is recalled and executed, the availability status of the machine is changed to busy on processing. After the process completion, all the parts are selected and labelled with the ID inherited by the parent cloth.

The Grasping Agent Procedures. The procedure is run by the fingers when the enabling condition holds, otherwise these mechanisms hold on indefinitely. Firstly the mechanisms back to the initial position, then the grasping device detaches a hanger from the hanging conveyor, and enables its clamp to follow the fingers. The tips of the three fingers have turbine fans that lift the fabric by means of vacuum. The fingers lift up and retract, so that the fabric hems shift between the hanger clamps. After that the grasping device freezes the hanger and hands the pattern over it. As soon as the confirmation by the hanger comes, the gripper communicates to the controller that everything is ready to move towards the loading point in the hanging conveyor. The resetting of all I/O channels concludes the procedure. The master device must be able to kill the execution of the procedures associated to the slave devices. The main routine of the gripper fingers envelops the operative procedure into a while loop: the escape condition is determined by the robot controller.

The Hanger Agent Procedure. The reconfigurable hanger is made up by three passive fingers attached to the hanger body device that are reconfigured by the gripper in a two-agents synchronous task. The associated procedure is very simple: each finger is bound to follow a tag placed on the corresponding grasping device clamp. The inverse kinematics settings of the hanger's fingers let them replicate only the position of the master tags, because the orientation is not an independent parameter for a 2 DOF mechanism.

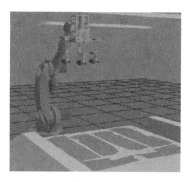

Fig. 7. 3D digital mock-up of the grasping system for cutting table unloading

The Robot Agent Procedure. The main procedure *grasp*, composed by elementary action procedures, is recalled each time a carrier is ready to be loaded with a fabric pattern, and groups the operations related to the hanger's grabbing, reconfiguring, loading and re-inlet into the inbound logistic system. With its first move, the robot gets ready to grab an empty carrier, that is always brought at the same point of the conveyor. The robot controller drives the fingers, so that they can attain the grabbing points on the current hanger. Once the hanger is secured to the gripper interface, the robot can move away from the grabbing position to the home position. The tool reference frame changes to the robot wrist frame: this same frame is indeed used by the gripper controller as the reference for calculating the fingers displacements and solve their inverse position kinematics problems. The robot moves the to the goal point and its controller orders the grasping device to reshape the hanger to the pattern grasping configuration. Actually, the robot controller is serving as a supervisor of the simultaneousness of the grasping device fingers' tasks. When the robot controller receives a suitable message, it assumes that the pattern has been successfully loaded and gives its agreement to the reloading of the hanger on the hanging conveyor. The manipulator ends the grasping procedure by moving back home.

5   Tests and Results

The production schedule is generated through a suitable database from realistic production information. Thanks to the modularity of this approach a database of all relevant parameters has been set, and specific input masks, as shown in Fig. 8, have been introduced in order to make the data input more intuitive to the end-users.

In the specific DES simulation environment the quantities and features of resources in a model can be modified through the batch processing of a configuration file. An application automates the process, by progressively generating a sequence of configurations that are closer and closer to an optimal solution: the optimization mechanism relies on the "Scatter Search" meta-heuristic approach and is applied to the output of each simulation run. The user must input a tentative solution, define the optimization drivers, the lower and upper bounds for the parameters to be optimized, that can be either discrete or continuous, and set one or more algebraic constraints on their values.

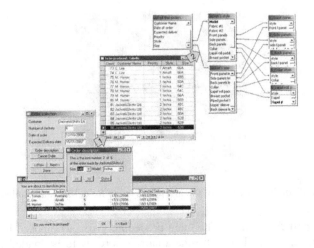

Fig. 8. Extraction of the production bills from a database

An articulated test campaign has been planned and several significant results have been derived. The amount of jackets produced in 40 hours in steady conditions is the driver of the layout performance optimization. Here after only some results concerning the influence of the dimensions of the production orders are presented.

The dimensions of lots made up of jackets with the same style and size has a key influence in product throughput and heavily impacts plant productivity. As an example, cut parts have to be sorted along their origin from a common batch before loading them on the robotized garment assembly cell: the smaller is the mean lot size, the longer will be the waiting time before a whole set of compatible parts is gathered up and processed.

The automation in the research of optimal solutions let investigate the plant performance when processing bills of orders made up of differently sized batches: along with the extreme conditions of unitary and mass production, the management of lots with mean dimensions of 2, 5, 10, 20 and 50 items (with 20% standard deviation) was simulated.

The optimization study helps to lay out the most suitable sets of resources for a certain production type, or even gives indication about the dynamic allocations of the production agents (i.e. the use of highly skilled human "jolly" resources). In particular the optimal number of carriers varies with the lot size (see Table 1), so that a dynamic carrier reservoir system would be implemented to face the variability on the composition of the order.

Table 1. Optimal number of carriers for several lots mean sizes

Mean Lot Size (20% st. dev.)	1	5	20	50	100
Optimal number of carriers	110	129	142	142	147

In the case of unitary-lot production, Fig. 9 reveals the inelasticity of system's response to the increasing of the overall work burden, i.e. there is a maximum launching rate of new items into production that cannot be exceeded; in case of batch production instead, the system succeeds in managing a wider throughput range although increasing the amount of work in progress, and thus the lead time. As a matter of facts, the cut parts originating from the same batch (style and size) are processed in along parallel paths have to be re-collected before concurring in the Garment Assembly cell: the smaller is the mean lot size, the most the production is paced by the parts' sorting process, that causes the saturation of the buffering capacity of the conveyor rings.

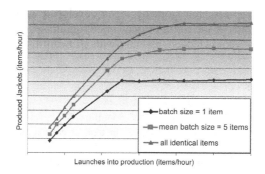

Fig. 9. Plant productivity as a function of lots mean size (with optimal number of carriers)

6 Conclusions

The paper introduces a new simulator environment for intelligent clothing manufacture. The competition between enterprises resorts to the process-added value of actually sold apparel, rather than to large products batches, requiring to run after buyers, with advertising or lower sale prices. High-standing clothes are noteworthy, as clients require personalized quality and quick service. The discussion offers hints to look after the integrated manufacturing approach and the influence on the process efficiency of new robotized resources developed within Leapfrog Integrated Project is specifically dealt with. The process description is based on a modular lay-out, to separate the effect of influence quantities and to investigate details, preserving the overall view of the process evolution.

One should emphasize the fact that, today, the clothing industries are work-intensive set-ups and extensively resort to the on-line operators versatility to modify production, while the process progresses; this possibly hinders the benefit of intelligent manufacturing, based on the concurrent run of the material and the information flows for adaptive flexibility: - at the organizational range (process-attuned managers): to select the fabrication agendas; - at the co-ordination range (decentralized controllers): to optimize the cloth bolts choice; - at the execution range (real-time supervisors): to adapt the material dispatching service.

The example discussion shows that flexible automation can deal with foregoing information on self-sufficient bases; actually, the benefits depend on a large number of cross-related facts and actual implementations, hard to be fixed, remain out of the reach of front-end operators. The area of high-standing garments, satisfying varying market requests, is exemplary case where automation provides critical support for quality certification.

The changes towards flexible lean automation, however, need be investigated in terms of realistic system behaviour and expected economic returns; simulation studies that integrate discrete events and 3D physics-based multi-body models are dominant help, to compare competing alternatives referring to actual production contexts and, moreover, to provide explanatory examples with training support immediately related to sets of feasible implementations.

Acknowledgments. The research work has been developed within the Leapfrog IP project funded by EU under the Sixth Framework Programme. The precious support of Kuka Italy is kindly acknowledged, together with all Leapfrog partners.

References

1. Acaccia, G.M., Callegari, M., Michelini, R.C., Molfino, R.M.: Simulational assessment of a modular assembly facility. In: Intl. Conf. on Concurrent Engineering and Electronic Design Automation, pp. 37–41 (1996)
2. Moss, S., Davidsson, P.: Multi-Agent-Based Simulation. Springer, Heidelberg (2001)
3. Michelini, R.C., Acaccia, G.M., Callegari, M., Molfino, R.M., Razzoli, R.: Knowledge based emulation simulation for flexible automation manufacturing. In: EUROSIM Conference, pp. 1259–1264 (1995)
4. Fontana, M., Rizzi, C., Cugini, U.: Computer-aided apparel tailoring with virtual simulation, J. Product Development 4(6), 600–625 (2007)
5. Acaccia, G.M., Chiavacci, A., Michelini, R.C., Callegari, M.: Benchmarking the Clothing Industry Effectiveness by Computer Simulation. In: 11th European Simulation Symposium and Exhibition: Simulation in Industry (ESS 1999), pp. 519–524 (1999)
6. Michelini, R.C., Acaccia, G.M., Callegari, M., Molfino, R.M.: XIMSIFIP: an expert simulation environment for factory automation. In: IFIP Transactions: Human Aspects in Computer Integrated Manufacturing, pp. 797–804. NorthHolland, Amsterdam (1992)
7. Bonsignorio, F., Molfino, R.M.: An object based virtual reality simulation tool for design validation of a new paradigm cloth manufacturing facility. In: Information Technology for Balanced Manufacturing Systems, vol. 220, pp. 301–308. Springer, Boston (2006)
8. Bruzzone, L.E., Molfino, R.M., Zoppi., M.: A discrete event simulation package for modular and adaptive assembly plants. In: 22nd Int. Conf. Modelling, Identification and Control, pp. 280–282. IASTED/ACTA Press (2003)
9. McNally, P., Heavey, C.: Developing simulation as a desktop resource. J. Computer Integrated Manufacturing 17(5), 435–450 (2004)
10. Qin, S.F., Lagoudakis, E., Kang, Q.P., Cheng, K.: Customer-Centric Strategy for E-Manufacturing in Apparel Industry. Applied Mechanics and Materials 10(12), 39–44 (2008)

A Lunar Surface Operations Simulator

Hari Nayar, Bob J. Balaram, Jonathan Cameron, Abhinandan Jain, Christopher Lim,
Rudranarayan Mukherjee, Stephen Peters,
Marc Pomerantz, Leonard Reder, Partha Shakkottai, and Stephen Wall

Jet Propulsion Laboratory, California Institute of Technology,
4800 Oak Grove Drive, Pasadena, CA 91109

Abstract. The Lunar Surface Operations Simulator (LSOS) is being developed to support planning and design of space missions to return astronauts to the moon. Vehicles, habitats, dynamic and physical processes and related environment systems are modeled and simulated in LSOS to assist in the visualization and design optimization of systems for lunar surface operations. A parametric analysis tool and a data browser were also implemented to provide an intuitive interface to run multiple simulations and review their results. The simulator and parametric analysis capability are described in this paper.

1 Introduction

The National Aeronautics and Space Administration (NASA) is leading an international partnership to develop and deploy a series of missions to return astronauts to the moon in 2025 [1]. In addition to habitation on, and exploration of the lunar surface, these missions, developed under NASA's Constellation Program, will be precursors for subsequent manned missions to Mars. To enable these missions, new launch, crew transport, lander, and surface mobility vehicles and lunar habitat systems are being designed. Simulators are playing a vital role in assisting in the mission design and planning, visualization and design optimization of these systems.

The Lunar Surface Operations Simulator (LSOS) is one of the simulators under development within the Constellation Program. As its name suggests, it models surface systems, their mechanical properties, dynamic interactions and operations. In addition to simulating the dynamic interactions during operations, for example, soil interaction or component motion, LSOS also models associated environmental, and system mechanical and non-mechanical processes. These include thermal, radiation and power transients, lighting and shadows, and terrain. LSOS's integrated architecture allows use of common models and enables interactions between components operating in different domains to be easily modeled. For example, the illumination, solar panel power and thermal models use a common sun model and incidence angle. Simulations and post simulation analyses have been recently performed within LSOS to show that it can be a powerful tool to assist both in the design and planning of missions, and in component design optimization.

LSOS has been built on and extended from previous simulation packages developed at the Jet Propulsion Laboratory. Its core physics simulation engine is the DARTS package originally developed to simulate the Cassini spacecraft [3]. DARTS is a multibody domain-independent dynamics engine. Subsequent development around DARTS

S. Carpin et al. (Eds.): SIMPAR 2008, LNAI 5325, pp. 65–74, 2008.

has led to supporting packages and simulators for a variety of space applications. These include Dshell [4], SimScape [8], ROAMS [5, 6], and DSENDS [7].

This paper gives an overview of LSOS. We start in the next section with a description of the models that have been developed within LSOS. We have used LSOS in a batch mode to perform parametric analysis. Procedures developed to enable this capability are described with an example in the section on Parametric Analysis. We finally conclude with a description of our current status and future plans.

The results from simulators like LSOS, combined with the analytical approaches by others [2] are essential for successful and timely development of NASA's vision for our return to the moon.

2   Models

Simulations in LSOS are composed from models of many components. Some of the more important component models are described in this section.

2.1   Vehicle Models

A number of prototype autonomous and teleoperated vehicles are have been developed for terrestrial demonstration of potential lunar surface operations. As development on and demonstrations of these vehicles for Lunar missions continue, they are being modeled and simulated in LSOS to facilitate visualizing and evaluating their performance under Earth and Lunar surface environmental conditions and to assist in design optimization.

The K-10 [9] built at the NASA Ames Research Center (ARC), ATHLETE [10] built at JPL and Chariot [11] built at the NASA Johnson Space Center (JSC) rovers are three prototypes being used in a series of field trials to demonstrate lunar operations capabilities. These vehicles, modeled in LSOS, are shown on Figure 1.

Fig. 1. The K-10 (left), ATHLETE (middle) and Chariot (right) rovers modeled in LSOS

A generalized infrastructure for vehicle modeling in LSOS has led to a streamlined process for modeling the variety of kinematic, dynamic and constraint properties found in these vehicles. Re-use of common elements has allowed us to reduce the complexity and improve the reliability of the modeling and simulation software. Each vehicle model is configured by assembling it from a library of components. The use of common components allows each unique vehicle to inherit many wheeled vehicle properties, for example, inertial sensors or mobility and navigation yet maintain their unique properties. The models are composed of detail elements of the vehicle including mass and inertia tensors of all rigid-body elements and joints, actuators and sensors.

2.2 Habitat Model

The Space Mission Analysis Branch [12] at the NASA Langley Research Center (LaRC) has been analyzing and developing models and scenarios of lunar surface systems for the Constellation Program. The development of a Lunar surface system architecture is a complex problem in which a wide variety of constraints have to be satisfied. Some design constraints are imposed from interactions with the supporting systems. For example the size of the habitat modules will have to fit within the space available in the launch vehicles.

Many other constraints have to be determined by evaluating performance under simulated operations. For example, the amount of power generated by the habitat solar panels depends on the location selected on the surface of the moon, the elevation and topography of the surrounding terrain, the kinematics and control of the solar panels, the efficiency of the solar panels and so on. In the design of systems as complex as the lunar habitat, the use of a simulator can assist in the design and optimization of components and the evaluation of overall performance.

Fig. 2. LSOS visualization of a potential Lunar habitat system from NASA LaRC

The LSOS team is working with lunar habitat designers at NASA LaRC to support the development of the lunar outpost. We have modeled the version of the lunar habitat shown on Figure 2 that was released in January 2008. Simulations were performed with this model for a power analysis assessment of the configuration. The model implemented in LSOS can place the static elements of the habitat on a terrain model at any user specified location. The supporting simulation sub-systems that enabled the power analysis simulation are described in the following sub-sections.

As the habitat design for the Lunar missions evolves, and as analytical and simulation needs arise, we will continue to update our habitat models and perform simulations and analysis to assist in the design of the lunar habitat.

2.3 Solar Panels

The current version of the lunar habitat implemented in LSOS has six solar panels. Each panel is mounted to a four degrees-of-freedom articulation system. The implementation

of the solar panel system in LSOS used an existing software component for modeling robot arms. Six such robot arms with identical kinematics but placed at the six specified base attachment points were used for modeling the solar panel arms and articulation.

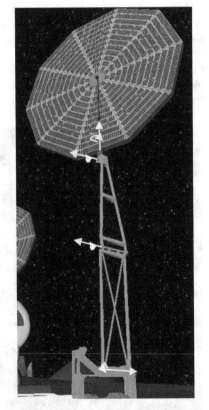

The configuration of the arms (shown on Figure 3) is a yaw joint at its base, a pitch joint at its elbow, a pitch joint at its wrist and a roll joint also at the wrist. The LSOS models derived the kinematics of the arms from the component graphics models we received from NASA LaRC. The LSOS models specify kinematics, and range of motion of the arm elements.

The objective in the control of the arms is to maximize the exposure of the solar panels to the sun while avoiding collisions between the arms and between arms parts and the habitat. Implicit in the goal of maximizing the solar panel exposure is the minimization of self-shadowing of the solar panels.

In our simulations, a simple algorithm was implemented for control of the solar panel arms. The motion of the sun with respect to the lunar habitat at the chosen location at the South Pole of the lunar surface is to traverse in a counter-clockwise direction very low on the horizon (between -3 degrees and +3 degrees) on a 27-day monthly cycle. Consequently, the solar

Fig. 3. Solar panel articulation in LSOS

panels should have their roll-axes vertical and be rotated to face the sun. The other three joints of the solar panel arms are periodically (four times during each monthly cycle) modified depending on the sun azimuth angle to translate the roll joint axis and improve the solar panel exposure to sunlight.

2.4 Terrain

Terrain models are an important component of surface simulations. LSOS uses the SimScape [8] package to incorporate terrain models. A number of terrain models have been generated for LSOS simulations. Among these are analog terrestrial field-trial locations at Meteor Crater in Arizona, USA and versions of lunar terrain models. Our lunar habitat simulator uses the recently released Goldstone Solar System Radar (GSSR) terrain model [13]. The GSSR terrain covers an area of about 300km by 600km at a 40m/pixel resolution. The terrain model was generated from radar images of the moon taken from the Earth. At the South Pole of the moon, the planned location of the lunar outpost, this terrain dataset is the best currently available.

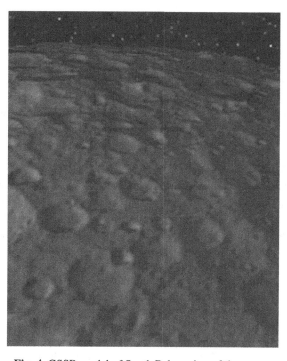

Fig. 4. GSSR model of South Pole region of the moon

Due to the process used in generating the GSSR terrain model, regions not viewable from the Earth (because they are obscured by terrain features) are *holes* in the terrain. In LSOS, these regions have been *filled* with interpolated values shown in red on Figure 4. While the 40m resolution of the GSSR terrain model is adequate for the habitat simulation, the terrain model will have to be enhanced to centimeter-level resolution to be good enough for accurate simulation of vehicle-terrain interactions.

2.5 Sun Propagation

LSOS uses the Spacecraft Planet Instrument C-matrix Events (SPICE) database and toolkit [14] to determine the locations of the moon, the sun and other planetary bodies at specified times during simulations. This data is used to compute the relative location of the sun with respect to specified locations on the surface of the moon at specified times.

The sun azimuth and elevation angle derived from the SPICE interface is available in the simulation environment for use by any algorithm. In the lunar habitat simulation, it is used to drive the roll angle value for each solar panel arm and for illumination modeling. In vehicle simulations, it is additionally used for computing heat radiation to the vehicle and ground, for solar panel lighting in the vehicle power analysis.

3 Parametric Analysis

One of the most powerful uses of LSOS is in performing parametric analysis to explore the behavior of systems as simulation parameters are varied. The software infrastructure to enable this was developed for the ROAMS [15] simulator to vary terrain and soil parameters and DSENDS [7] simulator to vary atmospheric conditions in entry, descent and landing simulations. This parametric analysis infrastructure was adapted for LSOS to orchestrate batch runs of lunar habitat simulations. In addition, the parametric analysis tools enable specification of parameters to vary the statistics of parameter variation, and data collection and storage from the simulations.

3.1 Parameters

Two parameters, height of the habitat and location of the habitat, were varied in a demonstration of parametric analysis applied to the lunar habitat simulation.

The height parameter placed the habitat at the specified height above the local terrain height (see Figure 5). In computing power generation, it was found that, because the sun is always low on the horizon, surrounding terrain features often obscure the solar panels from the sun. An advantage can be gained by increasing the height of the habitat because it raises the panels above the terrain shadows. This parameter was selected to determine the sensitivity of habitat height to the power generation. During the parametric analysis batch simulations, the height parameter was varied uniformly between 0 and 30m.

Fig. 5. The height parameter is measured from the local terrain height

Locations at the South Pole of the moon have been identified as likely landing sites for lunar missions. This is motivated by the possibility that ice may be found close to the surface at the bottom of craters and the sun may be visible year-round from selected locations. For these reasons, Shackleton Crater, located almost exactly at the South Pole of the moon is an ideal site. Choosing a specific location on the rim of Shackleton is not as easy a task because surrounding terrain features obscure some areas, the elevation of the rim and proximity to the South Pole varies at different locations.

The complex interaction of these properties makes the analytical determination of the best habitat location complex. Varying the location in multiple simulations and determining power generation for each location is an alternative approach to determine ideal locations for the placement of a habitat.

Figure 6 shows the locations around the rim of Shackleton that were selected for the parametric analysis. Thirty locations, approximately equally spaced, were selected. The coordinates for these locations were entered in a table. During the parametric analysis simulations, an index into the table was uniformly varied to select a particular location to use for the simulation.

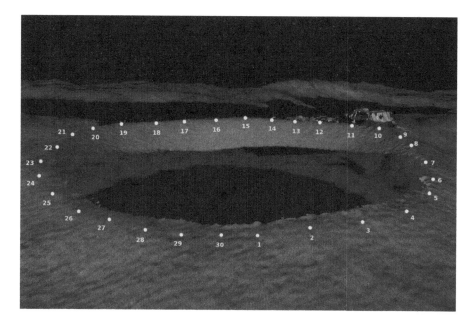

Fig. 6. Locations around the rim of Shackleton Crater varied as a parameter

3.2 Parametric Analysis Runs

A total of 200 simulations were run in the parametric analysis. Each simulation ran a one-month (720 hours) simulation with time incremented in one hour steps. The start time use in the simulations was March 7, 2011, GMT 01:00:00.

To illustrate the parametric analysis, a simple power model was implemented in the simulation runs. At each step, the power generated was computed by multiplying the exposed solar panel area by 400 Watts/m^2 to factor the solar power collected and converted into useful energy. This approximates the solar panel efficiency to be about thirty percent. A battery model with a capacity of 100000 Watt-hrs was used in the simulations to store the power generated. A constant drain on the battery of 200 Watts was also implemented to model power usage during surface operations. The simulations were initialized with the battery at fifty percent charged, i.e. with 50000Watt-hrs of energy. Data collected during the simulations include the time, habitat height and location, the sun azimuth and elevation angles, current power, battery charge and total accumulated power.

Data collected from the simulations was stored in HDF5 format. A browser, developed to retrieve data from the HDF5 store and selectively view the data, provides an intuitive interface to inspect the results from the simulations.

Screen shots from the data browser display are shown on Figure 7. A scatter plot of accumulated power versus location index for all the simulation runs is shown on

Figure 7a). For the simulation conditions used (terrain, habitat model, etc), the results indicate that locations 1-10 and 20-30 are generally better than locations 11-19. The browser allows the user to select simulations from the scatter plot to view in detail.

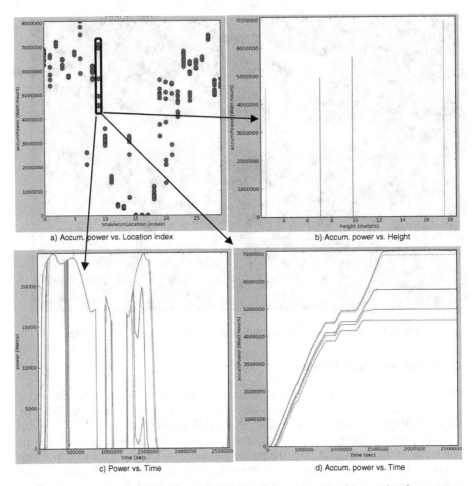

Fig. 7. Browser display of parametric analysis data: a) scatter plot of accumulated power versus location for all 200 simulation runs, b) Accumulated power versus height for selected simulation runs at location 9, c) Power versus time for selected simulation runs at location 9, and d) Accumulated power versus time for selected simulated runs at location 9

We can see from Figure 7b) that, not surprisingly, at location 9, increasing height improves power accumulation. Figure 7a), however, shows that power generation at some locations are more sensitive to height changes than at other locations. Figure 7c) and 7d) show that, at location 9, a terrain feature probably blocks the sun about 1600000 secs (about 444 hours or about 18.5 days) after the start of the simulation.

We used this simulation and parametric analysis example to illustrate the utility of applying high-quality simulations to assist the design of systems. The capability to select and view any parameter or simulation variable plotted against any other parameter or simulation variable can be used to identify hidden relationships in the data that may lead to new revelations to optimize designs.

4 Conclusions

We have presented, in this paper, preliminary results from our development of LSOS. It has been used to demonstrate the simulation of a variety of models and operational scenarios. We also describe a parametric analysis package to manage batch execution of multiple simulations with varying parameters. A demonstration of this capability is used to illustrate how simulations can be used effectively to aid in the optimization of designs.

Future development plans for LSOS include extensions to handle new lunar vehicle types, simulate more complex operations and scenarios, incorporate models of other physics-based processes, share models and data with other lunar mission simulators and support design and development activities and field trial planning for NASA lunar missions. Plans are also underway to generate high-resolution terrain models using re-construction techniques based on physical process models [16].

Acknowledgement

This work was carried out at the Jet Propulsion Laboratory, California Institute of Technology, under a contract with the National Aeronautics and Space Administration. We thank our our sponsor, Doug Craig from NASA Headquarters, and our collaborators at the United States Geological Survey (USGS), NASA Glen Research Center, NASA Langley Research Center, NASA Johnson Space Center, NASA Ames Research Center, NASA Marshall Space Flight Center and Jet Propulsion Laboratory for support in the development of LSOS.

References

1. Cooke, D., Yoder, G., Coleman, S., Hensley, S.: Lunar Architecture Update. In: AIAA NASA 3rd Space Exploration Conference, Denver, Colorado (February 2008)
2. Fincannon, J.: Lunar South Pole Illumination: Review, Reassessment, and Power System Implications. In: AIAA 5th International Energy Conversion Engineering Conference and Exhibit (IECEC), St. Louis, Missouri (June 2007)
3. Jain, A., Man, G.: Real-time simulation of the Cassini spacecraft using DARTS: functional capabilities and the spatial algebra algorithm. In: 5th Annual Conference on Aerospace Computational Control, Jet Propulsion Laboratory, Pasadena, CA (August 1992)
4. Biesiadecki, J., Henriquez, D., Jain, A.: A Reusable, Real-Time Spacecraft Dynamics Simulator. In: 6th Digital Avionics Systems Conference, Irvine, CA (October 1997)
5. Jain, A., Guineau, J., Lim, C., Lincoln, W., Pomerantz, M., Sohl, G., Steele, R.: ROAMS: Planetary Surface Rover Simulation Environment. In: International Symposium on Artificial Intelligence, Robotics and Automation in Space (i-SAIRAS 2003), Nara, Japan, May 19-23 (2003)

6. Jain, A., Balaram, J., Cameron, J., Guineau, J., Lim, C., Pomerantz, M., Sohl, G.: Recent Developments in the ROAMS Planetary Rover Simulation Environment. In: IEEE Aerospace Conference (March 2004)

7. Balaram, J., Austin, R., Banerjee, P., Bentley, T., Henriquez, D., Martin, B., McMahon, E., Sohl, G.: DSENDS - A High-Fidelity Dynamics and Spacecraft Simulator for Entry, Descent and Surface Landing. In: IEEE 2002 Aerospace Conf., Big Sky, Montana, March 9-16 (2002)

8. Jain, A., Cameron, J., Lim, C., Guineau, J.: SimScape Terrain Modeling Toolkit. In: Second International Conference on Space Mission Challenges for Information Technology (SMC-IT 2006), Pasadena, CA (July 2006)

9. Fong, T., Allan, M., Bouyssounouse, X., Bualat, M., Deans, M., Edwards, L., Flückiger, L., Keely, L., Lee, S., Lees, D., To, V., Utz, H.: Robotic Site Survey at Haughton Crater. In: 9th International Symposium on Artificial Intelligence, Robotics and Automation in Space (iSAIRAS), Los Angeles, CA, February 26-29 (2008)

10. Wilcox, B., Litwin, T., Biesiadecki, J., Matthews, J., Heverly, M., Morrison, J., Townsend, J., Ahmed, N., Sirota, A., Cooper, B.: ATHLETE: A Cargo Handling and Manipulation Robot for the Moon. Journal of Field Robotics 24(5), April 17 (2007) DOI: 10.1002/rob.20193

11. Ambrose, R.: Human-Robotics Interactions: Field Test Experiences from a collaborative ARC, JPL and JSC Team. In: AIAA NASA 3rd Space Exploration Conference, Denver, Colorado (February 2008)

12. Troutman, P.: The House of More Than a Decade of Tomorrows. NASA News and Features,
http://www.nasa.gov/topics/moonmars/features/troutman-architecture.html

13. Hensley, S.: Lunar Imaging from Goldstone. In: AIAA NASA 3rd Space Exploration Conference, Denver, Colorado (February 2008)

14. NASA's Navigation and Ancillary Information Facility (NAIF), SPICE
http://naif.jpl.nasa.gov/naif/aboutspice.html

15. Madison, R., Jain, A., Benenyan, G., Lim, C., Reder, L., Maimone, M.: Large Scale Rover Simulations: Supercomputing to Evaluate Rover Control Algorithms, Space 2005 (August 2005)

16. Gaskell, R., Husman, I.E., Collier, I.B., Chen, R.L.: Synthetic Environments for Simulated Missions. IEEE A&E Magazine (July 2007)

YARS: A Physical 3D Simulator for Evolving Controllers for Real Robots

Keyan Zahedi[1], Arndt von Twickel[2], and Frank Pasemann[2]

[1] MPI for Mathematics in the Sciences, Inselstrasse 22, 04103 Leipzig, Germany
zahedi@mis.mpg.de
[2] University of Osnabrück, Institute of Cognitive Science,
Albrechtstraße 28, 49076 Osnabrück, Germany
{arndt.von.twickel,frank.pasemann}@uni-osnabrueck.de

Abstract. This paper presents YARS (Yet Another Robot Simulator), which was initially developed in the context of evolutionary robotics (ER), yet includes features which are also of benefit to those outside of this field. An experiment in YARS is defined by a single XML file, which includes the simulator configuration, the (randomisable) environment, and any number of (mobile) robots. Robots are either controlled through an automatised communication, or by dynamically loaded C++ programs. Therefore, YARS, although still under active development, is comparable with commercial and open-source robot simulators which include a physics engine such as Webots and Breve but with a much stronger focus on requirements originating from the field of evolutionary robotics.

1 Introduction

The development of robots is time-consuming and, therefore, often very expensive. Especially in research, where budgets are limited, and various novel approaches are tested in hardware and software, simulators can play an important role in reducing development cost and time. Another advantage is that research groups can cooperate and exchange results, even if the physical robot platform is not available to all groups. These advantages only hold if the simulator does not require a high implementation effort for a new experiment and if the results obtained in simulation are portable to the physical platform.

In the context of evolutionary robotics (ER) [1] additional requirements must be fulfilled. A simulator is only advantageous if it is much (in the order of ten times) faster than real-time and if the results do not require additional porting effort. Another important criterion is the automatic set-up of the experiment after each evaluation to ensure compatibility of the fitness values.

There is a large number of robot simulators available, emphasising different aspects of robot simulation. Examples are Khepera 2.0 Simulator, Webots, Darwin2k, Adams, Yobotics, Gazebo, Breve, and USARSim [2,3,4,5,6,7,8,9,10]. So why is there a need for Yet Another Robot Simulator? The simulators mentioned above were reviewed by the authors before work on YARS was initiated, but not

S. Carpin et al. (Eds.): SIMPAR 2008, LNAI 5325, pp. 75–86, 2008.

Table 1. Comparison of simulators, evaluated with respect to evolutionary robotics as it is performed within the presented context (see fig. 1). The simulators listed here were chosen during the assessment phase of YARS because of their particular emphasis and as they were the most widely used simulators in the field of robotics. The entries $\ominus$ and $\oplus$ refer to a positive or negative evaluation, respectively. Evaluations given in brackets were not tested by the authors of this work, but obtained through available documentation. The evaluation of Webots refers to version 3, and might not be true for the current version 5. As none of the available simulators met all the requirements, YARS was initiated. Footnotes: 1) Available source refers to the possibility to include motor and sensor models, 2) Publication [10] states up to 300 times faster than real-time. This could not be validated with the examples provided in the evaluation version (Ver. 5, Mac OS 10.5.4, 2.5GHz Dual Core, 4GB RAM). Achieved maximum was ca. seven times faster than real-time. 3) Documentation states that Webots can be started as batch-process, 4) No statements made in the documentation, 5) Supervisor-concept available, but in Version 3 not well suited for evolution as performed in this context, i.e. with an external evolution- and evaluation-software, and the requirement to set and re-set the simulation externally.

Simulator	Speed	Optional GUI	Free	Auto. reset	Source avail.[1]
Webots	$[\ominus]^2$	$[\oplus]^3$	$\ominus$	$[\ominus]^5$	$\ominus$
Breve	$[\oplus]^4$	$[\oplus]$	$\oplus$	$[\ominus]^4$	$\oplus$
Adams	$\ominus$	$\ominus$	$\ominus$	$[\ominus]^4$	$\ominus$
Darwin2k	$[\ominus]$	$[\ominus]$	$\oplus$	$[\ominus]^4$	$[\oplus]$
Yobotics	$[\ominus]$	$\ominus$	$\ominus$	$[\ominus]$	$\ominus$
YARS	$\oplus$	$\oplus$	$\oplus$	$\oplus$	$\oplus$

chosen because of either cost, speed, or restricted usability for ER (for a discussion see tab. 1). The latter refers to setting up an experiment, and resetting it automatically after every evaluation of an individual. Additionally, customising and adding new sensors and actuators is either not possible or requires a high implementation effort, which excludes corresponding simulators for experiments such as those presented here. Furthermore, the evolution time can be reduced, if the evaluation of populations is distributed in a cluster. This is only possible if the simulator does not require GUI interactions and a running visualisation, two features which are not widely supported.

An additional feature which supports the distribution of the evaluation is the possibility to fully configure YARS either via command-line parameters, a configuration file or through network communication.

These requirements are a few of the features of YARS presented in this paper, which is organised as follows: the following section covers the approach of YARS and explains how it is well-suited for both, ER and mobile robot simulation in general. The third section explains the concept of YARS and describes its most prominent features. The fourth section introduces RoSiML, the XML description language of YARS. The fifth section gives an outlook of the future of YARS and the final section closes with a discussion.

2   Approach

In the context of ER, a simulator is used for four main reasons: 1. During evolution, hardware-damaging behaviours are likely to occur. 2. A simulator can run faster than real-time. 3. The state of the simulator can be precisely set by the experimenter, increasing the comparability of the fitness values of the individuals in a population. 4. For the analysis of the behaviour-relevant dynamics, it is essential to control all the parameters.

Yet, these reasons only hold if the simulator-reality gap does not lead to significant behavioural differences. Closing the gap is related to the precision of the simulator, which stands in contrast to the simulation speed, i.e. there is a trade-off. The central issue here is how precise must the simulator be to ensure the portability of the results and still remain fast enough to fulfil the requirements of ER.

In the approach followed here, it is not important if the characteristic curve of each motor is identical in simulation and reality, as a robust controller should compensate for these differences. Hence, the simulator is sufficiently precise if the observed behaviours in simulation and reality are qualitatively equivalent.

This has implications on the physics engine which is required in a number of experiments, e.g. walking [11,12,13] and gravity driven [14,15] machines. ODE [16] was chosen as the physics engine for YARS, because it is faster than real-time (depending on the complexity of the simulation, see next section for an example), numerically stable and well-documented. Numerically stable, in this case, means that the simulation will not crash, if the internal physics runs into computational singularities. For evolution, this type of simulator behaviour is very important. First, the singularities indicate hardware-damaging behaviour, which can be punished by the fitness-function. Second, for the next individual, the running simulator is simply reset and does not have to be restarted otherwise.

This advantage comes with a trade-off. ODE uses a first-order Euler integrator for the physics, a linear force model for the actuators, and only a Coulomb friction model, which together, result in a fast, numerically stable but not very precise simulation. In the approach followed here, this is not a drawback, as robust controllers are generated by including noise, exploiting the sensori-motor loop, and are evolved on an abstraction of the hardware. A sufficient abstraction is determined by comparing intermediate results on the simulated and real robot on the behaviour level. This approach leads to portable controllers, and hence, validates YARS for ER and robot development. The latter is briefly discussed in the next section, but the procedure is equivalent, except that the evolution is exchanged with other controller-generating or learning methods. An example is the use of YARS to simulate the RunBot [17] (see fig. 3(d)).

YARS has been used for over five years of research in numerous experiments. A small overview is presented in figure 3 (a more comprehensive list is given in [18]). This is only possible because it was designed to be general, while not requiring any programming knowledge. The last two statements are discussed in the following sections.

3   YARS

YARS was initially designed to connect to ISEE [18,19,20], an ER environment. Therefore, the early application was to connect to an external control program. For each robot, a UDP socket communication port is opened automatically and the morphological configuration of the robot is communicated through a hand-shake mechanism. Each description of a sensor and an actuator includes the mapping of the values. This can be used to adapt the pre- and post-processing of the controller automatically. Java and C++ classes are provided to connect other software by the same mechanism.

A reload mechanism in YARS supports on-line modification of the XML file. This enables the easy modification of the experiment's parameters and the observation of their influence without the need to halt the controller or to restart the simulation. This is an important feature in closing the simulator-reality gap. There is also the possibility to send the XML file through a socket communication port to YARS, which enables the co-evolution of environment, morphology and controller (see fig. 1). The same mechanism can be used to externally generate complex environments.

The properties discussed above, automatic communication and external configuration and control of YARS, enable YARS to connect to existing software

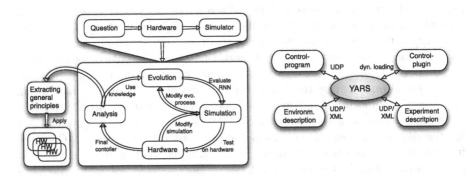

Fig. 1. Interactive evolutionary robotics. Left: The experiments begins with the definition of a question, e.g. insect-locomotion (see Octavio in text below and figure 3(c)). From this question, a well-suited hardware platform is defined, built and a simulation capturing the main physical properties is written in YARS. Recurrent neural networks are evaluated in simulation and the observations are used to modify the evolution parameters. Intermediate results are tested on hardware, and a comparison of the behaviour of the simulated and physical robot yields to modifications of the simulation parameters. Final results are extracted, generalised and may also be used as initial populations in other experiments. Right: YARS offers different possibilities for its controlled and configured. A control program can connect via a UDP connection to exchange sensor and motor commands, but can also be loaded dynamically during runtime. An experiment description is given as a command line parameter, or may be passed through a UDP port to YARS. The latter can be used to generate complex environment descriptions by an external tool.

with little effort, and are features from ER that make YARS attractive for robot simulation in general.

In ER, a large number of different controllers must be evaluated, until a good solution is found, i.e. the simulation speed is crucial. Currently, non-trivial simulations (e.g. Octavio, see fig. 3(c)) run between 10-70 times faster than real-time on a Pentium M 1.7 GHz. The high values result from the possibility to start YARS without visualisation or by reducing the refresh-rate of the rendering, while the lower bound is a consequence of the OpenGL rendering.

In closed-source simulators, actuators and sensors are problematic, as they can either not be extended at all, or require a large amount of implementation effort. YARS includes the most common sensors and actuators, which can be fully configured. Adding a new sensor or actuator is possible, as YARS is open-source (for details see sec. 5, Sensors)

Essential for the analysis of a controller is the ability to log data from the simulator. Sensor and motor values are available through the communication interface, pose of the objects can be written to a text file, and data can be displayed on-line, currently through a gnuplot interface.

RoSiML. Setting-up an experiment can be a very time-consuming process, and often requires programming knowledge or knowledge of 3D modelling languages such as VRML. We chose a different approach and designed our own description language: RoSiML (Robot Simulation Markup Language) [21,22]. This was done for one main reason. If the keywords of the description language are chosen with care, it is human-readable and does not require any programming knowledge.

Standardised 3D description languages, e.g. VRML and X3D, were not chosen, because they are too extensive in their possibilities, and require advanced programming knowledge. Their focus lies on scene descriptions and extending them to robotics requires heavy modifications, eliminating the advantage of available graphical development tools. XSLT [23] offers the possibility to convert

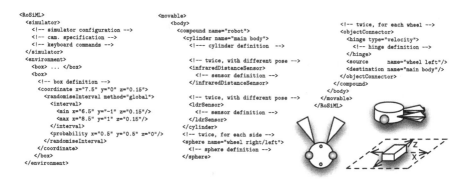

Fig. 2. YARS example: This figure shows snippets of RoSiML code and sketches of the robot. The snippets were taken from the SRN experiment discussed in the text below and shown in figure 3(b). An XML file is given to YARS either through command line, or through a UDP communication protocol (see fig. 1). A proximity sensor is simulated by five rays.

description languages, e.g. to convert VRML to RoSiML, but still requires additional manual modifications.

The first version of RoSiML was used in the German Research Foundation Priority Program 1125 as a general simulator description language to make descriptions exchangeable among the program members (e.g. [21,22]), independent of the simulation system.

The description of an experiment in RoSiML is divided into three main sections, the simulator, the environment and the movables (see fig. 2). The simulator section relates to the general configuration of YARS, e.g. update frequency of the physics and controller, keyboard commands, window size, camera position, etc. The environment section describes all static objects. Their position can be randomised at every reset, but remain fixed in their pose throughout the simulation run. The objects are basic geometric primitives (box, sphere, etc.) that are also used to define a movable. The movable section includes any number of movables, which are either controlled (see below) or passive. An example is a RoboCup [24] scenario in which groups of controlled robots act in a static environment interacting with a movable but otherwise passive ball. The concept of a moveable is detailed below.

Movables. A moveable is a generalised concept of a (mobile) robot. There are four possible types, *active*, *passive*, *controlled*, and *moving*, which are distinguished by their form of control and whether or not communication is established.

For each *active* movable, UDP socket communication is automatically established. Exceptions are *passive* movables, which do not require any form of control or communication. Both types are elaborated next.

In ER it is desirable to have a dynamic environment, i.e. other robots that interact with the robot and controller of interest. An example is an obstacle-avoidance controller that should not only avoid static but also moving obstacles. In this case, only the obstacle-avoider should be *active*, i.e. open to evolution/analysis/development, whereas the behaviour of the other robots remain unchanged. This case is covered by the *controlled* movable. YARS provides the possibility to dynamically load C++ classes. A string identifier in the XML file relates to the name of the C++ class, which contains the implementation of the controller. The *moving* movable is very similar to the *controlled* movable. The difference is that the outputs of the C++ program are forces which are applied directly to the body. The next paragraphs cover the concept of the morphology, sensors, and actuators of a movable.

Morphology. The morphology description of a movable is organised in a four-level tree (see fig. 2). The first-level node is named *body*, and it includes *compounds* and *connectors*. A compound is a group of connected rigid bodies or composites of rigid bodies, called objects for short. Connectors are active or passive joints between two objects. Inter-compound connectors are defined below the *body* node, intra-compound connectors within the compound. For each object, the physical parameters, e.g. weight and friction coefficients, must be specified.

Composites [16] allow the definition of complex rigid bodies. Trimesh objects will be included in a future release.

Sensors. Currently, different generic and specific sensors are implemented, both exteroceptive and proprioceptive. Exteroceptive sensors are attached and positioned relative to an object. Proprioceptive sensors are included in the actuator definition. The list of exteroceptive sensors includes: generic rotation sensor (3D compass), generic proximity sensor, two specific Sharp infra-red proximity sensors (DM2Y3A003K0F, GP2D12-37), generic light-dependent resistor sensor, and a generic directed camera sensor. The generic sensors are fully configurable, including noise. Available proprioceptive sensors are: joint (angular) position, joint (angular) velocity, joint force/torque, and an energy sensor. A special group are global sensors, which are not usually available in physical robots and which are used for the evaluation. Currently included are a global coordinate sensor and an ambient light sensor. Both were used to calculate the fitness in the examples discussed below.

Custom sensors can be added through modification of the source code, or may result from the combination of available sensors, e.g. a laser-scanner can be simulated by an array of proximity sensors.

Actuators. Actuators connect two rigid bodies, and are positioned relative to their source. Possible actuators are hinge, hinge2 (combination of two hinges), slider, ball joint, and a complex hinge. They are configurable in torque/force, max. deflection, damping and spring properties, and noise.

4 Examples

Aibo. The first example is an evolved neuro-controller for a fast quadrupedal walking behaviour [13] (see fig. 3(a)). The experimentation platform is the Sony Aibo robot [25]. A detailed 3D model of the Aibo is available, which enables the extraction of the body's proportions, but there are no specifications available about the motors and the weight distribution. This increases the difficulty of evolving a controller in simulation and porting it to the real hardware. Further challenges were the unknown friction coefficients and the non-trivial shape of the Aibo legs, which could not be simulated in detail. The solution to these problems were manifold. First, a few tests were conducted with the actual robot in order to get rough approximations of the motor torques. The second step was to find a good approximation for the weight distribution and morphology. The third step was to test intermediate evolution results on the real hardware, using the German Team framework [26], until the behaviour was qualitatively equivalent. With these techniques, the final solution only required minimal changes to a few synaptic weights in order to run on the physical hardware.

Octavio. Octavio is an example of a complex walking machine where a multitude of nonlinear mechatronic effects have to be taken into account in simulation to

(a) Fast Quadrupedal Walking [13]. Left: The physical robot platform Right: Simulated Aibo.

(b) Left: The randomised environment used in the SRN adaptive light-seeker experiment. Right: A swarm experiment.

(c) Octavio is a modular eight-legged walking machine. First different controllers for single-leg control were evolved [11] and then combined in a walking machine (left). Right: The physical platform.

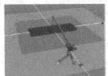

(d) RunBot is the fastest two-legged walking machine [17] (robot image was taken from the BCCN Göttingen site)

Fig. 3. YARS application examples

enable an efficient transfer of neuro-controllers to the real hardware. Octavio is a modular four-, six-, or eight-legged machine with autonomous legs with regard to control and energy supply (see fig. 3(c)). Each leg has three active and one passive joint of which each active one is equipped with a DC-motor-gear combination, a spring coupling, a pre-stressed spring, an angle, and a current sensor. Instead of using the motors as servo motors with the desired positions as input, controllers may take full advantage of the four states that the motor offers: forward torque, backward torque, relaxed and brake. Activation amplitude is determined by pulse-width modulation. On the one hand, this gives more power to the neuro-controller to e.g. save energy by making use of the relaxed mode; on the other hand it imposes a higher demand on the simulator in terms of transferability of controllers to hardware because effects like backlash, friction and inertia have a much more direct impact on performance. This is because they are not hidden from the neuro-controller by means of a black-box servo control. For successful transfers of neuro-controllers to hardware the usual strategy of reproducing weight distributions, including sensor- and motor noise etc. (see e.g. the Aibo example above) was not sufficient and the simulator therefore, had to be extended in several ways, of which a few examples are given here: simple models including static and dynamic joint friction which were derived from experiments, rotor inertia is taken into account as an energy storage that greatly influences the passive dynamics, pulse-width to maximum no-load velocity and maximum stall torque mappings were determined experimentally and backlash effects were quantified and included in the simulator. Going beyond the transferability of controllers from simulation to Octavio a comparability of artificial neuro-controllers with biological controllers in e.g. the stick insects is desired. To this end, simple muscle models based on biological data are implemented to take into account the neuro-muscular transform.

A detailed elaboration on the implementation of the neuromuscular transform will be subject of future publications.

Adaptive Light-Seeker. The adaptive light-seeker with the Self-Regulating Neuron (SRN) model [18,27] demonstrates the randomisation possibilities of an environment in YARS (see fig. 3(b)). The SRN model is an extension of the standard additive neuron model, which is motived by Ashby's Homeostat [28]. Coupled in an embodied and situated recurrent neural network, it enables adaptivity within such structures. To demonstrate this, an environment was chosen in which a light source has to be found under varying light conditions. The robot cannot distinguish between a light source and the ambient light in the raw sensor data. YARS enables the randomisation of the pose of any object in the environment and the value of the ambient light. The former feature was used to first evolve a light-seeker without ambient light. The obstacles were randomised such that a static, non-explorative behaviour, e.g. cyclic movements with increasing radius, would not lead to a good fitness, as the environment changes from generation to generation. In the next step, the ambient light was randomised. The result is a pure feed-forward SRN network that is able to find a light source under varying ambient light conditions, as a result of the homeostatic properties of the SRN and the interaction with the environment [18].

Another example, RunBot [17], not in the context of evolutionary robotics, is shown in figure 3(d).

5 Outlook

The current state of YARS is well suited for experimentation in- and outside the field of ER (see examples given in figure 3). With XML as the description language, researchers who may not be familiar with programming are able to create their experiments within YARS. The communication is established automatically, and sources in Java and C++ are available to connect YARS to other programs. Controllers can also be written directly in C++ and loaded dynamically during the start-up of YARS. Hence, YARS can also be used without any additional software, such as ISEE. Recompiling YARS to test new controllers/morphologies/environments is not necessary. Nevertheless, there are still considerable improvements currently under development or in planing phase.

Modularisation/Plug-in Concept. The entire source of YARS is built into one monolithic executable, with the exception of the C++ controllers which are loaded dynamically during runtime. The next step of the YARS development will split functional subgroups of YARS into shared libraries, which can then be easily exchanged without the need to recompile the entire system. Such functional groups are the physics engine, the visualisation, sensors, actuators, and logging. Each of them is discussed in the following paragraphs.

Visualisation. The ODE visualisation engine, drawstuff, was replaced by a faster OpenGL implementation which also supports multiple cameras. The next step is to make the visualisation optional at compile-time, and to allow the user to choose between different visualisations, i.e. none, minimal, such as OpenGL, or more comfortable such as e.g. wxWidgets. The more comfortable GUI will also allow graphical, interactive manipulation of the scene. As our focus was on exploiting the capabilities of simple sensors in the sensori-motor loop, textures for photo-realistic rendering has, so far, not been included, but will follow with the refactoring of the visualisation.

Physics. Current developments in the field of open-source physics engines tend towards impulse-based physics simulation [29]. Physics engines will be added after evaluation, if they meet the requirements and provide improvements.

Sensors/Actuator. A sensor and an actuator requires almost the same implementation effort in YARS. At this stage, first the XSD grammar has to be changed, followed by the parser, the internal representation, the simulation of the sensor/actuator, and finally the communication. Although well-structured, this is a considerable amount of implementation to add a new sensor/actuator. Under current planing is a plug-in concept to reduce this effort significantly and to support dynamic loading.

Logging/Plotting. The possibility to log and plot simulation variables is essential in order to analyse the quality of a controller or, as in the context in which YARS was developed, to understand the correlation between the neuro-dynamics and behaviour, given the sensori-motor loop. A template concept will support logging of data into any format, such that also exports to e.g. povray [30] will be possible.

Multi-OS. YARS runs on Linux (gcc 4.x), and is currently ported to Mac OS X 10.5 and Win32.

6   Discussion

YARS is a very flexible, highly configurable robot simulator. If physics is required and the on-line visualisation does not need to be highly sophisticated, it is currently, to the best of the authors' knowledge, the fastest available simulator. YARS' main contribution is simulation speed, but keeping the simulator-reality gap in mind, ensuring quick portability of simulation results to the physical platforms. Other contributions of the YARS development are easy integration of new sensors and actuators, and concerning evolutionary robotics; automating of communication, randomisation of the environment, and the possibility to reset the experiment through a communication channel. The experiment description file may also be passed to YARS through socket communication, which enables co-evolution of the environment, morphology and controller and enables generation of complex environments by external programs. YARS has also proven to be useful in experiments outside the field of ER, as in e.g. RunBots.

Therefore, YARS already has many desired features for research which is currently discussed in the field of ER, but also supports robotics development outside this field.

YARS is open-source and available from sourceforge: `http://sourceforge.net/projects/yars/`.

Acknowledgements. Steffen Wischmann contributed to the implementation of the early version of the YARS core. The generic communication interface between YARS and Hinton was designed and implemented by Björn Mahn. Verena Thomas implemented the dynamical loading of control programs, the OpenGL visualisation, and the virtual camera sensor.

This work was partly funded by the DFG grants CH 74/9, PA 480/4, PA 480/6.

References

1. Floreano, D., Urzelai, J.: Evolutionary robots with on-line self-organization and behavioral fitness. Neural Netw. 13(4-5), 431–443 (2000)
2. Michel, O.: Khepera simulator 2.0 (last visited: August 2008), `http://diwww.epfl.ch/lami/team/michel/khep-sim/`
3. Michel, O.: Webots (last visited: August 2008), `http://www.cyberbotics.com/products/webots/`
4. Leger, C.: Darwin2k (last visited: August 2008), `http://darwin2k.sourceforge.net/`
5. MSC Software: Adams (last visited: August 2008), `http://www.mscsoftware.com/products/adams.cfm`
6. Yobotics Inc.: Yobotics website (last visited: August 2008), `http://yobotics.com/`
7. Koenig, N., Polo, J.: Gazebo (last visited: August 2008), `http://playerstage.sourceforge.net/index.php?src=gazebo`
8. Klein, J.: breve: a 3d simulation environment for the simulation of decentralized systems and artificial life. In: Proceedings of Artificial Life VIII, the 8th International Conference on the Simulation and Synthesis of Living Systems, Sydney, Australia. MIT Press, Cambridge (2002)
9. Carpin, S., Lewis, M., Wang, J., Balakirsky, S., Scrapper, C.: Usarsim: a robot simulator for research and education. In: Proceedings of the 2007 IEEE Conference on Robotics and Automation (2007)
10. Michel, O.: Webots: Professional mobile robot simulation. Journal of Advanced Robotics Systems 1(1), 39–42 (2004)
11. von Twickel, A., Pasemann, F.: Reflex-oscillations in evolved single leg neurocontrollers for walking machines. Natural Computing 6(3), 311–337 (2007)
12. Manoonpong, P.: Neural Preprocessing and Control of Reactive Walking Machines Towards Versatile Artificial Perception-Action Systems. In: Cognitive Technologies. Springer, Heidelberg (2007)

13. Markelić, I., Zahedi, K.: An evolved neural network for fast quadrupedal locomotion. In: Xie, M., Dubowsky, S. (eds.) Advances in Climbing and Walking Robots, Proceedings of 10th International Conference (CLAWAR 2007), pp. 65–72. World Scientific Publishing Company, Singapore (2007)

14. Popp, J.: sphericalrobots (last visited: August 2008),
    http://www.sphericalrobots.org

15. Wischmann, S., Hülse, M., Pasemann, F.: (Co)Evolution of (de)centralized neural control for a gravitationally driven machine. Advances in Artificial Life, 179–188 (2005)

16. Smith, R.: ODE (last visited: August 2008), http://www.ode.org

17. Geng, T., Porr, B., Wörgötter, F.: Fast biped walking with a sensor-driven neuronal controller and real-time online learning. The International Journal of Robotics Research 25(3), 243–259 (2006)

18. Ghazi-Zahedi, K.M.: Self-Regulating Neurons. A model for synaptic plasticity in artificial recurrent neural networks. PhD thesis, University of Osnabrück (2008)

19. Zahedi, K., Hülse, M.: ISEE – integrated structure envolution environment (last visited: August 2008), http://sourceforge.net/projects/isee/

20. Hülse, M., Wischmann, S., Pasemann, F.: Structure and function of evolved neurocontrollers for autonomous robots. Connection Science 16(4), 294–296 (2004)

21. Laue, T., Spiess, K., Röfer, T.: Simrobot — a general physical robot simulator and its application in robocup. In: Bredenfeld, A., Jacoff, A., Noda, I., Takahashi, Y. (eds.) RoboCup 2005. LNCS (LNAI), vol. 4020, pp. 173–183. Springer, Heidelberg (2006)

22. Mayer, N., Boedecker, J., da Silva Guerra, R., Obst, O., Asada, M.: 3d2real: Simulation league finals in real robots. In: RoboCup 2006: Robot Soccer World Cup X, pp. 25–34 (2007)

23. Clark, J., Lipkin, D., Marsh, J., Thompson, H., Walsh, N., Zilles, S.: XSL Transformations (XSLT) Version 1.0. W3C (1999)

24. The RoboCup Federation: Robocup official site (last visited: August 2008),
    http://www.robocup.org

25. Sony: Sony aibo europe (last visited: August 2008),
    http://support.sony-europe.com/aibo/

26. Röfer, T., Laue, T., Burkhard, H.D., Hoffmann, J., Jüngel, M., Göhring, D., Düffert, U., Spranger, M., Altmeyer, B., Goetzke, V., von Stryk, O., Brunn, R., Dassler, M., Kunz, M., Risler, M., Stelzer, M., Thomsas, D., Uhrig, S., Schwiegelshohn, U., Dahm, I., Hebbel, M., Nistico, W., Schumann, C., Wachter, M.: Germanteam 2004 (2004) (last visited: August 2008), http://www.germanteam.org/GT2004.pdf

27. Zahedi, K., Pasemann, F.: Adaptive behavior control with self-regulating neurons. In: Lungarella, M., Iida, F., Bongard, J.C., Pfeifer, R. (eds.) 50 Years of Aritficial Intelligence. LNCS (LNAI), vol. 4850, pp. 196–205. Springer, Heidelberg (2007)

28. Ashby, W.R.: Desgin for a brain. Chapman & Hall Ltd., London (1954)

29. Bender, J.: Impulse-based dynamic simulation (last visited: August 2008),
    http://www.impulse-based.de/

30. Persistence of Vision Raytracer Pty. Ltd.: Povray – the persistence of vision raytracer (last visited: August 2008), http://www.povray.org/

A Software Platform for Component Based RT-System Development: OpenRTM-Aist

Noriaki Ando, Takashi Suehiro, and Tetsuo Kotoku

Intelligent Systems Research Institute,
National Institute of Advanced Industrial Science and Technology (AIST),
AIST Tsukuba Central 2, Tsukuba, Ibaraki 305-8568, Japan
{n-ando,t.suehiro,t.kotoku}@aist.go.jp,
http://www.openrtm.org/

Abstract. This paper proposes the RT-Middleware for robot system integration. "RT" means "Robot Technology" which is applied not only to industrial field but also to nonindustrial field such as human daily life support systems. We have studied modularization of RT elements and have developed software platform RT-Middleware which promotes application of RT in various field. Robotic system development methodology and our RT-Middleware concepts is discussed. The RT-Component which is a basic madular unit of RT-Middleware based system integration is derived from this discussion. A methodology of system development with RT-Components, and a framework to make component are shown.

1 Introduction

The progress of robotics research has accumulated vast amounts of knowledge and technology. Those technologies called "Robotic Technology (RT) [1]" have begun to be applied to various field including ubiquitous computing, intelligent room and service robot applications. However the applications of those technologies are not developed enough, and the system integration issues for those technologies are receiving increasing attention both by academia and industrial circles. Especially software takes the lead in robotic system integration methodology. As the supportive evidence of it, many software platforms for robots have been developed in the world in recent years.

We have studied software building block architecture for robot development, and the RT-Middleware (RTM) and RT-Component (RTC) has been proposed as the one of solution about it [2]. The purpose of the RT-Middleware is to establish basic technologies for integrating robot systems with a new function easily by using modularized software components named RT-Component. If robot systems with new functions can be constructed more flexibly, it can satisfy every users' needs individually which cannot be satisfied now. Thus, it is expected that the conventional robot industry mainly restricted to the manufacturing field will be expanded to the nonmanufacturing field like support robots for daily life.

The research on software platforms and libraries for robotic systems are performed actively in recent years. "Player/Stage" is a free software project for

S. Carpin et al. (Eds.): SIMPAR 2008, LNAI 5325, pp. 87–98, 2008.

research in robot and sensor systems. The Player, which is a robot server with robot control interface, and its simulation backends, Stage and Gazebo, are very widely used especially by mobile robotics researchers [3]. "ORCA" is an open-source framework for developing component-based robotic systems. It provides the means for defining and developing the software components as the building-blocks [4]. "CLARAty" (Coupled-Layer Architecture for Robotic Autonomy) is an integrated framework for reusable robotic software developed by JPL, University of Minesota and Carnegine Mellon University [5]. It defines interfaces for common robotic functionality and integrates multiple implementations of any given functionality. "MSRDS" (Microsoft Robotics Developer Studio) is software platform for robotics that is distributed by Microsoft. This platform is based on DSSP (Decentralized Software Services Protocol) that is SOAP based application protocol for lightweight services. This platform also provides Visual Programming Language (VPL) for robot developers.

The main differences between those software platforms and our RT-Middleware are characterized by the open specification and interoperability. The RT-Component, which is managed its lifecycle by the RT-Middleware, is a software component based on the open specification. Since the specification is opened, any software vendors can implement based on it, and because of the common specification, different implementation can be interoperable. We also have implemented RT-Middleware and RT-Component framework based on the specification, and the implementation named "OpenRTM-aist" is provided as an open source reference implementation.

In the following, first, the requirement of the software platform for component based RT-system development is discussed, and the basic concept of RT-Middleware is shown. Then, on the basis of the discussion, a component model of RT-Component is shown. Based on the proposed component model, the RT-Middleware and RT-Component framework is implemented. Finally, some RT-Middleware based systems are shown and the discussion and conclusion are given.

2   What Is Needed for RT Software Platform

In this section, the core architecture of the RT-Componet is discussed. In consideration of RT-specific features for software, the requirement for the component model for RT systems is clarified.

2.1   Code Reusability

The reusability has two meanings. One is reusability of user's code, the other is reusability of components. Users are unwilling to use the component framework which needs to remake all codes. In order to reuse a lot of software library developed until now, it is necessary to provide the framework for modularizing the existing software library easily. Therefore, framework needs to support various operating systems and various programming languages. After modularized as an component, the component should be used without any modification and re-compile of codes.

OpenRTM-aist provides a component framework and template code generator. User can easily embed their code in it and can make it reusable component. Since component framework provides various functionality such as lifecycle management, network communication including data-oriented and service-oriented interaction and runtime configuration, user can focus on his/her own main logic.

2.2   Various Granularity Support

Various granularity size of modules could be considered, when modularizing an RT element. A motor, a sensor, and a controller can be a fine granularity component respectivly. A vision system with some image processing algorithms, a several degrees of freedom manipulator arm and a mobile robot with some sensors are example of middle-fine granularity components. An application program might want to handle a humanoid robot, an intelligent room, etc. as a coarse grained module respectivly. The software platform needs to support various component grain size in the framework.

OpenRTM-aist's component model provides data-centric interaction method, which is mainly used for fine grained components, and service-oriented interaction method, which is mainly used for coarse grained components.

2.3   Active Module

Usually, a general distributed object works as a passive object that sends back return values to a method invocation. In this case, an object is modeled as interfaces that contain operations with input and output parameters and a return value. An internal activity model of an object is not considered.

On the other hand, some of modularized RT element has its own tasks like real-time feedback control in it, and it is necessary to collect required data RT-element itself, or to notify event to other elements when it happened.

In the RT-Component model, a component's business logic is associated with at least one execution entity named Execution Contexts. The Execution Context, which is a logical thread, executes user's logic implemented in the RT-Component framework.

2.4   Realtime Capabilities

Realtime capabilities of module activity are an indispensable function in RT systems especially in low level control layer. It is necessary not only in one component but also in composite component that is composed of some fine-grained components. For example, in order to make two or more modules cooperate in the real-time schedule, the time synchronization between modules is needed. Software platform for RT systems should satisfy these requirements.

Above mentioned Execution Context, which is a logical thread, is associated with RT-Component in run-time. Replacing by a execution context driven by a real-time thread, real-time execution of the RT-Component's can be possible.

2.5   Platform Independency

Here the platform contains some meanings such as operating systems, programming language, network middleware and communication media. As mentioned above, it is significant that platform supports multiple operating systems and languages for code reusability. Generally as for the code of a low level which controls hardware, C and C++ language are used, and a code of a high level, such as behavior and judgment of a robot will often be described by Java or script languages. In many cases, device drivers for robotic devices support a few operating systems and needs special communication media. Since a device and its device driver often depend on operating systems and communication media, the framework for modularizing it should not be dependent on them.

Currently OpenRTM-aist supports C++, Java, Python and C# languages on various UNIX, Mac OS X and Windows platforms. OpenRTM-aist's interoperability among these languages and OSs is realized by CORBA (Common Object Request Broker Architecture).

2.6   Social Requirement

The software platform has to be stable in the meaning of the quality of software code itself and the social continuity of the software. Needless to say that the code quality of the software platform is important. Additionally since many software components that are developed on the platform depend on the platform, continual existence of the platform is also important issue. The open source and copyleft strategy can be one of solution for it, and the open specification is the other solution.

OpenRTM-aist is an open source project, and it is released under LGPL license. We also opened its specification including component model and interface definition. Currently we released C++, Java and Python version of OpenRTM, and one private company released OpenRTM for C#, which is compatible with our OpenRTM-aist for C++, Java and Python. Multi-vendor environment gives the software platform diversity, optionality and continuousness. Additionally the specification itself has to be stable, so we have standardized the RT-Component specification in OMG (Object Management Group) [6].

3   Component Model

From the requirements mentioned above, we had studied about appropriate component model for RT-systems, and had defined the functionality in the component model. We call it RT-Component (RTC). Figure 1 shows the architecture block diagram of the RT-Component. The functionality of the RT-Component is as follows:

- Component metadata for dynamic component assembly.
- Component action and execution context for business logic execution.
- Data ports for data exchange between RTCs.

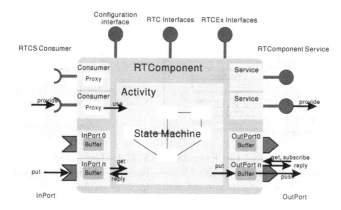

Fig. 1. The proposed architecture of RT-Component model. The RT-Component has a component body, common interface for metadata acquisition, component action, data ports, service ports and configuration interface.

- Service ports for service-oriented communication between RTCs.
- Configuration interface for runtime parameter setting.

3.1   Metadata Acquisition

The metadata acquisition capability, which realize querying and administering RTCs at runtime, is also known as "Introspection" (Figure 2). RTC has some interfaces to get metadata including profile, properties about ports. These capabilities can be used by other RTCs, tools or other application programs that support dynamic RTC composition. By using these metadata, application programs can obtain these metadata from RTC in runtime, and can make dynamic composition of RTCs in runtime. These metadata is also useful for components debugging tools and components composition tools. This functionality has two features, one is resource data model, the other is stereotype and interfaces. Resource data, which is a kind of data-only class, describes component profiles. Interfaces defines some methods to get or set profiles and properties.

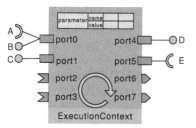

Name	MyManipulator0
Type	Periodic execution type
port0	Provide: A, Required: B
port1	Provide: C
Port2	DataPort: InPort, velocity, float x6
Port3	DataPort: InPort, position, float x6
Port4	Provide: D
Port5	Required: E
Port6	DataPort: OutPort, status int x1
Port7	DataPort: OutPort, velocity, float x6
ExecutionContext	Period: 10ms
Parameter	gain0(float x6), flag(int x1), dev_file(string)

Fig. 2. The RTC provides introspection interfaces to obtain metadata of the RTC. Other RTC or application can utilize the metadata to make dynamic RTC composition.

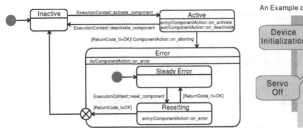

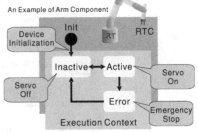

Fig. 3. The state machine of the Execution-Context. Each callback named "on_xxx" is invoked on related transition events and actions.

Fig. 4. The Component Action callbacks in which the component specific logic is implemented are invoked by the logical thread ExecutionContext

3.2   Component Action

The "Component Action" interface defines callbacks corresponding to the execution of the lifecycle operations of RTC. These callbacks would be invoked by the execution entity named "Execution Contexts" that is a logical thread object.

An RTC developer would implement Component Action's callback operations that would be invoked in each state of "Execution Context", in order to execute RT-component-specific logic. An RTC can participate in Execution Contexts, and an Execution Context can accept multiple RTC participants. As shown in Figure 3 and 4, an Execution Context performs a state transition between "Active" "Inactive" and "Error" state, and Component Action callbacks is invoked in appropriate timing in the state transition.

As mentioned above, the logic of an RTC and the logical thread is decoupled in the RTC model. This model is useful to implement tightly coupled RTCs in a single (real-time) thread. It is called the synchronous composite RT-Component.

3.3   Data Ports

In the low level real-time control layer, if a component is considered as the functional unit which consists of inputs, processing, and outputs like a control block diagram, it will be easy to perform a system configuration (Figure 5). This input/output model is not suitable for general usage of the distributed object model. Because an object which sends its data to other objects has to know all objects' complete interface definition. On the other hand, in such low level control layer, data type, number of data and unit of data are more important than interface definition. As shown in Figure 6, RT-Component adopted the publisher/subscriber model and defines it as InPort/OutPort.

OutPort supports some subscription types, "New", "Periodic" and "Flush." For example, the "New" subscription type means that an OutPort sends data to InPorts which subscribe it when a new data come from the Component Action.

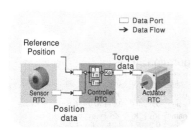

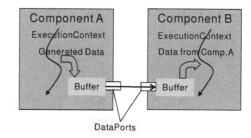

Fig. 5. A DataPort usage example. The DataPort is used for data-centric communication between components.

Fig. 6. The DataPort provides data-centric port for RTCs. The InPort receives data from the OutPort. The OutPort has some subscription types that control data pushing timing.

3.4 Service Ports

The software component should have enough interfaces to access to detailed functionality of the component from outside (Figure 7). The "Service Ports" provide endpoint to attach provided interfaces and required interfaces on it. Component developer can provide his/her own defined interface through the Service Port. The developer also can use provided interfaces by the other components through the Service Ports, as shown in Figure 8.

3.5 Configuration

The Configuration interface provides interfaces to administrate user defined RTC's parameters. As mentioned above, a component should not have the hard-coded configuration parameters which prevent reuse of the component.

The configuration consists of some configuration parameters as list of values with name, as shown in Figure 9. RTC is able to have some configurations as sets. This is called the Configuration Set. The Configuration Sets can be replaced in

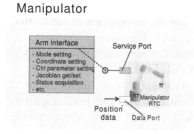

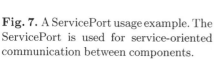

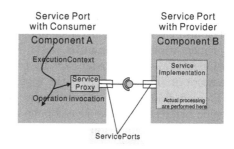

Fig. 7. A ServicePort usage example. The ServicePort is used for service-oriented communication between components.

Fig. 8. The ServicePort provides service-oriented communication between RTCs. User defined service objects can be exported through the ServicePort.

PID Controller

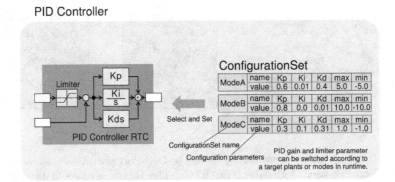

Fig. 9. The Configuration interface allows manipulation of configuration parameters in runtime. User can define some sets of the configurations.

runtime to adapt the RTC into the applications. For example, if an RTC realises PID controller with P-I-D gain as configuration parameters, the configuration set can be replaced or changed to adapt to the plant.

4   Implementation

4.1   OpenRTM-aist

According to the proposed RTC model, the "OpenRTM-aist (Open RT-Middleware distributed by AIST)" that is a component framework and middleware environment for RTCs have been implemented [7]. "OpenRTM-aist" consists of an RT-Component development frame work, a middleware including RTC manager and some tools. OpenRTM-aist is implemented on CORBA (Common Object Request Broker Architecture), because of its network transparency, OS/language independency and interoperability. Currently OpenRTM-aist supports C++, Java and Python languages on Windows, Linux and other UNIX-like operating systems. An RTC developer can choose appropriate language according to granularity, logic abstraction level and preference of language, and RTCs implemented on different languages are interoperable each other. OpenRTM-aist is also CORBA independent implementation, so it supports some CORBA implementation like omniORB, TAO, MICO and ORBexpress.

"OpenRTM-aist" provides a GUI tool to manage and administrate RTC on the network. The Figure 10 is the tool named "RtcLink."

The left side pane is "Name Service View" that show component list on the specific name server. The center pane is "System Editor" that is editor area to compose RTCs connection and to activate/deactivate RTCs. The right side pane is "Property View" to show the selected RTC's profile.

This GUI tool is implemented as an Eclipse plug-in. The Eclipse is a open-source project, and a lot of third party plug-ins is available. Since the Eclipse is one of the most widely used integrated development environment now, we have chosen the Eclipse as a platform of our tools.

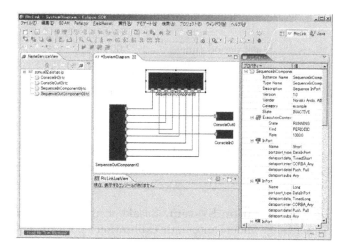

Fig. 10. RtcLink on Eclipse. RT-System online design tool running on Eclipse IDE.

4.2 RTM Based Systems

OpenRTM-aist already has more than 100 users, and some of national robotic projects in Japan adopts it as official platform. Here some of RTM based systems are shown.

Force Controled Manipulator. This is an example system, which consists of a force sensor RTC, a manipulator RTC, a joystick RTC and a dumper controller RTC, to show real-time capability of OpenRTM-aist.

As shown in Figure 12, these components are associated with same real-time thread, and each component's logic are executed synchronously in a 2 ms periodic task. Table 1 shows task execution time statistics in this experiment. The point is that these three devices components and one control component are not a

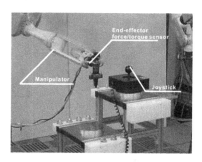

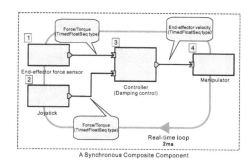

Fig. 11. Manipulator system equipment: End-effector force/torque sensor, manipulator, joystick

Fig. 12. A force controlled manipulator system using a synchronous composite component. Number in upper left of each block means execution order.

Table 1. Execution time of force controlled manipulator system

Task period time	2.00 ms
Maximum execution time	2.01 ms
Minimum execution time	1.99 ms
Mean execution time	2.00 ms
Standard deviation	4.41 μs

monolithic program but programs completely created separately. Furthermore, the point that these components were executed synchronizing in real-time is important.

Automatic LRF Calibration System. Sasaki et al. implemented their distributed LRF (laser range finder) automatic calibration algorithm on OpenRTM-aist [8](Figure 14).

This system consists of four type of RTC: LRF RTC, Tracker RTC, LRF Calibration RTC, Coordination Transform RTC. LRF sensors distributed on network are integrated by the network transparency capability of OpenRTM-aist.

Other RTCs. The following is an example of the components developed on OpenRTM-aist by OpenRTM-aist community.

- 3D recoginition and tracking RTCs by AIST and Applied Vision Co. Ltd.(Figure 15)
- Learning/inference RTCs baed on β-RNA by AdIn Research, Inc.
- LRF based human tracking RTCs by System Engineering Consultants Co., Ltd.
- Manipulator and bilateral tele-operation RTCs by AIST
- Input device RTCs (Game-pad, PHANToM, GUI, etc.) by AIST
- Dynamics simulator: OpenHRP3 by AIST(Figure 16)

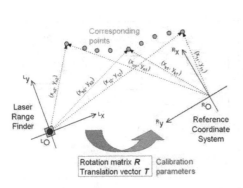

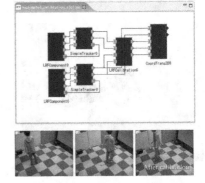

Fig. 13. The LRF automatic calibration algorithm. Relative.

Fig. 14. LRF automatic calibration and tracking system based on OpenRTM-aist

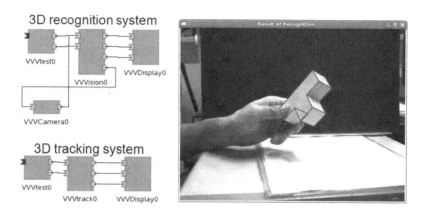

Fig. 15. 3D recognition and tracking RTCs. This system is based on VVV (Versatile Volumetric Vision) developed in AIST.

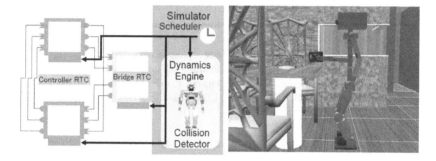

Fig. 16. The OpenHRP3 provides an environment for dynamics simulation for various types of robots including humanoid robots, manipulators and mobile robots. The controller RT-Component that is tested in the OpenHRP3 can be exported to the real robot without recompiling.

Currently a lot of RT-Components are being developed and circulation in a user community is also starting.

5   Conclusion

In this paper, we proposed component based robotic system integration scheme RT-Middleware and RT-Component. The functions required for the RT-Component which supports robot specific features were discussed and clarified. To realize component based robotic system development efficiently, RT-Component and its architecture was proposed. The "OpenRTM-aist", which includes RTC development framework, middleware and tools, have been implemented.

References

1. Japan Robot Association, Summary Report on Technology Strategy for Creating a Robot Society in the 21st Century (2001),
   http://www.jara.jp/e/dl/report0105.pdf
2. Ando, N., Suehiro, T., Kitagaki, K., Kotoku, T., Yoon, W.-K.: RT-Middleware: Distributed Component Middleware for RT (Robot Technology). In: IEEE/RSJ International Conference on Intelligent Robots and Systems (IROS 2005), pp. 3555–3560 (2005)
3. Gerkey, B.P., Vaughan, R.T., Stoy, K., Howard, A., Sukhatme, G.S., Mataric, M.J.: Most Valuable Player: A Robot Device Server for Distributed Control. In: Proceedings of the IEEE/RSJ International Conference on Intelligent Robots and Systems (IROS 2001), pp. 1226–1231 (November 2001)
4. Makarenko, A., Brooks, A., Kaupp, T.: Orca: Components for Robotics. In: IEEE/RSJ International Conference on Intelligent Robots and Systems (IROS 2006), Workshop on Robotic Standardization (2006)
5. Volpe, R., Nesnas, I.A.D., Estlin, T., Mutz, D., Petras, R., Das, H.: The CLARAty Architecture for Robotic Autonomy. In: Proceedings of the 2001 IEEE Aerospace Conference, Big Sky Montana, March 10-17 (2001)
6. Object Management Group, Robotic Technology Component Specification Version 1.0, formal/2008-04-04 (2008)
7. OpenRTM-aist official web site, http://www.openrtm.org
8. Sasaki, T., Hashimoto, H.: Hierarchical Framework for Implementation of Intelligent Space. In: Proceedings of the 33rd Annual Conference of the IEEE Industrial Electronics Society (IECON 2007), vol. 11, pp. 28–33 (2007)

A Software System for Robotic Learning by Experimentation

Iman Awaad[1], Ronny Hartanto[1], Beatriz León[2], and Paul Plöger[1]

[1] Bonn-Rhein-Sieg University of Applied Science
Grantham-Allee 20, 53757 Sankt Augustin, Germany
{iman.awaad,ronny.hartanto,paul.ploeger}@fh-bonn-rhein-sieg.de
[2] Universitat Jaume I, Castellon de la Plana, Spain
beatriz.leon@smail.inf.fh-bonn-rhein-sieg.de

Abstract. The goal of this work is to develop an integration framework for a robotic software system which enables robotic learning by experimentation within a distributed and heterogeneous setting. To meet this challenge, the authors specified, defined, developed, implemented and tested a component-based architecture called XPERSIF. The architecture comprises loosely-coupled, autonomous components that offer services through their well-defined interfaces and form a service-oriented architecture. The Ice middleware is used in the communication layer. Additionally, the successful integration of the XPERSim simulator into the system has enabled simultaneous quasi-realtime observation of the simulation by numerous, distributed users.

1 Introduction

Software solutions have developed from a simple algorithm to programs that might contain more than one algorithm, to groups of programs forming an application. Nowadays, these solutions might encompass numerous applications running on a number of machines. More often, these applications are developed independently and must be integrated into a single architecture. Along with these developments, the complexity in the task of designing and abstracting (or architecting) these architectures has also grown. Principles that guide the structuring of such distributed applications are necessary, as is the use of technology which facilitates their development.

The test bed for the software system presented in this work is the XPERO project, the goal of which is robot learning by experimentation. The task at hand is the integration of required applications, such as planning of experiments, perception of parametrized features, robot motion control and knowledge-based learning, into a coherent cognitive architecture. This allows a mobile robot to use the methods involved in experimentation in order to learn about its environment. The software applications are distributed due to both the processing power needed and the multidisciplinary cooperation inherent in robotics research.

The results of this work demonstrate that the framework is robust and flexible, and can be successfully scaled to facilitate the complete integration of the

S. Carpin et al. (Eds.): SIMPAR 2008, LNAI 5325, pp. 99–110, 2008.

necessary applications, thus enabling robot learning by experimentation. The cognitive architecture is itself beyond the scope of this paper. The design supports composability, thus allowing components to be grouped together in order to provide an aggregate service. Distributed simulation enables quasi real-time tele-observation of the simulated experiment by users and applications.

The following section will discuss and compare related work. Next, the necessary background information on the chosen approach is provided in the form of an overview of service-oriented architecture (SOA) [1] and component based software engineering (CBSE). The XPERSIF [2] system architecture and the component model which forms the basis for all components within the loop is then presented. An overview of the resulting architecture follows. As simulation was used from the start to speed up the pace of research [3] the solution used to distribute the simulation to numerous clients simultaneously is then presented. The results are presented in section 6 followed by a discussion of the work.

2   Related Work

In this section, we present an overview of robotic software systems (RSS) and relate them to this work.

As laid out in [4], RSS tend to fall within one of three categories, driver and algorithm implementations, communication middleware, and robotic software frameworks. Often, the borders between these categories are blurred. Comparisons between RSS within different categories is misleading as each is motivated differently and serves a different function – i.e. they are simply unlike each other except in their shared goal of increasing reusability in robotics. An attempt is made here to present an example RSS from each of the three categories above, and relate them to this work.

The Player project [5] is an excellent example of the first type of RSS described above (driver and algorithm implementations). It includes a robot device interface which serves as a hardware abstraction layer (HAL) for robotic devices, as well as the robot simulators Stage and Gazebo. They are all open source and free. Player allows the same interface to be used to control the robot by providing 'drivers' which translate the abstract commands available in the interface into robot-specific commands.

Middleware for Robotics (Miro) [6] is a distributed object-oriented framework for mobile robot control, based on CORBA. The overhead in terms of memory and processing power which results from the use of CORBA is a disadvantage of this solution. In addition, the complexity involved in understanding and learning to use it is also a hurdle. In comparison, the use of the much simpler and more efficient Ice middleware [7] by XPERSIF precludes such problems. Miro is an example of the second type of RSS.

Orca [8] is very much a robotic software framework. It is an open-source framework for developing component-based robotic systems. It uses a CBSE approach which allows building-blocks (components) to be developed and used together to create a more complex robotic system. The main motivation is the advancement of robotics research through the reuse of such building blocks. This is done by providing commonly-used interfaces, libraries and a repository of existing components. Orca's successor, Orca2, uses the Ice middleware.

While the use of the Player project would address the issue of robot control and perhaps simulation, it could not be used for the integration of a complete robotic system (such as the cognitive architecture presented here). The same can be said of Miro. Of the three RSS presented above, Orca is most similar to XPERSIF in that it is also a thin framework which utilizes the Ice middleware, provides a simple component model and uses simple and efficient communications patterns. An added advantage of the XPERSIF framework is its service-oriented nature. Despite being a mature project, Orca's repository does not provide interfaces, components or libraries which offer the more advanced functionalities relating to cognitive architectures. Section 6 presents the results of the XPERSIF framework and architecture which highlight the advantages of its design.

3 Approach

A CBSE approach has been used to encapsulate the functionalities of the robotic software and hardware systems into components. These components have been loosely coupled to form a SOA.

"Service-Orientation" is a design paradigm for architecting a distributed architecture which centers around loosely-coupled autonomous components and groups of components providing services in order to carry out a given task. The principles of this paradigm allow the separation of the business and application logic domains of an enterprise. They guide their structuring into the layers associated with a SOA model. Additionally, they provide tennets for the granularity and other characteristics towards which individual services should strive. SOAs are basically a collection of services. A service is well-defined and self-contained, and does not depend on the context or state of other services [1]. These services can be registered with a central registry which allows service requesters to discover them. This is the essence – the abstract idea of a SOA.

How a SOA is implemented can vary. An implementation approach based on that of traditional distributed architectures, or alternatively one utilizing "Web Services" (WS) which takes advantage of the Internet and its proprietary-free communications network may be adopted. Such a SOA might use document-style messages which are encoded in protocols such as the Simple Object Access Protocol (SOAP) to transport, process and route the payload which itself is represented in the Xtensible Markup Language (XML).

Components can be placed on various computers – dedicated application servers – to form a distributed architecture. Traditionally, Remote Procedure Calls (RPCs) are used for communication between components within such a distributed architecture. This is a point of difference between SOAs based on these distributed architectures and those based on WS, as the communication between services in the latter case is accomplished through document-style messages using protocols such as SOAP, which are as self-sufficient as possible (containing policy rules, meta-information and processing instructions for example). This tends to result in larger messages that are sent and received less frequently in comparison to RPC communication as used in traditional distributed architectures.

In this work, the traditional distributed architecture is used in the implementation of a SOA. Additionally, no workflow and orchestration (in the strict SOA sense) are used. These are not necessary as the architecture presented here has no need for service discoverability and the use of services within the architecture is static rather than dynamic. The composability of SOA is achieved through the use of the CBSE approach. CBSE adopts the doctrine of 'divide and conquer' by breaking down a system into functional or logical components. These components (and the services they provide) are accessed through their interfaces. The component model used for this work is defined in the following section.

4   Architecture

Components within the XPERSIF architecture are classified into one of three basic groups of components, namely *basic* components, *organizational* components responsible for managing a hierarchy of components, and *aggregate* components which are organizational components which appear as a single component but are composed of individual components which cooperate to provide the services of the aggregate component by using the facade software pattern.

A component's structure can be summarized by stating that it offers services as commands and operations (as defined below) and notifies its users of the final state of the service (Fig. 1). In order to provide this functionality several abstract interfaces are specified. Namely, the Operation interface (which provides functionality for component administration), the Subject interface (which provides a means to subscribe to notifications) and the Observer interface (which provides a means to receive notifications). The component-specific functionality is specified within the Component interface. As none of the components within the XPERO system are hard real-time components, this component model meets the soft real-time requirements in the simplest way possible. This is not to say that soft real-time systems are sufficient for robotics in general. Certainly in legged robots and where coordination between actuators are involved, a hard real-time system is essential. These three interfaces are thus sufficient for the requirements of the project.

Operations are used for services which complete q uickly, commands for those that need more time, and notifications serve to enable a call to a command to quickly return (thus enabling a non-blocking call) and to provide monitoring and error handling mechanisms. To prevent components from blocking, while at the same time allowing for tasks which may have varying duration, a differentiation is made between commands and operations. Both commands and operations return immediately, however, commands will start an asynchronous process which completes when the component notifies the original caller of the command's completion.

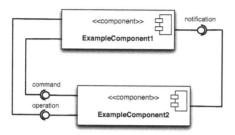

Fig. 1. The XPERSIF component model

Commands are used for tasks which may take time to complete, such as moving to a position for example or gripping an object. They are implemented as non-blocking RPCs. From a planning perspective, commands could be seen as planning operators and as such should have preconditions and effects so that a planner can make use of this information. These preconditions and effects may be seen as a contract. Operations, on the other hand, do not start an asynchronous process. Tasks such as getting the readings from the IR sensors or setting the maximum velocity are implemented as operations, as they take very little time to execute and pose no risk of blocking the component when they are called. This distinction has many effects on the architecture. It is useful to specify preconditions and effects for operations as well. For example, an operation which should deliver the shape of an object might specify as a precondition that the object is in view at a specified distance from the camera. The definition of such preconditions for operations would then form a contract (as with commands).

4.1 The XPERSIF Components

A component diagram depicting the data flow between the various components of the loop is shown in Fig. 2. The components here have been grouped according to their functionality. This diagram does not elaborate on the implementation of each of these components – for example, it does not mention which are applications and which are components that are grouped to form an application. They simply show the components of the loop and the data flowing between them. The LOOPMODEL component which is the organizational center of the loop is seen at the center of Fig. 2. It serves as an entry point to the loop for a graphical user interface (GUI) (or a console client as in the current implementation) which uses it to configure the loop. It is responsible for parametrizing, starting, monitoring and exiting the necessary components within the loop. For the sake of simplicity, the flow of the component status information from each component to the LOOPMODEL is not depicted.

The DESIGNOFEXPERIMENTS component is responsible for designing effective experiments when the robot is in the experimentation state. The GOALDESIGN module is responsible for the robot's actions when it is not in the experimentation state. Once a goal state for the robot has been formulated, the planner should

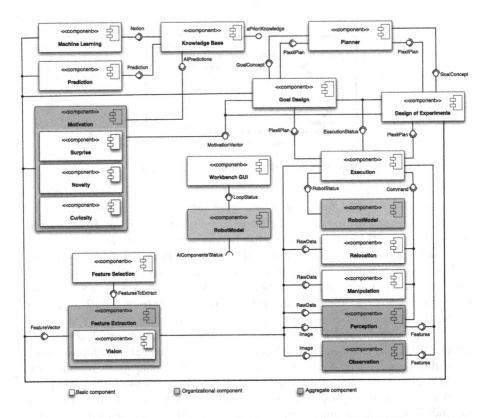

Fig. 2. A component diagram showing the data flow between XPERSIF components

produce a plan to achieve this goal, and the EXECUTION component should then execute this plan.

The robotic embodiment is itself represented by a group of components. As the embodiments are mobile manipulators, the components include a RELOCATION and a MANIPULATION component. In addition, a PERCEPTION component provides access to the embodiment's sensors. These components receive commands from the execution component and return monitoring information to it. A central point to query the embodiment's state is the ROBOTMODEL component. It is part of the organizational layer as it is responsible for starting those components which make up the robotic embodiment. These components make API calls to either the physical embodiment or to the simulated embodiment within the XPERSim simulator, thus, it may be seen as a form of tool-driven validation.

An overhead camera is often used within the cognitive loop both by the human researcher to tele-observe the experiment, and by the robot itself to provide ground truth. In the latter case, the view from the overhead camera is provided to the robot as a service (by the OBSERVATION component). Both this component and the PERCEPTION component are displayed as aggregate components in Fig. 2 as they use their own instances of the ROBOTFEATUREEXTRACTION meta-component. They are responsible for initializing the instances of this component and are the sole users of the interfaces.

The FEATUREEXTRACTION component takes as input the raw sensor data from the embodiment and the overhead camera, and extracts meaningful features (by default objects and their poses). Should the FEATURESELECTION component specify additional features to be extracted, this may be carried out by either the FEATURE-EXTRACTION component itself or the VISION component. The FEATUREEXTRACTION component generates a feature vector as the output of this process.

Components such as those of the MOTIVATION aggregate component and the MACHINELEARNING component receive these feature vectors and use them to generate their own outputs (curiosity and surprise values, a prediction, a notion, etc). For the sake of simplicity, the diagram in Fig. 2 shows only the data flowing into the knowledge base, although it serves as a central point for all components to query for data at anytime.

5   Distributing the Simulation

The integration of the XPERSim simulator [9] provided not only the means to conduct research but a means to validate the software system itself. This section details the efforts made to distribute the simulation for tele-observation by researchers and for processing by individual components. Although the implementation is specific to the XPERSim simulator, the same approach can conceptually be used for other simulators. This integration of XPERSim into XPERSIF allows the simulation to be run in a distributed setting.

XPERSim is a 3D simulator based on open source components, built by the authors, that quickly and easily constructs an accurate and photo-realistic simulation for robots of arbitrary morphology and of the environments within which they function. XPERSim achieves such high quality visualization by using the Object-Oriented Graphics Rendering Engine 3D (Ogre) engine to render the simulation whose dynamics are calculated by Open Dynamics Engine (ODE). Simultaneous multiple camera simulation of the rendered scene is possible at high frame rates. A library of sensors and actuators commonly-used in robotics is available.

The solution presented here uses a proven methodology (implemented in multi-player games for over a decade) which involves moving the rendering of images from the server-side to the client-side by sending out a subset of the scene information to ensure that all clients are operating synchronously [10]. This drastically reduces the amount of data being transmitted and is possible due to the scene-oriented nature of the XPERSim simulation. As mentioned previously, the Ogre 3D rendering engine uses scene-graphs to represent hierarchies, which simplifies the processing of objects or groups of objects. A scene-graph consists of nodes (with parent nodes and child nodes). If a parent node is translated or rotated, this transformation is applied to the child scene nodes as well.

The latency resulting from the distributed nature of the application is ameliorated by sending the node information from the simulator while the client is rendering the previous one – i.e. the server does not wait for the client to request the image but sends it continuously once it has subscribed. The method described above to distribute a simulation to multiple clients is implemented here by decoupling the physics and graphics engines from XPERSim to create an XPERSim Server (calculating dynamics) and a TeleSimView client (rendering the nodes at their new positions). The XPERSim Server sends out the positions and orientations of all scene-nodes to the clients that simply transform the specified nodes to the specified positions and orientations and in so doing produce the same scene in an efficient and real time manner.

In an effort to further reduce network latency, a one-way invocation is used to send the new frame. This can in fact be quite expensive when many such small messages need to be sent. This is because the run time taps into the OS kernel for each message and because each of these messages is sent out with its own message header [11]. To ameliorate this problem, batched one-way invocations are used. This allows the Ice run time to buffer these small messages until the XPERSim Server explicitly flushes them.

6   Results and Discussion

The XPERO project has provided XPERSIF with an invaluable testing ground. The success of the framework lies in whether all the requirements are met efficiently. This has been most clearly demonstrated in the efficient communication of the outputs from the various components throughout the loop. The most demanding of these outputs is the distribution of the simulated scene in a quasi real-time manner.

The evaluation of the software integration framework is first measured here qualitatively against various criteria such as flexibility, reusability, scalability, ease of use, level of documentation, and development time. After this evaluation, empirical results which highlight the success of the distributed simulation solution as tested during the running of the various other components are presented.

Flexibility of the framework was the core criterion in the development process. It is manifested not only by the ease of changing implementations independently of the abstract interfaces (e.g. using different planning algorithms beneath the same interface) but also by the ease with which components use each other's services. Flexibility was enhanced by the use of the organizational components which centralize the point at which changes might need to be made. Even a change of interfaces would be simple enough to propagate. The flexibility was further enhanced through the adherence to the SOA principle of service-stateless. The services offered through the component interfaces are at a level of granularity which enables their use under different control flow scenarios which have been specified within the project.

Reusability has been achieved by allowing various existing implementations of an application to be reused beneath the interfaces. Numerous instances of components (such as VISION) also contributed to the reusability of a component.

Scalability has been ensured through the use of the component-based approach and through the consistent use of simple and efficient communication patterns.

Ease of development was facilitated by the use of a single basic component model (augmented as need be for organizational components). The simplicity in design of this basic component model, which is nonetheless robust and efficient in propagating information through the various layers, is an achievement in itself. It allowed the system to be easily debugged and facilitated error handling which results in a *robust* system. The implemented base applications also contributed to the ease of integration of components and applications. This ease of development also contributed to the *extensibility* of the architecture. The framework was designed with future needs in mind (e.g. a workbench for robot learning by experimentation, the use of stereo vision, of multiple robots, etc). This includes the facilitation of implementing a change in the experimentation process. The use of the GOALDESIGN and DESIGNOFEXPERIMENTS modules to orchestrate the loop allows such changes to be confined to these components. The interfaces of the remaining components are abstract enough to not need amendments.

The level of *documentation* is accurate and consistent at a variety of levels including the source code, installation and user guides for the various versions which have so far been released to the project partners. This holds for both the XPERSim and the XPERSIF projects. The Ice middleware too, has a high level of documentation which is both extensive and easy to reference.

Sliding autonomy [12] is, in the case of this work, a valuable criterion, as the evaluation of the functional performance of the architecture must be carried out from the viewpoint of both the researcher and the robot (the two XPERSIF users), and often must be carried out from both points of view simultaneously. The ability to use XPERSIF under varying levels of autonomy is a necessity. The use of the LOOPMODEL component to parametrize the experiment and the enabling of placeholders for the application (e.g. allowing a pre-generated plan to be used through the interface) provided this varying degree of autonomy.

With the exception of XPERSim, the framework was evaluated using placeholder components that were implemented using the various component models and performed as the components would, observing the relevant components, publishing their own outputs and receiving notifications. These components helped validate the XPERSIF specifics as a whole system was tested.

Distribution of the simulation through the integration of XPERSim into the XPERSIF architecture was successfully achieved. The scalability of the implementation described above was evaluated by measuring the impact on the quality of the simulation by varying the number of subscribers to the tele-observation service during the execution of various other applications. The initial efforts to distribute the simulation provided the image's color pixel values, in the BGR format, as a sequence of integers. In addition to the image itself, the width and height of the image, as well as the time to which it belongs, were also sent. A set of experimental evaluations was carried out (Fig. 3 details the experimental setup) to measure the time in seconds which is needed to receive a new image of size 416 x 600 pixels. For this set of evaluations, the image was sent from

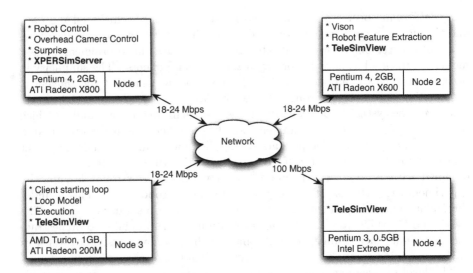

Fig. 3. The experimental setup used to obtain the empirical results for distributed simulation below. Depicted here is the specification for the four nodes along with the components which ran on them during the measurement process. Nodes 2 and 3 each ran one TelesimView client while Node 4 ran additional clients as needed.

the machine running at Node 1 to the machine running at Node 3. The round trip time needed to deliver the image was measured at 9.5346 seconds (i.e. at a frame rate of <1 fps). Using the approach described above, the time measured between receiving two subsequent images was 0.0046 seconds (i.e. 217 fps).

Table 1 shows the measurements made when one, three, five and then ten clients are subscribed to the service. All experiments were repeated three times, measuring the time it took for 60 frames to be delivered to the TeleSimView client. It is worth noting that the size of the image to be rendered is inconsequential. As nodes are being sent and not an image, it is the number of nodes within a scene that affects the time and not the image size. For the test case above, 15 nodes were transmitted (representing the Khepera robot and the four cubes). Using this information, the scene may be rendered from the viewpoint of any number of cameras.

A number of issues are currently being addressed. In the current implementation of the XPERSim simulator, no distinction is being made between parent

Table 1. The time in seconds between receiving two subsequent images using the batched one-way invocation method

Trial	1 client	3 clients	5 clients	10 clients
1	0.0039 s	0.0039 s	0.0219 s	0.0227 s
2	0.0023 s	0.0172 s	0.0128 s	0.0352 s
3	0.0075 s	0.0036 s	0.0120 s	0.0448 s
Mean	0.0046 s	0.0082 s	0.0156 s	0.0342 s

nodes and child nodes. It is recommended however that this distinction be made as it would reduce the number of nodes whose data needs to be transmitted (transmit parent nodes only and nodes which can be moved separately from the hierarchy – a gripper for example which, despite being a member of the robot node, may be moved on its own). In the setup above, for example, the number of nodes being transmitted would be reduced from 15 to just eight. Additionally, the TeleSimView client is being upgraded to use the latest version of Ogre.

7   Discussion

The resulting software framework easily and efficiently allows the integration of components (both software and hardware) with heterogeneous platforms and languages. The use of CBSE allows the software architecture to maximize concurrency in the application development process of the various research groups. The adoption of the SOA approach in the design of the framework has produced a system which is highly flexible and maintainable. The framework is data-centric with communication of the data playing a significant role in the design. The simplicity of the communication patterns contributes to the efficiency and flexibility of the framework. The data itself which is exchanged between components is abstracted in such a way as to maintain interfaces which are as simple as possible. Additionally, the solution for the tele-observation of experiments is a significant contribution to the framework as a whole. The architecture thus developed has successfully enabled effective, simultaneous, quasi-realtime observation of the simulation by numerous, distributed users.

The component model and communication patterns on which the framework is built are basic, lending themselves to providing the base of frameworks for the design of heterogenous robot systems. The differentiation made between commands and operations and the associated data structures contribute to the value of the framework. Although the Ice middleware has been used successfully in the implementation presented here, the component model itself remains independent of it and this in turn enables users to choose any other middleware. The methods used to distribute the simulation, although implemented here with XPERSim, may be adopted by other simulators.

The implementation of additional mechanisms to support real-time are a top priority in the further development of the framework, for example, implementing methods to ensure Quality of Service (QoS). Extending the framework to allow for multiple agents simultaneously is an on-going endeavor. The use of WS SOA approaches to enable a more loosely-coupled system is under investigation.

Acknowledgements

The work described in this article has been partially funded by the European Commission's Sixth Framework Programme under contract no. 029427 as part of the Specific Targeted Research Project XPERO ("Robotic Learning by Experimentation"). The authors express their gratitude to Karl-Heinz Sylla for his guidance and to the researchers of the XPERO project for their feedback and support. The authors gratefully acknowledge the reviewers' comments.

References

1. Erl, T.: Service-Oriented Architecture: Concepts, Technology, and Design. Prentice Hall PTR, Upper Saddle River (2005)
2. Awaad, I., Leon, B.: Xpersif: A component-based software integration framework for robotic learning by experimentation. Technical report, University of Applied Sciences Bonn-Rhein-Sieg (2008)
3. Bratko, I.: Initial experiments in robot discovery in xpero. In: International Conference on Robotics and Automation Workshop on Concept Learning for Embodied Agents (2007)
4. Makarenko, A., Brooks, A., Kaupp, T.: On the benefits of making robotic software frameworks thin. In: IEEE/RSJ International Conference on Intelligent Robots and Systems Workshop (2007)
5. Gerkey, B., Vaughn, R.T., Howard, A.: The player/stage project: Tools for multi-robot and distributed sensor systems. In: Proceedings of International Conference on Automation and Robotics, pp. 317–323 (2003)
6. The Miro Group, Miro Manual Version 0.9.4 (2006)
7. Henning, M.: Massively multiplayer middleware. Association for Computing Machinery Queue Magazine 1(10) (2004)
8. Makarenko, A.: The ORCA manual 2.7.0 (2007)
9. Awaad, I., Leon, B.: Xpersim: A simulator for robot learning by experimentation. In: Proceedings of this conference (2008)
10. Funkhouser, T.A.: Ring: A client-server system for multiuser virtual environments. In: Proceedings of the SIGGRAPH Symposium on Interactive 3D Graphics, Association for Computing Machinery SIGGRAPH, pp. 85–92 (1995)
11. Henning, M., Spruiell, M.: Distributed Programming with Ice. ZeroC Inc. Revision 3.2 edn. (2007)
12. Brookshire, J.D.: Enhancing multi-robot coordinated teams with sliding autonomy. Master's thesis, Carnegie Mellon University (2004)

A Mobile Robot Control Framework: From Simulation to Reality

Stephen Balakirsky, Frederick M. Proctor, Christopher J. Scrapper, and Thomas R. Kramer

National Institute of Standards and Technology Gaithersburg, MD USA 20899

Abstract. In order to expedite the research and development of robotic systems and foster development of novel robot configurations, it is essential to develop tools and standards that allow researchers to rapidly develop, communicate, and compare experimental results. This paper describes the Mobility Open Architecture Simulation and Tools Framework (MOAST). The MOAST framework is designed to aid in the development, testing, and analysis of robotic software by providing developers with a wide range of open source robotic algorithms and interfaces. The framework provides a physics-based virtual development environment for initial testing and allows for the seamless transition of algorithms to real hardware. This paper details the design approach, software architecture and module-to-module interfaces.

1 Introduction and Related Work

The usefulness of simulation for developing control systems is well established. The role of simulation is to provide convincing sensor measurements in response to a controller's actuator outputs in an environment observable to developers. Ideally the simulation should be accurate enough so that performance parameters tuned in simulation work as well in the real world. In practice, attaining this level of simulation is often more costly than real-world testing, and simulators that respond plausibly if not accurately are acceptable. Plausible simulation then complements real-world testing to minimize the time and effort needed to build controllers that work well. Several such simulation systems exist; several of which are open source, including the Unified System for Automation and Robot Simulation (USARSim)[1][1] and the Stage and Gazebo components of Player/Stage [2].

While the typical simulation system allows one to directly connect and experiment with servo-level controllers, they in general lack any form of intelligence

---

[1] No approval or endorsement of any commercial product by the National Institute of Standards and Technology is intended or implied. Certain commercial equipment, instruments, or materials are identified in this report in order to facilitate understanding. Such identification does not imply recommendation or endorsement by the National Institute of Standards and Technology, nor does it imply that the materials or equipment identified are necessarily the best available for the purpose.

S. Carpin et al. (Eds.): SIMPAR 2008, LNAI 5325, pp. 111–122, 2008.

or ability to interpret sensor readings and issue meaningful commands. For this reason, it is necessary to connect the simulation engine to a control framework. Several such systems exist in the literature and on the web. Perhaps the most popular of which is the Player portion of Player/Stage.

Player/Stage combines a robot server interface, called Player, with a simulation system, called Stage, so that Player-enabled robots can be easily interchanged with each other and their simulated counterparts. The Player interface is installed on robotic vehicles, providing an interface to the robot's sensors and actuators over a TCP/IP network. Stage simulates a population of robotic vehicles and sensors in a 2-D environment. Gazebo is a 3-D counterpart provided for outdoor simulation. While Player started as a robot interface with drivers that directly control hardware, it has grown to include several abstract drivers since then. These abstract drivers use other drivers, instead of hardware, as the sources for data and the sinks for commands. Several well-known algorithms are now included with the system thus providing services such as way-point navigation and obstacle avoidance.

Several component-based architectures have been developed. These include the middleware project RT-Middleware [3] and the component architecture OCRA [4]. These architectures provide a component specification that prescribes a component's interfaces, activity, and input/output ports. They do not provide a functional architecture. In the case of RT-Middleware, a graphical tool may be used to interconnect various components and create a fully functional robotic system.

USARSim provides robot and sensor models and a standardized actuator/raw-sensor level interface for communicating with a physics-based simulation engine. Many of the robots and sensors have been validated against their real counterparts. In addition, USARSim supports a Player driver that allows algorithms coded to its interface specification to utilize Player to communicate with real hardware.

A new entry to the robot simulation/control arena is Microsoft Robotics Developer Studio (MSRDS) [5]. MSRDS includes support for simulation and implements services to control robotic platforms. While MSRDS is not as mature as Player/Stage or USARSim, it promises to build a library of services that will be available to robot developers.

1.1   Adding an Architecture: MOAST

Player, USARSim, and MSRDS focus on the interfaces to mobile robots that allow developers to build their own controllers, with portability across robots that support Player or MSRDS made easier. Rt-Middleware and OCRA provide a component level specification. None of the systems defines an overall architecture or high-level interface specification that guides the development of robot controllers. We have found that an architecture is essential to the efficient development of intelligent systems. An architecture assigns roles and responsibilities among controllers and dictates what services are necessary. It defines module timing, data and control interfaces, and planning extents. An architecture also provides the framework in which the rest of the intelligent system resides and dictates the rules that the modules must follow. For these reasons, we built the Mobility Open Architecture Simulation and Tools Framework (MOAST). MOAST begins with a well defined architecture, and adds simulations, services, and controllers. The entire MOAST framework is intended to provide tools to lead a researcher through all of the phases of development and testing of an autonomous agent system.

MOAST is made up of the following components:

1. A reference model architecture that dictates how control responsibilities are divided between modules.
2. Communication interface specifications that dictate how and what modules will communicate.
3. Sample control modules for the control of a sample simulated robotic platform. These modules include sensor processing, world modeling, and behavior generation for 4 levels of the hierarchical architecture and provide a complete control system.
4. Validated sensors and robot models in the simulation.
5. Tools to aid in development and debug of the control system.

The remainder of this paper will address the components of MOAST. Section 2 describes the reference model architecture that is utilized by MOAST. Section 3 describes the various services and capabilities that are provided by the framework, Section 4 describes how MOAST transitions from simulation to real hardware. Finally, Section 5 describes future work and concludes the paper.

2   Reference Model Architecture

The capabilities of the MOAST framework are encapsulated in components that are designed based on the 4D/RCS Reference Model Architecture [6][7]. The RCS reference model architecture is a hierarchical, distributed, real-time control system architecture that decomposes a robotic system into manageable pieces while providing clear interfaces and roles for a variety of functional elements.

Figure 1 depicts the general structure of each echelon (level) of the 4D/RCS hierarchy. Each echelon in 4D/RCS contains a systematic regularity and is composed of control nodes that perform the same general type of functions: *sensory processing* (SP), *world modeling* (WM), *value judgment* (VJ), and *behavior generation* (BG). Sensory processing is responsible for populating the world model with relevant facts. These facts are based on both raw sensor data and the results of previous SP (in the form of partial results or predictions of future results). WM must store this information, information about the system self, and general world knowledge and rules. Furthermore, it must provide a means of interpreting and accessing this data. BG computes possible courses of action to take based on the knowledge in the WM, the system's goals, and the results of plan simulations. VJ aids in the BG process by providing a cost/benefit ratio for possible actions and world states.

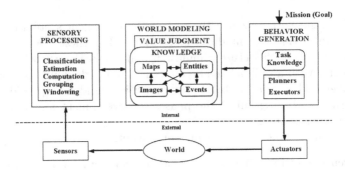

Fig. 1. Generic 4D/RCS Control Node

The principal difference between control nodes at the same echelon is in the set of resources managed, while the principal difference between nodes at different echelons is in the knowledge requirements and the fidelity of the planning space.

This regularity in the structure enables flexibility in the system architecture that allows scaling of the system to any arbitrary size or level of complexity [8].

2.1 Generic Module

While 4D/RCS provides a reference model for the architecture, MOAST is an implementation of that architecture. Therefore, specific responsibilities, knowledge requirements, and interfaces have been designed for each control module. Each control module is based upon a generic core controller that is shown in Figure 2. The MOAST hierarchical decomposition in terms of its control modules is depicted in Figure 3.

The control module core has the following flow:

1. **Initialize:** The initialization opens any communication buffers, places the system in a safe known state, and initializes any control parameters.
2. **Read Command:** Command information is received, and the system is prepared to execute the command. When a new command is received, the old command is immediately replaced by this command.
3. **Read Config:** Configuration information is received, and the system is prepared to change its settings. A separate configuration channel is provided to allow for control parameters to be changed without interrupting the current controller. For example, a user may want to change a system's cycle time without interrupting a complex control function.
4. **Handle Command State Tables:** All of the modules run on a fixed cycle time. Therefore, command functions must either guarantee that they finish in under the cycle time, or provide for being re-entrant. Although this text refers to the command execution as being finite state machine (FSM) based, search based planning systems have also been implemented under this framework.
5. **Handle Config State Tables:** Requests to change configuration settings are carried out similarly to handling command state tables.

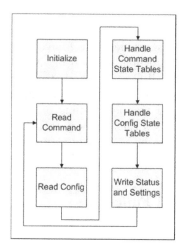

Fig. 2. Generic core of control module

6. **Write Status and Settings:** The current module status and the configuration's settings are sent out over communication buffers.

2.2   RCS Library

Support for developing software conforming to the 4D/RCS methodology is provided by the RCS Library [9]. The RCS library includes portable utilities for creating and synchronizing real-time tasks following the 4D/RCS architecture. Code generation and diagnostics tools simplify much of the application setup

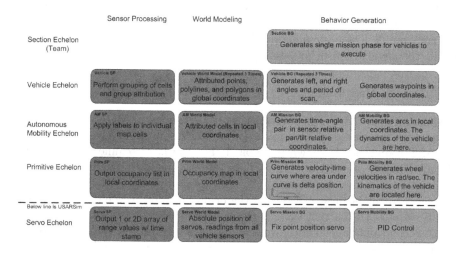

Fig. 3. Modular decomposition of MOAST framework that provides modularity in broad task scope and time

and debugging. Communication between RCS control modules is provided by the Neutral Message Language (NML), a software library for communication ported to a variety of platforms including Linux, Solaris, VxWorks, LynxOS, QNX, Windows and MacOS. Applications using NML define a message vocabulary as C++ classes and call C++ methods to open buffers, read and write messages. Java bindings are also available. NML applications running on one platform can communicate with ones running on any other platform. The location of buffers and processes that connect to them is selected at run time, and a running application can be extended to communicate with new processes dynamically. NML source code is freely available at [10] and documented in [9].

3   MOAST Provided Functions

The development and maintenance of an advanced mobile robot require expertise ranging from sensor processing, path planning, and communications protocols, to basic auto repair. While many of the algorithms for accomplishing these functions are well known, freely available code that implements these functions tends to be incompatible with other code or robotic platforms. This necessitates interface and functional tweaks before the code modules become useful.

Part of the original design philosophy of MOAST was to provide "out of the box" functionality that would reduce the breadth of expertise required to conduct research with mobile robots. The developers of MOAST have taken many well known algorithms and implemented them within the 4D/RCS framework. The result is a fully functional framework that allows researchers and students to immediately begin to experiment with functional robots in both simulated and real environments. Researchers are then free to examine the code modules that address functions in their areas of expertise. The hope is that as improvements are made, the researchers will contribute the improved modules back to the community. The basic functionality of the mobile robot may be broken down in the the areas of sensor processing and mobility.

3.1   Sensor Processing

The majority of the sensor processing work performed in MOAST is in the detection of obstacles. The decomposition of this responsibility by echelon in the MOAST framework is shown in Table 1. For the laser scanner, the Primitive (Prim) Echelon provides a series of data tuples as shown in Figure 4. The data is available over the communications interface and includes the location of the device when the beam was fired and the beam hit point in vehicle relative coordinates. Under the current system, the laser is constrained to be fixed mounted and facing straight ahead of the vehicle in a level orientation. While this presents an instantaneous snapshot of the environment, the data tends to be noisy, and encompass a very small region.This data is further processed to produce a cellular height map of the environment as shown in Figure 5. Due to the mounting constraint on the laser, whenever the vehicle is driving on a flat level surface the

Table 1. Sensor processing requirements and responsibilities

Data Out	Description
Primitive Echelon laser scan data	Beam start and hit point
Autonomous Mobility Echelon height map	Cellular map of 2.5D elevations
Autonomous Mobility Echelon obstacle probability	Cellular map of obstacle probabilities
Vehicle Echelon obstacle map	Concave hull of obstacle areas from AM

height of every cell that has been observed is either the height of the floor or the height of the laser above the floor.

While the external representation is transmitted as a cellular height map, internally, the cell's height, range, hits history, and obstacle probability are stored. The model for the terrain being observed is like a 3D bar chart, where solid blocks of various heights extend through cells in the XY plane. The height of each cell records the estimated distance its block extends above the local XY plane. The height is negative if the top of the block is below the XY plane. The range of a cell records the largest distance from which a cell has been seen to contain an obstacle. Some obstacles are seen only when they are close to the sensor. It is desired to avoid having the system decide that an obstacle no longer exists because it is not seen when the system is farther away than its range. It is expected that if a cell containing an obstacle is viewed from within the cell's range, the obstacle will be seen again, but if the cell is viewed from beyond its range,

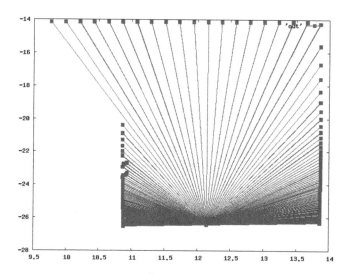

Fig. 4. Laser range data from Prim includes the start and end of each beam

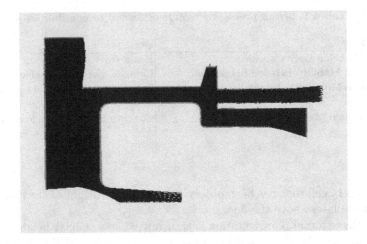

Fig. 5. Cellular height map generated from laser data. Yellow represents cells that have never been seen, and cells that are observed are shown in shades of aqua based on their height. Due to the mounting configuration of the laser, only heights of "ground," shown as very dark aqua (i.e. black), or heights of above the laser, shown as bright aqua, are displayed (hard copies of this paper should be printed in color).

the obstacle might not be seen. The range is used in setting the hits history, as described below.

The hits for a cell encodes the seven most recent viewings of the cell. A cell is regarded has having been viewed whenever a ladar ray passes through it (the cell is not seen) or bounces off an obstacle in it (the cell is seen).

Obstacle probability is a real number from 0.0 to 1.0. It represents the system's best estimate of the chances that the cell is occupied by an obstacle. A separate map of obstacle probability is exported over a communication channel for use by other modules.

3.2   Mobility

The mobility functions consist of a family of planning algorithms that are able to compute obstacle free paths for Ackerman, skid-steered, and omni-drive ground robot platforms as well as helicopter-like air platforms and sub-like underwater vehicles. When examining the planning systems, it is useful to note the knowledge

Table 2. Mobility planning requirements and responsibilities

Plan Out	Command In	Knowledge In
Prim actuator/motor commands	Constant curvature arcs	Kinematics
AM constant curvature arcs	Way-points	Dynamics
Vehicle way-points	Named location	*a priori* map
Section vehicle actions	Behaviors	Vehicle Capabilities

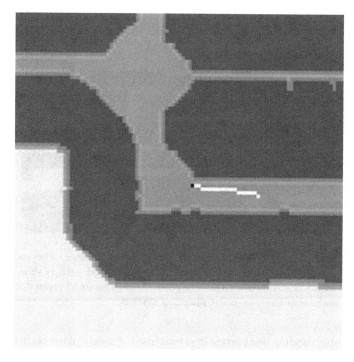

Fig. 6. Cellular obstacle map generated from obstacle probability data. Yellow represents cells that are unknown. Green represents free-space, orange represents the edge of obstacles, and red represents obstacles. The obstacles are grown by half the vehicle width to allow for the planner to plan on a point-sized robot. The white path represents the planned path for the platform and the platform's current location is shown as the black dot (hard copies of this paper should be printed in color).

required by each module as well as the module's output format, i.e., the form the plan takes. This information is represented in Table 2.

At the lowest echelon, the output of the planning system consists of actuator and motor commands that are sent through MOAST's generic interface known as SIMware [11]. These commands are platform steering type dependent and consist of such things as left and right wheel velocities for a skid-steered vehicle or steering curvature and velocity for an Ackerman steered vehicle. This module requires a series of obstacle free constant curvature arcs as input. In addition to the command input, the module requires knowledge of the specific robot kinematics. Item such as wheelbase, tire diameter, and minimum turning radius must be provided.

An additional way-point interface exists into the planning hierarchy. This interface accepts a series of way-points as its commands and computes a series of obstacle-free constant curvature arcs as output. This module reads in the obstacle probability map from the sensor processing chain and also has knowledge of the vehicle dynamics. A graphical example of this module's output is shown in Figure 6.

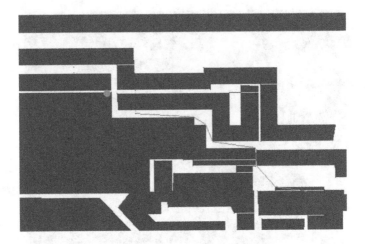

Fig. 7. Vector-based *a priori* map used by the *a priori* planner. The red areas are obstacle polygons and the white is free space. The computed path is shown in green, and the robot location is shown with a large green circle. The small green dots represent the planning horizon of the way-point planning system.

This planning module has two main strengths. It quickly plans realistic smooth paths with appropriate speeds and curve radii while keeping within the allowed deviation and avoiding obstacles. Second, it plans paths dynamically in environments with moving obstacles (such as other vehicles). Weaknesses of this planner stem primarily from not getting enough sensory information and not attempting to use all the information available.

If *a priori* data is available, then a planning module exists to take advantage of this data. This module ingests *a priori* vector data and computes a visibility graph based plan that starts at the way-point planner's planning horizon and terminates at a named point (for example an address). This system currently reads .mif formatted vector data. An example of the plan output is shown in Figure 7. The system accepts a named point as its input and outputs a list of way-points for the platform to follow.

Finally, a planning system capable of coordinating groups of vehicles exists. This planner accepts behavior based commands (i.e. explore, or deliver packages) and coordinates the actions of several platforms to accomplish the tasks. The system accepts the behavior command as its input and outputs named points and tasks for the platforms to accomplish. The system must have knowledge of individual platform capabilities.

4   Migration to Real Hardware

The Servo Echelon in Figure 3 is implemented outside of MOAST by real or simulated vehicles. To limit the spread of vehicle-specific source code into MOAST, an external middleware layer was built that bridges different controllers to different vehicles or vehicle simulations. This Simulation Interface Middleware (SIMware) defines a software application programming interface (API) based on the notion of "skins" that customize an environment to particular controllers and simulations or real vehicles [11]. Skins are divided into superior skins that interface SIMware to vehicle controllers, and inferior skins that interface SIMware to simulations or real vehicles. Programmers build a SIMware middleware layer by instantiating a particular superior skin that interfaces to a controller, instantiating a particular inferior skin that interfaces to a robot and sensor environment, and defining configuration information specific to each skin.

Inferior skins have been created that communicate with the simulator USAR-Sim, the Player interface library, and directly to smart motor drives. This has allowed for the direct application of simulated code to real platforms. Since all of the interfaces above the Servo Echelon do not change, no modifications to the algorithms under test are necessary. In fact, by using a validated simulation engine such as USARSim, the authors have been able to migrate the entire MOAST framework from simulation to an ATRV platform without changing any lines of code. In addition, real/virtual operation is possible where part of the system operates in simulation while other aspects are run on real hardware. This has been demonstrated with the use of real mobility and simulated perception. In this case, mobility planning algorithms are able to take advantage of perceived attributes that may not be available from the current generation of perception algorithms.

5   Future Work and Conclusions

The MOAST framework has been used to control virtual robots in both urban search and rescue environments and manufacturing settings, and physical robots (automated guided vehicles) on real shop floors. By utilizing the Player inferior skin of SimWare, identical algorithms that have been tuned in simulation are being experimented with on real hardware in identical environments. The idea is to validate performance in both the real and virtual worlds in order to verify simulated models and control system utility.

In addition, new algorithms are constantly being added to the framework. Work is progressing on Simultaneous Localization and Mapping (SLAM) as well as the inclusion of a true 3D world model. The MOAST website highlights the latest improvements.

References

1. USARSim, http://www.sourceforge.net/projects/usarsim
2. The Player Project, http://playerstage.sourceforge.net
3. Ando, N., Suehiro, T., Kitagaki, K., Kotoku, T., Woo-Keun, Y.: Rt-middleware:distributed component middleware for rt (robot technology). In: Proceedings of the 2005 IEEE/RSJ International Conference on Intelligent Robots and Systems, pp. 3933–3938. IEEE, Los Alamitos (2005)

4. Brooks, A., Kaupp, T., Makarenko, A., Williams, S., Oreback, A.: Towards component-based robotics. In: Proceedings of the 2005 IEEE/RSJ International Conference on Intelligent Robots and Systems, pp. 163–168. IEEE, Los Alamitos (2005)
5. Microsoft Robotics Studio, http://msdn.microsoft.com/robotics
6. Albus, J.: Outline for a theory of intelligence. IEEE Transactions on Systems Man and Cybernetics 21, 473–509 (1991)
7. Albus, J.: 4D/RCS reference model architecture for unmanned ground vehicles. In: Proceedings IEEE International Conference on Robotics and Automation, pp. 3260–3265 (2000)
8. Balakirsky, S., Scrapper, C.: Planning for on-road driving through incrementally created graphs. In: Proceedings IEEE Conference on Intelligent Transportation Systems (2004)
9. Gazi, V., Moore, M.L., Passino, K.M., Shackleford, W.P., Proctor, F.M., Albus, J.S.: The RCS Handbook: Tools for Real-Time Control Systems Software Development. John Wiley and Sons, Chichester (2001)
10. The Real-Time Control Systems Library, http://www.isd.mel.nist.gov/projects/rcslib
11. Scrapper, C.J., Proctor, F.M., Balakirsky, S.: A simulation interface for integrating real-time vehicle control with game engines. In: Proceedings of the ASME Computers in Engineering Conference, September 3-7 2007, Las Vegas, Nevada USA, pp. DETC2007-34495 (2007)

Implementing Flexible Parallelism
for Modular Self-reconfigurable Robots

Mirko Bordignon, Lars Lindegaard Mikkelsen, and Ulrik Pagh Schultz*

Maersk Institute – Modular Robotics Lab, University of Southern Denmark
Campusvej 55, DK-5230 Odense M, Denmark
mirko@mmmi.sdu.dk, llm@simac.dk, ups@mmmi.sdu.dk
http://modular.mmmi.sdu.dk/

Abstract. Modular self-reconfigurable robots are drawing increasing interest due to their nature as a versatile, resilient and potentially cost-effective tool. Programming modular self-reconfigurable robots is however complicated by the need for closely coordinating the actions of each module with those of its neighbors. In this paper, we investigate the need for a flexible set of concurrency primitives with which to express control algorithms, while respecting the constraints posed by the physical structure. We present two solutions for the ATRON self-reconfigurable robot built over TinyOS and the Java Virtual Machine. Both solutions are based on the principle of split-phase operations, and both address the need for a structured, language-neutral way to express the desired control flow, while retaining the flexibility needed to efficiently cope with the constraints specific to highly physically concurrent robotic systems.

1 Introduction

Modular self-reconfigurable robots are robotic devices capable of changing their own shape. They are usually built from multiple physically distinct modules that can manipulate each other in order to perform shape change. Additionally, they can fulfill a range of other more conventional tasks, like locomotion [1,2,3,4,5]. Envisioned applications for this kind of system includes space exploration, operations in occluded environments and in general tasks where versatility and resilience to unanticipated failures can represent key advantages [6].

One of the unique characteristics of this kind of system, which makes it particularly difficult to program, is the tight coupling of multiple entities within a single physical ensemble. This coupling imposes a strict coordination among the operations of single modules, resulting in algorithms that contain detailed sequences of control steps to be carefully translated by developers into code. We observe that this issue is particularly acute in many self-reconfiguration sequences. While a number of conventional programming techniques can be adopted, we in this paper define more appropriate concurrency primitives by explicitly modeling

---

* This work was supported by The Danish Council for Technology and Production and Sun Microsystems.

S. Carpin et al. (Eds.): SIMPAR 2008, LNAI 5325, pp. 123–134, 2008.

and exploiting specific features of these robotic systems. We show that software written using such tailored constructs is closer to the original control algorithms and more time efficient than the counterparts employing traditional methods. The contribution of our work includes two implementations of programming interfaces (APIs) for modular robots: one built over TinyOS [7] using nesC [8] and targeting resource-constrained devices, like modular robots equipped with simple microcontrollers; the other built over Java and providing a suitable alternative for common computing platforms, including those hosting simulation environments. The APIs are shown to provide an advantage for implementing common sequences of reconfigurations for the ATRON robot, both in simulation and on the physical system. Although our work is motivated by and targeted to modular self-reconfigurable robots, we expect that a similar approach would be applicable for many other types of robotic systems.

The rest of the paper is organized as follows. First, Sec. 2 describes the ATRON hardware, and discusses issues in programming the ATRON robot by means of a few examples. Sec. 3 presents the main contribution of this paper: a conceptual model suitable for expressing concurrent control and two implementations of a set of concurrency primitives that enable a direct and efficient controller implementation. Last, Sec. 4 presents related work and Sec. 5 concludes and outlines directions for future work.

2   The ATRON Self-reconfigurable Robot

2.1   The ATRON Platform

The ATRON self-reconfigurable robot is a 3D lattice-type robot [2,10]. Fig. 1 (left) shows an example ATRON car robot built from 7 modules. As a concrete example of self-reconfiguration, this car robot can change its shape to become a snake (a long string of modules) capable of traversing obstacles; part of this self-reconfiguration sequence is illustrated in the rest of Fig. 1 ending in an 8-shape that is easily transformed into the snake shape. An ATRON module has one degree of freedom, is spherical and is composed of two hemispheres which can be rotated relatively to each other. A module may connect to neighbor modules using its four actuated male and four passive female connectors. The connectors are positioned at 90 degree intervals on each hemisphere. Eight infrared ports,

Fig. 1. Self-reconfiguration on the ATRON robot [9]

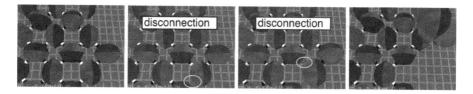

Fig. 2. USSR simulation of a self-reconfiguration step on the ATRON robot [9]

one below each connector, are used by the modules to communicate with neighboring modules and sense distance to nearby obstacles or modules. A module weighs 0.850kg and has a diameter of 110mm. The single rotational degree of freedom of a module makes its ability to move very limited: in fact a module is unable to move by itself. In the current hardware revision a module has 128KB of flash memory for storing programs and 4KB of RAM for use during execution of the program. Modules have until now been programmed in ANSI C using a simple, low-level API that provides non-blocking operations for e.g. controlling the actuators of each module.

Simulation of the ATRON robot is supported by our simulator for self-reconfigurable robots, see Fig. 2 for an example. This simulator, named the "Unified Simulator for Self-Reconfigurable Robots" (USSR), is designed to support a wide variety of self-reconfigurable robots [11,12], which currently includes the ATRON, Odin, and M-TRAN systems [2,3,13]. It is based on a physics engine and hence allows simulation of dynamic interaction with the environment, such as friction and object manipulation, but is also precise enough to simulate self-reconfiguration. The simulator is implemented in Java but provides a lightweight interface for controllers written in ANSI C. The control API for the simulated ATRON basically mirrors the low-level C API, except that each module can be configured to use blocking or non-blocking operations; as most of the users found the blocking API easier to use, it is currently the default.

2.2   Basic Requirements in Controller Development

We are interested in providing a flexible means of expressing the actions of a single module. General approaches to controlling the ATRON self-reconfigurable robot include, among the others, rule-based techniques [14], metamodules [15], and role-based control [16]. These approaches however deal with issues like task selection, distribution of behaviors across the ensemble, and management of the relationships among modules. We will instead focus on the basic expressive requirements for a single module based on practical experience developing ATRON controllers.

In order to reason about concrete cases, we now present two examples with different expressive requirements. First, we consider again the self-reconfiguration sequence depicted in Fig. 1. As is often the case for self-reconfiguration operations, the control algorithm running on each module resembles a sequence of steps involving connections and disconnections from other modules, rotations, and communication. For example, the start of the self-reconfiguration sequence causes the module acting as the "front axle" of the car (i.e., the module connected to the two "front wheels") to perform the following actions:

1. rotate 90 degrees in clockwise direction
2. wait for the right wheel to be connected to rest of the structure
3. disconnect the right wheel
4. rotate 90 degrees in clockwise direction
5. wait for the left wheel to be connected to rest of the structure
6. disconnect the left wheel

An easily recognizable feature of this kind of control algorithm is the temporal interdependency among actions involving physical changes: the module cannot rotate (step 4) before being disconnected from the previously attached left wheel, otherwise it will collide with the rest of the structure; likewise it has to explicitly wait (step 5) for a connected module to be ready to be disconnected, otherwise it will fall due to premature disconnection. This interdependency is implicitly stated by the algorithm's progression through subsequent steps, each of them fully terminating before letting the next one begin. As we elaborate in Sec. 3, this seems to suggest a natural implementation as a program consisting of a similar sequence of commands making use of traditional blocking semantics.

As a second example, we consider a subsequence of a controller implementing a two-dimensional surface reconfiguration [9]. The steps under analysis are depicted in Fig. 2 as a USSR simulation, and the module performing them is the one starting in the lower portion of the surface (leftmost picture) and ending in the higher one (rightmost picture). Informally speaking, once the module has received the message triggering the self-reconfiguration behavior it needs to disconnect from two of the modules it is attached to, then notify a neighbor unit that it is ready to be moved. At this point another module will rotate so as to move it to the destination position. Disconnecting from the two modules is ideally done in parallel, since this is more time efficient, but this is not possible using standard blocking semantics. Conversely, the subsequent rotation operations must not begin until both disconnections have completed.

3   Flexible Concurrency Primitives

3.1   Analysis

Control algorithms such as the described self-reconfiguration sequences typically involve operations with inherently different runtime behaviors:

- *synchronous commands*, immediately completed upon return from execution, similarly to a standard procedure call;
- *asynchronous commands*, started by the execution of a synchronous procedure, and completed after a possibly undetermined amount of time upon the occurrence of a specific condition (analogous e.g. to asynchronous I/O in standard computer systems);

– *asynchronous events*, occurring with a timing possibly independent from the user defined control flow (similarly e.g. to interrupt requests).

Returning to the running example outlined at the end of the last section, the 2D-surface reconfiguration subsequence is comprised of the following steps: (1) wait for a start message to arrive, (2) disconnect from the two modules on the left side, and (3) send a message to notify the next module. The first step is triggered by an asynchronous event, as a self-reconfiguration request can arrive at any time. The second step involves issuing an asynchronous disconnection command, which as all actuator operations starts by setting a target state and completes when this state is reached, with a delay determined by physical load, battery level, etc. The third step can either be performed as a synchronous command or an asynchronous one, depending on the specific hardware used to send the message. In the case of the half-duplex infrared channel used for neighbor-to-neighbor communication in the ATRON it is an asynchronous operation (it starts with a channel acquisition request and completes after a grant event). Whether operations execute in sequence or in parallel can have a significant impact on performance: on the ATRON robot a (dis)connection operation takes about 2.5 seconds, while a 90 degrees rotation can take between 1.5 and 4 seconds [9]. Given the number of steps involved in a self-reconfiguration sequence (68 for the car-to-eight sequence of Figure 1), parallelizing temporally unconstrained operations, like the two disconnections in step no. 2, can bring significant speedups.

A conventional way to ensure that an operation will be performed after the completion of a previous one is by means of *blocking* semantics, sometimes also referred to as *synchronous* [17]. An execution environment embodying this semantic paradigm yields control to the statement following a blocking call after the latter is deemed to be completed, thus making the calling context appear to block until then. This convenience usually implies that a number of issues, like for example stack management, are dealt with by the environment, be it an operating system or some programming language facility. Environments providing a blocking semantics are usually implemented as threaded systems, but such an implementation can be overly expensive in terms of resources on small embedded systems like most modular, self-reconfigurable robots. Moreover, although it is clear that the 2D self-reconfiguration sequence could easily be implemented using a standard blocking style interface, it is not obvious how to program the parallel and more time efficient version, even if the blocking API was supplemented by non-blocking versions of the same procedures.

An alternative approach is to first tackle the need for parallelism, and then to impose sequentiality constraints. Instead of focusing on self-contained, blocking-to-completion calls, we can shape the ATRON programming interface after a non-blocking, *split-phase* semantics, directly modeling the nature of long running-operations composed of a start request and a separate completion event. By exposing both the invocation and the completion phases we allow finer-grained control over the system's operations. This makes it possible and relatively straightforward to implement, for example, the parallel version of the example algorithm.

3.2   An Extended ATRON Platform

To implement a simple and extendable programming environment for the
ATRON we ported the TinyOS operating system to the ATRON hardware [7].
This not only allows us to program in an event-based fashion using the nesC
language [8], but also provides numerous benefits in terms of stability and modularity. For instance, compared to our previous ATRON API which performed
most of the operations within interrupt handlers, we can now exploit a mechanism similar to bottom-half handling [18] in order to keep the system responsive
even under intensive interrupt load. Moreover, by basing our programming environment upon an event-based system we made it open to extensions: it is
now easy to implement further abstractions over a non-blocking, split-phase semantics as it emulates the behavior of the hardware. This allowed us, as we
will illustrate later, to extend the system in order to support a simple form of
threading, and provides a suitable ground for further experimentation.

Following the TinyOS philosophy our port models the ATRON hardware as a
collection of components, each accessible through interfaces where the completion of split-phase operations are signalled using events (i.e. callbacks registered
statically at compile time). Component libraries from both the standard TinyOS
distribution and from the contributors' community can be directly reused on the
ATRON: we were for example able to use a standard sensor network dissemina-
tion protocol in order to diffuse messages within an ATRON ensemble.

Using TinyOS and nesC, we can now precisely express the concurrency we
require for the 2D-metamodule example. The overall control flow is outlined
in Fig. 3 as a finite state machine (FSM) along with the corresponding nesC
implementation. Event handlers are declared using the keyword event, whereas
synchronous operations are executed immediately using the keyword call, or
defined within the body of a task procedure scheduled for later execution with
the keyword post. In the example the overall control flow starts with a message
sparking a Receive.receive event, after which a task is posted that initiates
the disconnection operations. When both operations are done, a notify message
is sent using the task notifyCompletion. Please note how we need to maintain
explicitly shared state information, a side effect known as "stack ripping" [17].

3.3   Augmenting the Event-Driven Model: Stackless Threads

We note that a significant drawback of the purely event-based programming
model is the hard-to-follow control flow. Instead of being linearly expressed
within the body of a single procedure, it is fragmented among several handlers
executed in a reactive fashion upon event occurrences. This well-known problem
forces the code to resemble an FSM (Fig. 3), where state is explicitly maintained
as global variables, and events can trigger state transitions [19]. With this programming style it is therefore difficult to write the code for even slightly complex
control algorithms, and it is even harder to infer an algorithm's control flow afterwards from the source code, making debugging and maintenance difficult.
As this applies even to experienced programmers, not surprisingly our initial

```
event message_t* Receive.receive(...) {
    if ((NeighborMsg*)rcvdMsg->info ==
        START_RECONFIGURATION) {
        if (!reconfigurationStarted)
            post startReconfiguration();
    } ...
} task void startReconfiguration() {
    reconfigurationStarted = TRUE;
    call Connector4.retract();
    call Connector6.retract();
} event void Send.sendDone(...) {
    notificationSent = TRUE;
}
```

```
event void Connector4.retractDone(...) {
    connector4retracted = TRUE;
    if (connector6retracted)
        post notifyCompletion();
} event void Connector6.retractDone(...) {
    connector6retracted = TRUE;
    if (connector4retracted)
        post notifyCompletion();
}

task void notifyCompletion() {
    ((NeighborMsg*)sendMsg)->info
        = DISCONNECTION_COMPLETED;
    call Send.send(sendMsg, ...);
}
```

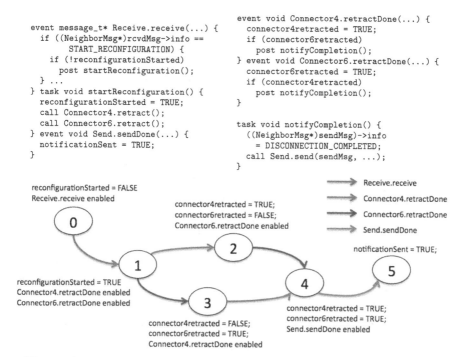

Fig. 3. The purely event-driven nesC code and the corresponding state machine

experience with event-based programming in nesC is that fellow roboticists in our lab had a hard time producing reasonably bug-free, working code.[1]

To simplify programming those cases where arbitrary parallelism is intertwined with traditional sequential execution, we need to be able to explicitly block and wait for a condition to be true. This can be the completion of a subroutine, the arrival of an event and more generally any boolean condition we could express. With such a flexible composition system, custom blocking calls can easily be tailored for the application at hand, or alternatively a single procedure can be written in which operations are started asynchronously but checks are inserted to enforce the temporal constraints.

We implemented such a paradigm by making use of so-called *stackless threads*, also known as protothreads after a popular implementation of this concept [20]. Instead of operating a full context switch every time a thread blocks and yields control to the scheduler, just the local continuation (see [20]) is saved so that execution can restart from the yield point the next time the thread is scheduled. The advantage of this technique is that all thread-like procedures rely on a single stack, which is unwound at every task switch. This makes systems with tight resource constraints able to benefit from blocking-style constructs, as every thread just requires memory for the local continuation and scheduling information (5 bytes, in our current implementation). Conversely, in a full multithreaded

---

[1] This observation is based on the implementation effort at USD Modular Robotics Lab concerning participation in the ICRA'08 Planetary Contingency Challenge.

```
blockingTask(reconfigurationSubsequence) {        blockingTask(disconnect) {
  blockingTaskBegin();                              blockingTaskBegin();
  /*1*/ blockingWaitUntil(triggerReceived);         call Connector4.retract();
  /*2*/ runBlockingTask(disconnect);                call Connector6.retract();
  /*3*/ runBlockingTask(notifyDone);                blockingWaitUntil(call Connector4.get()
  blockingTaskEnd();                                  == CONNECTOR_RETRACTED &&
}                                                     call Connector6.get()
                                                      == CONNECTOR_RETRACTED);
event message_t* Receive.receive(...)               blockingTaskEnd();
{                                                  }
  if ((NeighborMsg*)rcvdMsg->info ==
      START_RECONFIGURATION) {                     blockingTask(notifyDone) {
    triggerReceived = TRUE;                          blockingTaskBegin();
  } ...                                             ((NeighborMsg*)sendMsg)->info
}                                                     = DISCONNECTION_COMPLETED;
                                                    call Send.send(sendMsg, ...);
event void Send.sendDone(...) {                     blockingWaitUntil(notificationSent);
  notificationSent = TRUE;                          blockingTaskEnd();
}                                                  }
```

Fig. 4. The 2D reconfiguration subsequence implemented with stackless threads

system a conservative amount of memory would need to be allocated for each thread, to prevent the stack from overflowing if the worst-case call sequence happens during its execution (e.g., because of nested interrupt requests). As many modular robotic systems, including ours, are designed around simple microcontrollers with a very limited amount of RAM (as low as 1 KB [4]), this solution represents a viable option. Fig. 4 shows the subsequence of Fig. 3 reimplemented with stackless threads: we can easily distinguish the three original control steps in the main thread reconfigurationSubsequence. To achieve this compact form, we subsumed the underlying event-based system by explicitly blocking on flags (triggerReceived) on the components state (call Connector4.get()), and on the completion of similar constructs (disconnect). Our preprocessor-based implementation automatically saves and restores the local continuation in a way similar to the original implementation proposed in [20]. Additionally, it transparently allocates and manages the control structures of the threads and performs the scheduling as needed, by means of a purposely developed scheduler component. The main drawback is dictated by the reliance on a single stack which must be unwound whenever a thread blocks: this implicitly means that eventual automatic variables (with procedure scope) are not properly saved and restored across context switches. A common workaround is to use local variables declared as static [20], or to simply use global variables.

3.4   Java Futures as Concurrency Constructs

The stackless thread implementation is designed for use in resource-limited systems. In less constrained ones these primitives can be provided at a higher level of abstraction. In the case of Java, threads are normally used to express concurrency. They are however inappropriate for fine-grained parallelism: separate thread classes and signalling through wait and notify combined with the overhead of creating a new thread for each operation makes this overly cumbersome. To provide a higher level abstraction, we encapsulate the concurrency control primitives using objects. We observe that *futures* provide a convenient

```
interface Future {                        // sequential
 void block();                            receive(START_RECONFIGURATION).block();
 boolean isCompleted();                   // parallel
 void onCompletion(Action a);             Futures.waitFor(openConnector(4),
}                                           openConnector(6));
                                          // sequential
interface Action {                        send(...,DISCONNECTION_COMPLETED).block();
 void execute();
 void timeout();                          // completion handler
}                                         rotate(90).onCompletion(
                                           new ActionImpl() {
class Futures {                             void execute() { ... }
 static void waitFor(Future f1,             void timeout() { ... }
   Future f2) { ... }                      }
 ...                                      );
}
```

Fig. 5. The ATRON future API: definition and examples

abstraction for the concurrent control primitives of the ATRON robot: a future is an object that represents the result of an unfinished computation [21]. Concretely, split-phase operations return a future object that can be used to synchronize on whether the operation has completed. The ATRON Java interface for futures is shown in Fig. 5 (left) along with examples of API usage (right). Rotating or actuating a connector returns an object that implements the interface Future which allows the caller to (1) block waiting for the operation to complete, (2) query whether the operation is completed, and (3) specify an action to run when the operation is completed. Synchronizing on the completion of a future can for example be done using the static method Futures.waitFor that blocks waiting for the two future arguments to complete. In general, encapsulating the execution of split-phase operations into futures allows arbitrary dependencies to be expressed using standard object-oriented programming techniques.

We have implemented a futures-based ATRON API on a prototype Java-enabled ATRON module as well as in the USSR simulator. The prototype Java-enabled ATRON module is the result of integrating a Sun SPOT processor board [22] within a standard ATRON module: the Sun SPOT controls the standard ATRON electronics over an SPI connection. This "SunTRON" module is programmed using the CLDC-compliant Squawk Java virtual machine, allowing the standard Java thread model to be used when programming controllers. Both implementations of the future-based ATRON API are based on a scheduler that manages Java threads: each future is represented by a Java thread and the scheduler decides which threads to activate based on the state of the hardware. While the simulator-based implementation provides a futures-based version of the full ATRON API, the SunTRON-based implementation is still preliminary and only provides an API subset, including e.g. futures-based control of the actuators.

4   Related Work

In order to simplify the programming of modular robots forming highly distributed and tightly coordinated systems, there is a growing interest in the development of high-level languages and programming environments. A principal aim of these approaches is to deal with the coordination among the individual modules in a larger robot, through abstractions like roles [23,24] and localized spatial pattern matching [25], so as to provide overall control of the robot. Our work is complementary in that it concerns coordination of actions on a single module; even if generalized to a distributed setting, our work is complementary in the sense that we are not concerned with the decision of whether to initiate an action, only the orchestration of the action once it has been initiated. Similarly, existing work on software architecture for modular robots [26,27] deals with the distributed coordination of services, not sequencing of actions.

We use low-level API primitives such as events or threads to implement our concurrency primitives. Alternatively, a language with explicit concurrency primitives such as occam-π can be used, which allows the programmer to directly specify whether to perform operations in sequence of concurrently [28,29]. This approach is however tied to a specific language and virtual machine, whereas our conceptual approach is more generally applicable and has thus far been implemented for nesC and Java without the need for language extensions. Nevertheless, we are investigating to what extent similar, more powerful concurrency primitives can be provided in our implementation framework.

5   Conclusions and Future Work

In this paper we have shown how to design an API that resolves the concurrency and coordination issues in programming modular self-reconfigurable robots. Our implementations of this design span from low-end robots with a minimal TinyOS kernel to high-end robots with a full Java VM. Concretely, we have both ported TinyOS to the ATRON robot to enable controlled concurrent programming through a mix of event-driven and threaded semantics and implemented a Java-based version of our API inside the USSR simulator and on the prototype Java-enabled ATRON modules. In general, although the work presented in this paper has been instantiated for a specific type of modular robot (the ATRON), we believe that the challenges that we address are common to the larger group of systems that we define as *physically interlocked systems* [24], meaning systems made of different, independent computational entities whose behavior is influenced by and closely coordinated with that of their immediate, physical neighbors.

In terms of future work, we are interested in generalizing our model to a distributed scenario, such as the one shown in the metamodule self-reconfiguration

Fig. 6. Distributed sequentiality and concurrency in self-reconfiguration

sequence of Fig. 6. Here, several modules sometimes need to disconnect within the same time step, and similarly to the case for one module this can be done either in sequence or in parallel. For this reason, we are interested in providing a distributed API supporting split-phase operations on local, neighboring modules. Adding distributed operations naturally necessitates dealing with partial failures, but would simplify programming self-reconfiguration sequences.

Acknowledgements

We would like to thank Danish Shaikh for building the SunTRON modules.

References

1. Castano, A., Chokkalingam, R., Will, P.: Autonomous and Self-Sufficient CONRO Modules for Reconfigurable Robots. In: Proc. Int. Symp. on Distributed Autonomous Robotic Systems (DARS 2000), Knoxville, TN, USA (2000)
2. Jørgensen, M.W., Østergaard, E.H., Lund, H.H.: Modular ATRON: Modules for a self-reconfigurable robot. In: Proc. IEEE/RSJ Int. Conf. on Intelligent Robots and Systems (IROS 2004), Sendai, Japan (2004)
3. Murata, S., Yoshida, E., Tomita, K., Kurokawa, H., Kamimura, A., Kokaji, S.: Hardware Design of Modular Robotic System. In: Proc. IEEE/RSJ Int. Conf. on Intelligent Robots and Systems (IROS 2000), Takamatsu, Japan (2000)
4. Zykov, V., Chan, A., Lipson, H.: Molecubes: an Open-Source Modular Robotics Kit. In: Proc. IROS 2007 Wksh. on Self-Reconfigurable Robots & Systems and Applications, San Diego, CA, USA (2007)
5. Yim, M., Duff, D.G., Roufas, K.D.: PolyBot: a Modular Reconfigurable Robot. In: Proc. IEEE Int. Conf. on Robotics and Automation (ICRA 2000), San Francisco, CA, USA (2000)
6. Yim, M., Shen, W.M., Salemi, B., Rus, D., Moll, M., Lipson, H., Klavins, E., Chirikjian, G.S.: Modular Self-Reconfigurable Robot Systems [Grand Challenges of Robotics]. IEEE Robotics and Automation Magazine (March 2007)
7. Levis, P., Madden, S., Polastre, J., Szewczyk, R., Whitehouse, K., Woo, A., Gay, D., Hill, J., Welsh, M., Brewer, E., Culler, D.: TinyOS: An Operating System for Wireless Sensor Networks. In: Ambient Intelligence. Springer, Heidelberg (2005)
8. Gay, D., Levis, P., von Behren, R., Welsh, M., Brewer, E., Culler, D.: The nesC Language: A Holistic Approach to Networked Embedded Systems. In: Proc. ACM SIGPLAN Conf. on Programming Language Design and Implementation (PLDI 2003), San Diego, CA, USA (2003)
9. Brandt, D., Christensen, D.J., Lund, H.H.: ATRON Robots: Versatility from Self-Reconfigurable Modules. In: Proc. IEEE Int. Conf. on Mechatronics and Automation (ICMA 2007), Harbin, China (2007)
10. Lund, H.H., Beck, R., Dalgaard, L.: Self-reconfigurable Robot with ATRON Modules. In: Proc. Int. Symp. on Autonomous Minirobots for Research and Edutainment (AMiRE 2005), Fukui, Japan (2005)
11. Schultz, U.P.: Unified Simulator for Self-reconfigurable Robots (USSR), http://modular.mmmi.sdu.dk/wiki/USSR
12. Christensen, D.J., Brandt, D., Støy, K., Schultz, U.P.: A Unified Simulator for Self-Reconfigurable Robots. In: Proc. IEEE/RSJ Int. Conf. on Intelligent Robots and Systems (IROS 2008), Nice, France (2008)

13. Garcia, R.F.M., Støy, K., Christensen, D.J., Lyder, A.: A Self-Reconfigurable Communication Network for Modular Robots. In: Proc. Int. Conf. on Robot Communication and Coordination (RoboComm 2007), Athens, Greece (2007)

14. Brandt, D., Østergaard, E.H.: Behaviour Subdivision and Generalization of Rules in Rule-Based Control of the ATRON Self-Reconfigurable Robot. In: Proc. Int. Symp. on Robotics and Automation (ISRA 2004), Querétaro, Mexico (2004)

15. Christensen, D.J., Støy, K.: Selecting a Meta-Module to Shape-Change the ATRON Self-Reconfigurable Robot. In: Proc. IEEE Int. Conf. on Robotics and Automation (ICRA 2006), Orlando, FL, USA (2006)

16. Støy, K., Shen, W.-M., Will, P.: Using Role Based Control to Produce Locomotion in Chain-Type Self-Reconfigurable Robots. IEEE/ASME Trans. on Mechatronics, special issue on Self-Reconfigurable Robots (2002)

17. Adya, A., Howell, J., Theimer, M., Bolosky, W.J., Douceur, J.R.: Cooperative Task Management Without Manual Stack Management. In: Proc. 2002 USENIX Annual Tech. Conf., Monterey, CA, USA (2002)

18. Rusling, D.A.: Kernel Mechanisms: Bottom Half Handling. In: The Linux Kernel. The Linux Documentation Project (TLDP) (1996-1999)

19. Kothari, N., Millstein, T., Govindan, R.: Deriving State Machines from TinyOS Programs using Symbolic Execution. In: Proc. Int. Conf. on Information Processing in Sensor Networks (IPSN 2008), St. Louis, MO, USA (2008)

20. Dunkels, A., Schmidt, O., Voigt, T., Ali, M.: Protothreads: Simplifying Event-Driven Programming of Memory-Constrained Embedded Devices. In: Proc. ACM Conf. on Embedded Networked Sensor Systems (SenSys 2006), Boulder, CO, USA (2006)

21. Baker Jr., H.C., Hewitt, C.: The incremental garbage collection of processes. In: Proc. 1977 Symp. on Artificial Intelligence and Programming Languages, Rochester, NY, USA (1977)

22. Sun Microsystems: Project Sun SPOT, http://www.sunspotworld.com

23. Støy, K., Shen, W.-M., Will, P.: Implementing Configuration Dependent Gaits in a Self-Reconfigurable Robot. In: Proc. IEEE Int. Conf. on Robotics and Automation (ICRA 2003), Taipei, Taiwan (2003)

24. Schultz, U.P., Christensen, D.J., Støy, K.: A Domain-Specific Language for Programming Self-Reconfigurable Robots. In: Proc. Wksh. on Automatic Program Generation for Embedded Systems (APGES 2007), Salzburg, Austria (2007)

25. De Rosa, M., Goldstein, S.C., Lee, P., Campbell, J.D., Pillai, P.: Programming Modular Robots with Locally Distributed Predicates. In: Proc. IEEE Int. Conf. on Robotics and Automation (ICRA 2008), Pasadena, CA, USA (2008)

26. Zhang, Y., Roufas, K.D., Yim, M.: Software Architecture for Modular Self-Reconfigurable Robots. In: Proc. IEEE/RSJ Int. Conf. on Intelligent Robots and Systems (IROS 2001), Maui, Hawaii (2001)

27. Zhang, Y., Yim, M., Eldershaw, C., Roufas, K.D., Duff, D.G.: Attribute/Service Model: Design Patterns for Distributed Coordination of Sensors, Actuators and Tasks. In: Proc. Wksh. on Embedded Systems Codesign (ESCODES 2002), San Jose, CA, USA (2002)

28. Barnes, F., Welch, P.H.: Communicating Mobile Processes. In: Proc. Conf. on Communicating Processes Architectures (CPA 2004), Oxford, UK (2004)

29. Jacobsen, C.L., Jadud, M.C.: Towards Concrete Concurrency: occam-pi on the LEGO Mindstorms. In: Proc. ACM Tech. Symp. on Computer Science Education (SIGCSE 2005), St. Louis, MO, USA (2005)

Real-Time Software for Mobile Robot Simulation and Experimentation in Cooperative Environments

Andreu Corominas Murtra[1], Josep M. Mirats Tur[1],
Oscar Sandoval[1], and Alberto Sanfeliu[1,2,*]

[1] Institut de Robòtica i Informàtica Industrial, IRI (UPC-CSIC). C/Llorens i Artigas,
4-6, 2nd floor, Barcelona, Spain
{acorominas,jmirats,osandoval,asanfeliu}@iri.upc.edu
www-iri.upc.es
[2] Universitat Politècnica de Catalunya, UPC. Barcelona, Spain

Abstract. This paper presents the software being developed at IRI (Institut de Robòtica i Informàtica Industrial) for mobile robot autonomous navigation in the context of the european project URUS (Ubiquitous Robots in Urban Settings). In order that a deployed sensor network and robots operating in the environment cooperate in terms of information sharing, main requirements are real-time performance and the integration of information coming from remote machines not onboard the robot. Moreover, the project involves a group of eleven industrial and academic partners, therefore software integration issues are critical. The proposed software framework is based on the YARP middleware and has been tested in real and simulated experiments.

Keywords: Mobile robot software, real-time, sensor networks.

1 Introduction

Research in robotics is experiencing a steady incoming of new hardware components, platforms and devices, with the aim of overcoming perception and actuation limitations of current robotic systems. These hardware novelties need software to be operative, but developing such a software is a time consuming and error prone task. Therefore, good practices in software development are required in robotic laboratories in order to economize engineering time and share results and modules between research teams. Also, simulation of robot systems is a generalized task that saves a lot of power and human energies, but the danger of recoding algorithms for both simulation and experimentation arises. All these topics have been recently discussed within the robotic research community [1,2,3,4].

* Research conducted at the Institut de Robòtica i Informàtica Industrial of the Universitat Politècnica de Catalunya and Consejo Superior de Investigaciones Científicas. Partially supported by Consolider Ingenio 2010, project CSD2007-00018, CICYT project DPI2007-61452, and IST-045062 of the European Community Union.

S. Carpin et al. (Eds.): SIMPAR 2008, LNAI 5325, pp. 135–146, 2008.
© Springer-Verlag Berlin Heidelberg 2008

In the last years some interesting middlewares have been presented which can be downloaded as open source software [5,6,7,8]. These projects coincide on being real-time oriented and based on fully independent processes running in the same machine or in a network of computers, thus they require a fast and robust inter-process communication tool to operate.

Our context is that of the URUS european project [9] involving open research fields such as network robot systems and cooperative robotics. Different experiments, as transport of goods or evacuation of people, are envisaged in outdoor urban scenarios, involving a camera network recently deployed on the URUS environment and a team of heteregeneous robots running in it. In order to be successful with the software integration and experimentation a good software practice and a process communication approach are mandatory.

In this work we present a software framework based on the YARP middleware [10]. YARP was initially written for people working with humanoid robots hence involving a lot of hardware devices to be controlled. We do use YARP in our context to provide communication capabilities between different processes of the whole system, whether these processes are running onboard the same robot or not. Therefore, our framework is developed with the aim of being executed in a decentralized network of computers, being flexible to accept an heterogeneous set of devices and algorithms and being independent of whether the data sources are real or simulated platforms and devices, or files with stored off-line data.

This paper is organized as follows: section 2 overviews the whole software structure, section 3 presents the knowledge basis of our system while section 4 focuses on the involved processes and their designed hierarchy. In section 5 the graphical user interface is presented. Real-time experiments, both simulated and real, are presented in section 6, validating the operability of the presented software. Finally, section 7 summarizes the main conclusions of the work.

2   Framework Overview

The proposed software framework has the main goal of providing a mobile robot with autonomous navigation capability. Moreover, our mobile robot is thought to be running in a cooperative environment, that is, an area where other mobile robots are also operating and where a sensor network is deployed. The whole system should provide a set of services in an urban environment such as transportation of goods and people, cleaning or surveillance. Figure 1 shows the proposed navigation software framework in this context including hardware devices providing data (grey boxes), processes running concurrently (white boxes), and YARP connections (black arrows) building a network of processes that exchange data. This figure also indicates with an asterisc the processes that are running in a remote machine (not on-board the robot) and, thus, a wireless link is required to connect them to on-board processes. The running mode variable indicates if the robot is tele-operated (RM=0), executing a path (RM=1) or following a visual target (RM=2).

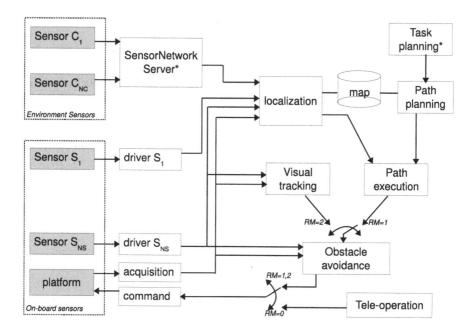

Fig. 1. Network of processes building up the proposed software framework for autonomous navigation in cooperative environments. Grey boxes are devices while white boxes are processes. Processes running in a remote machine are marked with *.

Our design divides the proposed software in three parts: knowledge-basis, processes and graphical user interface. The *knowledge basis* is a set of classes implementing the data base and methods to deal with it, representing all that the mobile robot 'knows'. In our context, this refers to the environment model (map) and the methods to efficiently operate with it. *Process classes* implement the core of this software design. These classes are organized in a three-level hierarchy in order to exploit C++ modularity and inheritance. This set of classes implements the basic process loop (layer 1), the process network (layer 2) and the specific device drivers and algorithms (layer 3). Finally, the *graphical user interface* (GUI) provides a mean to display real-time data while allowing the user to drive the robot in a tele-operation running mode.

3 Knowledge Basis

The set of classes implementing the a priori knowledge of the robot builds up the knowledge basis. In our map-based navigation case, this a priori knowledge is given by a map of the environment and different geometric methods to operate with it. This map could also be implemented off-board, as a data server providing answers to requests about distances, angles or line-of-sights. However, since some navigation algorithms perform thousands or even millions of operations per second related to the map, the "server approach" is unfeasible for real-time applications. This fact forces us to load the knowledge basis to the local memory of the computers where processes requiring it are running.

In the context of our network robot system the map is described in a data file of about $40KB$, using a compatible format with Geographical Information Systems (GIS). The model represents the environment as a list of obstacles, each one described with metric and semantic information. When a robot initializes, it requests the map to a map server. The map server replies sending the map file and the robot loads it to a program variable, thus the knowledge basis is now in the local memory and processes requiring it have faster access to their methods.

For other applications this knowledge basis could be a dictionary, as a set of objects to be identified, or a set of faces to be recognized (parameterized or not). Obviously, if there were no real-time constraints in our application, we could implement this knowledge basis as a data base server running in a machine not onboard the robot.

4   Processes

The hierarchy of the classes implementing processes is organized in three layers. The first layer defines a basic process class. A second layer implements the interfaces, defining data packets and connections between processes, thus the process network is completely stablished. This second layer is based on the communication capabilities of the YARP middleware. Finally, the third layer of the hierarchy implements specific algorithms and drivers to control devices.

Figure 2 shows the C++ class hierarchy for the involved processes in our framework. In the next subsections we detail each layer of this hierarchy.

4.1   Layer 1: Basic Process Class

This single class defines a generic process as an independent thread. The protected variables of this class are listed below:

```
int status; //=0 when process runs ok. Otherwise is an error code
int partnerId; //id of the partner responsible of that process
int machineId;  //id of the machine where this process is running
char label[20];  //short label identifying the process
int sleepPeriod; //sleep period [us] to regularize loop period
ofstream logFile; //file to print log messages
ofstream dataFile; //file to print data
timeval timeStamp; //time stamp of the process output data
int processThreadID; //thread id
pthread_t processThread; //thread variable
```

This variable set has been found as the minimum common set that all our processes need to be operative. The variable status indicates if a process is running with no trouble (status=0) or if some error or unexpected situation is encountered

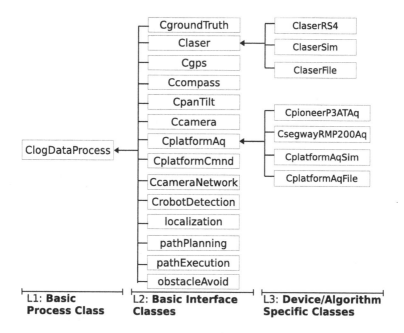

Fig. 2. Hierarchy of classes involved in the process implementation. Claser and CplatformAq (acquisition) basic interfaces are unfolded to their related specific classes for illustrative purposes. Boxes are classes and arrows imply inheritance relation.

(status=errorCode). The variable partnerId identifies which partner is responsible of the process among a group of partners working in the project. The variable machineId carries the identification of the machine on which the process is running. The label string is used to shortly define the process as, for instance, 'gps', 'frontLaser' or 'obstacleAvoidance'. The sleepPeriod integer, defined in microseconds, is the pause that the process will execute to regularize its output to a given output frequency, specially for those cases where process stuff is very low and data output is not required to be fast. Two files are also members of a process, one to keep log messages during execution and the other to save process data. Both, log messages and process data are always printed with a time stamp value provided by the variable timeStamp (TS). Last two variables are needed to run the process as a separate thread.

For this basic process class, we have the following public member functions:

```
ClogDataProcess(int ptid, int rid, char *labelStr); //constructor
virtual ~ClogDataProcess(); //destructor
int writeLogFile(char *msg);//prints message with TS to logFile
int writeDataFile(char *msg);//prints message with TS to dataFile
virtual void printAlive(); //prints alive message to std output
virtual void process()=0; //Main method processing the data
virtual void printData()=0; //prints data content to dataFile
```

```
virtual void sendData()=0; //sends data content (publish data)
void startRun(); //Throws the thread calling the run() method
void endRun(); //Cancels the run() this process
static void *run(void *thisPnt); //Main loop
```

The proposed set of public member functions is also designed to satisfy the minimum common needs for all the processes. The constructor initializes the status to −1, sets the variables partnerId, machineId and labelString, and opens the logFile and the dataFile. Destructor will close these files. We have also the member functions writeLogFile() and writeDataFile(), that print a given message in the log/data file with the current time stamp. The virtual member function printAlive() prints a basic alive message to the standard output. If desired, it can be overridden to print a more specific alive message. After that, we find three pure virtual member functions that are just named in this class but not implemented. The process() member function will contain all the process work and it will be implemented in the last layer of the hierarchy, that of the device/algorithm specific classes. The other two functions will be implemented in the second layer of the hierarchy: the printData() member function printing the whole data packet that the process outputs to the dataFile, and the sendData() member function sending a data packet through a communication channel (publishes data). Finally, there are three member functions implementing the starting of the thread, its main loop and its end or cancel condition. The run() member function is the main loop of the thread and it is detailed in the following code:

```
while (1)
{
        thisProcess->process();//main job of this process
        thisProcess->printData();//prints data to data file
        thisProcess->sendData();//writes data to output ports
        sleep(thisProcess->sleepValue);//adjusts output frequency
}
```

Please note that in this basic process class neither the process connections nor the data packets are still defined, since each process uses a different number of inputs and outputs and works with different kind of data. The second layer of the hierarchy will define and manage these issues.

4.2   Layer 2: Basic Interface Classes

Classes in the second layer implement communication between processes, that is, they define the network connecting processes and data packets passing through that network. This layer is motivated by the fact that several implementations of a given algorithm or sensor driver use the same inputs and outputs and manage the same data packets. The idea within this layer is to define, for each interface class, which are the required inputs, the provided outputs, and the format of the data packets going through these inputs and outputs. It is only in this layer where

Fig. 3. Concept of the localization basic class. Inputs, outputs and data packets are defined at this basic interface layer.

YARP, the chosen middleware, is used to support the communication network. Such a layer is critical since we are working in a project involving several industrial and academic partners, and is in this layer where integration guidelines must be carefully respected [11]. Only if we faithfully follow these guidelines we will enjoy the integration work as an assembling of "little black boxes".

As an illustrative example we show the localization basic class, implementing the communication layer for all specific localization algorithms. Figure 3 shows this class as a black box accepting inputs from several real-time observations and outputing a data packet containing the estimations of the robot pose, velocities and related uncertainties. Hence, the localization basic class is in charge of putting a localization specific module in the right place within the network of processes.

To fully implement an interface, we need to define the format of the data packets provided by each interface. With this aim, we have designed a set of structs named xPacket for each content format travelling throughout the process network. Moreover, we have a set of classes inheriting yarp ports, specialized to send or receive a given data packet. In figure 3, the localization basic class has, for instance, a laserReceiverPort, an object in charge of receiving real-time observations from a laser driver process, always storing the last one. In the output side, the localization process, publishes a localization data packet through a localizationSenderPort, with the format specified in figure 4.

In terms of integration, and following the illustrative localization case, a given process P requiring real-time localization data only has to incorporate a "localizationReceiverPort" object and connect it to the output port of the localization process. Doing this, the process P has available in its local memory the last estimation of the robot position, published by the localization process.

However, these interface classes do not implement the process() member function presented at section 4.1, thus they 'do nothing', but the robot has to sense and move. The next section details the third layer of the presented software framework, where specific algorithms and drivers are implemented.

4.3   Layer 3: Specific Device/Algorithm Classes

This last layer of the hierarchy implements the specific processes of drivers controlling hardware and algorithms for navigation tasks, that is, it implements the member function process() that remainded a pure virtual function in the first

int TSsec	int TSmsec	int robotId	int status

double x	double y	double z	double θ	double α	double ϕ

double $\dot{x}$	double $\dot{y}$	double $\dot{z}$	double $\dot{\theta}$	double $\dot{\alpha}$	double $\dot{\phi}$

double σ_x^2	double σ_y^2	double σ_z^2	double σ_{xy}^2	double σ_θ^2	double dT

Fig. 4. Output data packet for the localization. All specific localization algorithms publish the same data packet. Grey fields form the common header of all data packets.

and second layers of the hierarchy. It is precisely in this layer where robotic researchers have to program their own algorithms to solve the different navigation tasks. The only restriction when programming a specific device or algorithm class is to agree with the related interface, a fact that appears naturally in object oriented languages as C++, when class inheritance is used.

For each basic interface related to a device family, we have a class implementing a simulation of that device family, a class reading off-line data for that device family, and a class for each physical device that we have in our laboratory. For instance, the basic class being in charge of the acquisition of the platform data (CplatformAq), has four inherited classes implementing the above mentioned cases: CplatformAqSim, CplatformAqOffLine, CplatformAqSegwayRMP200, CplatformAqP3AT (see figure 2).

The key point of the proposed software architecture is that all these four specific classes inherit the basic CplatformAq class, thus from the point of view of communications, these four classes have the same interface and manage the same data packets, and, therefore, for a process requiring platform data it is completely transparent which kind of platform (simulated, off-line or real) is currently providing the real-time data. To keep the real-time in off-line executions, the sleepPeriod of the process reading a data file is adapted at each iteration according to the time stamp increment between the two last data rows.

This approach facilitates also the integration work. For instance, a team requiring the localization data for its task allocation research do not worry on which specific algorithm is performing the localization. This team only needs to incorporate a localizationReceiverPort to its module and to connect this port to the output port of the localization process.

5   Graphical User Interface

The developed graphical user interface allows monitoring the navigation experiments. Figure 5 shows a snapshot of this GUI for a simulated case.

On the right side of the screen snapshot in figure 5 we can see a map representing the $10000m^2$ campus outdoor area where the robots are expected to operate.

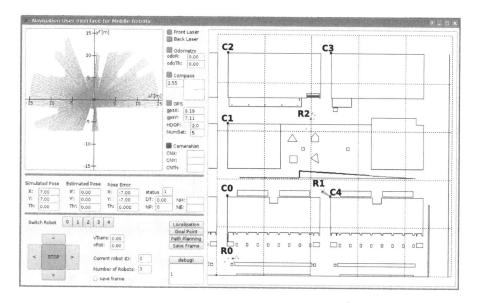

Fig. 5. GUI snapshot

In this map, we can see three robots (R0..R2) as red dots and five fixed cameras (C0..C4) as black squares. We can also see simulated GPS data for robots R0 and R2 positions as green spots on the map layout (R1 was out of gps coverage), and how the camera network process is detecting robot R1 with camera C4 and is sending range-bearing observations, each one depicted as a green segment.

On the left of the snapshot (figure 5), we can see the simulated onboard sensor data for the selected robot (R0 in this case). Leds near each sensor label indicate whether the status of the sensor driver is ok (green) or if some problem occurs on providing data (red). In the shown case, the cameraNetwork led is in red since there are no detections for R0 (the selected robot), since it is out of the camera network coverage. On the bottom left there are also the control buttons to move the robots and to change the selection of the current robot.

6   Real-Time Experiments. Position Tracking Example

6.1   Simulated Experiments

We first show a simulated experiment on position tracking. The localization filter is a process fusing data coming from six simulated device processes: platform acquisition (odometry), front laser, back laser, compass, gps and camera network observations. Moreover, during this execution we have a process moving the platform and updating the simulated ground truth and the GUI. All these processes run in real-time, providing and receiving data through the YARP network. The localization filter process do not worry about where are the computers providing data arriving to its data ports (see figure 3) and whether these data is

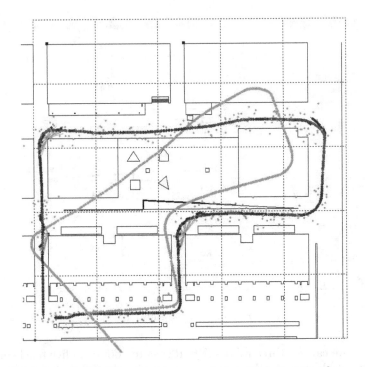

Fig. 6. Simulation of a position tracking experiment. Red poses are for ground truth. Blue poses are the output of the filter. Green poses form the odometry path. Little green dots are GPS data. Green segments are camera detections.

simulated or real. This localization process is completely ready to be exported to a real experiment with no change on the code. Figure 6 shows the map frame after the execution of this simulated experiment.

6.2   Real-World Experiments

This experiment is a position tracking experiment of the segway platform RMP-200 of figure 7 (left). This position tracking is processed at real-time, since the filter output rate was about $3Hz$ and the maximum robot speed was about $0.5m/s$. Since the overall camera network infrastructure and robot detection algorithms are not yet fully operative, the localization filter only fuses onboard sensor data, coming from a front laser, a back laser and the odometry of the platform. However, the robot position is sent throughout the ouput port(see figure 3) and a remote computer connected to this port can see the position of the robot. In this experiment we have validated that the proposed software is operative in real conditions, but also we have ascertained that integration of the provided localization service can be easily done if a receiver process incorporates a localizationReceiverPort object and connects it to the output port of the localization process. Figure 7 (right) shows the map frame after the execution of this real experiment.

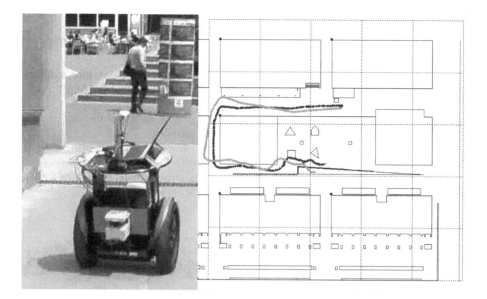

Fig. 7. Left: The segway robot with two lasers and one computer onboard. Right:Real position tracking experiment. Blue poses are the output of the filter. Green poses form the odometry path.

7   Conclusions

This paper presents a software architecture to solve navigation tasks for autonomous mobile robots operating in cooperative environments. We mean by a cooperative environment an area where a sensor network is deployed and a team of robots operates in it. This network robot system is the context of the URUS european project where eleven industrial an academic partners are developing joint research. Both engineering and social contexts of this project force to develop software following three main aims: real-time constraints for mobile robot navigation techniques, easiness on integration software modules and decentralized computing approach.

Real-time constraints in navigation techniques is a mandatory issue if we want that the robots operate autonomously in such environment. Easiness on integration is due to the fact that the proposed experiments demonstrating the validity of the whole project involve several partners and several robotic fields such as computer vision, data fusion or human-robot interaction. Finally, a network robot system approach implies that a set of computers are physically (wired or wireless) and logically connected to share any kind of data that each process requires and provides.

The proposed approach, based on the YARP middleware, satisfies these three aims and has been already tested in simulation and in a preliminary real outdoor experiment, showing its potentialities, specially in terms of integration.

References

1. Bruyninckx, H.: Robotics Software: The Future Should Be Open. IEEE Robotics and Automation Magazine 15, 9–11 (2008)
2. Brugali, D., Schlegel, C., Stumpfegger, T., Tansley, S.: In: Third International Workshop on Software Development and Integration in Robotics, SDIR 2008, Pasadena, USA (May 2008)
3. Fitzpatrick, P., Metta, G., Natale, L.: Towards Long-Lived Robot Genes. Journal of Robotics and Autonomous Systems 56, 29–45 (2008)
4. Makarenko, A., Brooks, A., Kaupp, T.: On the Benefits of Making Robotic Software Frameworks Thin. In: Proceedings of the IEEE/RSJ International Conference on Intelligent Robots and Systems (IROS), San Diego, California (October 2007)
5. http://orca-robotics.sourceforge.net/
6. http://www.orocos.org
7. http://playerstage.sourceforge.net/
8. http://eris.liralab.it/yarp/
9. Sanfeliu, A., Andrade-Cetto, J.: Ubiquitous networking robotics in urban settings. In: Proceedings of the IEEE/RSJ IROS Workshop on Network Robot Systems, Beijing, China (October 2006)
10. Metta, G., Fitzpatrick, P., Natale, L.: YARP: Yet Another Robot Platform. International Journal on Advanced Robotics Systems 1(3), 43–48 (2006)
11. Barbosa, M., Ransan, M.: URUS Communication Protocol. tech. rep. (September 2007)

Knowledge Processing Middleware

Fredrik Heintz, Jonas Kvarnström, and Patrick Doherty

Dept. of Computer and Information Science
Linköping University, 581 83 Linköping, Sweden
{frehe,jonkv,patdo}@ida.liu.se

Abstract. Developing autonomous agents displaying rational and goal-directed behavior in a dynamic physical environment requires the integration of a great number of separate deliberative and reactive functionalities. This integration must be built on top of a solid foundation of data, information and knowledge having numerous origins, including quantitative sensors and qualitative knowledge databases. Processing is generally required on many levels of abstraction and includes refinement and fusion of noisy sensor data and symbolic reasoning. We propose the use of *knowledge processing middleware* as a systematic approach for organizing such processing. Desirable properties of such middleware are presented and motivated. We then argue that a declarative stream-based system is appropriate to provide the desired functionality. Different types of knowledge processes and components of the middleware are described and motivated in the context of a UAV traffic monitoring application. Finally DyKnow, a concrete example of stream-based knowledge processing middleware, is briefly described.[1]

1 Introduction

When developing autonomous agents displaying rational and goal-directed behavior in a dynamic physical environment, we can lean back on decades of research in artificial intelligence. A great number of deliberative and reactive functionalities have already been developed, including chronicle recognition, motion planning, task planning and execution monitoring. Integrating these approaches into a coherent system requires reconciling the different formalisms they use to represent information and knowledge about the world. To construct these world models and maintain a correlation between them and the environment, information and knowledge must be extracted from data collected by sensors. However, most research done in a symbolic context tends to assume crisp knowledge about the current state of the world while information extracted from the environment often consists of noisy and incomplete quantitative data on a much lower level of abstraction. This causes a wide gap between sensing and reasoning.

Bridging this gap in a single step, using a single technique, is only possible for the simplest of autonomous systems. As complexity increases, one typically requires a combination of a wide variety of methods, including more or less standard functionalities such as various forms of image processing and information fusion as well as

---

[1] This work is partially supported by grants from the Swedish Aeronautics Research Council (NFFP4-S4203), the Swedish Foundation for Strategic Research (SSF) Strategic Research Center MOVIII and the Center for Industrial Information Technology CENIIT (06.09).

S. Carpin et al. (Eds.): SIMPAR 2008, LNAI 5325, pp. 147–158, 2008.

application-specific and possibly even scenario-specific approaches. Such integration is often done ad hoc using a variety of mechanisms within a single architecture, partly by allowing the sensory and deliberative layers of a system to gradually extend towards each other and partly by introducing intermediate processing levels.

We propose using the term *knowledge processing middleware* for a principled and systematic framework for organizing incremental and potentially distributed processing of knowledge at many levels of abstraction. Rather than being a robotic architecture itself, knowledge processing middleware should provide an infrastructure for integrating the necessary components in such an architecture and managing the information flow between these components. It should support incremental processing of sensor data and facilitate generating a coherent view of the environment at increasing abstraction levels, eventually providing knowledge at a level natural to use in symbolic deliberative functionalities. It should also support the integration of different deliberation techniques.

In the next section, an example scenario is presented as further motivation for the need for a systematic knowledge processing middleware framework. Desirable properties of such frameworks are investigated and a specific stream-based architecture suitable for a wide range of systems is proposed. As a concrete example, our framework DyKnow is briefly described. We conclude with some related work and a summary.

2   A Traffic Monitoring Scenario

Traffic monitoring is an important application domain for autonomous unmanned aerial vehicles (UAVs), where tasks such as detecting accidents and traffic violations and finding accessible routes for emergency vehicles provide a plethora of cases demonstrating the need for an intermediary layer between sensing and deliberation.

One approach to detecting traffic violations uses a formal declarative description of each type of violation. This can be done using a chronicle [1], which defines a class of complex events using a simple temporal network where nodes correspond to occurrences of high level qualitative events and edges correspond to metric temporal constraints. For example, to detect a reckless overtake, events corresponding to changes in qualitative spatial relations such as $beside(car_1, car_2)$ and $on(car, road)$ might be used. Creating such representations from low-level sensory data, such as video streams, involves a great deal of work at different levels of abstraction which would benefit from being separated into distinct and systematically organized tasks. Figure 1 provides an overview of how this processing could be organized. We emphasize that this is intended to illustrate one potential use for knowledge processing middleware rather than to propose a specific robotic architecture to be used in UAV applications.

At the lowest level, a helicopter state estimator uses data from an inertial measurement unit (IMU) and a GPS sensor to determine the current position and attitude of the UAV. This information is fed into a camera state estimator, together with the current angles of the pan-tilt unit on which color and infrared cameras are mounted, to determine the current camera state. The image processing system uses the camera state to determine where the cameras are currently pointing. The two video streams can then be analyzed in order to extract vision objects representing hypotheses regarding moving and stationary physical entities, including their approximate positions and velocities.

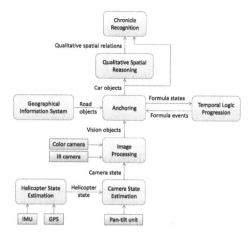

Fig. 1. Incremental Processing

Each vision object must be associated with a symbol for use in higher level services, a process known as *anchoring* [2,3]. Identifying which vision objects correspond to vehicles is also essential, which requires knowledge about normative sizes and behaviors of vehicles. Behaviors can be described using formulas in a metric temporal modal logic, which are incrementally progressed through states that include current vehicle positions, velocities, and other relevant information. An entity satisfying all requirements can be hypothesized to be a vehicle, a hypothesis that may be withdrawn if the progressor signals that the entity has ceased to satisfy the normative behavior.

As an example, vehicles usually travel on roads. Given that image processing provides absolute world coordinates for each vision object, the anchoring process can query a geographic information system to determine the nearest road segment and derive higher level predicates such as *on-road(car)* and *in-crossing(car)*. These would be included in the states sent to the progressor as well as in the vehicle objects sent to the next stage of processing, which involves deriving qualitative spatial relations between vehicles such as *beside(car$_1$, car$_2$)* and *close(car$_1$, car$_2$)*. These predicates, and the concrete events corresponding to changes in the predicates, finally provide sufficient information for the chronicle recognition system to determine when higher-level events such as reckless overtakes occur.

In this example, a considerable number of distinct processes are involved in bridging the gap between sensing and deliberation and generating the necessary symbolic representations from sensor data. However, to fully appreciate the complexity of the system, we have to widen our perspective. Towards the smaller end of the scale, we can see that a single process in Figure 1 is sometimes merely an abstraction of what is in fact a set of distinct processes. Anchoring is a prime example, encapsulating tasks such as the derivation of higher level predicates which could also be viewed as a separate process. At the other end of the scale, a complete UAV system also involves numerous other sensors and information sources as well as services with distinct knowledge requirements, including task planning, path planning, execution monitoring, and reactive procedures.

Consequently, what is seen in Figure 1 is merely an abstraction of the full complexity of a small part of the system. It is clear that a systematic means for integrating all forms of knowledge processing, and handling the necessary communication between parts of the system, would be of great benefit. Knowledge processing middleware should fill this role, by providing a standard framework and infrastructure for integrating image processing, sensor fusion, and other data, information and knowledge processing functionalities into a coherent system.

3 Knowledge Processing Middleware

As stated in the introduction, any form of knowledge processing middleware should provide a principled and systematic framework for bridging the gap between sensing and deliberation in a physical agent. While it is unlikely that one will ever achieve universal agreement on the detailed requirements for such middleware, the following requirements have served as important guiding principles.

First, the framework should *permit the integration of information from distributed sources*, allowing this information to be processed at many different levels of abstraction and transformed into a suitable form for use by a deliberative functionality. In traffic monitoring, the primary input will consist of low level sensor data such as images, a signal from a barometric pressure sensor, a GPS signal, laser range scans, and so on. There might also be high level information available such as geographical information and declarative specifications of traffic patterns and normative behaviors of vehicles. The middleware must be sufficiently flexible to allow the integration of these sources into a coherent processing system. Since the appropriate structure will vary between applications, a general framework should be agnostic as to the types of data and information being handled and should not be limited to specific connection topologies.

Many applications, including traffic monitoring, provide a natural abstraction hierarchy starting with quantitative sensor signals, through image processing and anchoring, to representations of objects with both qualitative and quantitative attributes, to high level events and situations where objects have complex spatial and temporal relations. Therefore a second requirement is the *support of quantitative and qualitative processing* as well as a mix of them.

A third requirement is that *both bottom-up data processing and top-down model-based processing should be supported*. Different abstraction levels are not independent. Each level is dependent on the levels below it to get input for bottom-up data processing. At the same time, the output from higher levels could be used to guide processing in a top-down fashion. For example, if a vehicle is detected on a particular road segment, then a vehicle model could be used to predict possible future locations, which could be used to direct or constrain the processing on lower levels.

A fourth requirement is support for *management of uncertainty*. Many types of uncertainty exist, at the quantitative sensor data level as well as in the symbolic identity of objects and in temporal and spatial aspects of events and situations. It should be possible to use different approaches in different architectures implemented with knowledge processing middleware, and to integrate multiple approaches in a single application.

Physical agents acting in the world have limited sensory capabilities and limited resources. At times these resources may be insufficient for satisfying all currently executing tasks, and trade-offs may be necessary. For example, reducing update frequencies would cause less information to be generated, while increasing the maximum permitted processing delay would provide more time to complete processing. Similarly, an agent might decide to focus its attention on the most important aspects of its current situation, ignoring events or objects in the periphery, or to focus on providing information for the highest priority tasks or goals. Resource-hungry calculations can sometimes be replaced with more efficient but less accurate ones. Each trade-off will have effects on the quality of the information produced and the resources used. A fifth requirement on knowledge processing middleware is therefore support for *flexible configuration and reconfiguration*. This is also necessary for context-dependent processing. For example, one may initially assume that vehicles follow roads. If a vehicle goes off road, this simplifying assumption must be retracted and processing may need to be reconfigured.

It should be possible to provide an agent implemented using knowledge processing middleware with the ability to reason about trade-offs and reconfigure itself without outside help, which requires introspective capabilities. Specifically, the agent must be able to determine what information is currently being generated as well as the potential effects of any changes it may make in the processing structure. Therefore a sixth requirement is for the framework to provide a *declarative specification of the information being generated and the processing functionalities that are available*, with sufficient content to make rational trade-off decisions.

To summarize, we believe knowledge processing middleware should support declarative specifications for flexible configuration and dynamic reconfiguration of context dependent processing at many different levels of abstraction.

4 Stream-Based Knowledge Processing Middleware

The previous section focused on a set of requirements, intentionally leaving open the question of how these requirements should be satisfied. We now go on to propose *stream-based* knowledge processing middleware, one specific type of framework which we believe will be useful in many applications. A concrete implementation, DyKnow, will be discussed later in this paper.

Due to the need for incremental refinement of information at different levels of abstraction, we model computations and processes within the stream-based knowledge processing framework as active and sustained *knowledge processes*. The complexity of such processes may vary greatly, ranging from simple adaptation of raw sensor data to image processing algorithms and potentially reactive and deliberative processes.

In our experience, it is not uncommon for knowledge processes at a lower level to require information at a higher frequency than those at a higher level. For example, a sensor interface process may query a sensor at a high rate in order to average out noise, providing refined results at a lower effective sample rate. This requires knowledge processes to be decoupled and asynchronous to a certain degree. In stream-based knowledge processing middleware, this is achieved by allowing a knowledge process to declare a set of *stream generators*, each of which can be *subscribed* to by an arbitrary number of processes. A subscription can be viewed as a continuous query, which creates a distinct asynchronous *stream* onto which new data is pushed as it is generated. The contents of a stream may be seen by the receiver as data, information or knowledge.

Decoupling processes through asynchronous streams minimizes the risk of losing samples or missing events, something which can be a cause of problems in query-based systems where it is the responsibility of the receiver to poll at sufficiently high frequencies. Streams can provide the necessary input for processes that require a constant and timely flow of information. For example, a chronicle recognition system needs to be apprised of all pertinent events as they occur, and an execution monitor must receive constant updates for the current system state at a given minimum rate. A push-based stream system also lends itself easily to "on-availability" processing, i.e. processing data as soon as it is available, and the minimization of processing delays, compared to a query-based system where polling introduces unnecessary delays in processing and the risk of missing potentially essential updates as well as wastes resources. Finally, decoupling also facilitates the distribution of processes within a platform or between different platforms, another important property of many complex autonomous systems.

Finding the correct stream generator requires each stream generator to have an identity which can be referred to, a *label*. Though a label could be opaque, it often makes sense to use structured labels. For example, given that there is a separate position estimator for each vehicle, it makes sense to provide an identifier i for each vehicle and to denote the (single) stream generator of each position estimator by $position[i]$. Knowing the vehicle identifier is sufficient for generating the correct stream generator label.

Even if many processes connect to the same stream generator, they may have different requirements for their input. As an example, one could state whether new information should be sent "when available", which is reasonable for more event-like information or discrete transitions, or with a given frequency, which is more reasonable with continuously varying data. In the latter case, a process being asked for a subscription at a high frequency may need to alter its own subscriptions to be able to generate stream content at the desired rate. Requirements may also include the desired approximation strategy when the source knowledge process lacks input, such as interpolation or extrapolation strategies or assuming the previous value persists. Thus, every subscription request should include a *policy* describing such requirements. The stream is then assumed to satisfy this policy until it is removed or altered. For introspection purposes, policies should be declaratively specified.

While it should be noted that not all processing is based on continuous updates, neither is a stream-based framework limited to being used in this manner. For example, a path planner or task planner may require an initial state from which planning should begin, and usually cannot take updates into account. Even in this situation, decoupling and asynchronicity are important, as is the ability for lower level processing to build on a continuous stream of input before it can generate the desired snapshot. A snapshot query, then, is simply a special case of the ordinary continuous query.

4.1 Knowledge Processes

For the purpose of modeling, we find it useful to identify four distinct types of knowledge process: Primitive processes, refinement processes, configuration processes and mediation processes.

Primitive processes serve as an interface to the outside world, connecting to sensors, databases or other information sources that in themselves have no explicit support for stream-based knowledge processing. Such processes have no stream inputs but provide a non-empty set of stream generators. In general, they tend to be quite simple, mainly adapting data in a multitude of external representations to the stream-based framework. For example, one process may use a hardware interface to read a barometric pressure sensor and provide a stream generator for this information. However, greater complexity is also possible, with primitive processes performing tasks such as image processing.

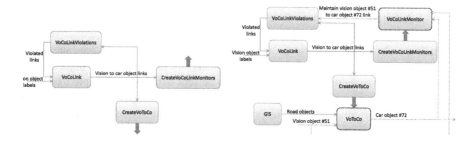

Fig. 2. Before creating vision object   **Fig. 3.** VisionObject#51 linked to CarObject#72

The remaining process types will be introduced by means of an illustrating example from the traffic monitoring scenario, where car objects must be generated and anchored to sensor data collected using cameras. This example shows one of many potential solutions that can be implemented with the help of knowledge processing middleware and has been successfully used in test flights with an experimental UAV platform [4].

In the implemented approach, the image processing system produces *vision objects* representing entities found in an image, having visual and thermal properties similar to those of a car. A vision object state contains an estimation of the size of the entity and its position in absolute world coordinates. When a new vision object has been found, it is tracked for as long as possible by the image processing system and each time it is found in an image a new vision object state is pushed on a stream.

Anchoring begins with this stream of vision object states, aiming at the generation of a stream of *car object* states providing a more qualitative representation, including relations between car objects and road segments. An initial filtering process, omitted here for brevity, determines whether to hypothesize that a certain vision object in fact corresponds to a car. If so, a car object is created and a *link* is established between the two objects. To monitor that the car object actually behaves like a car, a maintenance constraint describing expected behavior is defined. The constraint is monitored, and if violated, the car hypothesis is withdrawn and the link is removed. A temporal modal logic is used for encoding normative behaviors, and a progression algorithm is used for monitoring that the formula is not violated.

Figure 2 shows an initial process setup, existing when no vision objects have been linked to car objects. As will be seen, processes can dynamically generate new processes when necessary. Figure 3 illustrates the process configuration when VisionObject#51 has been linked to CarObject#72 and two new refinement processes have been created.

The first process type to be considered is the *refinement process*, which takes a set of streams as input and provides one or more stream generators producing refined, abstracted or otherwise processed values. Several examples can be found in the traffic monitoring application, such as:

– VoCoLink – Manages the set of links between vision objects and car objects, each link being represented as a pair of labels. When a previously unseen vision object label is received, create a new car object label and a link between them. When a link is received from the VoCoLinkViolations process, the maintenance constraint of

the link has been violated and the link is removed. The output is a stream of sets of links. A suitable policy may request notification only when the set of links changes.
- VoToCo – Refines a single vision object to a car object by adding qualitative information such as which road segment the object is on and whether the road segment is a crossing or a road. Because quantitative data is still present in a car object, a suitable policy may request new information to be sent with a fixed sample frequency. Using a separate process for each car object yields a fine-grained processing network where different cars may be processed at different frequencies depending on the current focus of attention.
- VoCoLinkMonitor – An instantiation of the formula progressor. Monitors the maintenance constraint of a vision object to car object link, using the stream of car object states generated by the associated VoToCo. The output is false iff the maintenance constraint has been violated.

The second type of process, the *configuration process*, takes a set of streams as input but produces no new streams. Instead, it enables dynamic reconfiguration by adding or removing streams and processes. The configuration processes used in our example are:

- CreateVoCoLinkMonitors – Takes a stream of sets of links and ensures VoCoLinkMonitor refinement processes are created and removed as necessary.
- CreateVoToCos – Takes a stream of vision to car object links and ensures VoToCo refinement processes are created and removed as necessary.

Finally, a *mediation process* generates streams by selecting or collecting information from other streams. Here, one or more of the inputs can be a stream of labels identifying other streams to which the mediation process may subscribe. This allows a different type of dynamic reconfiguration in the case where not all potential inputs to a process are known in advance or where one does not want to simultaneously subscribe to all potential inputs due to processing cost. One mediation process is used in our example:

- VoCoLinkViolations – Takes a stream of sets of links identifying all current connections between vision objects and car objects. Dynamically subscribes to and unsubscribes from monitor information from the associated VoCoLinkMonitors as necessary. If a monitor signals a violation (sending the value "false"), the corresponding link becomes part of the output, a stream of sets of violated links.

In Figure 2 the VoCoLinkViolations mediation process subscribes to no streams, since there are no VoCoLinkMonitor streams. In Figure 3 it subscribes to the stream of monitor results of the maintenance constraint of the new VisionObject#51 to CarObject#72 link.

This example shows how stream-based knowledge processing middleware can be applied in a very fine-grained manner, even at the level of individual objects being tracked in an image processing context. At a higher level, the entire anchoring process can be viewed as a composite knowledge process with a small number of inputs and outputs, as originally visualized in Figure 1. Thus, one can switch between different abstraction levels while remaining within the same unifying framework. In previous work it has been shown how stream-based knowledge processing middleware can provide support for the different functional levels in the JDL Data Fusion Model [5].

4.2   Timing

Any realistic knowledge processing architecture must take into account the fact that both processing and communication takes time, and that delays may vary, especially in a distributed setting. As an example, suppose one knowledge process is responsible for determining whether two cars are too close to each other. This test could be performed by subscribing to two car position streams and measuring the distance between the cars every time a new position sample arrives. Should one input stream be delayed by one sample period, distance calculations would be off by the distance traveled during that period, possibly triggering a false alarm. Thus, the fact that two pieces of information arrive simultaneously must not be taken to mean that they refer to the same time.

For this reason, stream-based knowledge processing middleware should support tagging each piece of information in a stream with its *valid time*, the time at which the information was valid in the physical environment. For example, an image taken at time t has the valid time t. If an image processing system extracts vision objects from this image, each created vision object should have the same valid time even though some time will have passed during processing. One can then ensure that only samples with the same valid time are compared. Valid time is also used in temporal databases [6].

Note that nothing prevents the creation of multiple samples with the same valid time. For example, a knowledge process could very quickly provide a first rough estimate of some property, after which it would run a more complex algorithm and eventually provide a better estimate with identical valid time.

The *available time*, the time when a piece of information became available through a stream, is also relevant. If each value is tagged with its available time, a knowledge process can easily determine the total aggregated processing and communication delay associated with the value, which is useful in dynamic reconfiguration. Note that the available time is not the same as the time when the value was retrieved from the stream, as retrieval may be delayed by other processing.

The available time is also essential when determining whether a system behaves according to specification, which depends on the information actually available at any time as opposed to information that has not yet arrived.

5   DyKnow

A concrete example of a stream-based knowledge processing middleware framework called DyKnow has been developed as part of our effort to build UAVs capable of carrying out complex missions [7,8,5]. Most of the functionality provided by DyKnow has already been presented in the previous section, but one important decision for each concrete instantiation is the type of entities it can process. For modeling purposes, DyKnow views the world as consisting of *objects* and *features*.

Since we are interested in dynamic worlds, a feature may change values over time. To model the dynamic nature of the value of a feature a *fluent* is introduced. A fluent is a total function from time to value, representing the value of a feature at every time-point. Example features are the speed of a car, the distance between two cars, and the number of cars in the world.

Since the world is continuous and the sensors are imperfect the exact fluent of a feature will in most cases never be completely known, instead it has to be approximated. In DyKnow, an approximation of the value of a feature over time is represented by a *fluent stream*. A fluent stream is a totally ordered sequence of *samples*, where each sample represents an observation or an estimation of the value of the feature at a particular time-point.

To satisfy the sixth requirement of having a declarative specification of the information being generated, DyKnow introduces a formal language to describe knowledge processing applications. An application declaration describes what knowledge processes and streams exists and the constraints on them. To model the processing of a dependent knowledge process a *computational unit* is introduced. A computational unit takes one or more samples as inputs and computes zero or more samples as output. A computational unit is used by a dependent knowledge process to create a new fluent generator. A *fluent generator declaration* is used to specify the fluent generators of a knowledge process. It can either be primitive or dependent. To specify a stream a *policy* is used.

The DyKnow implementation sets up stream processing according to an application specification and processes streams to satisfy their policies. Using DyKnow an instance of the traffic monitoring scenario has successfully been implemented and tested [4].

6   Related Work

There is a large body of work on hybrid architectures which integrate reactive and deliberative decision making [9,10,11,12,13]. This work has mainly focused on integrating actions on different levels of abstraction, from control laws to reactive behaviors to deliberative planning. It is often mentioned that there is a parallel hierarchy of more and more abstract information extraction processes or that the deliberative layer uses symbolic knowledge, but only a few of these approaches are described in some detail [14,15,16].

We now focus on some approaches providing general support for integrating sensing and reasoning as opposed to approaches tackling important but particular subproblems such as symbol grounding, simultaneous localization and mapping, or transforming signals to symbols. With general support we mean that a system explicitly supports at least a few of the requirements, and does not prevent any of the remaining requirements from being met. However, the explicit support for the requirements often widely differ.

4D/RCS is a general cognitive architecture which can be used to combine different knowledge representation techniques [17]. It consists of a multi-layered hierarchy of computational nodes each containing sensory processing, world modeling, value judgment, behavior generation, and a knowledge database. The idea of the design is that the lowest levels have short-range and high-resolution representations of space and time appropriate for the sensor level while higher levels have long-range and low-resolution representations appropriate for deliberative services. Each level thus provides an abstract view of the previous levels. Each node may use its own knowledge representation and thereby support multiple different representation techniques. However, the architecture does not, to our knowledge, explicitly address the issues related to connecting different representations and transforming one representation into another. These are fundamental issues which stream-based knowledge processing middleware explicitly supports. However, it ought to be possible to combine the two approaches and implement the 4D/RCS architecture using DyKnow.

The CoSy Architecture Schema Toolkit (CAST) built on top of the Boxes and Lines Toolkit (BALT) is a tool for creating cognitive architectures [18]. An architecture consists of a collection of interconnected subarchitectures (SAs). Each SA contains a set of processing components that can be connected to sensors and effectors and a working memory which acts like a blackboard within the SA. A processing component can either be managed or unmanaged. An *unmanaged* processing component runs constantly and directly pushes its results into the working memory. A *managed* process, on the other hand, monitors the working memory content for changes and suggests new possible processing tasks. Since these tasks might be computationally expensive a *task manager* uses a set of rules to decide which task should be executed next based on the current goals of the SA. One special SA is the *binder* which creates a high-level shared representation that relates back to low-level subsystem-specific representations [19]. It binds together content from separate information processing subsystems to provide symbols that can be used for deliberation and action.

The BALT middleware provides a set of processes which can be connected either by 1-to-1 *pull* connections or 1-to-N *push* connections. With its push connections and its support for distributing information and integrating reasoning components it can be seen as a basic stream-based knowledge processing middleware. A difference is that it does not provide any declarative policy-like specification to control push connections. CAST further adds support for a structured way of processing data on many levels of abstraction and the binder supports an explicit integration of representations from several SAs. A difference compared to DyKnow is the lack of a declarative specification of the processing of an architecture.

7 Summary

As autonomous physical systems become more sophisticated and are expected to handle increasingly complex and challenging tasks and missions, there is a growing need to integrate a variety of functionalities developed in the field of artificial intelligence. A great deal of research in this field has been performed in a purely symbolic setting, where one assumes the necessary knowledge is already available in a suitable high-level representation. There is a wide gap between such representations and the noisy sensor data provided by a physical platform, a gap that must somehow be bridged in order to ground the symbols that the system reasons about in the physical environment in which the system should act.

When physical autonomous systems grow in scope and complexity, bridging the gap in an ad-hoc manner becomes impractical and inefficient. At the same time, a systematic solution has to be sufficiently flexible to accommodate a wide range of components with highly varying demands. Therefore, we began by discussing the requirements that we believe should be placed on any principled approach to bridging the gap. As the next step, we proposed a specific class of approaches, which we call stream-based knowledge processing middleware and which is appropriate for a large class of autonomous systems. This step provides a considerable amount of structure for the integration of the necessary functionalities, but still leaves certain decisions open in order to avoid unnecessarily limiting the class of systems to which it is applicable. Finally, DyKnow was presented to give an example of an existing implementation of such middleware.

References

1. Ghallab, M.: On chronicles: Representation, on-line recognition and learning. In: Proc. KR 1996, pp. 597–607 (1996)
2. Coradeschi, S., Saffiotti, A.: An introduction to the anchoring problem. Robotics and Autonomous Systems 43(2-3), 85–96 (2003)
3. Heintz, F., Doherty, P.: Managing dynamic object structures using hypothesis generation and validation. In: Proc. Workshop on Anchoring Symbols to Sensor Data (2004)
4. Heintz, F., Rudol, P., Doherty, P.: From images to traffic behavior – a UAV tracking and monitoring application. In: Proc. Fusion 2007, Quebec, Canada (2007)
5. Heintz, F., Doherty, P.: A knowledge processing middleware framework and its relation to the JDL data fusion model. J. Intelligent and Fuzzy Systems 17(4) (2006)
6. Jensen, C., Dyreson, C. (eds.): The consensus glossary of temporal database concepts. In: Temporal Databases: Research and Practice (February 1998)
7. Doherty, P., Haslum, P., Heintz, F., Merz, T., Nyblom, P., Persson, T., Wingman, B.: A distributed architecture for autonomous unmanned aerial vehicle experimentation. In: Proc. DARS 2004 (2004)
8. Heintz, F., Doherty, P.: DyKnow: An approach to middleware for knowledge processing. J. Intelligent and Fuzzy Systems 15(1), 3–13 (2004)
9. Bonasso, P., Firby, J., Gat, E., Kortenkamp, D., Miller, D., Slack, M.: Experiences with an architecture for intelligent, reactive agents. J. Experimental and Theoretical AI 9 (1997)
10. Arkin, R.C.: Behavior-Based Robotics. MIT Press, Cambridge (1998)
11. Pell, B., Gamble, E.B., Gat, E., Keesing, R., Kurien, J., Millar, W., Nayak, P.P., Plaunt, C., Williams, B.C.: A hybrid procedural/deductive executive for autonomous spacecraft. In: Proc. AGENTS 1998, pp. 369–376 (1998)
12. Atkin, M.S., King, G.W., Westbrook, D.L., Heeringa, B., Cohen, P.R.: Hierarchical agent control: a framework for defining agent behavior. In: Proc. AGENTS 2001, pp. 425–432 (2001)
13. Scheutz, M., Kramer, J.: RADIC – a generic component for the integration of existing reactive and deliberative layers for autonomous robots. In: Proc. AAMAS 2006 (2006)
14. Lyons, D., Arbib, M.: A formal model of computation for sensory-based robotics. Robotics and Automation, IEEE Transactions on 5(3), 280–293 (1989)
15. Konolige, K., Myers, K., Ruspini, E., Saffiotti, A.: The Saphira architecture: a design for autonomy. J. Experimental and Theoretical AI 9(2–3), 215–235 (1997)
16. Andronache, V., Scheutz, M.: APOC - a framework for complex agents. In: Proceedings of the AAAI Spring Symposium, pp. 18–25. AAAI Press, Menlo Park (2003)
17. Schlenoff, C., Albus, J., Messina, E., Barbera, A.J., Madhavan, R., Balakrisky, S.: Using 4D/RCS to address AI knowledge integration. AI Mag. 27(2), 71–82 (2006)
18. Hawes, N., Zillich, M., Wyatt, J.: BALT & CAST: Middleware for cognitive robotics. In: Proceedings of IEEE RO-MAN 2007, pp. 998–1003 (2007)
19. Jacobsson, H., Hawes, N., Kruijff, G.J., Wyatt, J.: Crossmodal content binding in information-processing architectures. In: Proc. HRI 2008, Amsterdam, The Netherlands (2008)

Towards Automated Online Diagnosis of Robot Navigation Software

Alexander Kleiner[1], Gerald Steinbauer[2], and Franz Wotawa[2,*]

[1] Institut für Informatik, Albert-Ludwigs-Universität Freiburg
Georges-Köhler-Allee, D-79110 Freiburg, Germany
kleiner@informatik.uni-freiburg.de
[2] Institute for Software Technology, Graz University of Technology
Inffeldgasse 16b/II, A-8010, Austria
{steinbauer,wotawa}@ist.tugraz.at

Abstract. Navigation software of autonomous mobile robots comprises a number of software modules that typically interact in a very complex way. Their proper interaction and the robustness of each single module strongly influence the safety during navigation in the field. Particularly in unstructured environments, unforeseen situations are likely to occur causing erroneous behaviors of the robot. The proper handling of such situations requires an understanding of cause and effect within the complex interactions of the system.

In this paper we present a method for the automatic modeling of navigation software components and their interactions by observing their communication patterns. The learned model is used online for model-based reasoning (MBR) in order to increase system robustness during runtime.

We evaluated the approach on three different robot systems whose software components are communicating via the widely used IPC (Inter Process Communication) architecture. Our results demonstrate the systems capability of automatic system learning and diagnosis without a priori knowledge.

1 Introduction

Control software of autonomous mobile robots comprises a number of software modules which interact in a very complex manner. With increasing complexity, design and implementation errors are likely to occur, causing failures during runtime. Such failures can have different symptoms, such as module crashes, deadlocks, and misinterpreted data leading to hazardous decisions of the robot. In order to enable truly autonomous robots long-term operating without or limited human intervention, such as planetary rovers exploring Mars, and rescue robots searching for victims in unknown terrain, their navigation software requires the capability to detect, localize, and to recover failure situations.

---

* Corresponding author.

S. Carpin et al. (Eds.): SIMPAR 2008, LNAI 5325, pp. 159–170, 2008.

In [1,2] the authors presented a MBR (model-based reasoning) framework for the control software of autonomous robots using consistency-based diagnosis techniques introduced by Reiter [3]. In this work models were created manually by humans analyzing the structure of the software. However, for large or partially unknown systems, manual modeling turns out to be suboptimal. Therefore, the automatic model creation, either by formal specification or system observation, is desirable.

In this paper we present an extension of previous work that allows to automatically derive models by observing the communication behavior of component-orientated navigation software. The basic idea is first, to learn communication patterns under normal conditions, and second, to detect and localize failures during runtime by comparing these patterns to observed communications. The algorithm generates a communication graph encoding software modules by vertices and module interactions by edges. Each edge is defined by a particular message type, e.g., reading of a laser range finder, or a position computed by the localization module, and the condition under which the message occurs, e.g., triggered, sporadic, or periodic with a specific frequency. From this graph structure, a set of logical clauses is extracted based on a component-based modeling schema [4]. Furthermore, for each edge an *observer* is generated that is parameterized according to the learned communication behavior of the link. During runtime, observers continuously monitor communications between the modules. If they observe abnormal patterns, the diagnosis engine is automatically triggered for reasoning the failure.

The model learning approach has been tested with the control software of the *Lurker* robots [5] used in the RoboCup Rescue league, a multi-robot team of *Zerg* robots [6] used in the RoboCup Rescue simulation league, and the Telemax robot designed for the TechX challenge [7]. The control software of these systems utilizes the *IPC* communication framework [8], which is a very popular event-based communication library used by a number of robotic research labs worldwide.

MBR has been actively studied in the past. The Livingstone architecture by Williams and colleagues [9] was used on the space probe *Deep Space One* to detect failures in the hardware and to recover from them. It has also been successfully applied to fault detection and localization in digital circuits and car electronics, and for software debugging of VHDL [4]. In [10] the authors show the application of MBR to the diagnosis of a group of robots in the health care domain. The system model comprises interconnected finite state automata. In [11] MBR was presented for monitoring component-based software. The behavior of software components was modeled by Petri nets, where nodes represented the state of components, and transitions the interactions. Verma and colleagues [12] utilized particle filters to estimate the state of the robot and its environment. These estimates together with a model of the robot were used to detect failure situations.

The reminder of this paper is structured as follows. In Section 2 the model learning from observed communication and in Section 3 the model-based diagnosis are discussed. In Section 4 we present experimental results and conclude in Section 5.

2   Model Learning

Systems based on IPC use an event-based communication paradigm, i.e. software modules provide data by publishing events, and other modules subscribe for these events in order to receive the data shortly after submission. Typically a central module is in charge of handling all communication, which can also be utilized for recording and monitoring events. For example, the central server of IPC is able to record the type of the event, the time the event was published or consumed, the content of the event, and the names of the publishing and the receiving modules. In our implementation we use this data for creating a model of the system. Please note that if an event is consumed multiple times, each consumption is separately recorded.

Figure 1 depicts the recorded events while running a simple control software example that comprises only five modules with a simple communication structure. In the example there are two data paths, one for processing self-localization, and another one for object tracking. Whereas the software modules *Odometry*, *Vision*, and *SelfLoc* provide data on a regular basis, the *Tracker* module provides data only if objects have been detected in the data published by the *Vision* module. Figure 1 shows the timing of event publishing, and Figure 2 the extracted communication graph. Communication graphs are not only useful for diagnosis, they also expressively visualize the relations between modules of larger or partially unknown software. In the following, the model learning algorithm will be described based on this example.

2.1   The Communication Graph

At a first step the algorithm extracts a communication graph from the data, where nodes represent different software modules, and edges different events that are exchanged between the modules. Each event is represented by at least one

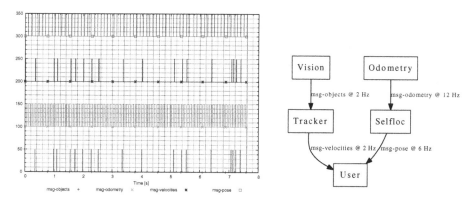

Fig. 1. Recorded communication of the example robot control software. The peaks indicate the occurrence of the particular event.

Fig. 2.   Communication graph learned from the recorded data of the example control software

edge, whereas edges can also connect to multiple receiving modules originating from a single publishing module. Formally, the communication graph can be defined as following:

Definition 1 (CG). *A communication graph (CG) is a directed graph with the set of nodes M and the set of labeled edges C, where:*

- *M is a set of software modules sending or receiving at least one event.*
- *C is a set of connections between modules, the direction of the edge points from the sending to the receiving module, the edge is labeled with the name of the related event.*

Please note that the communication graph may contain cycles. Usually such cycles emerge from hand shaking mechanisms between two modules. The algorithm for the creation of the communication graph can be formalized as following:

computeGraph
Input: a set of recorded events E
Output: a set of nodes M and edges C

1. Let M be the empty set.
2. Let C be the empty set.
3. For all $e \in E$:
    (a) If $p(e) \notin M$ add $p(e)$ to M.
    (b) If $c(e) \notin M$ add $c(e)$ to M.
    (c) If $(p(e), c(e), l(e)) \notin C$ add $(p(e), c(e), l(e))$ to C
4. Return M and C.

The algorithm starts with an empty set of nodes M and edges C and then iterates trough the set E of all recorded communication events. If either the sender or the receiver is not in the set of nodes, the sender or the receiver is added. If there is no edge pointing from the sending to the receiving node with the proper label, a new edge with the appropriate label is added between the two modules. The functions $p(e)$, $c(e)$, $l(e)$ return the publisher, the consumer and the label of an event c. Moreover, we define the two functions $in : CO \mapsto 2^C$ and $out : CO \mapsto 2^C$ which return the edges pointing to and from a node.

2.2   The Communication Behavior

In a next step the behavior or type of each event connection is determined. For this purpose we consider the output and input edges of the publishing node, and the recorded timing of each communication via these edges. We distinguish the following event types: triggered event connection (1), periodic event connection (2), bursted event connection (3), and random event connection (4). In order to describe the behavior of a connection formally, we define a set of connection types $CT = \{periodic, triggered, bursted, random\}$ and a function $ctype : C \mapsto CT$ which returns the type of a particular connection $c \in C$. The type of an event connection is determined by tests like measurements of the mean and the standard deviation of the time between the occurrence of the events on the connection, and comparison and correlation of the occurrence of two events. The criteria used to assign an event connection to one of the four categories are summarized below:

Triggered. In order to determine whether an event connection is triggered, events on connection $c \in out(m)$ are correlated to events on the set of input connection of the software module $I = in(m)$. If the number of events on connection c, which are correlated with an event on a particular connection $t \in in(m)$, exceed a certain threshold, connection t is named as trigger by connection c. The correlation test checks for the occurrence of the trigger event prior to the observed event. If connection c is correlated with at least one connection $t \in in(m)$, connection c is categorized as a triggered connection. Usually, such connections are found in modules performing calculations only if new data is available.

Periodic. On a periodic event connection the same event regularly occurs with a fixed frequency. We calculate from time stamps of event occurrences a discrete distribution of the time difference between two successive events. If one particular time difference can be found with low variance, the connection is classified as periodic and parameterized with the detected frequency. For a pure periodic event connection one gets a distribution close to a Dirac impulse. Usually, such connections are found for modules providing data at a fixed frame rate, such as a module sending data from a video camera.

Bursted. A bursted event is similar to the periodic event, whereas its regular occurrence can be switched on and off for a period of time. An event connection is classified as bursted if there exist time periods where the criteria of the periodic event connection holds. Usually, such connections are found with modules which do specific measurements only if the central controller explicitly enables them, e.g., the generation of a complete 3d laser scan requiring the motion of an actuator for some while.

Random. For random event connections none of the above categories match and therefore no useful information about the behavior of that connection can be derived. Usually, such connections are found in modules which provide data only if some specific circumstance occur in the system or its environment.

In the case of the above example, the algorithm correctly classified the event connections *odometry*, *objects* and *pose* as periodic and the connection *velocity* as triggered with the trigger *objects*.

2.3   The Observers

In order to be able to monitor the actual behavior of the control software, the algorithm instantiates an observer for each event connection. The type of the observer is determined by the type of the connection and its parameters, estimated by the methods described before. An observer raises an alarm if there is a significant discrepancy between the currently observed behavior of an event connection and the behavior learned beforehand during normal operation. The observer provides as an observation O the atom $ok(l)$ if the behavior is within the tolerance and the atom $\neg ok(l)$ otherwise. Where l is the label of the corresponding edge in the communication graph. The observations of the complete control software OBS are the union of all individual observations

$$OBS = \bigcup_{i=1}^{n} O_i$$

where n is the number of observers.

Observers can be instantiated for either triggered, periodic, bursted, or random connections. The *trigger* observer raises an alarm if within a certain timeout after the occurrence of a trigger event no corresponding event occurs or if the trigger event is missing prior the occurrence of the corresponding event. In order to be robust against noise, the observer uses a majority vote for a number of succeeding events. The *periodic* observer raises an alarm if there is a significant change in the frequency of the events on the observed connection. The observer checks if the frequency of successive events does vary significantly from the specified frequency. For this purpose, the observer estimates the frequency of the events within a sliding time window. The *bursted* observer is similar to the periodic observer. It differs in the fact that it starts the frequency check only if events occur and does not raise an alarm if no events occur. Finally, the *random* is a dummy observer which always provides the observation $ok(l)$. This observer is implemented for completeness.

2.4   The System Description

The communication graph together with the type of the connections is a sufficient specification of the communication behavior of the robot control software. This specification can be used in order to derive a system description for the diagnosis process. It is a description of the desired or nominal behavior of the system. In order to be able to be used in the diagnosis process, the system description is automatically written down as a set of logical clauses. We use Horn-clauses only for efficiency reasons. This set can easily be derived from the communication graph and the behavior of the connections. The algorithm to derive the system description can be formalized as following:

computeSD
Input: the communication graph with nodes M and connections C
Output: a set of clauses

1. Let SD be the empty set.
2. For all $c \in C$:
   If $host(p(c)) \neq host(c(c))$
   (a) If $ctype(c) = triggered$ add

$$\neg AB(p(c)) \bigwedge_{t \in trigger(c) \wedge t \in in(p(c))} ok(t) \wedge$$

$$\wedge \neg AB(host(p(c))) \wedge \neg AB(host(c(c))) \rightarrow ok(c)$$

to SD
Else add

$$\neg AB(p(c)) \wedge \neg AB(host(p(c))) \wedge \neg AB(host(c(c))) \rightarrow ok(c)$$

to SD

Else

(b) If $ctype(c) = triggered$ add

$$\neg AB(p(c)) \bigwedge_{t \in trigger(c) \wedge t \in in(p(c))} ok(t) \rightarrow ok(c)$$

to SD
Else add

$$\neg AB(p(c)) \rightarrow ok(c)$$

to SD

3. For all $m \in M$:
Add

$$\bigwedge_{c' \in out(m)} ok(c') \rightarrow \neg AB(m)$$

to SD

4. Return SD.

Functions $p(c)$ and $c(c)$ return the publishing and receiving module of an event connection c. Function $host(m)$ returns the host computer on which a particular module m is executed. The algorithm starts with an empty set SD. For every event connection, clauses are added to the system description by two steps. In the first step, a clause for forward reasoning is added. The clause specifies if a module works correctly and if all related inputs and outputs behave as expected. Depending on the type of connection, we add the following clause to SD: If connection c is *triggered*, we add a clause expressing that if the module and all related inputs work as expected, also the output works as expected. Otherwise, a clause expressing that if the module works as expected, also the output works as expected, is added (see Line 2). The negation $\neg AB(m)$ denotes that module m is not abnormal, i.e. working as expected, and atom $ok(c)$ denotes that connection c behaves as expected. Moreover, if the host of the sending and receiving modules of connection c is different, a fact expressing that the network interfaces of these modules have to work correctly, is added, e.g., $\neg AB(host(p(c))$.

In a second step, a clause for backward reasoning is added. The clause specifies if all output connections c' of module m behave as expected, the module itself has to behave as expected (see Line 3).

Figure 3 depicts the system description obtained for the above example control software. Clauses 1 to 4 describe the forward reasoning. Clauses 5 to 8 describe the backward reasoning. Clause 3 states that the module *Tracker* works correctly only if a velocity event occurs exclusively after a trigger event. For instance, Clause 6 states that if all output connections of module *Odometry* work as expected, consequently the module itself works correctly.

1. $\neg AB(\mathit{Vision}) \rightarrow ok(\mathit{objects})$
2. $\neg AB(\mathit{Odometry}) \rightarrow ok(\mathit{odometry})$
3. $\neg AB(\mathit{Tracker}) \wedge ok(\mathit{objects}) \rightarrow ok(\mathit{velocities})$
4. $\neg AB(\mathit{Selfloc}) \rightarrow ok(\mathit{pose})$
5. $ok(\mathit{objects}) \rightarrow \neg AB(\mathit{Vision})$
6. $ok(\mathit{odometry}) \rightarrow \neg AB(\mathit{Odometry})$
7. $ok(\mathit{velocities}) \rightarrow \neg AB(\mathit{Tracker})$
8. $ok(\mathit{pose}) \rightarrow \neg AB(\mathit{Selfloc})$

Fig. 3. The system description automatically derived for the example control software

3 Model-Based Diagnosis

For the detection and localization of faults we use the consistency-based diagnosis technique of Reiter [3]. In order to be able to detect and localize a fault, the method needs a model of the correct behavior of the system (the obtained system description), recent observations of the system, and assumptions whether the components of the systems work correctly. The basic idea is that if we assume all components to work correctly (expressed by the according literals $\neg AB$), and if the prediction of the (correct) behavior of the model differs from the actual observations of the system, there is a failure in the system. If the method discovers such a contradiction, a fault is detected. Formally, we define this by:

$$SD \cup OBS \cup \{\neg AB(m) | m \in M\} \models \perp.$$

Such a consistency-check for Horn-clauses can be performed in linear time using the LTUR algorithm [13].

So far we only know that a fault occurred but not which module(s) are its root cause(s). In order to localize the module(s) responsible for the detected fault, we have to calculate a diagnosis Δ. Where Δ is a set of modules $m \in M$ we have to declare as faulty (change $\neg AB(m)$ to $AB(m)$) in order to resolve the above contradiction. Formally, we define this by:

$$SD \cup OBS \cup \{AB(m) | m \in \Delta\} \cup \{\neg AB(m) | m \in M \setminus \Delta\} \not\models \perp.$$

This is similar to human reasoning. The algorithm of Reiter implements an efficient way to manipulate the assumptions in order to calculate the diagnosis. Intuitively one can say that a diagnosis Δ is an explanation for an observed misbehavior. We use our implementation[1] of this diagnosis process for the experimental evaluation of the models. Please refer to [1,2] for more details on the diagnosis process.

Consider the following simple situation for the example control software. If a fault occurs in module *Vision*, the fact that no more events of the type *objects* are produced is recognized by an observer. This is expressed by the observation $\neg ok(\mathit{objects})$. i If we use the system description of Figure 3, the actual

---

[1] The implementation can freely be downloaded at
   http://www.ist.tugraz.at/mordams/.

observations, and the assumption that all modules work as expected, we are able to derive $ok(objects)$ by the clause 1. This contradiction shows that we have detected a fault. In order to localize the root cause of the fault we retract assumptions about working modules. For instance, if changing assumption $\neg AB(Tracker)$ to $AB(Tracker)$ it is still possible to derive $ok(objects)$ by clause 1. Therefore, the set containing only module *Tracker* does not resolve the contradiction and is therefore not a diagnosis. Such checks for inconsistencies are done by a call of a theorem prover, e.g., the LTUR algorithm. But if we change assumption $\neg AB(Vision)$ to $AB(Vision)$, we can not derive $ok(objects)$ by clause 1 anymore. Therefore, the set $\Delta = \{Vision\}$ resolves the contradiction and is therefore a valid diagnosis. Please note that every superset of a diagnosis is also a diagnosis.

4   Experimental Results

In order to show the potential of the proposed model learning, the approach has been tested on three different types of navigation software. We evaluated whether the approach is able to derive an appropriate model reflecting all aspects of the behavior of the system. The derived model was evaluated by the system engineer who has developed the system. Moreover, we injected artificial faults like module crashes in the system, and evaluated if the fault can be detected and localized by the derived model.

Autonomous Exploration Robot Lurker. We recorded the communication of the navigation software of the rescue robot Lurker [5] while it was autonomously exploring an unknown area. The robot is shown in Figure 4 (a).

The control software of this robot is far more complex as in the simple example since it comprises software modules enabling autonomous exploration of rough terrain. Figure 4 (a) shows the communication graph derived from the recorded data. The numbers in the labels of the edges denote the average frequency of events on the connections. Please note that a frequency of 0 Hz means the actual frequency is below 1 Hz. From the communication graph and the categorized

(a)   (b)   (c)

Fig. 4. Three autonomous navigation systems that have been evaluated. (a) The rescue robot Lurker, (b) the Telemax robot, and (c) a team of four Zerg robots during exploration in the USARSim environment.

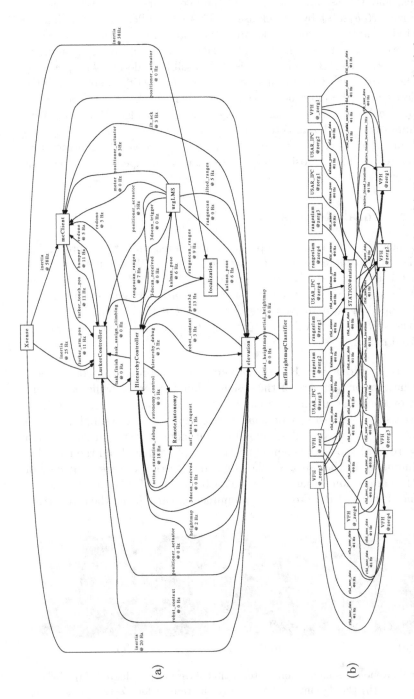

Fig. 5. Two learned communication graphs. (a) Communication graph of the central module for the multi robot scenario with the Zerg robots. (b) Communication graph of the Lurker robot. The name of the host a module is running on is depicts in the label of the node.

event connections, a system description with 70 clauses with 51 atoms and 35 observers was derived. After a double check with the system engineer of the control software it was confirmed that the automatically derived model maps the behavior of the system.

Autonomous Exploration Robot Telemax. In this experiment we record data from the navigation software of the autonomous Telemax robot, shown in Figurer 4 (b), which has been designed for the *TechX Challenge*. The communication was recorded from active software modules for controlling the robot to detect, enter, and operate an elevator.

The communication graph and the system description were derived from the recorded data. The communication graph comprises 18 nodes (software modules) and 51 edges (connections). From the communication graph and the categorized event connections a system description with 63 clauses with 63 atoms and 51 observers was derived. Due to space limitation we omit the picture of the graph in this paper. A review of the system engineer confirms that the generated graph and system description reflect the desired structure and behavior of the system.

Autonomous Exploration with a Group of Zerg Robots. In this experiment we record data during an autonomous exploration run of a group of four Zerg robots within the USARSim environment used in the RoboCup Rescue Virtual Robot League [14]. The robots are shown in Figure 4 (c).

A central control station coordinates the exploration of the individual robots. The central station module and the control software of the robots run on different hosts. From the recorded communication of the central software we extract the communication graph, the categorized event connections and a system description with 48 clauses with 44 atoms and 36 observers was derived. Figure 4 (b) shows the communication graph derived from the recorded data.

This system description was used in a diagnosis experiment. During an autonomous exploration run we switched-off the network interface of robot 3 and 4. This failure situation was immediately recognized by 3 observers which raised an alarm. The output of all observers (36 literals) together with the above obtained system description have been insert into the diagnosis engine. Based on the system description and the observations, the engine concluded the correct root cause of the problem, i.e., the network interface of robot 3 and 4: $AB(zerg3)$ and $AB(zerg4)$. It has to be noted that these root causes could not be directly observed. This result clearly shows the benefit of model-based diagnosis for the robustness of robot navigation software.

5   Conclusion and Future Work

In this paper we presented an approach which allows the automated learning of communication models for robot navigation software. The approach is able to automatically extract a model of the behavior of the communication within component-orientated navigation software. Moreover, the approach is able to derive a system description which can be used for model-based diagnosis. The approach was successfully tested on *IPC*-based navigation software like the one used by the rescue robot Lurker. Since *IPC* is widely used, our approach is instantly usable on many different robot systems.

The presented implementation can be extended for model learning on any component-based system using an event-based publisher-subscriber mechanism for communication. Currently, we are working on a port for *Miro*-based systems. In future work, we will work on methods that also analyze the content of messages, e.g., methods that are able to distinguish between data under normal and abnormal conditions. We believe that more context knowledge will further increase the robustness of model-based reasoning.

References

1. Steinbauer, G., Wotawa, F.: Detecting and locating faults in the control software of autonomous mobile robots. In: 16th International Workshop on Principles of Diagnosis (DX 2005), Monetrey, USA, pp. 13–18 (2005)
2. Steinbauer, G., Mörth, M., Wotawa, F.: Real-Time Diagnosis and Repair of Faults of Robot Control Software. In: Bredenfeld, A., Jacoff, A., Noda, I., Takahashi, Y. (eds.) RoboCup 2005. LNCS (LNAI), vol. 4020, pp. 13–23. Springer, Heidelberg (2006)
3. Reiter, R.: A theory of diagnosis from first principles. Artificial Intelligence 32(1), 57–95 (1987)
4. Friedrich, G., Stumptner, M., Wotawa, F.: Model-based diagnosis of hardware designs. Artificial Intelligence 111(2), 3–39 (1999)
5. Kleiner, A., Dornhege, C.: Real-time Localization and Elevation Mapping within Urban Search and Rescue Scenarios. Journal of Field Robotics (2007)
6. Ziparo, V., Kleiner, A., Nebel, B., Nardi, D.: RFID-based exploration for large robot teams. In: Conference on Robotics and Automation, pp. 4606–4613 (2007)
7. DTSA: Techx challenge (2008),
   http://www.dsta.gov.sg/index.php/TechX-Challenge
8. Simmons, R.: Structured Control for Autonomous Robots. IEEE Transactions on Robotics and Automation 10(1) (1994)
9. Muscettola, N., Nayak, P.P., Pell, B., Williams, B.C.: Remote agent: To boldly go where no AI system has gone before. Artificial Intelligence 103(1-2), 5–48 (1998)
10. Micalizio, R., Torasso, P., Torta, G.: On-line monitoring and diagnosis of a team of service robots: A model-based approach. AI Communications 19(4) (2006)
11. Grosclaude, I.: Model-based monitoring of component-based software systems. In: 15th International Workshop on Principles of Diagnosis, Carcassonne, France, pp. 155–160 (2004)
12. Verma, V., Gordon, G., Simmons, R., Thrun, S.: Real-time fault diagnosis. IEEE Robotics & Automation Magazine 11(2), 56–66 (2004)
13. Minoux, M.: LTUR: A Simplified Linear-time Unit Resolution Algorithm for Horn Formulae and Computer Implementation. Information Processing Letters 29, 1–12 (1988)
14. Balakirsky, S., Carpin, S., Kleiner, A., Lewis, M., Visser, A., Wang, J., Ziparo, V.A.: Towards heterogeneous robot teams for disaster mitigation: Results and Performance Metrics from RoboCup Rescue. Journal of Field Robotics 24(11-12), 943–967 (2007)

A Common Framework for Co-operative Robotics: An Open, Fault Tolerant Architecture for Multi-league RoboCup Teams

Luís Mota[1,2] and Luís Paulo Reis[2]

[1] Instituto Superior de Ciências do Trabalho e da Empresa (ISCTE), Portugal
luis.mota@iscte.pt
[2] NIADR - LIACC, Universidade do Porto, Portugal

Abstract. Research in the RoboCup domain has grown considerably since the beginning of this initiative more than ten years ago. Much of this growth is due to the existence of different leagues, that allow the focussing of research in specific and heterogeneous issues.

This specialisation of research has, though, proven to have some drawbacks: research subjects become very specific, and one loses the ability of properly generalising, and sharing, the obtained results.

This paper presents an architecture that aims at being open, enabling the development of independent components that can easily be ported between application environments. This architecture, called Common Framework, relies on standardised interfaces, protocols and communication channels between components. Besides allowing the free association of heterogeneous components, like real and simulated back-ends, it also considerably eases the introduction of principles of redundancy and fault tolerance.

1 Introduction

RoboCup is an international initiative to promote Artificial Intelligence, Robotics, and related fields. It fosters research by providing a standard problem where a wide range of technologies can be integrated and examined. RoboCup uses the soccer game as a central topic of research, aiming at innovations to be applied for socially significant problems and industries. Research topics include design principles of autonomous agents, multi-agent collaboration, strategy acquisition, real-time reasoning, robotics, and sensor-fusion.

The ultimate goal of the RoboCup initiative is "By the year 2050, develop a team of fully autonomous humanoid robots that can win against the human world soccer champion team." This is certainly an ambitious goal, but research in co-operative robotics has been accumulating results that allow the community to continue believing in this challenge.

The RoboCup initiative has known how to attract research to a wide array of scientific problems, by creating different leagues that address specific and multiple questions. In the robotic soccer domain, in brief, there are simulation

S. Carpin et al. (Eds.): SIMPAR 2008, LNAI 5325, pp. 171–182, 2008.

leagues (2D and 3D) that abstract from all the hardware-related problems and allow focussing on higher-level problems; heterogeneous real robot leagues, in small and middle size, foster research in hardware development and player interaction and coordination; the standard platform league allows different teams to deploy different strategies in a standardised environment; and, finally, the humanoid league enables research on questions related to biped movement and playing skills. Furthermore, other initiatives such as the different Rescue and RoboCup@Home leagues extend the multi-robot research to domains in search and rescue and domestic scenarios, allowing the development of work in different, unrelated domains.

This diversity of application domains has certainly been responsible for attracting a wide and heterogeneous research community for this popular challenge, but these characteristics, associated with it's strong competitive side, has also had some drawbacks. Namely, research teams, in order to stay competitive in the leagues they participate in, have normally focussed on a single league, trying to exploit it's prevailing details. This specialization temptation has made it rare that teams simultaneously maintain competitive teams in different leagues, such as, e.g., simulation and middle size.

This natural specialisation tendency has brought noticeable drawbacks: teams achieve results that, though being competitive, are not easily generalisable and consequently shared between different leagues. E.g., is is not common to see high level results from the simulation leagues applied to middle size teams, where the same kind of challenges arise. This is certainly an undesirable result, which we try to deal with in this paper.

In section 2, a new robotic architecture that intends to be applicable to different leagues is presented. This architecture, which was named "Common Framework", relies on a multi-agent system (MAS) paradigm that is presented in section 3. The different components taking part in this MAS need to communicate using a language that is presented in section 4. Finally, some considerations about our proposed future work and conclusions are presented in sections 6 and 7.

2   Common Framework for Co-operative Robotics

This paper addresses the problem of developing a common approach to co-operative robotics with applications in domains where complex co-operative tasks must be performed by autonomous agents, like the different RoboCup competitions.

2.1   Requirements

The proposed architecture needs to address a set of requirements, in order to comply with it's goals, as follows:

Open Architecture. The architecture should be open, allowing the real-time addition and withdrawal of components without compromising it's stability;

General Application. High-level components should be applicable to different leagues without further customisation;
Redundancy. The architecture should allow the coexistence of redundant components, which may be co-ordinated, or selected, by other components.

2.2   Architecture Layout

Since the architecture of the Common Framework is designed to be open and to include different components in real-time, these components must be able to communicate through a standardised interface, shared by all. The communication channels and protocols must also be common among all components.

The Common Framework includes a knowledge representation structure capable of representing organised information pertaining to the robotic soccer domain. In order to control different (simulated and real) robots, the Common Framework needs specific components that deal with each agent's perception and action capabilities. Low-level skills and perception mechanisms will be designed for each type of robot, while high-level actions can be chosen through the same, league-independent, decision-making component. A general action vocabulary will be developed to enable the low-level action components to understand high-level decision-making, whereas a perception vocabulary will address the representation of state-of-the-world information.

In order for the Common Framework to be truly flexible, allowing the integration and replacement of components in real time, it requires a flexible architecture that can be modified both in real and compile time. It is argued in the next section that the best way to answer these requirements is through a multi-agent system.

3   Multi-Agent System Architecture

In this paper, it is proposed to use a multi-agent system (MAS) for the control of each player. Thus, one team would be a system of multiple multi-agent systems. In each of the players, the same kind of components will exist (perception, action, decision, etc.), taking part on a MAS while using standardised communication. Each component might be implemented using a different programming language, or even be running in different machines, with distinct operating systems, as seen on Fig. 1. The components can arbitrarily vary in number, and even be redundant. This paper presents a proposal of the system to implement, making possible to exploit a scenario as depicted in this figure.

In order for the different components to interact freely, it is necessary that they have a way of knowing/discovering each other. With this purpose, there will be a communication management agent (ComMAg) that will keep information on the existing components, as seen on section 3. Furthermore, this architecture requires a standardised communication language, for the expression of perception, action and state-of-the-world information. This language, described in section 4, will include basic concepts, such as regions, locations and time, as well as soccer related items.

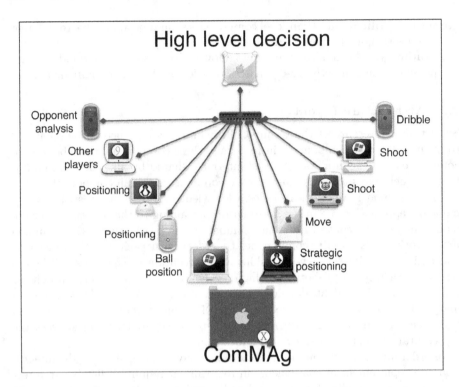

Fig. 1. Proposed architecture: arbitrary services, both in nature and quantity, can connect to the system

The communication management agent (ComMAg) was designed to keep information on all the existing agents, namely the addresses where these are accessible, and the type of service they provide. The agents will be accessible only through sockets, in order to keep the implementation simple and to allow maximum flexibility in the access: thus, these components could be implemented in any programming language, provided that they respect the communication interface. To achieve interoperability, the address for each agent must be known, as well as the port where it will be listening to connections, and the type of Service the agent provides. The necessary information is depicted in Fig. 2.

Fig. 2. Information needed for registering with the ComMAg

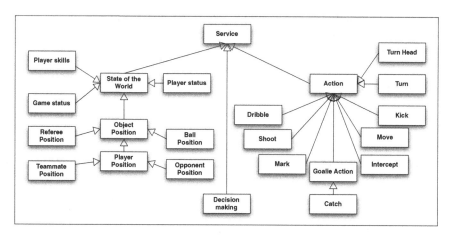

Fig. 3. Proposed hierarchy of soccer-related services

To precisely characterise each agent's services, a taxonomy of services that defines the concrete abilities of each agent must be created. Different agents will be able to supply more general or more specific services, e.g., an agent might be solely capable of executing a dribble, or of executing any type of physical action. Thus, the characterisation of the service might be done by a class in an upper level of the hierarchy (more general service), or further down (more specific). The proposed service hierarchy is summarised in Fig. 3.

The role of the ComMAg will be vital in the bootstrapping step, when the players are being launched: each component will register it's services, and components that need other services to operate will look for the necessary components by querying the ComMAg. After this bootstrapping phase, the ComMAg could stay inactive, since the other components will be able to communicate directly among themselves. The ComMAg agent can, however, play another very important role, as argued in section 3.1: if, during the game, the ComMAg would keep track of the functioning of each of the components, it would be able to detect possible malfunctioning situations. Such an ability could be exploited in order to make the system fault tolerant.

3.1 Fault Management

In this architecture, where components may be arbitrarily added to the system, and where redundant components are expected to exist, it is most appropriate to include a fault management mechanism.

To ensure that the components are behaving properly, the Common Framework expects each component to re-register with the ComMAg on a pre-defined schedule. If some component fails to do so after the elapsed time has passed, the ComMAg can assume that the component is malfunctioning, and react by trying to re-launch the agent using the registered *launchCommand*, included in the information sent by the agent for registration (see Fig. 2). If the component repeatedly fails to launch, it will simply be withdrawn form the registration directory. This component will cease to exist, and all interactions will have to be re-routed to other existing components.

4   Framework Language

The open and flexible architecture of the Common Framework demands that the various components are able to communicate according to a least commitment principle, since various components might be programmed in different languages, or be hosted in different machines. Thus, there has to be a standard interface to the components, and the exchange of messages also has to be pre-defined and standardised.

Furthermore, these concepts have to be integrated in a more general framework that allows their meaningful exchange between components. The components will need, e.g., to ask for the execution of actions, to demand the answering of queries, or to subscribe to important information sources. These communication primitives can be supplied by some agent communication language, like FIPA-ACL [1], which is an international standard, endorsed by IEEE, and supplies all the necessary primitives.

4.1   Language Requirements

The most fundamental concepts are the ones pertaining to the description of the world and the possible actions of the players. These concepts should be modelled in an abstract way that should apply to different leagues and settings. This conceptualisation is visible in figures 4 and 5. The language underlying the Common Framework will have to address a set of requirements in order to be able to fulfil it's role. These requirements will be described hereafter.

State of the world concepts. The language needs to be able to express information about all the objects existing on the field, namely physical static objects, such as flags, the field and it's regions, as well as dynamic objects such as the ball, the players and, possibly, a referee.

In the dynamic and fast changing domain of robotic soccer, the perception is always imperfect and error-prone. Therefore, the expression of locations must also be able to include information about the related uncertainty.

Robotic soccer actions. There is obviously also the need for the expression of the actions that can be executed by the agents. Such actions should be modelled from a high level point of view, and include ball manipulation (kicks, shots), movement without ball (moving to a position, turn in a direction), as well as moving of the head, i.e., of the part of the robot where the usually existent cameras are located.

These requirements were considered closely and the resulting modelling can be seen in figure 4 (general view of the framework's contents), figure 5 (close view of the player's characterisation and description of the existing actions) and figure 6 (concepts related to positioning and associated uncertainties).

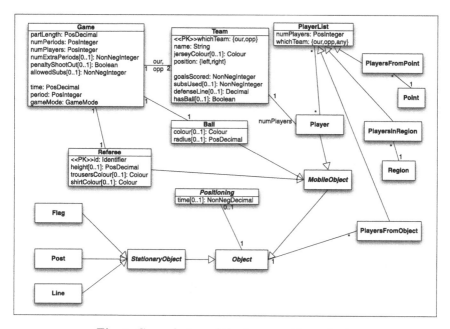

Fig. 4. General view of the framework's contents

4.2 Language Syntax

The model of the Common Frameworks needs its' concepts to be exchangeable through messages. Therefore, a syntax has to be defined that allows the different concepts in the model (instances, actions, access to attributes,...) to be expressed in a textual format.

The usage of well established agent systems' content languages, like FIPA-SL[2] or KIF[3] was considered, but was abandoned due to very different reasons:

- neither SL nor KIF allow the usage of Object Oriented concepts like methods;
- KIF has no support for actions;
- SL has very few available tools, namely a parser for C++.

Therefore, the proposed way to deal with OO-concepts is to create a simple, new approach to their expression is a textual format, which will now be presented.

Instances of Classes. The different classes in the model will need to have a way of expressing instances. With this purpose, it is suggested that the instances are expressed through S-expressions, with the class name as the first element and every attribute labelled by it's name following a colon, e.g. ':name'. Using this formalism, an example of an Absolute Positioning would be as follows:

```
(AbsolutePositioning :x 10.3 :y -23.67 :yaw 0.23456)
```

In terms of FIPA-ACL, these instances can be understood as propositions representing objects, and can be used, e.g., in the replies to queries.

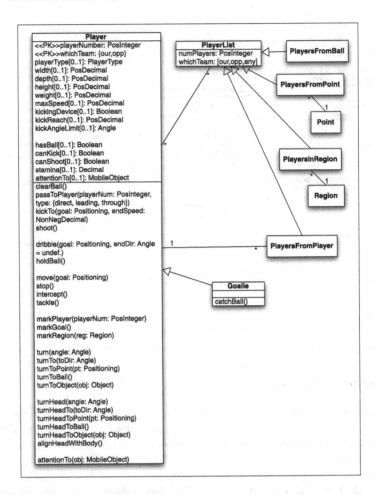

Fig. 5. View of the player's characterisation and description of the existing actions

Access to Class Attributes. When querying parts of the state of the world, there will be the need to refer specific values of attributes, e.g., the positioning of a player. This need will be satisfied through a new primitive (val), which will be followed by the name of the sought class and attribute, and by the primary key to the class, when needed. As an example, the positioning of player five in the opponent team would include the player number and the team, since these are the primary key to this class:

```
(val Player positioning :playerNumber 5 :whichTeam opp)
```

To refer to the present time in the game, the expression would be even simpler, since there is only one game and therefore there is no need for the primary key:

```
(val Game time)
```

This attribute access mechanism corresponds to FIPA-ACL's referential expressions, and can be used as the content of a query.

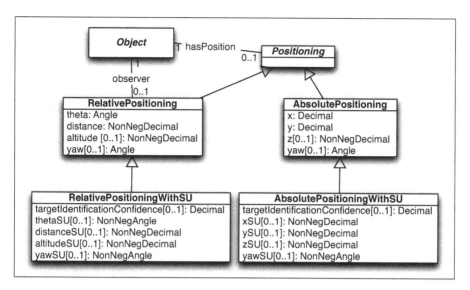

Fig. 6. Concepts related to positioning and associated uncertainties

Execution of Methods. The Player class defines methods modelling the possible actions of a player. These methods will need to be invoked by the high level decision component. With this purpose, the primitive *exec* is introduced. This primitive will need as parameters the name of the class, the primary key to the instance to which the method should apply, and the method's arguments. As an example, in order for player 3 to turn to player 4, the following formulation is necessary:

```
(exec Player turnToObject :playerNum 3
:whichTeam our
:obj (Player :playerNum 4 :whichTeam our))
```

These method execution expressions can be considered action expressions, and therefore used as the content of FIPA-ACL requests.

5   Related Work

Several authors have dealt with the concept of mobile robotic middleware in recent years. Some relevant approaches will be described in the current section.

Orocos [4,5] intends to be a middleware for mobile robotics, strictly following free software best practices. It aims at being general purpose, and replace all proprietary drivers and control software shipped with the hardware. It also provides different software patterns to deal with common tasks, such as localisation determination. This framework has originated in an EU-funded project and has been developed for several years. The framework is in no way related to robotic soccer or the RoboCup initiative.

Miro [6,7] is also a proposal for a middleware for mobile robotics, from a research team that has significant RoboCup experience[8]. The middleware, however, does not seem to have any specific adaptation for this domain. Similarly to Orocos, the framework is based on Corba[1] principles. General purpose functionalities, such as mapping and localisation, are included in the framework.

Another middleware proposal[9] also originates from a team with RoboCup experience, but also pays no special attention to the domain, as it intends to be general-purpose and adaptable to different domains. The framework has three components, to deal with action and perception primitives, state-of-the-world, and high-level architectures, such as petri nets and state machines.

These different approaches intend to be of general application, with no specific support or adaptation for the RoboCup domain. From the point of view of a team working specifically on the robotic soccer domain, this generality brings disadvantages: the action and perception primitives are very basic, not covering essential actions like (different types of) kicks nor concepts like an off-side line, that become very difficult to deal with.

Moreover, these frameworks are normally extendable, therefore not providing a fixed set of primitives, nor a standardised soccer-specific vocabulary, as is the case with the Common Framework. This openness is undesirable, since it allows teams to develop league and team specific solutions and models, which will impair the sharing of results between teams and leagues.

Additionally, the reliance of Orocos and Miro on Corba shows that the frameworks are primarily intended to be used with Java and C++, since Corba offers little or no support for other languages like Prolog. The Common Framework relies simply on sockets, and can therefore be used with any programming language.

6   Future Work

Having achieved a complete definition of the Common Framework and it's underlying language, the next step will be to develop a pilot implementation in the 2D-simulation league. We intend to use public available implementations of well tested teams (e.g. UvA TriLearn [10] and Helios [11]) as our primary code source. At least two of these teams will be used, in order to show the interoperability of the architecture. Namely, it will be possible to simultaneously use code from different sources in the same agent.

Further on, it is intended to use the framework, with exactly the same controller agent, in the scope of the Mixed-Reality league [12] , which uses actual, micro-sized robots.

As the framework becomes more stable and mature, it will also be used to control a team of robots in the Mid-size league [13] , where new challenges linked to the usage of different, possibly failing sensors and actuators will arise, allowing the architecture to show the whole of it's potential.

---

[1] http://www.corba.org

7 Conclusion

This paper has introduced a new architecture, a Common Framework for Co-operative Robotics, for the development of multi-robot teams. It aims at being open, flexible, redundant and fault tolerant. These qualities are inherent to the design of the Framework as a system of multiple multi-agent systems, where the enrolment of each player's components is managed by a centralised Communication Management Agent.

The existing components will communicate among themselves on basis of a shared modelling of the RoboCup domain, whereas the necessary conversations will need to comply to well-defined protocols that rule the development of meaningful interactions.

This open architecture allows the implementation of agents with arbitrary, redundant and reusable components. The components' relative independence also allows their separate development by diverse programming teams for posterior integration. Other advantages are the real-time addition and withdrawal of components, as well as tolerance to failures, and the usage of the same high-level agents in different environments (e.g. different leagues or real and simulated back-ends).

References

1. FIPA Technical Committee: FIPA ACL message structure specification. Technical report, Foundation for Intelligent Physical Agents (2002)
2. FIPA Technical Committee: FIPA SL content language specification. Technical report, Foundation for Intelligent Physical Agents (2002)
3. Genesereth, M.R., Fikes, R.E.: Knowledge interchange format, version 3.0 reference manual. Technical report, Computer Science Department, Stanford University (1992)
4. Bruyninckx, H.: Open robot control software: the orocos project. In: IEEE International Conference on Robotics and Automation (2001)
5. Bruyninckx, H., Soetens, P., Koninckx, B.: The real-time motion control core of the orocos project. In: IEEE International Conference on Robotics and Automation (2003)
6. Enderle, S., Utz, H., Sablatnög, S., Simon, S., Kraetzschmar, G., Palm, G.: Miro: Middleware for autonomous mobile robots. In: IFAC Conference on Telematics Applications in Automation and Robotics (2001)
7. Utz, H., Sablatnög, S., Enderle, S., Kraetzschmar, G.: Miro—middleware for mobile robot applications. IEEE Transactions on Robotics and Automation 18(4), 493–497 (2002)
8. Mayer, G., Kaufmann, U., Clauss, M., Hartmann, C., Monsch, M., Ruland, T., Seibold, B., Sitter, C., Wolf, F., Palm, G.: The ulm sparrows 2006 - team description paper. Technical report, University of Ulm (2006)
9. Ramos, N., Barbosa, M., Lima, P.: Multi-robot systems middleware applied to soccer robots. In: ROBOTICA 2007 - 7th Portuguese Robotics Festival (2007)
10. Kok, J.R., Vlassis, N., Groen, F.: Uva trilearn 2004 team description. Technical report, University of Amsterdam (2004)

11. rctools Web Page, http://rctools.sourceforge.jp/akiyama/
12. Gimenes, R., Mota, L., Reis, L.P., Lau, N., Certo, J.: Simulation meets reality: A co-operative approach to robocup's physical visualization soccer league. In: Neves, J., Santos, M.F., Machado, J.M. (eds.) EPIA 2007. LNCS (LNAI), vol. 4874. Springer, Heidelberg (2007)
13. Moreira, A.P., Costa, P., Scolari, A., Sousa, A., Marques, P.: 5dpo-2000 team description for robocup 2006. Technical report, University of Porto (UP) (2006)

Multilevel Testing of Control Software for Teams of Autonomous Mobile Robots

Sebastian Petters, Dirk Thomas, Martin Friedmann, and Oskar von Stryk

Technische Universität Darmstadt, Department of Computer Science
Hochschulstr. 10, D-64289 Darmstadt, Germany
{petters,dthomas,friedmann,stryk}@sim.tu-darmstadt.de,
http://www.sim.tu-darmstadt.de

Abstract. Developing control software for teams of autonomous mobile robots is a challenging task, which can be facilitated using frameworks with ready to use components. But testing and debugging the resulting system as taught in modern software engineering to be free of errors and tolerant to sensor noise in a real world scenario is to a large extend beyond the scope of current approaches. In this paper multilevel testing strategies using the developed frameworks RoboFrame and MuRoSimF are presented. Testing incorporating automated tests, online and offline analysis and software-in-the-loop (SIL) tests in combination with real robot hardware or an adequate simulation are highly facilitated by the two frameworks. Thus the efficiency of validation of complex real world applications is improved. In this way potential errors can be identified early in the development process and error situations in real world operations can be reduced significantly.

1 Introduction

Development of control software for teams of autonomous robots imposes many challenges on the developer. The software is usually highly complex, containing modules for very different tasks (like motion generation, sensor data fusion or behavior control). To ensure operation of such systems, each module of the control software must (1) be free of errors and (2) tolerate noise and errors from other sources. A special class of robots targeted at in this paper are "lightweight" robot systems characterized by inertially stabilized high motion dynamics and limited onboard sensing and computing capabilities due to payload restrictions like small humanoid robots, small unmanned aerial or marine vehicles.

As autonomous mobile robots are operated in environments with large uncertaines, the software must be tolerant to noise and disturbances. To examine the abilities of an autonomous robot all individual modules of the control software as well as the complete system have to be tested extensively. Testing the software for autonomous mobile robots is a complicated challenge, which can only be met if the developer is equipped with appropriate tools. One major problem when testing such software is the fact, that the source of an error is often not obvious. An error can usually be caused by one of the modules involved, or it can be

S. Carpin et al. (Eds.): SIMPAR 2008, LNAI 5325, pp. 183–194, 2008.

caused by external influences like changing environmental conditions. Errors in the control software can also be shadowed by such external influences, so that such an error does not become obvious. E.g. if the tracking of an oject fails, the reason may be in the vision module, a calculation error in the world model, in the behavior control or an unexpected input like a falsely recognized new other object in the scene. It may also be possible that an error exists in the sensor fusion module which is misinterpreted as an effect of noisy sensor data.

In this paper several ways of ensuring the quality of robot control software through testing are discussed. These methods include component tests of the control software before using it, testing the software with software-in-the-loop (SIL) simulations, monitoring the performance of the control software during real world operations and using offline evaluation afterwards. Crucial for the efficiency of such tests is the availability of a robot middleware with potential capabilities for flexible monitoring and remote debugging as well as simulations of the robots capabilities for sensing of and interacting with the physical world on different levels of detail depending on the current SIL test.

For facilitating the testing process, the used software architecture should therefore in general provide the following features:

- Extendable testing framework to allow implementation of new component tests,
- modular design to test different parts of the control software independently,
- flexible and easy to use communication mechanisms to enable data exchange with a remote computer for debugging,
- an extendable graphical user interface for visualization,
- built-in features allowing offline debugging e.g. a recording/playback tool,
- and a simulation framework allowing different layers of realism.

2   Existing Technologies

2.1   Robot Control Software

In the last decades several architectures for robot control software have emerged. All of them try to facilitate the challenging and thus error-prone task of the developers by providing solutions for common problems as tested and ready to use components. Current approaches especially differ in the targeted robot platforms and the scope, for which components are provided.

Frameworks like Microsoft Robotics Studio [1] and the CORBA [2] based Miro [3] are focused on systems with a significant amount of computational power, e.g. multi processor systems, and provide effective communication mechanisms. For "lightweight" robot systems with only very limited onboard computational power these frameworks have the disadvantage of a relatively large overhead which further restricts computational resources available to robot control software.

Robot device interfaces try to standardize the access to sensors and actors by providing an easy to use driver layer. CLARAty [4] for example contains reusable components which can easily be adapted to different robot platforms but does not support teams of robots. The Player Project [5] provides an interface to access different hardware over a network and supports multiple programming languages i.e. C++, Java and Python. There exists drivers for the simulation frameworks Stage (2D) and Gazebo (3D) [6], which allows development of robot control software without the real hardware. URBI [7] follows a similar approach, but only supports a C++ like scripting language. These device interfaces do not perform very well in the development of complex robot control applications for teams of autonomous robots due to the lack of flexible communication mechanisms which are essential for modular large scale applications.

Integrated robot control software architectures like Webots [8] or Saphira [9] allow the development of software for robots like the Pioneer 2DX, Bioloid (Robotis), AIBO (Sony) and Nao (Aldebaran Robotics), mainly for educational or research purposes. They contain graphical user interfaces and a simulator and provide components to construct own robots from commonly used sensors and actuators. Webots also allows the development of sofware for swarms of robots and evolutionary algorithms. Due to the focus on a specific plaform, it is not possible to develop software for teams of heterogeneous robots.

2.2 Robot Simulations

Most existing 3D simulations rely on external packages for physics simulation. Very often the Open Dynamics Engine (ODE) [10] is used, e.g. in Webots [8], SimRobot [11] or Gazebo [6]. Other packages used are PhysX [12] by NVIDIA (used in the Microsoft Robotics Studio [1]) or game engines like the Unreal Engine [13] (used in USARSim [14]).

Depending on the current testing task, requirements on the robot simulation vary widely. High physical accuracy may be necessary under some circumstances (e.g. for motion optimization), but not important for other scenarios (e.g. testing of team coordination). Also physics-based robot simulation may impact the real time performance severly. Often there is a tradeoff between accuracy of the simulation and size of the team.

If a simulation depends on external packages for physics simulation or other purposes, adjusting the accuracy (and thus the real-time performance) of the simulation is complicated. One solution to this problem is using different simulations, e.g. Gazebo [6] for 3D physics simulation and Stage for 2D simulation of large teams. As long as the simulations provide the same interface to the control software (as is given in the Player/Stage/Gazebo project), this approach is practicable. If this precondition is not fulfilled, it becomes necessary to model the robots and to provide suitable connections to the control software for each simulation.

2.3 Testing Strategies

Automated tests are a widely used tool in software engineering today. In contrast to formal verification, which is not feasible for complex systems, automated tests check the correctness of a software component for a predefined set of samples.

Testing can only be used to detect the effects of errors, but not the reasons for the errors. The absence of failed tests is not a proof for the correctness of the software as long as the perfomed tests do not cover all possible inputs and internal states.

To ensure a specified functionality automated unit-, regression-, integration- and stress-tests [15] are used during the development process of software components and applications. But even if there are many tools available to simplify the process of testing, studies show their acceptance heavily depends on the time needed to setup up and perform the tests [16]. As a consequence usefull tools actively have to support the developers by keeping the efforts of testing to a minimum.

2.4   Summary of Existing Technologies

Existing solutions for robot control software and 3D simulation packages aim at supporting the developers by providing easy to use components. The process of testing and validating the resulting system in real world applications is nevertheless mostly beyond the scope of the current approaches, especially for scenarios where multiple heterogeneous robots interact with each other. The capabilities of first approaches using logfiles and graphical user interfaces for later offline analysis [17] are quite limited. For a more detailed analysis during runtime, the debugging mechanisms should be tightly integrated into the whole system, easily accessible via small interfaces and with a low processing overhead.

The previously mentioned testing strategies from software engineering are only applicable to the low-level functionality of robot control software. It is impossible to specify test cases which cover all possible input data which could occur in an environment which is far from being fully predictable because of the infinite many situations of sensing of and interaction with the physical world. Due to potential hardware wearing, numerous automated tests with the real robot system may not be desired. For this reason the standard strategies of software engineering are only of limited use to test robot control software.

In situations where multiple components are developed independently, it is also necessary to enable tests of individual components. Depending on the test case it may also be desired to simplify the surrounding system by partly replacing other components using an adequate simulation matching the current situation. This approach reduces the overall complexity of the test scenario and thus facilitates the identification of the source of an error.

3   Developed Technologies

3.1   RoboFrame

RoboFrame [18,19] has been developed in the authors group to meet the special requirements of heterogeneous teams of lightweight autonomous robots. The source code is available for non-commercial research and educational usage. It is implemented in object oriented ANSI C++ and contains a platform abstraction layer to support Windows 2000/XP/Vista/CE as well as various Linux and Unix derivates and Mac OS X as underlying operating system. Due to short development cycles of new robot hardware components and fast changing requirements caused by complex scenarios, RoboFrame provides flexible communication mechanisms and easy exchangeable modules, which encapsulate algorithms for image processing, world modeling, behavior control and motion generation. Modules can be added to multiple threads, which can be executed at a given frequency or if new data to process arrives.

For data exchange between the modules in one application a shared memory can be used. The preferred way of data exchange of smaller data packages is a message based communication, which allows transparent communication even via network. Messages can be of arbitrary type or complex data structures to support any kind of application specific message. To handle application specific messages advanced serialization mechanisms are provided. Modules can request messages from other modules without having to worry about the current process layout. All data packages automatically get a source address to identify the sender of a message and are timestamped.

For communication via network, both unreliable, but fast UDP and reliable TCP is supported. Depending from the required reliability and performance, the appropriate protocol can be selected. Usually the faster UDP is used for team communication between the robots while TCP is used for debugging or remote control connections.

For debugging, monitoring and remote control purposes a graphical user interface (GUI) which allows connections to multiple robots is part of RoboFrame. All messages within an application or additional data for debugging purpose, which is only generated if requested, can be send to the GUI and can be visualized in their respective context by application specific dialogs. It is also possible to send data to an application, i.e. to reconfigure the application or a module or to test certain modules.

The GUI also contains a dialog to record messages sent from the connected applications. The messages can be replayed for later analysis or can be sent to the application. This allows repetitive tests with the same data and thus enables the investigation of changes made to the modules.

In contrast to other existing architectures RoboFrame itself does not make any assumptions about the applications on top of it. Neither any message types nor any modules are provided by the framework itself. Instead RoboFrame enforces the development of components which can be reused in different applications.

3.2 MuRoSimF

The **Multi-Robot-Simulation-Framework** [20] enables to create simulations for heterogeneous teams of autonomous mobile robots. A key feature of MuRoSimF is that algorithms used for the simulation (e.g. simulation of robot motions or sensors) can be exchanged transparently. As algorithms for the same purpose exist on different levels of physical detail resp. computational complexity (e.g. robot motion simulation based on kinematics or multibody system dynamics), simulations can be tailored to be adequate to a given testing task with respect to the level of detail and precision of simulation as well as number of robots simulated simultaneously at real-time.

MuRoSimF provides several algorithms for simulation of biped, quadruped and wheeled locomotion on different levels of detail. Algorithms for the simulation of external sensors like cameras and laser scanners as well as for internal sensors like gyroscopes, accelerometers and joint encoders are provided. All can be extended or replaced.

3.3   Integration of Simulation and Control Software

Simulations created with MuRoSimF can be connected easily to control programs based on RoboFrame. External software can be connected to the simulation using serial communication (virtual or real RS232 connections as well as TCP). MuRoSimF provides so called *controllers* which are software modules allowing to communicate with sensor and actuators of the simulated robots. Within the control application modules exist which can communicate with the respective controllers of the simulation. When connecting the control software to the simulation instead of the real hardware, only these modules have to be adapted while the core modules of the application remain the same. In case the real robot is connected by RS232 to the control computer, the connection to the simulation will be completely transparent, as RS232 is provided as a way of communication.

Many robot designs (e.g. [21]) incorporate special controller hardware for real time control of a reflex layer (e.g. gait generation and control for walking robots or motion control for wheeled vehicles). Such controllers have significant parts of software of their own. To enable the SIL-testing of this software, it is possible to recompile the central functions into a dynamic link library and execute these functions within the simulation.

The simulation framework also provides the capability to extract information from the scenario like ground truth data of the simulated objects. These information can be used to bypass some processing components in the real application to simplify the complexity of the application for testing purposes.

4   Multilevel Testing Strategies

In this section strategies for testing the control software for teams of autonomous robots will be discussed. Depending on the abstraction level of the software modules under consideration of a test, different approaches will be most useful. The following three testing strategies might all be carried out either *without any hardware*, with *real robots* or with *simulated robots*: (i) component tests, (ii) online testing, (iii) offline testing.

Even if these testing strategies are common knowledge in modern software engineering it may be more or less difficult to perform these tests depending on the software architecture. The used software architecture and tools can vastly reduce the required affords to setup different types of test scenarios. Using a message based communication it becomes very handsome to alter the data flow of the application and to intercept or inject messages during runtime.

In the scenario of a team of autonomous soccer playing humanoid robots described later on some testing strategies are used as showcases. This scenario provides many challenges, as (1) noisy off-the-shelf sensors and limited onboard computation capacity, (2) the software involved has a high degree of complexity and different levels of abstraction and (3) communication between the robots is unstable. Similar challenges can be found in many other real world applications (e.g. cooperative search and rescue, exploration operations). The software architecture for the example scenario consists of several modules like image processing, world modeling, behavior control, motion generation and inter-robot communication (cf. Fig. 1).

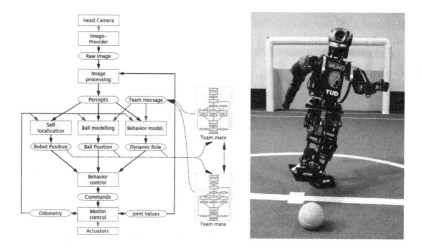

Fig. 1. Software architecture (left) for a team of autonomous soccer playing humanoid robots (right). Modules are depicted as boxes, messages as ellipses. Inter-robot communication is not stable and may be faulty.

4.1   Component Tests

In a deterministic and finite dimensional world unit tests would have a code coverage of nearly 100%. However, this is not ture for such a complex, real world application, since the efforts for creating unit tests for high level functionality are highly increasing. Therefore it is only applicable to parts of the software. In general the low level functionality which involves less source code is better testable using component tests than complex high level functionality.

To ensure the correctness of the message passing system, serialization mechanisms and the shared memory subsystem of `RoboFrame` these parts are covered by a set of component tests.

A prime example for unit tests in robotics are mathematical operations. Their tests do not involve any hardware and the functions are easily testable - mostly even in very small unit, which makes it even simpler to write the component tests. Since algorithms based on mathematical formulars are also better testable than other high-level functionality, some of the application specific models are also covered by component tests, e.g. the odometry model accumulates the odometry of the robot which is measured multiple times per second. Several internal robot modelings, e.g. the relative ball model and the self localization, are based on the integrated odometry model which performs the computations required by other models for different time intervals. A set of unit tests assures its correct functionality.

But other component tests might utilize simulated robots to assure that e.g. inter-robot communication of their own localization is working flawlessly. But the component test is neither implying that there is really any self localization done nor that the robot is really walking or driving around. Therefore an adequate simulation, which provides oracle data of exact robot poses and a simplified odometry reduces the amount of software to be covered by testing enormously by factoring out the influence of the not used code.

4.2   Online Testing

For several high level components unit testing is not a feasible approach. This also applies to cases where the data to check vary in a non-trivial matter e.g. because of noisy input data. A human can easily determine the correctness of the computed output data, where implementing a unit test would be quite expensive if not impossible. Therefore the application architecture must provide a rich set of features to monitor and debug a running application. Especially in mobile robotics the demand to work remotely is significant.

A good example to demonstrate the online testing capabilities of `RoboFrame` is the self localization in the scenario of Fig. 2. The humanoid robot uses an articulated, directed camera to determine it's position and orientation on the soccer field using a particle filter method. The self localization is based on a large set of input data: on one side the odometry model feed by the internal sensors, on the other side various objects recognized by an image processor software like goals, poles, field lines etc. Determining the quality of self localization is not only a test for correctness but even more a benchmark for accuracy of the localization method.

A component test can by its definition only detect the effects of an error but not the reason itself. For this test a different strategy must be used which involve the judgment of a human. Due to the large amount of data the GUI must be capable of visualizing these information in a way a human can easily comprehend any necessary details. These testing strategy allows a human to test a high level component based on the comprehensive visualization.

4.3   Offline Testing

In some scenarios it is not feasible to do testing online in real time. Even the best visualization might not be suitable when the state changes frequently. Furthermore it is not possible to use a debugger during online test to track down the reason of an error. Therefore the third testing strategy involves the logging and replay capabilities of `RoboFrame`.

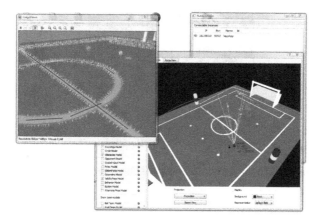

Fig. 2. Graphical user interface visualizing the detected field lines (white lines), position and orientation computed by the self localization (blue arrow) and the ground truth information provided from a ceiling camera or simulator (black arrow)

Any messages saved to a logfile during a former online test can later be replayed and visualized with the same tools used for the live testing which have been described before. This allows feeding the application with e.g. saved sensor messages to repeatedly test the components with the same known input data.

4.4 Software in the Loop Testing

As described in Sect. 3.3 `RoboFrame` and `MuRoSimF` provide communication capabilites allowing SIL-testing of the control software. Depending on what kind

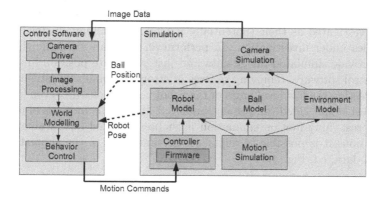

Fig. 3. Data exchange between control application and simulation. Solid lines indicate data similar to the data exchanged with the real robot. Dashed lines are additional informations provided by the simulation. The simulation can be extended to teams of robots by duplicating the robot data models and attaching the new models to the simulation algorithms used.

Fig. 4. Evaluation of a robot's walking motion. The simulated robot is augmented with the trajectories of feet and hip.

of SIL-test is to be performed, different information may be transfered from the simulation to the control application. MuRoSimF is capable of providing *adequate* simulations for a wide variety of testing-scenarios. For testing the complete software the simulation can act as a replacement for the real robot's sensing and motion capabilities, processing motion requests from the control application and providing camera images in response.

Besides the normal sensor information of the robot, the simulation can provide any information on the state of the simulation, like position of simulated robots or ball. This ground truth data can be used in multiple ways. A simplified structure of robot control software and simulation is shown in Fig. 3.

One possibility is to verify the performance of a robot's self localization. To do this a complete robot is simulated and the simulation provides further information on the robots current position and orientation. This information is compared to the output of the self localization modules of the control application.

Another possibility is testing behavior and communication for a team of robots. In this case, the function of the image processing parts of the robots are not investigated as their (potentially wrong) output may shadow errors in the modules under investigation. To perform an adequate test, the simulation will not provide simulated image data and just propagate position information to the control software, removing sources of errors not under investigation.

When testing the low level parts of the robot control software, even less information must be provided (and thus) simulated. If only the motions of the robot are of interest, only motion simulation must be simulated. For evaluation of a robot's actions it is possible to augment the simulation of the simulation with additional data, c.f. Fig. 4.

4.5   Selection of Adequate Testing Strategy

The choice to select one of the strategies for a specific test is always left to the developer of the application. Each and every of the depicted types of testing options have their advantages and disadvantages for a specific purpose as summarized in Table 1.

Table 1. The suitability of the test strategies for different test goals. (+) marks good, (-) marks bad suitability, (o) marks uncertain.

Test strategies	Ensure correct computations	Evaluate algorithms with noisy input data	Track down source of an error
Component tests	+	o	-
Online test	-	+	o
Offline test	-	+	+

5   Summary and Outlook

Existing approaches used in modern software engineering are only of limited use for meeting the challenges involved in testing software for a team of autonomous mobile robots operating in an uncertain environment. They must be extended by further testing techniques. Depending on the application the developers have to consider which testing strategy fits each part of the software best.

The software architecture RoboFrame was designed to meet the special requirements stated at the end of Sect. 1. It enables multilevel testing from unit testing over live testing of heterogeneous teams to offline testing with recorded real world input data. Due to the message based communication mechanisms and the dynamic runtime configuration of the framework the efforts to set up a test environment are highly reduced compared to other approaches. The framework MuRoSimF enables an adequate robot simulation for each different scenario. The algorithms vary from complex dynamics simulation for testing the motion generation in the loop to simple kinematics but providing ground truth data to concentrate on high level team behavior tests. Furthermore, any of the algorithms can be replaced by custom implementations to provide tailored solutions for any requirement. The source code of RoboFrame and MuRoSimF is available at no cost for research and educational purposes from the authors. Both developed software frameworks actively support the developers in testing and debugging their applications and thus improve the efficiency which speeds up the development process and results in a higher reliability of the final application.

References

1. Microsoft Robotics Studio (2007), http://msdn.microsoft.com/robotics/
2. OMG Object Management Group. CORBA - Common Object Request Broker Architecture (2007), http://www.corba.org
3. Utz, H., Sablatnög, S., Enderle, S., Kraetzschmar, G.K.: Miro – middleware for mobile robot applications. IEEE Trans. on Robotics and Automation 18(4), 493–497 (2002)
4. Nesnas, I., Wright, A., Bajracharya, M., Simmons, R., Estlin, T., Kim, W.S.: CLARAty: An architecture for reusable robotic software. In: SPIE Aerosense Conference, Orlando, FL (April 2003)

5. Gerkey, B.P., Vaughan, R.T., Howard, A.: The Player/Stage project: Tools for multi-robot and distributed sensor systems. In: Intl. Conf. on Advanced Robotics (ICAR), Coimbra, Portugal, 30 June - 3 July 2003, pp. 317–323 (2003)

6. Koenig, N., Howard, A.: Gazebo - 3D multiple robot simulator with dynamics (2003), `http://playerstage.sourceforge.net/gazebo/gazebo.html`

7. Gostai. Urbi - Universal Real-time Behavior Interface (2008),
`http://www.urbiforge.com`

8. Michel, O.: Cyberbotics ltd. - webots(tm): Professional mobile robot simulation. Intl. Journal of Advanced Robotic Systems 1(1), 39–42 (2004)

9. Konolige, K.: Saphira robot control architecture. Technical report, SRI International (2002)

10. Smith, R.: ODE - Open Dynamics Engine (2007), `http://www.ode.org`

11. Laue, T., Spiess, K., Röfer, T.: SimRobot - a general physical robot simulator and its application in RoboCup. In: Bredenfeld, A., Jacoff, A., Noda, I., Takahashi, Y. (eds.) RoboCup 2005. LNCS (LNAI), vol. 4020, pp. 173–183. Springer, Heidelberg (2006)

12. AGEIA PhysX website (2007), `http://www.ageia.com/physx/`

13. Epic games, unreal engine (2007), `http://www.epicgames.com`

14. Carpin, S., Lewis, M., Wang, J., Balakirsky, S., Scrapper, C.: USARSim: a robot simulator for research and education. In: Proc. of the 2007 IEEE Intl. Conf. on Robotics and Automation (ICRA) (2007)

15. Ntafos, S.C.: A comparison of some structural testing strategies. IEEE Trans. Softw. Eng. 14(6), 868–874 (1988)

16. Ng, S.P., Murnane, T., Reed, K., Grant, D., Chen, T.Y.: A preliminary survey on software testing practices in Australia. In: Proc. Australian Softw. Eng. Conf (ASWEC 2004), Washington, DC, USA, p. 116. IEEE Computer Society, Los Alamitos (2004)

17. Figueiredo, J., Lau, N., Pereira, A.: Multi-agent debugging and monitoring framework. In: First Proc. IFAC Workshop on Multivehicle Systems (MVS 2006), Brazil (2006)

18. Petters, S., Thomas, D., Stryk, O.v.: RoboFrame - a modular software framework for lightweight autonomous robots. In: Proc. Workshop on Measures and Procedures for the Evaluation of Robot Architectures and Middleware of the 2007 IEEE/RSJ Int. Conf. on Intelligent Robots and Systems, San Diego, CA, USA, October 29 (2007)

19. Petters, S., Thomas, D.: RoboFrame website (2008), `http://www.roboframe.info`

20. Friedmann, M., Petersen, K., von Stryk, O.: Scalable and adequate simulation for motion and sensors of heterogeneous teams of autonomous mobile robots. In: Carpin, S., et al. (eds.) Proc. 1st Intl. Conf. on Simulation, Modeling and Programming for Autonomous Robots (SIMPAR 2008), Venice, Italy, November 2008. LNCS (LNAI). Springer, Heidelberg (2008)

21. Friedmann, M., Kiener, J., Petters, S., Sakamoto, H., Thomas, D., von Stryk, O.: Versatile, high-quality motions and behavior control of humanoid robots. International Journal of Humanoid Robotics, pages accepted (to appear, 2008)

ppPDC Communication Framework – A New Tool for Distributed Robotics

Grzegorz Polaków and Mieczyslaw Metzger

Faculty of Automatic Control, Electronics and Computer Science
Silesian University of Technology,
Akademicka 16, 44-100 Gliwice, Poland
{grzegorz.polakow,mieczyslaw.metzger}@polsl.pl

Abstract. Parallel processing Producer-Distributor-Consumer (ppPDC) transmission scenario is proposed and developed for improving communication features of the Ethernet-based switched industrial networks. First version of ppPDC-based communication infrastructure was developed in the LabVIEW graphical programming platform as a flexible and low cost framework. Further development of the framework turned it into a fully functional real-time middleware, which has the main advantage of running the message processing in the protocol stacks in parallel, thus minimising the impact of nodes processing times on network efficiency. The proposed ppPDC-based communication infrastructure, amongst many other possible uses such as intelligent multiagent systems, can be well-suited in distributed robotics.

Keywords: communication infrastructure, distributed robotics, middleware for robotics, producer-distributor-consumer, real-time ethernet.

1 Introduction

Nowadays the autonomous, intelligent and networked systems are very essential in distributed robotics. A distributed robotic system deals with multiple autonomous robots or multiple sensor/actuator system under automatic control. Even if each component of distributed system can operate autonomously reacting to its local environment the whole robots community must cooperate to accomplish some desired tasks. Hence in the distributed robotic system the reciprocal communication should be treated as a major tasks.

An overview of problems dealing with Intelligent Autonomous Systems focused on industrial robotics and its applications was presented at the beginning of the third millennium [1]. A typical representative problem is a combined use of reactive and deliberative subsystems in multirobot systems [2] as well as a cooperation through an implicit communication in multi robot systems with an application for simulated soccer robot team [3]. An interesting distributed multi robot application is presented in [4] for supporting the elderly and disabled people for which is difficult to move their body to take some objects.

Programming multirobot distributed system is a difficult and challenging task. A very interesting idea of programming by demonstration lets a robot system to learn

S. Carpin et al. (Eds.): SIMPAR 2008, LNAI 5325, pp. 195–206, 2008.
© Springer-Verlag Berlin Heidelberg 2008

new behaviours from a human operator demonstration [5]. An object-oriented and distributed approach for programming flexible manufacturing systems equipped with robots is proposed in [6]. In this approach a general framework deals with remote access to the robot controller, remote programming and monitoring. Some theoretical background for programming software for distribute robotic systems based on team formation example was presented in [7].

Agent and multi agent systems (AMAS) are strictly connected with distributed robotic system in, for example, soccer league from the one (entertainment) hand and in industrial applications from the other hand. Basic notions for AMAS can be found for example in [8], [9], [10], and [11], while chosen examples of AMAS applications in robotics, manufacturing control and process control was presented in [12], [13], [14], [15], [16], [17], [18].

The foundation for contemporary automation and robotic systems is the use of communication networks in the distributed systems [19], [20], [21]. While instrumentation manufacturers actively promote their own communicational solutions, such as for example Fieldbus, Profibus, WorldFIP, Modbus, ControlNet, or DeviceNet standards, there is a concurrent tendency to use the widely known Ethernet standard [22], [23], [24] as a basis for both horizontal and vertical process data transmission (see for example [25]). Newly emerging networking media, ie. wireless communication standards, present even more attractive possibilities, also for distributed robotic systems [26].

In this paper the Ethernet-based communicational middleware is presented, which employs modified producer-distributor-consumer scheme for distributed control of robotic systems. The paper is organised as follows. At first the motivation for developing the middleware is stated, and the current technological state-of-art is briefly described as a basis for the following presentation of the proposed ppPDC protocol. The methodology of ppPDC's implementation in already existing control systems is also presented. The paper is summarised by a concluding remarks and propositions of future work.

2 Motivation

The main assumption behind the contribution, introduced by this work, is the existence of the similarity between classical, known from cybernetics, star topology of communicational networks and the internal structure of many of distributed control and multirobot systems. This analogy of structures suggests that it may be possible to implement communication in such control systems directly as a computer network using star topology. Communication in the network can be than performed using native low-level protocols specific to the given network standard. Protocols of higher layers are to be designed in such case to take specific characteristics of the used physical medium into account.

The idea is presented in the Fig. 1. In nearly all of the robotic environments it is possible to distinguish a set of components, distributed spatially and/or logically, which are having the same priority, while being controlled by another privileged component. Whether it is a manipulator consisting of a set of sensors and actuators controlled by central unit, or a manufacturing line employing multiple robots controlled locally, but globally synchronised by superior system, or, especially, a team of soccer robots connected to the PC when learning or diagnosed – the topology of star can easily be distinguished.

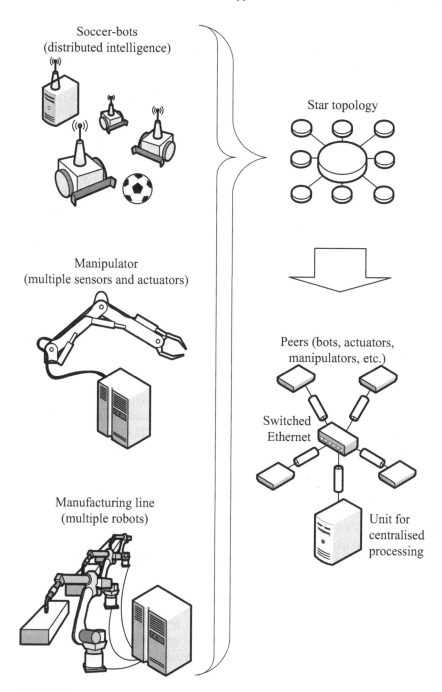

Fig. 1. The main idea of the ppPDC application in a distributed robotics environment

Issues considered and described in the literature usually are connected to the highest level of inter-robots communication (see e.g. [27, 28]), i.e. swarm intelligence, grouping of the units, or positioning. Low level aspect of the physical communication is in this context often omitted and treated as implicit, transparent and already existing; it is high level of communication which is stressed explicitly (as in [29]). However, it turns out that ensuring properly quick and efficient communication between components of the system is not trivial and requires extensive planning. Typically, for communication in robotics specialised retail industrial networks are used (e.g. Profibus-DP optimised for remote I/O, Swiftnet for aircraft applications, or CANopen in automotive industry) [30]. The downside of such products is that they are restricted in many ways, including their high price, potential patent claims, and closed standards. Reconfiguration and adaptation of such network is therefore highly limited, which is particularly undesirable in research applications.

Time determinism and network's efficiency are guaranteed by the properly designed data exchange scheme. The most popular communication schemes include token ring, master-slave, producer-consumer and producer-distributor-consumer [31], [32]. Some of the techniques are used in conjunction to ensure some specific network propertied (e.g. Profibus uses multi master–slave scheme, where current master is designated using the token passing technique). In general however, all of these techniques were designed primarily as the method of multiple access for shared medium, implementing the functionality of the data link layer of the ISO OSI model. Meanwhile, networking technologies evolved, and currently the most popular group of standards in use is the IEEE802 family working using the star topology implemented with the switching technique of IEEE802.1D. The flagship of the IEEE802 is the IEEE802.3, widely known as the Ethernet. The Ethernet standard gained bad opinion in the industrial networking society due to its CSMA/CD (*Carrier Sense Multiple Access with Collision Detection*) method, which solves collisions in the shared medium using random delays, which effectively makes it impossible to predict transmission times. However, CSMA/CD method is obsolete since switching technology became popular and nowadays Ethernet networks use the star topology. This technological leap was noticed, and now it is widely considered that transmission times in Ethernet networks are determinable [23]. But still, it remains unnoticed, how great is the potential of the queuing technology of modern switches, which are specialised fast computers designed to fulfil one duty i.e. reliable storing and forwarding Ethernet frames [33].

The ppPDC proposed protocol bridges the gap as it is designed to work on top of the Ethernet network built using the switching technology, and heavily relies on the functionality provided by the underlying physical network and its switching device. The ppPDC middleware enables time determined communication between spatially distributed control system components in agent-systems friendly way, which is especially well fitted for the distributed robotic systems. Currently, the ppPDC protocol is implemented with the visual language of the National Instruments LabVIEW, but its thorough documentation and openness allows to implement it with any programming language and in any Ethernet-enabled hardware.

3 Parallel Processing Producer – Distributor – Consumer

The parallel processing Producer–Distributor–Consumer communication scheme is heavily based on the traditional Producer–Distributor–Consumer scheme used in retail FIP, Swiftnet and FF (all standardized in the IEC61158 norm) networks, however it is modified to work in star topology based networks, in which a switching device is able to relieve network nodes of some of the protocol tasks.

The middleware consists of:

- the ppPDC protocol layer which implements the functionality of the distributed database of cyclic variables and allows to send and receive acyclic messages;
- the hardware layer which is supposed to be an Ethernet network working according to IEEE802.3 norm with the IEE802.1D switching technology.

Both layers are connected implicitly due to encapsulation of the ppPDC frames in UDP messages and TCP streams, which are transparently encapsulated in IP datagrams, which at least are passed to the LLC layer of the underlying Ethernet network.

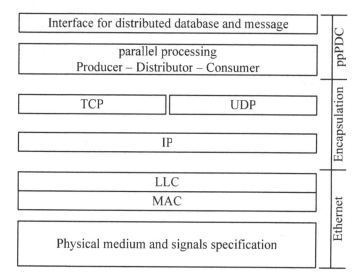

Fig. 2. The layer model of the communicational framework using ppPDC communication scheme

3.1 ppPDC Protocol for Distributed Database

The ppPDC data distribution scheme is the result of works on implementation of the classical PDC scheme in Ethernet networks. During the development it turned out, that some of the functionalities of the PDC scheme are redundant. The PDC scheme fulfils a double role in the networking stack. On one hand, it is the internal mechanism of distributed database of variables and messages, and on the other hand it manages the shared physical medium to avoid frame collisions. In switched networks functionality of medium access control is performed by hardware and it can be dropped from the protocol itself.

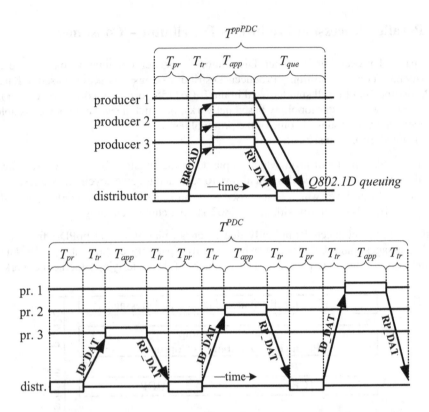

Fig. 3. Comparison of sequences of transmissions between PDC and ppPDC communicational schemes

The ppPDC scenario keeps the original idea of division of network nodes into two groups i.e. *producers* and *consumers*, while the communication between all the nodes is maintained by the additional privileged node called *the distributor*. It is the order of transmission of frames which was changed in the ppPDC protocol. In the PDC scheme, network frames are broadcasted sequentially and all the nodes are only allowed to answer to the explicit commands of the distributor, which asks the producers to broadcast values of variables they produce, accordingly to the predefined required periods. In the ppPDC there is only one request of the distributor which is common for all the producers (Fig. 3). Answers to this request are sent as quickly as possible, but with no specific coordination, so in the utmost case the answers can be even sent at the same exact time. In networks based on a shared medium it would cause multiple frame collisions. However, when network is switched accordingly to the IEEE802.1D standard, all the nodes are located in the separate domains of collisions, and messages they send are received by the switching device, stored in its memory, queued and orderly and timely delivered (T_{que} in Fig. 3) to the distributor node.

Due to this change in the ppPDC scheme, summarised time of network messages processing (T_{app} and T_{pr} in Fig. 3) which is the largest element of the total message round-trip-time ([23], [24]), is significantly lowered because of the parallel processing of the frames (in contrary to the sequential processing in the PDC scheme). The price for the parallel processing capability is the dependence of the high layer protocol on the low layer physical infrastructure.

3.2 Physical Media Supported

The main requirement of the ppPDC middleware is that the physical layer should be based on switching instead of the one of the CSMA family method. Effectively, the requirement limits possible physical layer technologies to a subset of Ethernet networks working in the full-duplex mode with the hardware switch. Popular solutions fulfilling this requirement include amongst others networks built with the 10/100/1000BASE-T copper cabling and newer 1000BASE-X fibre optic cables.

All the IEEE802 family standards are encapsulated in such a way, that from the higher network layer's point of view they are seen as a LLC (*Logical Link Control*) interface. Those of IEEE802 standards, which use CSMA access methods are time non-determined as the introduce random time delays. Due to the encapsulation, the ppPDC protocol cannot determine whether the low level layer is time determined (switched) or not. Because of this, it is also possible to implement the ppPDC protocol on top of CSMA-based network, and while the main property of determined time transmissions will be lost, logical functionality will be still the same. In cases when time efficiency is not required, the ppPDC can still be implemented for its distributed database capabilities. Such physical layers include older IEEE802.3 cabling standards like 10BASE2 working with the CSMA/CD method or modern wireless networks of the IEEE802.11 family working according to the CSMA/CA (*Carrier Sense Multiple Access with Collision Avoidance*) method, as in case of soccer robot system in Fig. 1.

3.3 Methodology for Implementation

Implementation of the presented ppPDC middleware in an already existing robotic system consists of few stages. The first step is an identification of occurrence of the star topology in the considered system. Fig. 1. presents examples of systems which are well suited to the ppPDC framework. Generally, the protocol may be used in all the systems which consist of a set of equally privileged components which should exchange small portions of data. The type of exchanged data depends on the characteristics of the specific system, it may be simple numerical type as in case of sensors and actuators in the robotic manipulator, or it may be advanced AI language as in the case of soccer robots learning. Such a wide range of possibilities is achievable due to capabilities of the ppPDC middleware. On one hand it is able to exchange small portions of information between network nodes in fast, reliable and time determined manner. On the other hand, the principle of work of the ppPDC, which employs broadcasting of messages containing values of all variables and all messages in the system, corresponds to the well known structure of knowledge from multi-agent systems i.e. blackboard system (see [10], [11]). It is very advantageous property of the ppPDC, as it makes implementation of the artificial intelligence-based control systems more user-friendly.

After the identification of star topology in the system, the type of data to be exchanged should be determined, so the central table of knowledge of the system can be built using this data type. This table, filled with the most recent values, will be cyclically broadcasted with the ppPDC protocol.

The last stage of the implementation process is ensuring that all the identified star nodes have the capability of TCP and UDP communication on top of Ethernet-based network. Network connecting all this nodes should be built, and additional node have to be connected to the network to fulfil the role of the distributor and control the communication process. In the most simple case nodes should be LabVIEW capable, so already developed software library could be used, but in general proper programming of the nodes can be done with any programming language (see [16], [17]).

Proper implementation by following all the above steps results in the fully time determined communication between all specified nodes. Achieved cycle times are relatively short and depend mainly on the protocol stacks' processing times in the distributed nodes (T_{app} in Fig. 3), as the times of physical signal propagation (T_{tr} in Fig. 3) and queing and forwarding (T_{que} in Fig. 3) are relatively small, and are of order of tens of microseconds ([23], [33]). If protocol stacks are programmed efficiently in low level programming language, achieved times of ppPDC protocol broadcasting cycle are short enough to close control loops and even directly control and position motors and manipulators.

4 Preliminary Tests

A preliminary experiment was conducted to compare the performance of the two specifically implemented protocols – the first based on the classical PDC and the second based on the proposed ppPDC communicational scheme. A research setup consisted of four typical desktop computers connected to an Ethernet network. All the computers had exactly the same hardware configuration (Intel Celeron 2.2GHz, 256MB RAM, Realtek RTL8139 Ethernet adapter) and worked under the control of the Windows XP operating system. A programming environment chosen for the experiment was National Instruments LabVIEW. The Ethernet network was based on the cat. 5A cabling, connecting all the computers to the hardware switch (Asmax BR-604), work modes of all the adapters were set to full-duplex with 100Mbit/s data rate. IP addresses of the PCs were set to private ones, router worked as a NAT, while all the packet forwarding from/to outside networks were disables, which created the model of a typical industrial Ethernet network without any outside traffic.

A schematic drawing of achieved structure of research setup is presented in the Fig. 4. Double connections between the PCs and the router are drawn to underline the fact that the network works in the full-duplex mode, which is a requirement for the ppPDC scheme to work effectively.

For this tests, protocols were slightly modified by disabling time synchronisation of the beginnings of the cycles. In effect, all the communication performed by the protocols was not synchronised according to the control algorithms, but was instead performed as fast as it was physically possible. Observation of network traffic allowed to determine achievable times of network cycles durations. The observation was done by capturing the traffic and registering the moments when frames starting the cycle occurred (ie. ID_DAT #0 for PDC protocol and BROAD for ppPDC protocol) - periods between this frames were treated as the cycle duration times.

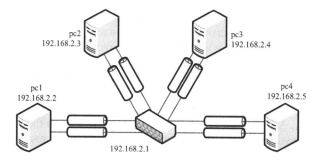

Fig. 4. The research setup for preliminary tests

The main idea of the test was determining dependence of the cycle duration on the number of variables exchanged in the cycle for both classical PDC protocol and the proposed ppPDC. Tests were performed for the communication containing 1, 2, 4, 8, 16, 32, 64, 128 and 256 variables equally distributed amongst the PCs connected with the protocol. Each gathered single result was plotted as the data point in the time-number of variables plane. Resulting clouds of points were fitted to the linear function with the least squares method (proof for the fact that expected character of the relation is linear was conducted but is not included here due to the limited space). Visualisation of achieved results is presented in the Fig. 5.

Coefficients of the formulas describing dependence of cycle times on the number of variables are as follows:

$$T^{PDC} = 0.001446n - 0.002532 , \qquad (1)$$

$$T^{ppPDC} = 0.0002194n + 0.001023. \qquad (2)$$

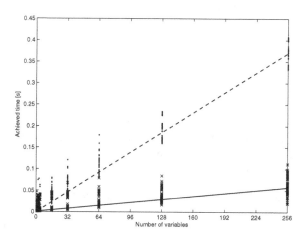

Fig. 5. Comparison of achieved cycle times of PDC (dots, dashed line) and ppPDC (crosses, continuous line) communicational schemes depending on number of exchanged variables

It should be noted that the achieved results are heavily influenced by the performance of the native Windows XP networking protocol stack. Duration of physical data transmission is in this cases only a fraction of total cycle time, as the most time consuming part of the communication is the processing of the data in the protocol stacks. However, the main idea of the ppPDC communication scheme is the parallelisation of the frames processing to minimise the impact of the processing times on the total communication cycle duration, and achieved results are a perfect illustration of this ppPDC's property. As it is seen in the formulas (1) and (2) and in the Fig. 5, parallelisation of the processing times in the distributed consumer nodes results in shortening total communication times by nearly one order of magnitude.

5 Concluding Remarks and Future Work

This paper presents the results of research on the communication middleware for AI-based control of multi-robot systems. Proposed protocol employs the data distribution scheme specifically designed for the star topology-based switched networks and proved useful when implemented on top of the popular and cheap Ethernet networks. The efficiency of the middleware is comparable with the retail products, while the systems using it stay open and highly reconfigurable. Use of the classical TCP and UDP protocols allows the ppPDC to be compatible with a great number of already existing tools and hardware.

Preliminary test results and pilot implementation (see [17]) show that the ppPDC scheme is very promising. The middleware is currently under further development and research. Laboratory tests are being conducted to determine exact efficiency under wide range of hosting operating systems and underlying hardware networks of varying standards. Depending on the parameters of switching device (memory, processing power) used in the physical layer, exact limits of data sizes and cycle times of the knowledge table broadcasting are also being determined.

Acknowledgments. This work was supported by the Polish Ministry of Science and Higher Education, grant no. N N514 296335.

References

1. Pagello, E., Arai, T., Dillmann, R., Stentz, A.: Towards the Intelligent Autonomous Systems of the third millennium. Robotics and Autonomous Systems 40, 63–68 (2002)
2. Carpin, S., Ferrari, C., Pagello, E.: Map focus: A way to reconcile reactivity and deliberation in multirobot systems. Robotics and Autonomous Systems 41, 245–255 (2002)
3. Pagello, E., D'Angelo, A., Montesello, F., Garelli, F., Ferrari, C.: Cooperative behaviors in multi-robot systems through implicit communication. Robotics and Autonomous Systems 29, 65–77 (1999)
4. Jia, S., Lin, W., Wang, K., Takase, K.: Network Distributed Multi-Functional Robotic System Supporting the Elderly and Disabled People. Journal of Intelligent and Robotic Systems 45, 53–76 (2006)
5. Aleotti, J., Caselli, S., Reggiani, M.: Leveraging on a virtual environment for robot programming by demonstration. Robotics and Autonomous Systems 47, 153–161 (2004)

6. Pires, J.N., Sa da Costa, J.M.G.: Object-oriented and distributed approach for programming robotic manufacturing cells. Robotics and Computer Integrated Manufacturing 16, 29–42 (2000)
7. Hu, X., Zeigler, B.: Model Continuity to Support Software Development for Distributed Robotic Systems: A Team Formation Example. Journal of Intelligent and Robotic Systems 39, 71–87 (2004)
8. Wooldridge, M., Jennings, N.R.: Intelligent agents: theory and practice. The Knowledge Engineering Practice 10(2), 115–152 (1995)
9. Jennings, N.R., Sycara, K., Wooldridge, M.: A Roadmap of Agent Research and Development. In: Autonomous Agents and Multi–Agent Systems, vol. 1, pp. 7–38. Kluwer Academic Publishers, Boston (1998)
10. Weiss, G. (ed.): Multiagent Systems. A Modern Approach to Distributed Artificial Intelligence. MIT Press, Cambridge (1999)
11. Knapik, M., Johnson, J.: Developing Intelligent Agent for Distributed Systems. Mc Graw–Hill, New York (1998)
12. Van Dyke Parunak, H.: A practitioners' review of industrial agent applications. Autonomous Agents and Multi-Agent Systems 3(4), 389–407 (2000)
13. Marik, V., McFarlane, D.: Industrial Adoption of Agent-Based Technologies. IEEE Intelligent Systems, 27–35 (January/February 2005)
14. Fletcher, M., Brennan, R.W., Norrie, D.H.: Modelling and reconfiguring intelligent holonic manufacturing system with Internet-based mobile agents. Journal of Intelligent Manufacturing 14, 7–23 (2003)
15. Kotak, D., Wu, S., Fleetwood, M., Tamoto, H.: Agent-based holonic design and operations environment for distributed manufacturing. Computers in Industry 52, 95–108 (2003)
16. Polaków, G., Metzger, M.: Agent-Based Approach for LabVIEW Developed Distributed Control Systems. In: Nguyen, N.T., et al. (eds.) KES-AMSTA 2007. LNCS (LNAI), vol. 4496, pp. 21–30. Springer, Heidelberg (2007)
17. Metzger, M., Polaków, G.: Holonic Multiagent-Based System for Distributed Control of Semi-industrial Pilot Plants. In: Mařík, V., Vyatkin, V., Colombo, A.W. (eds.) HoloMAS 2007. LNCS (LNAI), vol. 4659, pp. 338–347. Springer, Heidelberg (2007)
18. Choinski, D., Metzger, M., Nocon, W., Polaków, G.: Cooperative Validation in Distributed Control Systems Design. In: Luo, Y. (ed.) CDVE 2007. LNCS, vol. 4674, pp. 280–289. Springer, Heidelberg (2007)
19. Piper, C., Johnson, A.: From fieldbus to.NET: an overview of today's network-based automation technologies. Hydrocarbon Processing, 37–44 (March 2004)
20. Lian, F.-L., Moyne, J.R., Tibury, D.M.: Performance evaluation of control networks. IEEE Control System Magazine, 66–83 (February 2001)
21. Husemann, R., Pereira, C.E.: A multi-protocol real-time monitoring and validation system for distributed fieldbus-based automation applications. Control Engineering Practice 15, 955–968 (2007)
22. Skeie, T., Johannessen, S., Brunner, C.: Ethernet in Substation Automation. IEEE Control System Magazine, 43–51 (June 2002)
23. Lee, K.C., Lee, S.: Performance evaluation of switched Ethernet for real-time industrial communications. Computer Standards & Interfaces 24, 411–423 (2002)
24. Decotignie, J.-D.: Ethernet-Based Real-Time and Industrial Communications. Proceedings of the IEEE 93(6), 1102–1117 (2005)
25. Vitturi, S.: On the Use of Ethernet at Low Level of Factory Communication System. Computer Standards & Interfaces (23), 267–277 (2001)

26. Wang, J., Premvuti, S.: Resource sharing in distributed robotic systems based on a wireless medium access protocol (CSMA/CD-W). Robotics and Autonomous Systems 19, 33–56 (1996)
27. Balch, T., Arkin, R.C.: Behavior-based formation control for multirobot teams. IEEE Transactions on Robotics and Automation 14(6), 926–939 (1998)
28. Reynolds, C.W.: Flocks, Herds, And Schools: A Distributed Behavioral Model. Computer Graphics (ACM) 21(4), 25–34 (1987)
29. Fernández-Madrigal, J., Galindo, C., González, J., Cruz-Martín, E., Cruz-Martín, A.: A software engineering approach for the development of heterogeneous robotic applications. Robotics and Computer-Integrated Manufacturing 24(1), 150–166 (2008)
30. Felser, M., Sauter, T.: The Fieldbus War: History or Short Break Between Battles? In: 4th IEEE International Workshop on Factory Communication Systems, Västerås, Sweden, pp. 73–80 (2002)
31. Yang, T.C.: Networked control system: a brief survey. IEE Proceedings: Control Theory and Applications 153(4), 403–412 (2006)
32. Chávez, M.L., Thomesse, J.-P.: Fieldbuses and Real-Time Mac Protocols. IFAC Intelligent Components and Instruments for Control Applications, Buenos Aires, Argentina, 41–46 (2000)
33. Loeser, J., Haertig, H.: Low-latency Hard Real-Time Communication over Switched Ethernet. In: Proceedings of 16th Euromicro Conference on Real-Time Systems, Catania, Sicily (July 2004)

The Experimental Robotics Framework

João Xavier and Helder Araújo

Institute of Systems and Robotics - ISR, University of Coimbra, Portugal
smogzer@gmail.com, helder@isr.uc.pt

Abstract. In this article is introduced a framework for the development
of reusable software components for Human Robot Interaction (HRI): the
Experimental Robotics Framework. Normally human-robot interfaces are
discarded as they stop being useful and because of that lots of work put
into those architectures is lost. Our software plans to change that, and
provide a platform that will enable interfaces to be reused. We explain
the architecture and design rationale of the framework, and demonstrate
it with some use cases. The developed framework is available on-line with
a LGPL license.

Keywords: OpenGL, GUI, Player, fast prototyping.

1 Introduction

Most human-robot interfaces are discardable and technologically limited (2D,
static, closed source, have steep learning curves, etc) as they serve only to perform a single experiment. The software described herein plans to change that situation and provide a state-of-the-art platform - 3D, dynamic, component based,
open-source - that will enable interfaces to be reused and improved over time by
its users.

In this article we explain the architecture and design rationale of that software
- the Experimental Robotics Framework (ERF) - and demonstrate it with some
use cases. ERF is not only about reusing components, it is also a platform for
creating and exploring new paradigms of interaction; joining researchers from
different domains, even from outside the robotics world, and also from different
robotics middle-ware communities, to do their interaction experiments under a
common platform. We expect that this software will make it easier to perceive
how algorithms work by having a mix of algorithms interacting with the environment, which can create a fertile environment for creativity, learning and
serendipities. As way of measuring the adoption of the platform, the new users
already developed visualizations for the inner methods of operation of the navigation algorithm VFH and new components for visualizing point clouds.

This article is organized as follows. Section 2 presents the related work.
Section 3 describes the software platform. Experiments demonstrating the con-
cepts used in the article are in 5. Future improvements are suggested in Section 6.
Final remarks are given in Section 7.

S. Carpin et al. (Eds.): SIMPAR 2008, LNAI 5325, pp. 207–221, 2008.
© Springer-Verlag Berlin Heidelberg 2008

2   Related Work

Good practices in usability ensure the users have a good experience with the HRI. Some articles discussing and evaluating interfaces are [1,2,3,4,5,6,7,8], our work builds on features that were available on those publications. The advantages of 3D interfaces for controlling robots are discussed in [9], the obvious advantage are the natural representation in 3d of objects that makes them easier for users to recognize, and avoiding the need to cast 3d objects as 2d objects that is a common trend in multi-robot interfaces.

A taxonomy for categorizing human-robot interaction is presented in [10]. Of the models available in this taxonomy our model would be in the "one operator to multiple robots". Both [11,12] have developed 3D HRIs for interfacing of a single user to multiple robots with support for motion planning and robot trajectory generation for target tracking. Their interfacing strategy is the following: first the operator selects which robots to use, then the operator selects which objects to be acted on, and finally the operator selects a task to perform. A Graphical User Interface (GUI) to operate GPS-enabled robots is described in [13]. They raise an interesting issue: the problem of objects appearing twice if sensed by different robots. To solve it they use heuristics to avoid drawing the same object twice if observed by more than one robot. While the core ERF library avoids addressing this issue as it does not have a canonical solution, the Markov Localization module that is part of PlayerViewer3D chooses as the robot reference frame the most likely particle from the particle filter set to represent the robot localization and disambiguate the robot pose. The previous three references use the OpenGL User Interface library (GLUI) for widgets and the OpenGL C++ Toolkit(GLT) for loading textures and object interaction or "picking". In ERF we use the Fast-Light Toolkit (FLTK) for widgets and implement our own procedures for 3d model and texture loading. In [14] are studied the conditions under which the collaborative human involvement in shared HRI will not jeopardize scalability of a network of robots. In our work this issue is not handled as we consider that it is a concern of the underlying sensor layer, that in our case is Player [15].

At present the modalities supported by ERF are mouse and keys, and Finite Stage Grammar (FSG) based ones - like speech or text. Other GUI solutions that also use multi-modality appeared on the fields of teaching [16] and alternative interfaces for the handicapped people [17].

Other fields that use HRI are the ones of Virtual Reality (VR) and Augmented Reality (AR). Multi-robots tele-operation using an intermediate functional representation of the real remote world by means of VR are present in [18,19,20,21,22] A VR-based operator interface was developed by NASA in [23] to remotely control complex robotic mechanisms. The authors concluded that VR interfaces can improve the operator situational awareness and provide valuable tools to help understand and analyze the vehicle surroundings, and plan command sequences.

Ar-Dev [24] is an AR application that superimpose graphics of a robot sensor readings over a real-world environment in real-time. Due to the modality of ERF a tool like Ar-Dev is possible to build using ERF, since it is possible to choose the order by which drawing happens, rendering the camera captured texture first and then superimposing the robots.

3   Overview of the Software Architecture

ERF provides a shared library that contains a collection of useful C++ classes (depicted in Fig.1) that enables the user to compose HRI applications by gluing components together. A composed HRI application is defined in a XML configuration which states what components get loaded into the framework. A full picture of the layout of the working system is displayed in Fig.2.

Next are described some important functionality blocks of our platform.

3.1   The Managers

These entities are responsible for the bookkeeping of the structures they manage. They use reference counting techniques so that duplicating instances are avoided whenever possible to ensure a frugal resource management. Examples of this is the sharing of access to a Player proxy by more than one plugin, or the reuse of a single OpenGL display list to draw the same object by multiple components. All Managers can be created as singletons, which is a software design pattern that assures they are unique and have lazy initiation (are only instantiated once, in the first time they are called).

3.2   Multiple Robot Interfacing

Multiple robot interfacing is the ability to tele-operate one or more robots (which are Player Clients) from a single HRI instance. This feature raises a synchronicity issue: when to check for new data on every remote robot without wasting precious CPU cycles ? The obvious solution would be to run all clients on a single thread and each time check for new data on each proxy, on each client. Experience demonstrated that this solution does not extend computationally to more than

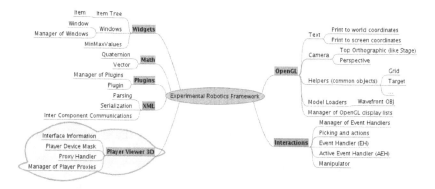

Fig. 1. A mind-map of the hierarchy of classes in ERF

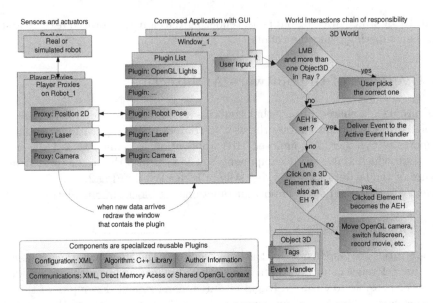

Fig. 2. Layout of a composite application of ERF and the user interaction chain of responsibility (on the right)

3 robots, so a solution that extends to more robots was devised. This solution is to make each Player Client run on its own thread and each client signals the application whenever they have new data on one of its proxies. The application can then proceed to use the new acquired data to redraw the world.

3.3   Multiple Windows Display

ERF can have each component draw its data on separate windows or combine them in a single window. A common setup is to have a world window where everything is displayed, and separate windows for video cameras. From the programmer point of view, the window is a container of components. In order to draw the world, the components are visited sequentially and each draws the data from their sensors.

When accessing multiple sensors from multiple robots the data is produced at very fast rates. This drawing operation would add up cause the blocking of the system. This problem makes it far from optimal to draw asynchronously, i.e. every time that new data arrives. To address this problem the drawing of the windows is done synchronously, at fixed intervals and only if there is new data to display. This interval by default is $0.10s$ but it can be modified by the user, the option of redrawing when the CPU is idle is also available, and the window also redraws whenever there is user input that changes the state of the world.

3.4   Inter-component Messaging

In order to remove code redundancies the components are specialized in certain tasks e.g. the manager of zones that comprises all the methods that can be applied to polygonal zones. Components can query one another for information or to execute some method. The queries are XML formatted data, normally in the form of a question. This message is passed through all components with the matching ID or library name until a positive reply ($error = 0$) is reported. The components reply to queries with both a XML message and an error message - that reports problems ($error < 0$), no problems ($error = 0$), or a component reserved report message ($error > 0$).

By using the XML API for messaging and for parsing configuration files we keep the overall simplicity of the framework API. The XML communication approach is adequate for rapid prototyping and communication of small structures, but it is not appropriate for large data sets, like big matrices such as images, which are better exchanged either sharing the textures in the OpenGL contexts or accessing the memory of other components directly. Direct memory access if achieved by querying the manager of plugins for the required plugin and then casting the plugin to the C++ Class that implements the interface that has the data and methods that we want to access.

3.5 Awareness and Contexts in ERF

Awareness means to know something or to be aware of a danger. There are two kinds of awareness that ERF provides, the situational and the spatial. Situational awareness is important for robots to identify that a certain event is taking place, normally based on the robot sensor data. An example of this is a person entering the laser range and being tagged as "person", which will signal a spatial event. Spatial awareness is important to identify certain places, like an elevator or dangerous zones, like stairs. ERF makes this knowledge of the world available for all the robots so they can cooperate in high level tasks.

Due to the dynamical nature of ERF it is possible to load new components into the framework or send XML messages between components when awareness events take place.

A concept that is fundamental for modelling and implementing awareness is tagging. Tags are the way world entities are identified so robot components identify and use them. Components can query or monitor the Manager of Objects for the existence of an Object3D with specific tags - e.g. "is there any person ?" - and further take actions on the Object3D, e.g. follow the "person".

3.6 Component System

Components extend the functionality of the application and are identified by their library name which specifies the type of component and by an id field defined in the XML configuration, which specifies the unique key that the component can be refered to during runtime. As there is a clear and simple interface for the services that each component implements, the development is possible without the need to read and understand the source of the rest of the composite application. Components are provided with default configurations so that they can run out of the box, imposing a minimal need to know their parameters.

When the application finalizes, the component states can be serialized again to the configuration file. Components are free to do anything, like adding widgets to the HRI, adding new entities to the world, communicating with the Player server, accessing other component data, etc. From the point of view of the developer, components inherits from the base Plugin C++ class. Other abilities, like XML messaging or serialization (saved) also need to be inherited from other base classes.

The component class can also contain extra information provided by the author: the author e-mail, the web-page and a description of the component.

During the component lifetime the following methods are called if they are implemented:

1. initialize - is called after the windows are shown and OpenGL contexts are created.
2. run - is called at each iteration, the method will draw or process data.
3. clean - is called just before the component is removed from the framework.

3.7 Serialization

Serialization is the process of writing data structures to XML so that they can be saved to disk or across the network, this procedure allows for the data structures can be restored again in other initializations. Serialization is implemented by converting the C++ data to XML and back to C++ by defining correspondences between the C++ data types and the XML data. The Serialization structure is also used to convert data to XML so that it can be communicated between components.

3.8 Multi-modality Interaction

The inputs ERF supports are distincted by those that need to be converted to finite state grammars (FSG) and those who do not. Speech recognition, text input either scripted or interactive, are in the class of FSG, while the GUI and key-combinations do not need to be convert to FSG. All components that must make use of one of these kind of inputs must implement the rational of the interactions in their code.

3.9 GUI Interaction with the 3D World

The GUI interaction involves two entities, the Event Handler(EH), and the Object3D. The Event Handler is a entity that can intercept the chain of input events in order to execute methods. An Object3D is an entity in the world that is clickable, and that can be an EH.

To make any C++ class an EH the developer only has to inherit from the EH virtual base class. Then when it becomes the AEH (normally because a user clicked it when no other AEH was active) the input of the user are then redirected to the AEH. From the information of the user input - keyboard or mouse - the AEH

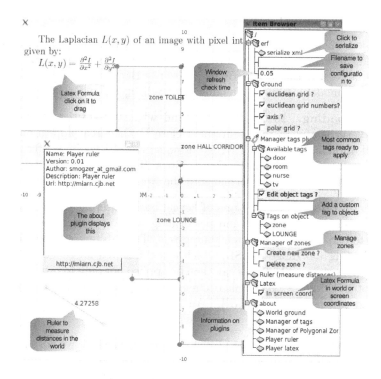

Fig. 3. Some generic components. On the right is the item tree that displays possible actions and data of the components. Of particular interest is the possibility of showing Latex formulas with the transparent background.

can decide what actions to take. The `AEH` knows the type of `Object3D` clicked by looking at its `Tags`, which can be either be attributes, names, etc.

An example of an interaction using the mouse is: pressing the Left Mouse Button (LMB) to select a robot - which is both an `Object3D` and `EH` - making him the `Active Event Handler` (AEH) and then clicking on a person - that is just an `Object3D` - delivers the event to the robot because the robot is the AEH. The robot EH can then display a pop-up with the options of actions that the robot can perform on the clicked person. A simplified explanation of how interaction is processed is demonstrated as the chain of responsibility represented in the rightmost diagram of Fig.2.

3.10 Item Tree

The item tree shows a hierarchical tree of FLTK item, that represent the loaded components, like the one depicted in Fig.3. The branches of the tree are the components and the leafs are their services and data. By clicking in each service, a callback can be executed that performs an action, e.g. showing a pop-up sub-menu of the component or give instructions to a robot.

3.11   Simplified OpenGL

Some complex OpenGL tasks are made simpler using ERF, like selecting objects in the world, drawing text and working with textures, applying GLSL shaders to textures, accessing the Frame Buffer Object (FBO) extension for rendering to textures, 3d model loading, managing display lists, moving a camera, etc.

3D Model Loading. To better understand what the entities in the robot world it is very helpful to represent them close to their real appearance. The pragmatical approach offered in ERF is to model the objects in a software that is appropriate for 3D modelling such as Wings 3D [25] and load an exported modeled model in the .obj [26] format into the world.

GPU Kernel Filters. The process of kernel based filtering consists of going through each pixel on an image and performing some operation on that pixel that is related to the values of neighbor pixels. These filters are coded in the OpenGL Shading Language (GLSL) which is a C inspired language specialized for graphics processing. The filters can then be applied not only to bitmap images but to robot world maps (grayscale occupancy grids), as they can be casted as textures and processed on the GPU. An API for loading GLSL kernels and applying those kernels to textures is provided.

Camera. The camera was idealized for mobile robotics, where we normally view from the top to give commands and move around the world. The camera has two view modes: a top orthographic mode and a perspective projection mode.

The center of the screen is common to both views, this means that if the user moves the scene center while in top view, and then switches to perspective view, the center of the screen in perspective view is updated to the top view center. The rationale is that the user uses the top view to navigate quickly around the world and switches to the perspective view to have a better understanding of what is in the center of the view, and rotate around it.

4   ERF Configuration Files

Configuration files define which components are loaded into the framework and their initial parameters. Composing interactions has two major steps: 1) writing the configuration files that describe the HRI composed application, and 2) launching the application composer that will glue all the components specified in the configuration file.

In order to expand our platform so that software developed by third parties can expand the framework itself (not the components) it is required that those extensions inform the ERF XML parser how to parse their unique XML entities.

This is accomplished with a "addParser" xml element on top of the configuration file. An example of this is the Player Viewer 3d (PV3D) that informs the XML parser how to parse elements like the "handlers" element. When PV3D starts it will load a set of plugins from the XML configuration file and associate them with Player proxies in order to create the final composite application.

To launch ERF the user has to specify one or more configuration files like:

```
$ erf ground.erf.xml laser.pv3d.xml sonar.pv3d.xml
```

There are two combinable approaches to write a PV3D configuration file: in the first approach the user specifies what plugins are loaded and precisely what Player Devices they will use; in the second approach the user provides device handlers. The Device Handlers are masks of Player Devices that will establish correspondence between a range of Player Devices and PV3D plugins. This latter technique works by specifying a mask using the syntax of a Player device, with the addition of wild-cards in place of the driver name or interface index; for selection of multiple devices - e.g. `laser:sicklms200:*` which means all the devices with a laser interface, a specific driver called sicklms200 and all possible indexes. The plugins associated with the handler will be loaded if any devices with that description are found; then the plugin information is added to a final XML configuration file with all the plugins that are going to be loaded. This concept is useful for example to load plugins for a simulator world full of robots. In Fig. 4 is shown a typical configuration file with handlers; the handler for the laser device is further exposed in Fig. 5.

```
<erf XMLns:pv3d="http://miarn.sf.net"
 XMLns:xi="http://www.w3.org/2001/XInclude">
<plugin library="libpv3d_glob" id="pv3d">
  <playerClient host="localhost" port="6665"/>
    <playerDeviceMask interface="laser">
      <xi:include href="laser.pv3d.XML"/>
    </playerDeviceMask>
</plugin>
<plugin library="libpv3d_lights"/>
<plugin library="libpv3d_ground"/>
</erf>
```

Fig. 4. A XML file describing the a composite application in the PV3D component

```
<plugin library="libpv3d_laser" id="laser">
  <playerDeviceMask host="localhost" port="6665"
   interface="laser" index="0"/>
  <parentNode interface="position2d" index="0"/>
  <fillLaserCspace>1</fillLaserCspace>
  <drawLaserCspace>1</drawLaserCspace>-->
  <skinFile>skins/laser_sick.obj</skinFile>
</plugin>
```

Fig. 5. A XML file describing the visualization of a laser, notice that when called from inside an handler the playerDeviceMask is replaced by the found device information

The handler approach can still not be enough for specific experiments, so another option is to make the program output a XML configuration file generated by the handlers. The user can then further customize this configuration file for his needs.

ERF avoids the need for users to remember the syntax of configuration files by providing relax-ng schemas for each individual component type. This way the user can use real-time auto-completion and validation using the Emacs editor in the nXml mode. An example of this feature is provided in a video on the MIARN site [27].

5   Examples of Composite Applications

This section demonstrates the composing of applications from distinct fields in robotics. The examples are the following: a) Scene perception; b) Multi-robot tele-operation; c) Mixing a real and a simulated world; d) Simulation of a camera projection; e) Sparse 3D reconstruction visualization; f) kernel filters in GLSL applied to images.

5.1   Example of Scene Perception

This example consists of representing the perception that a robot has of the world, which is depicted in Fig.6.a. This task requires the visualization of a laser device, and two scene interpretation components, one for people detection and another for geometric features. Both scene interpretation components use the Player Fiducial devices, that communicate the data of the fiducials to the visualization component. These Player Scene Interpretation plugins for Player were also developed by the author of this article, in a previous project [28] and are also on-line. Due to the reusable nature of the ERF framework the components of this example can be combined with others, like the tele-operation one, which would allow the robots to navigate while perceiving the scene.

5.2   Example of Tele-Operation

In this example the HRI accesses three mobile robots in the Stage simulator (it could also have been in the real world), it is depicted in Fig.6.b. Each robot has either a laser or a sonar sensor on top. Two robots have 3D models, the Nomad and the Robchair (a robotic wheelchair); the third robot only shows the geometry of the robot that is also its collision envelope. Note in this example the widget for position control, which can establish limits to the velocities of the robot and a joystick like interface to the robot, which is a customized FLTK [29] widget. The position component also provides a `Event Handler` for controlling the robot in the world, in the form of a target. By dragging the target over the "ground" `Object3D` it is possible to give a way-point for the robot to navigate to (in position mode) or interface with the velocities of the robot in a joystick like style (in velocity mode).

5.3   Example of Mixing a Real and a Simulated World

Hardware-in-the-loop and human-in-the-loop are two possibilities for experimenting and debugging systems that are possible by accessing either real or simulated devices and combining them together under the same interface. This is demonstrated in Fig.6.c where a real-world camera is operating in a simulation environment.

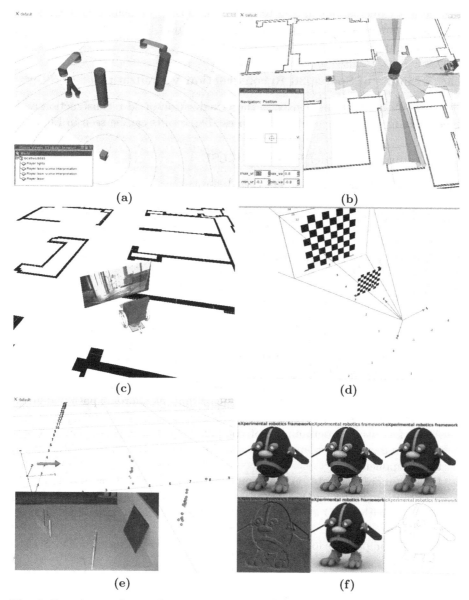

Fig. 6. Experiments from different robotics domains: a) Scene interpretation from laser data, b) multi-robot tele-operation, c) mixing simulation and a real camera; d) a simulation of a camera, e) sparse 3d reconstruction, f) a tile of different kernels implemented in GLSL

5.4   Example of Simulating a Camera Projection

In computer vision experiments is hard to work in ideal conditions as cameras have distortion and are expensive. Simulation offers the advantage of working with perfect cameras, not having to deal with noise. In OpenGL is possible to render the content of a camera to a frame-buffer object (FBO). This FBO result can then be applied to a texture as seen in Fig.6.d.

5.5 Example of Sparse 3d Reconstruction Visualization

This example serves to demonstrate the visualization of 3d reconstruction and camera ego-motion from sparse 2d features. The results can be seen in Fig.6.e.

5.6 Example of Kernel Filters in GLSL

The result of application of different kernels implemented as GLSL filters to ERF logo are depicted in Fig.6.f . The filters were applied individually, screenshots were of them taken and the resulting mosaic was composed.

6   Future Improvements

The future improvements are:

- Create a component to draw and manipulate bezier curves in OpenGL (useful for robot path planning).
- Create a component that is a run-time component editor, a loader and can change the order the components are visited.
- Explore the potential of the GPU in mobile robotics applications that use grid maps. To explore the potential of algorithms like Voronoi path planning, Vector Field Histogram, etc.
- Allow for visual programming of components, like connecting outputs to inputs in a graphical manner, this will need some sort of introspection from the components.
- Develop more computer vision components and interfaces for exploring the possibilities offered by OpenCV.
- Integrate with the Open Dynamics Engine (ODE) for starting a robot simulator based on ERF.
- Develop components for integration with a cognitive platform such as SOAR [30].

7   Conclusion and Contributions

In this work is contributed an Open Source freely available framework for developing Human Robot Interfaces - the Experimental Robotics Framework (ERF). ERF provides a common framework where a community of researchers can share common interfaces and algorithms. Because the component paradigm is simple to understand and very expandable the chance their work gets exposed and continued by others is greater.

The main features of ERF are:

1. It is very adaptable to the user needs, it supports : Multi-robot, multi-context, multi-modal, multi-windows.
2. It is the start of a full featured package for computer vision using the GPU and the CPU with interaction and scene interpretation.
3. The approach to graphical user interfacing is abstracted in a way that is very easy to the developers to create interactions with the entities of the world.
4. In the classroom this software can encourage learning due to its interactivity, graphics, ease of use and Latex formula display, which can even be used to present algorithms in an interactive way.
5. Provides a wide selection of components, that can also be used as templates for devising new ones. The components range from generic ones to computer vision, to mobile robotics;
6. World awareness is also modeled so that the framework can react to world events by signaling components that spatial of situational events are taking place and have the components react to these events.

With the availability of this framework for free on the Internet the process of designing 3D interactive GUIs for robotics related sciences is now much more accessible to everybody. The developed software is having wide acceptance and good feedback by the Player robotics community. Because the developed software is updated on a regular basis the reader is invited to visit the site [27] for an updated version.

Acknowledgments

This work is supported by the European Commission grant FP6-IST-2004-027268 attributed to the POP project.

References

1. Steinfeld, A.: Interface lessons for fully and semi-autonomous mobile robots. In: IEEE Conference on Robotics and Automation (2004),
   `citeseer.ist.psu.edu/steinfeld04interface.html`
2. Steinfeld, A.M., Fong, T.W., Kaber, D., Lewis, M., Scholtz, J., Schultz, A., Goodrich, M.: Common metrics for human-robot interaction. In: Human-Robot Interaction Conference. ACM Press, New York (2006)
3. Scholtz, J., Antonishek, B., Young, J.: Evaluation of a human-robot interface: Development of a situational awareness methodology. In: International Conference on System Sciences (HICSS), vol. 05 (2004)
4. McDonald, M.J.: Active research topics in human machine interfaces. Intelligent Systems and Robotics Center Sandia National Laboratories, Tech. Rep. (2000)
5. Lakshmi, S.S.: Graphical user interfaces for mobile robots. University of Kansas, Tech. Rep. (2002), `citeseer.ist.psu.edu/612670.html`
6. Persson, A.: Multi-robot operator interface for rescue operations. Master's thesis, Orebro University (2005)

7. Fong, T.W., Thorpe, C.: Vehicle teleoperation interfaces. Autonomous Robots 11(1), 9–18 (2001), citeseer.ist.psu.edu/fong01vehicle.html
8. Song, D.: Systems and algorithms for collaborative teleoperation. Ph.D. dissertation, Department of Industrial Engineering and Operations Research, University of California, Berkeley (2004)
9. Lin, I.-S., Wallner, F., Dillmann, R.: Interactive control and environment modelling for a mobile robot based on multisensor perceptions. Robotics and Autonomous Systems 18(3), 301–310 (1996)
10. Yanco, H.A., Drury, J.: Classifying human-robot interaction: An updated taxonomy. In: IEEE Conference on Systems, Man and Cybernetics (October 2004), www.cs.uml.edu/~holly/papers/
11. Clark, C., Frew, E.: An integrated system for command and control of cooperative robotic systems. In: 11th International Conference on Advanced Robotics, Coimbra, Portugal (June 2003)
12. Jones, H., Hinds, P.: Extreme work groups: Using swat teams as a model for coordinating distributed robots. In: Conference on Computer Supported Cooperative Work (November 2002)
13. Jones, M.S.H.: Operating gps-enabled robots with an opengl gui. Dr. Dobb's Journal, 16–24 (January 2003)
14. Makarenko, A., Kaupp, T., Grocholsky, B., Durrant-Whyte, H.: Human-robot interactions in active sensor networks. In: IEEE International Symposium on Computational Intelligence in Robotics and Automation (CIRA 2003), Kobe, Japan, July 2003, pp. 247–252 (2003)
15. Gerkey, B., Vaughan, R.T., Howard, A.: The player/stage project: Tools for multi-robot and distributed sensor systems. In: Proc. 11th International Conference on Advanced Robotics, Coimbra, Portugal, pp. 317–323 (2003), playerstage.sf.net
16. Ishii, H.S.M.: A step toward a human-robot cooperative system. Artificial Life and Robotics (1997)
17. Xu, H., Brussel, H.V., Moreas, R.: Designing a user interface for service operations of an intelligent mobile manipulator. Telemanipulator and Telepresence Technologies IV 3206(1), 12–21 (1997)
18. Kheddar, A., Coiffet, P., Kotoku, T., Tanie, K.: Multi-robots teleoperation - analysis and prognosis. In: 6th IEEE Int. Workshop on Robot and Human Communication, IROS, Sendai, Japan, September 1997, pp. 166–171 (1997), citeseer.ist.psu.edu/kheddar97multirobots.html
19. Kheddar, A., Fontaine, J., Coiffet, P.: Mobile robot teleoperation in virtual reality. In: IEEE IMACS CESA 1998, Nabeul-Hammamet, Tunisie (April 1998), citeseer.ist.psu.edu/kheddar98mobile.html
20. Aucoin, N., Sandbekkhaug, O., Jenkin, M.: Immersive 3d user interface for mobile robot control. In: Proc. IASTED Int. Conf. on Applications of Control and Robotics, Orlando, pp. 1–4 (1996), citeseer.ist.psu.edu/379953.html
21. Stuart, R.E.K., Chapman, G.: Interactive visualization for sensor-based robotic programming. In: Systems, Man, and Cybernetics, vol. 12(15), pp. 761–766 (1997)
22. Michael Schmitt, F.: Virtual reality-based navigation of a mobile robot. In: 7th IFAC / IFIP / IFORS / IEA Symposium on Analysis, Design and Evaluation of Man-Machine Systems, pp. 377–382 (1999)
23. Nguyen, L., Bualat, M.: Virtual reality interfaces for visualization and control of remote vehicles. In: IEEE Conference on Robotics and Automation (2002)
24. Collett, T., MacDonald, B.: Augmented reality visualisation for player. In: ICRA, Orlando CA (2006), www.ece.auckland.ac.nz/~robot

25. Wings 3d modeller, `http://wings3d.org`
26. Wavefront obj format, `csit.fsu.edu/~burkardt/data/obj/obj_format.txt`
27. Modules for intelligent autonomous robot navigation, `miarn.sf.net`
28. Xavier, J., Pacheco, M., Castro, D., Ruano, A., Nunes, U.: Fast line arc/circle and leg detection from laser scan data in a player driver. In: Proc. IEEE Int. Conf. on Robotics and Automation, Barcelona (2005)
29. The fast light toolkit, `fltk.org`
30. Laird, J.E., Newell, A., Rosenbloom, P.S.: Soar: an architecture for general intelligence. Artif. Intell. 33(1), 1–64 (1987),
    `http://portal.acm.org/citation.cfm?id=27702`

Where Am I? A Simulated GPS Sensor for Outdoor Robotic Applications

Benjamin Balaguer and Stefano Carpin

School of Engineering
University of California Merced
5200 North Lake Road, Merced CA 95343, USA
{bbalaguer,scarpin}@ucmerced.edu

Abstract. Advances in the field of robotic simulations in general and the complexity of virtual outdoor environments in particular have created a demand for accurate simulated open-air localization devices. In this paper, we answer this request by presenting the implementation of a simulated Global Positioning System receiver for the popular USARSim platform. The engineering tradeoff of speed versus accuracy is encountered throughout the design process and discussed comprehensively in the paper. Along the lines of a validation methodology we developed in recent years, the simulated sensor is implemented and extensively analyzed in a real/simulated scenario, where data logged from a real robot is evaluated against the data acquired in simulation.

1 Introduction

With the continuously growing focus on multi-robot cooperation and improvements in computer hardware, algorithmic techniques, and computer animation, robotic simulators are gaining momentum within the robotics community. Indeed, robotic simulators are now capable of simulating multiple blocks of an outdoor urban environment, comprised of a multitude of robots, victims, fires, collapsed structures, rivers, bridges, and more [1]. The typical assortment of sensors for robots operating in similar real world environments more and more often includes a Global Positioning System (GPS) receiver in order to ease the localization task. Henceforth, in order to create a faithful simulation environment, we designed a simulated GPS sensor that is, to the best of our knowledge, the first of its kind in comparable simulation systems. In fact, our goal is not to merely convert Cartesian coordinates into latitude and longitude components, but rather produce a realistic sensor that exhibits the same properties of current GPS receivers.

Even though the paper's aim is to provide a standard methodology for the construction of a simulated GPS sensor for outdoor robotic applications, we implemented our framework inside the Unified System for Automation and Robot Simulation (USARSim)[1]. USARSim has become a popular real-time three

---

[1] This system was formerly known as Urban Search and Rescue Simulator. The name change reflects the much broader applicability it gained through the years.

S. Carpin et al. (Eds.): SIMPAR 2008, LNAI 5325, pp. 222–233, 2008.

dimensional simulator thanks to widespread validation effort from the community [2][3][4] and its utilization in the yearly RoboCup Rescue Simulation League [5][6]. USARSim is an open-source extension to the Unreal Tournament (UT) game engine that, consequently, only requires a modestly priced UT license. The game engine takes care of rendering scenes and computing physics while UnrealScript, an object-oriented programming language similar to C++, allows for the addition and modification of actors (e.g. robots, actuators, sensors) in the simulation. Since the sensor's implementation will exclusively be performed in UnrealScript, it is important to keep some of its drawbacks in mind; namely its slow computational speed and lack of floating point number precision.

This paper builds upon a validation methodology we developed for USARSim in the past and that has proved to be highly effective in order to close the loop between simulation and reality. In short, our approach consists in performing the same experiment in simulation and with the real world system, and to quantitatively compare the results. This effort may sometimes be costly, because it entails developing accurate models of the robotic systems at hand, but it has proved to be a formidable tool in order to assess which conclusions can be extrapolated from simulation to reality and which ones do not generalize. Part of the USARSim success draws from the abundance of these validation efforts, and this paper, besides illustrating the technical details of GPS simulation, can be read as a working example of the robot simulators validation process we advocate.

2   Methodology and Implementation

2.1   Satellite Tracking

Since a real GPS module receives signals from satellites, the first cornerstone to simulate a GPS receiver is to establish a relationship between the GPS sensor and the orbiting satellites. The most realistic method to establish this relationship is by tracking GPS satellites. The three governing North American aerospace institutions, namely the National Aeronautics and Space Administration (NASA), the North American Aerospace Defense Command (NORAD), and the Air Force Space Command (AFSPC), collectively promote the usage of the Simplified General Perturbations Satellite Orbit Model 4 (SGP4) for satellite tracking, the details of which are found in [7]. In fact, the SGP4 algorithm has gained a strong reputation among amateurs and professionals and quickly became the standard satellite tracking model, resulting in sustained research and constant improvements [8][9].

While the details of SGP4, which can be found in the referenced publications, are beyond the scope of this paper, we will provide a very brief and high-level description of the orbital model. The algorithm takes as input a NASA/NORAD Two-Line Element (TLE) [10], a date, and a time and outputs the location of the satellite defined by the TLE at the given date and time. Real-time satellite tracking can consequently be achieved by continuously running SGP4 with the current date and time. The TLE format, a sample of which is given in Figure 1,

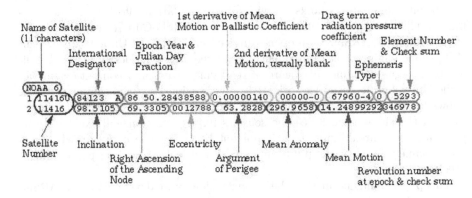

Fig. 1. Sample TLE File with Format Descriptions (modified from [10])

provides the orbital information necessary to reconstruct the orbit of a satellite (see Figure 2) that can then be used to approximate the satellite's location. The SGP4 algorithm parses the TLE data and calculates the satellite's orbital state vectors, the result of which is usually expressed as latitude, longitude, and altitude components. Manifestly, the precision of SGP4 is strongly correlated to the accuracy of the TLE data. To that effect, the AFSPC publishes and maintains a database of TLE files available to approved users on the space track website [11].

Even though there already exists a plethora of satellite trackers implemented with SGP4, available both as online visualization tools [12][13] and comprehensive software suites [14][15][16], we constrained our search to user-friendly, reusable, open-source, and lightweight systems since we were, originally, looking to port the code to UnrealScript. After experimenting with a multitude of implementations and choosing GLSat [17], we realized that translating the code to

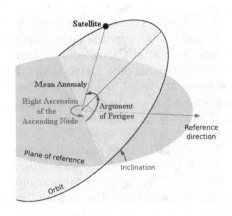

Fig. 2. Reconstructing a Satellite Orbit from a TLE-File

UnrealScript was impossible due to poor floating point precision. Indeed, the UT engine is only capable of keeping track of seven decimal places, rendering live satellite tracking inaccurate. In addition, the amount of time spent calculating satellite positions took too much time away from other simulated components.

We circumvented the aforementioned problem by switching to an offline approach for satellite tracking. More specifically, we modified the GLSat program to take in the following parameters: a TLE file comprised of one or more satellite, a date, a time, and the amount of time during which satellite positions should be tracked. The program then computes all the satellite positions, starting from the given date and time, over the time interval with a pre-defined time step, and creates a configuration file that can be read by UnrealScript. The configuration file is then read-in and stored in appropriate data structures when the simulation starts, effectively yielding a lookup table of satellite positions, based on time. Even though this method requires greater user interaction and does not reflect real satellite positions for large time steps, it alleviates computational burden - a primordial aspect of robotic simulations. It is worthwhile noting that this approach allows flexible researchers to use any configuration file (for applications where it does not matter if satellite positions do not reflect the current date and time), while more stringent researchers can go through the process of generating their own configuration files (for applications requiring the proper satellite positions for a given time interval). The reader should observe that in order to render faithful simulation, the system we have developed does not perform a generic simulation of a GPS, but rather offers the possibility to locate the simulation in time, i.e. it extracts the position of the GPS satellites at a given point in time. In this way the correlation between simulation and real world systems becomes more binding.

2.2   Signal and Noise Model

With the simulation now capable of determining the satellites' location, we introduce signal and noise models. Real GPS receiver precision depends on the number of satellite signals received by the unit (i.e. the more satellites seen by the receiver, the better the accuracy of the location) as well as the geometric arrangement of the satellites (i.e. the dilution of precision) [18]. For the purpose of this paper and due to the additional computational burden of integrating dilution of precision calculations, we solely base our noise model on the number of satellite signals received by the GPS receiver. Consequently, the first step in our model is to determine the number of satellites observed by the simulated GPS sensor; a two-step process. First, the angle of elevation between the current sensor location and each satellite position is calculated. Any satellite yielding an elevation angle less than five degrees is discarded. The process eliminates all the satellites that would require sending a signal through the earth's surface (i.e. negative elevations) as well as the satellites that are too low to consider (i.e. elevations between zero and five degrees). Eliminating satellites based on their elevation, through a set of straightforward equations, is of foremost importance to guarantee that the next elimination process is computationally friendly.

Second, ray tracing is performed from the GPS receiver to each of the satellites' location to further eliminate some of the observed satellites. If the ray trace hits an environment entity (e.g. buildings, vehicles) on its way to a satellite then that satellite is discarded, otherwise it becomes one of the satellites seen by the GPS sensor. Ray tracing being a computational burden [19], the first elimination process assures that it will not be used needlessly. The proposed line-of-sight signal model provides a very crude approximation, but modeling realistic signal strength taking into account possible deflections would surely result in an intractable scenario.

As previously discussed, the amount of noise in a GPS sensor measurement needs to be proportional to the number of satellites available. We, once again, favor a computationally-friendly modular approach that allows researchers to effortlessly change the noise function as they see fit. Indeed, the currently implemented noise function, described below, can be swapped by another; thus allowing improvements or specific noise functions emulating different GPS receivers. Since experiments have shown GPS noise to have Gaussian distribution [18], we exploit the Box-Muller method [20] to generate Gaussian-distributed random numbers. More specifically, we use two configuration variables to dictate the maximum and minimum amount of localization error, in meters, when four and twelve satellites are available to the sensor, respectively. The reader shoud note that four is the minimum number of satellites required for a GPS fix, while twelve is habitually the maximum. The two configuration variables are especially important for users looking to effortlessly simulate different GPS receivers without having to change code or recompile the simulation environment. For example, both Wide Area Augmentation System (WAAS) capable and WAAS-incapable GPS receivers can be simulated by simply modifying the parameters.

Mathematically, the two configuration variables give the sensor two points on a curve with respect to the number of satellites observed. Our noise function linearly interpolates between those two points to create a function of error, in slope-intercept form, based on the number of satellites seen. First, the slope, m, of the linear function is calculated, using the two configuration variables maxNoise and minNoise as shown:

$$m = \left(\frac{\text{maxNoise} - \text{minNoise}}{4 - 12} \right). \tag{1}$$

Then, the y-intercept, b, of the linear function is derived using the slope:

$$b = \text{maxNoise} - (4 * m). \tag{2}$$

Finally, Equation 3 calculates a standard deviation, σ, for the Gaussian number generator by using the current number of satellite seen by the simulated GPS sensor. More specifically, the Gaussian random number generator is used with a mean of zero and a standard deviation of a third of the maximum noise, guaranteeing that, in 99.7% of the cases, the error produced will be within plus or minus of the maximum error.

$$\sigma = \left(\frac{m * \text{SatelliteSeen} + b}{3} \right) \tag{3}$$

Even though the proposed method might seem simplistic, it is efficient to compute and provides very good results, as will be described in the experimental section of the paper.

2.3   Implementation Details

The satellite tracker, along with the signal and noise models, encompasses the majority of the simulated GPS methodology but leaves a few open issues. One of the main dilemmas when using a GPS sensor in virtual environments is the mapping of a virtual location to a real one. Since many virtual worlds do not inherently possess latitude and longitude coordinates, we propose and have implemented three different methods to allocate a GPS coordinate to a virtual world, each with different levels of precedence. First, world developers can add a specially-created tag when building the virtual environment and modify its properties to reflect the desired latitude and longitude coordinates. The placement of the tag will define a reference GPS coordinate that can be used to determine the latitude and longitude of any point on the map. Second, configuration variables can be set inside the USARSim initialization file to provide the reference GPS coordinate of the (0,0) Cartesian coordinate in the virtual world. Third, the GPS sensor class can be modified to link the (0,0) Cartesian coordinate with a GPS coordinate. All of these methods solve the same problem and have been added for user-friendliness and backward compatibility with old virtual environments.

Once the amount of noise, in meters, has been established using the aforementioned techniques, latitudinal and longitudinal components have to be calculated and returned by the sensor - calculations that require a couple of assumptions. The first, aimed at lowering computationally intensive instructions, assumes a flat earth and, consequently, provides a straightforward translation between distance and degrees, using the surface distance per degree change conversion. In other words, under the flat-earth assumption, a one degree change corresponds to a specific change in distance, allowing conversions from meters to degrees. The second assumption involves the global coordinate frame of the virtual world. We assume that all X-axis motion is converted to latitude and that all Y-axis motion is converted to longitude. While, in most cases, the global X-axis points to the North, it is worthwhile noting that this is not always the case due to singularities that may occur. Indeed, as shown in Figure 3, the sensor handles singularities that occur at the earth's poles (at 90 degree North and 90 degree South) and on the longitude (at 180 degree West and 180 degree East). In other words, and as an example, driving along the X-axis at 89 degrees and 59.9 minutes will increase the latitude component of the GPS until 90 degree North is reached. At that point, the latitude component will decrease (meaning that the global X-Axis now points to the south). These singularities exist and are taken into account due to the flat nature of virtual worlds and the spherical shape of the earth.

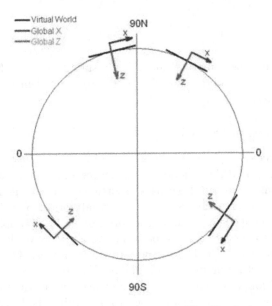

Fig. 3. Singularity Representation with Flat-Earth Assumption

3 Experimental Results

We conducted a set of experiments aimed at validating the simulated GPS sensor by using a real/virtual testbed similar to [21]. More specifically, we teleoperate a real P3AT robot, equipped with a Holux M1000 GPS receiver, at various

Fig. 4. Picture of the real P3AT (left) next to a screenshot of the simulated P3AT (right) in the experimental environment

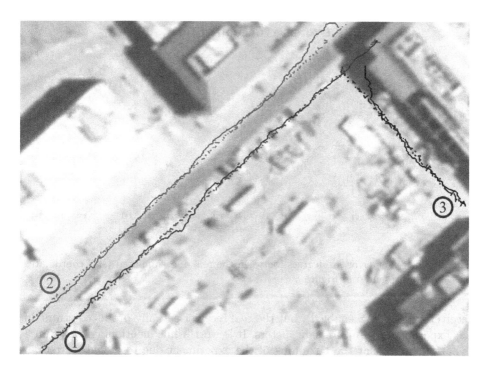

Fig. 5. Plot of GPS latitude and longitude coordinates in Google Earth for three different runs. Each run is labeled from 1 to 3 and comprised of two paths. The solid line indicates the path of the real robot whereas the dotted line shows the path of the simulated robot. Run 1 was performed from North-East to South-West, Run 2 was performed from South-West to North-East, and Run 3 was performed from North-West to South-East.

distances from buildings outside the University of California, Merced quad. During each run, lasting between two and ten minutes, data comprised of the latitude, longitude, and number of satellites observed by the receiver is logged to a file. To facilitate the correspondence between the real and simulated robot motions, we limited our experiments to straight paths, thus decreasing time-dependent mechanical differences between the robots. Once the runs were performed using the real robot, they were replicated in simulation, in real-time, with the extensively-utilized USARSim P3AT, equipped with the simulated GPS sensor. A simplified virtual representation of the UC Merced quad was built to that effect, only including major landmarks such as buildings and significant ground slopes. Some of the experimental results are shown in Figure 5, 6, and 7.

As can be seen from Figure 5, the latitude and longitude components reported by the simulated sensor are very close to those reported by the real receiver. The difference between the two paths stem from the noise model parameters used during the experiment. Indeed, the simulated run used a maximum noise parameter of three meters (the advertised accuracy of the Holux M1000 GPS

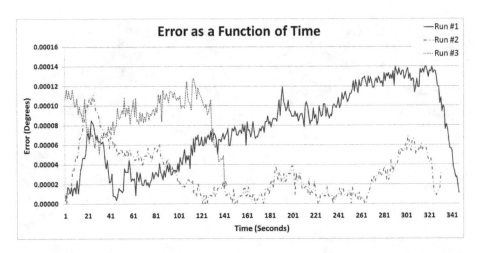

Fig. 6. Plot of the error, in degrees, between the real and simulated GPS coordinates for each run presented in Figure 5

receiver with WAAS enabled), but the real receiver actually produced errors, in our experiments, of up to eight meters. It is worthwhile mentioning that Run 3 is particularly off at the beginning of the experiment due to a cold start from the receiver; a typical GPS feature (i.e. they take time to initially localize) that was not modeled in our simulated GPS.

A plot of the error difference, in degrees, between the real and simulated GPS coordinates is given in Figure 6 for each of the three runs presented in this paper. Equation 4, exploited for each time step, gives insight into how the plots were created. The primary insightful result from Figure 6 is the fact that, for each of the three runs presented, the error between the simulated GPS sensor and the Holux M1000 GPS receiver did not surpass 0.00014 degrees, a testament to the accuracy of the simulated sensor. Furthermore, the error for Run 1 and Run 2 varies the most at the beginning and towards the end of the runs. This behavior is explained by the inertial difference between the real robot and the simulated one. Indeed, the real robot requires a lot more time to reach a given speed than its simulated counterpart. The same behavior is observed at the end of Run 3. The beginning of Run 3 possesses an unusually high error due to the previously-discussed cold start.

$$\sqrt{\left(\mathrm{Real_{Latitude} - Sim_{Latitude}}\right)^2 + \left(\mathrm{Real_{Longitude} - Sim_{Longitude}}\right)^2} \quad (4)$$

Figure 7 shows, for each run, the number of satellites seen by the real and simulated GPS receivers. The significant aspect of the data is that the simulated plot follows, in terms of shape, the real plot. Two additional comments can be made. First, the simulated sensor sees, in most cases, more satellites

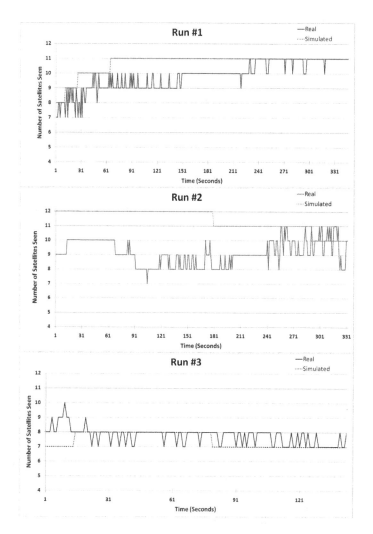

Fig. 7. Plot of the number of satellites seen as a function of time for each run. The runs correspond to the ones presented in Figure 5.

than its real counterpart. Second, the simulated sensor is much more linear and experiences fewer changes in the number of satellites seen. Both of these facts can be explained by the simplified virtual representation of the environment and the signal model. Since only major landmarks were included in the virtual world, small objects (e.g. trees, benches, stairs) interfered with the real receiver but not the simulated one. Additionally, the line-of-sight signal model does not take into account signal reflections, i.e. the reason for the oscillating number of satellites seen by the real receiver.

4   Conclusion and Future Work

In this paper, we presented a complete methodology supporting the creation of a simulated GPS sensor, supplemented by a USARSim implementation and experimental results comparing real and simulated data. The simulated results are close to the real receiver, especially when taking into account the assumptions made and the focus on computation friendliness over accuracy. In fact, the USARSim GPS sensor was selected and used in the 2008 RoboCup Rescue Simulation League in July 2008, where its robustness was successfully put to the test in a highly competitive scenario. Moreover, a DARPA Urban Challenge team has expressed the desire to use the sensor along with USARSim.

A few research opportunities stem from this work both in terms of improvements and extensions. Some improvements can be made within the noise and signal models, provided that they are not too demanding for the engine. More specifically, a great improvement would be to incorporate the dilution of precision as part of the noise model. In addition, getting real-time satellite tracking working, perhaps through the use of C++ dynamic library, would create a better all-in-one solution. Alternatively, porting the implementation to a different simulator, such as the new Microsoft Robotics Studio Simulator, could allow for more rigorous noise and signal models and the integration of real-time satellite tracking.

References

1. Balakirsky, S., Scrapper, C., Balaguer, B., Farinelli, A., Carpin, S.: Virtual Robots: progresses and outlook. SRMED (2007)
2. Carpin, S., Stoyanov, T., Nevatia, Y., Lewis, M., Wang, J.: Quantitative assessments of USARSim accuracy. In: Proceedings of PerMIS (2006)
3. Wang, J., Lewis, M., Hughes, S., Koes, M., Carpin, S.: Validating USARSim for use in HRI Research. In: Proceedings of the Human Factors and Ergonomics Society 49th Annual Meeting, pp. 457–461 (2005)
4. Pepper, C., Balakirsky, S., Scrapper, C.: Robot Simulation Physics Validation. In: Proceedings of PerMIS (2007)
5. Balakirsky, S., Lewis, M., Carpin, S.: The Virtual Robots Competition: vision and short term roadmap. SRMED (2006)
6. Carpin, S., Wang, J., Lewis, M., Birk, A., Jacoff, A.: High fidelity tools for rescue robotics: Results and perspectives. In: Robocup Symposium (2005)
7. Hoots, F., Roehrich, R.: Spacetrack Report No. 3 - Models for Propagation of NORAD Element Sets. Project Spacetrack Reports, Peterson (1988)
8. Vallado, D., Crawford, P., Hujsak, R., Kelso, T.: Revisiting Spacetrack Report #3. In: AIAA/AAS Astrodynamics Specialist Conference (2006)
9. Kelso, T.: Validation of SGP4 and IS-GPS-200D Against GPS Precision Ephemerides. In: AAS/AIAA Space Flight Mechanics Conference (2007)
10. Definition of Two-Line Element Set Coordinate System,
    http://spaceflight.nasa.gov/realdata/sightings/SSapplications/Post/
    JavaSSOP/SSOP_Help/tle_def.html

11. Space Track The Source for Space Surveillance Data,
    http://www.space-track.org/
12. NASA Science@NASA J-Track 3D,
    http://science.nasa.gov/realtime/jtrack/3d/JTrack3D.html
13. Real Time Satellite Tracking, http://www.n2yo.com/?k=20
14. Magliacane, J.: Portable PREDICT Plus! A Satellite Tracking, Pacsat Yakking, APRS Hacking, Linux Packing Mini Application Suite You Can Carry with You. CQ-VHF Magazine (2005)
15. Owen, M., Knickerbocker, C.: Nova for Windows, Real Time Tracking of an Unlimited Number of Satellites. Northern Lights Software Associates (2006)
16. Stoff, S.: Orbitron - Satellite Tracking System. Quick Starting Guide (2005)
17. Haupt, M.: Applicability of OSS to Space Thermal Engineering Open Source Software for Engineering Purposes. In: European Workshop on Thermal and ECLS Software (2003)
18. Kaplan, E., Hegarty, C.: Understanding GPS: Principles and Applications. Artech House Publishers, Norwood (2005)
19. Shirley, P., Morley, K.: Realistic Ray Tracing. AK Peters, Wellesley (2003)
20. Box, G., Muller, M.: A Note on the Generation of Random Normal Deviates. The Annals of Mathematical Statistics 29, 610–611 (1958)
21. Balaguer, B., Carpin, S., Balakirsky, S.: Towards Quantitative Comparisons of Robot Algorithms: Experiences with SLAM in Simulation and Real World Systems. In: IROS 2007 Workshop (2007)

An Emphatic Humanoid Robot
with Emotional Latent Semantic Behavior

Antonio Chella[1], Giovanni Pilato[2], Rosario Sorbello[1], Giorgio Vassallo[1],
Francesco Cinquegrani[1], and Salvatore Maria Anzalone[1]

[1] Dipartimento di Ingegneria Informatica, Università degli Studi di Palermo, Italy
{chella,sorbello_rosario,gvassallo}@unipa.it
[2] ICAR – Istituto di CAlcolo e Reti ad Alte Prestazioni Italian National Research Council
(CNR)
g.pilato@icar.cnr.it

Abstract. In this paper we propose an Entertainment Humanoid Robot model
based on Latent Semantic Analysis, that tries to exhibit an emotional behavior
in the interaction with human. Latent Semantic Analysis (LSA), based on vector
space allows the coding of the words semantics by specific statistical computations applied to a large corpus of text. We illustrate how the creation and the
use of this emotional conceptual space can provide a framework upon which to
build "Latent Semantic Behavior" because it simulates the emotional-
associative capabilities of human beings. This approach integrates traditional
knowledge representation with intuitive capabilities provided by geometric and
sub-symbolic information modeling. To validate the effectiveness of our approach we have simulated an Humanoid Robot Robovie-M on *dInfoBots* a linux
based framework developed in our Mobile Robot Lab.

Keywords: Humanoid Robot Architecture, Entertainment Robot, Machine
Learning Applications, 3D Robot Simulation, Human Robot Interaction.

1   Introduction

The ability Robot environment interaction is one of the most relevant topics for a
large set of applications in the entertainment field. However the classical rule-based
models are often too restrictive. To overcome the limitations of totally symbolic
knowledge representation systems, there has been much research, involving hybrid
symbolic/sub-symbolic systems. Many attempts have been made to merge connectionist and symbolic approaches [10][11]; some work, often concerning robotics,
faces the problem of linking a conceptual level to a symbolic one [2].

On the other hand, the ability to recognize and understand emotions plays an important role for a *natural* and *spontaneous* human robot communication. The interaction of the entertainment robots with human and the environment should not be
mechanical and deterministic in order to avoid a predictable and trivial behaviour. To
reach this goal many approaches try to use ethological or emotional models [15][16].

In the last years, many efforts have been made towards the design of knowledge
representation system providing 'intelligent' interaction with the environment [13][14].

S. Carpin et al. (Eds.): SIMPAR 2008, LNAI 5325, pp. 234–245, 2008.
© Springer-Verlag Berlin Heidelberg 2008

Many models try to incorporate ethological or emotional models for use in entertainment robot based on a behavioral system approach [15][16].

At the same time, Latent Semantic Analysis (LSA), is a paradigm, extensively used in last years, aimed at extracting and representing the meaning of words by statistical computations applied to a large corpus of texts [12]. LSA is founded as the vector space method: words are coded as vectors in a large dimensional semantic space S [8][12] while the semantic similarity between them can be computed using a geometric distance measure between their representative vectors.

One of the most interesting features of the Latent Semantic Analysis technique is that it is capable of simulating several human cognitive phenomena (word-categorization, sentence-word semantic priming, discourse comprehension, judgments of essay quality, etc.)[8].

Besides, it has been shown in [3] that it is possible to label the basis vectors of the semantic space S generated by using the LSA paradigm. This allows to see this space as an entirely data-driven "conceptual space"; hence, it is not necessary introducing any hierarchical structure, since orthonormality of basis vectors guarantees independency between their represented concepts.

This leads to a technique that allows the building of a data-driven "conceptual space" where words, documents, and concepts, represented as their verbal description, can be mapped [3]. Besides, using this space it is possible to simulate a set of human psycholinguistic cognitive phenomena that involve association capabilities and semantic similarity measures [8][12].

In particular Landauer and Dumais [4][5] assert that behind this paradigm there is a fundamental theory for knowledge acquisition and representation. Hence, this choice allows also coding, in some way, the intuitive - associative component of human brain. Roughly speaking, if it is possible to verbally describe a concept, an object, and so on, te concept, the object or whatever can be straightforwardly mapped into S. This allows overcoming the limitations of classic rule-based robot behaviors, providing a robot architecture of associative operation.

Objects in the real world, and words in sentences, are usually interconnected by complex relations. These relations can be partially captured by complex data structures and functions. However a more simple way could be let automatically emerge these latent associations from data creating a high-dimensional vector space where objects can be mapped and relations among them will emerge as geometric distances in this space.

The particular interpretation [3] of the Latent Semantic Analysis methodology contributes to better design a humanoid robot equipped with a conceptual space that is capable to act and modify his behavior coherently with the perceived world sensations also when the rule-based knowledge base is not capable to properly manage the interaction.

In this paper we try to merge the use of LSA-based "conceptual spaces" to the robot behavioral categories. To reach this goal we link a subset of words and sentences, coded in this data driven conceptual space, to specific behavioral categories.

We present a humanoid robot architecture capable to interact with the environment, whose input stimuli are coded using an "hidden semantic layer". Such a layer is usually not reached by explicit logical relations or predicates of classical rule-based paradigms and can be modeled as a vector space built using the LSA paradigm [3][8][12] .

Our aim is to create an *empathic* robot (EMPYBOT) for an entertainment application. Such robot should be capable to feel emotions triggered by environmental situations or of other people behaviors. According to an "empathy mechanism" the robot may activates a behavior which is related to the inferred emotion.

As a simple example of this behavior consider a man talking to his robot pet dog and saying "I love playing football", and the humanoid, taking advantage of the hidden semantics, associates the sentence of his owner with the triggering of a specific behavior, which consists of searching for a ball and carrying it to his owner.

This kind of behavior may be compared to the Latent Semantic Indexing paradigm, where the answer of the system is given by the association of a document whose vector coding is close to the input stimulus given by the user query. According to the Thagard theory about empathy analogies[6], we take the idea to provide the robot, during the training phase, with a sub-symbolic encoding about achiveable situations and their potential correlated emotions.

This sub-symbolic encoding allows the construction of an analogical mapping between the current situation and some aspects of the knowledge gained during previous emotional situations.

Ortony, Clore and Collin's theory [1] states that emotions are essentially descriptors of the people reaction to some events happened in the environment. Since environment can be described by tokens, the use of a technique capable to encode words in an emotional space allows inferring emotions not only from verbal communications but also from environmental stimuli.

To reach this goal, we choose a set of words or sentences related to the environments knowable by the pet robot. Then, the LSA technique with a modified version of TSVD is applied [3].

We link a subset of words, which represent concepts used for the space creation, with a set of behaviors or sequences of desired behaviors. Each time an input stimulus arises, it is mapped in the conceptual space. This mapping activates the most suitable behavior, which is closely related to the stimulus. If more than one behavior is activated, only one of them is randomly chosen.

This last choice has been done in order to implement a non-deterministic mechanism like in chat-bot systems, when a random answer (among a set of possible, coherent answers) is chosen to allow a natural, non trivial, more interesting interaction with an user.

The remainder of the paper is organized as follows: in section 2 it is illustrated a conceptual interpretation of data driven semantic space; in section 3 it is described the architecture of the emphatic robot; in section 4 is shown the *dInfoBots* simulator; in section 5 the simulated emphatic humanoid robot and the experimental results are presented; finally in section 6 conclusions and future work are outlined.

2 The Data-Driven Semantic Space Creation

One of the most widespread methodologies for the induction of semantic spaces from data is the Latent Semantic Analysis (LSA) approach [5].

The paradigm is based on the vector space method: given a text corpus of N documents and M words, LSA defines a mapping between the M words and the N

documents into a continuous vector space S, where each word, as well as each document is associated to a vector in S[5].

Let **A** be the $M \times N$ matrix whose (i, j)-th entry is the square root of the sample probability of the i-th word belonging to the j-th document. The Singular Value Decomposition of the matrix **A** is performed, so that **A** is decomposed in the product of three matrices: a column-orthonormal $M \times N$ matrix **U**, a column-orthonormal $N \times N$ matrix **V** and a $N \times N$ diagonal matrix **Σ**, whose elements are called singular values of **A**.

$$\mathbf{A} = \mathbf{U\Sigma V}^{\mathrm{T}} \tag{1}$$

Let us suppose that **A**'s singular values are ranked in decreasing order. Let R be a positive integer with $R < N$, and let $\tilde{\mathbf{U}}$ be the $M \times R$ matrix obtained from U by suppressing the last $N-R$ columns, $\tilde{\Sigma}$ the matrix obtained from Σ by suppressing the last $N-R$ rows and the last $N-R$ columns and $\tilde{\mathbf{V}}$ be the $N \times R$ matrix obtained from **V** by suppressing the last $N-R$ columns. Then

$$\tilde{\mathbf{A}} = \tilde{\mathbf{U}}\tilde{\Sigma}\tilde{\mathbf{V}}^{T} \tag{2}$$

is a $M \times N$ matrix of rank R. It can be shown [3][3], that, according to the illustrated procedure, $\tilde{\mathbf{A}}$ is the best rank R approximation of **A** (among the M×N matrices) with respect to the Hellinger distance, defined by

$$d_H(\mathbf{X}, \mathbf{Y}) = \sqrt{\sum_{i=1}^{M} \sum_{j=1}^{N} \left(\sqrt{x_{ij}} - \sqrt{y_{ij}}\right)^2} \tag{3}$$

which allows to interpret the TSVD technique as a statistical estimator.

The two matrices $\tilde{\mathbf{U}}$ and $\tilde{\mathbf{V}}$ obtained after truncated decomposition reflect a breakdown of the original relationships identified by **A** into linearly independent vectors. The R columns of $\tilde{\mathbf{U}}$ constitute a basis of a semantic space S, which can be interpreted as a "conceptual space". The term "conceptual space" may be confusing, since it recalls the well known Gardenfors conceptual spaces [9]. Gardenfors spaces have to be "manually" built by extracting from the knowledge base the quality dimensions, so they could be not the optimal choice, for practical reasons, in order to describe the knowledge base of a robot. The conceptual interpretation of the semantic space allows the automatic building of "conceptual spaces" by sub-symbolic processing of the raw sample data, so that the fundamental "latent semantic concepts" rise spontaneously. These fundamental co-ordinates will be represented by the orthonormal basis generated by the application of the LSA methodology, using the Hellinger distance instead of the Frobenius distance.

More formally, the independent R dimensions of the $\mathbf{R}^R$ space can be labeled, in order to characterize the "fundamental" concepts residing in the data driven space. The technique is to identify, for each column of the matrix $\tilde{\mathbf{U}}$ the words associated to the components with the highest value these words will constitute a label for each axis. Emotional states and external situations can be verbally described and mapped into this semantic space. Besides, an associative capability is simulated between a generic verbal-coded stimuli s_i and a generic emotion e_j with a closeness geometric distance given by the cosine between s_i and e_j.

3   The Architecture of the Emphatic Humanoid Robot

The architecture, as shown in figure 1, is organized in three main areas:

A. *The Sub-conceptual Area*: which processes perceptual data coming from the humanoid sensor;
B. *The Emotional Area*: it is a "conceptual space of emotional states" which constitutes the sub-symbolic representation of emotions, acquired during the training phase. This area gives to the robot empathic capability;
C. *The Behavioural Area*: it activates a non-deterministic behavior related to the humanoid emotional state.

3.1   The Sub-conceptual Areaz

The sub-conceptual area receives inputs from robot sensors system and sends commands to the robot's actuators.

This area is composed of two modules: *MotionModule* and *PerceptualModule*.

A.   The *MotionModule* controls the robot actuators in order to execute the motion request by Behavioural Area.
B.   The *PerceptualModule* processes raw sensor data coming from robot sensors to obtain information about the environment.

In order to make the model as similar as possible to an human being, we have considered five input channels for the Perceptual Module associable to the five human senses: the *sight* channel, the *touch* channel, the *sound* channel, the *taste* channel and the *olfaction* channel.

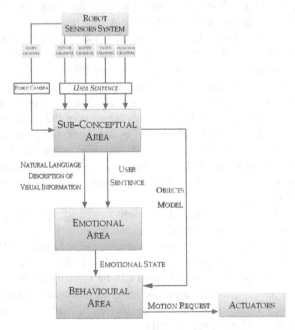

Fig. 1. A snapshot of the Architecture of the Emphatic Humanoid Robot

Being a simulated architecture, it will constitute a framework for the future development of a real humanoid robot equipped with ad-hoc sensors in order to completely simulate human senses.

The perceptual features extracted through the processing of inputs from the sensing channels are subsequently associated to their English description. (e.g. the recognized object *teddy-bear* corresponds to the description :"I can see a teddy-bear"). The use of a verbal description for all the perceptions coming from the external environment allows their straightforward mapping into the Emotional Area. The natural language descriptions associated to the sense channels are merged together and constitute the input for the conceptual area.

3.2 The Emotional Area

The emotional area allows the humanoid robot to discover emotional analogies between the current status and the previous knowledge of the robot; both of them are mapped in the "semantic space of emotional state".

An ad hoc corpus of documents dealing with emotions has been built and used in order to infer a "semantic space of emotional states". Emotional states have been coded in this space using proper subsets of verbal description of emotional situations (environmental stimuli, context, spoken message, and so on.) that evoke them. This represents the knowledge base of the robot about emotional state. Environmental incoming stimuli are encoded in natural language words and subsequently mapped in this space in order to find empathic analogies. In the following subsections the process of data collection, the space induction, and the inference of emotional state process are illustrated.

The Data Collection

The set of documents used has been obtained trough an accurate selection of excerpts associated to feelings. We have selected the following emotional expressions: *sadness, fear, anger, joy, surprise, love* the *neutral* state has also been considered. A large amount of documents has been selected from several publicly available on-line sources. The excerpts have been organized in homogeneous paragraphs both for text length and emotion. A matrix has been organized where the 6 emotional states and the *neutral* state have also been coded according to the LSA paradigm. A corpus of 1000 documents, equally distributed among the seven states, has been built. This set of documents represents the affective knowledge base of the system.

The "Emotional State Space" Creation

Each document has been processed in order to remove all words in literature named "stopwords" that do not carry semantic information like articles, prepositions and so on. According to the technique outlined in section two, a **87x1000** terms-documents matrix (**A**) has been created where $M=80+7$ is the number of words plus the emotional states and $N=1000$ is the number of excerpts. The generic entry a_{ij} of the matrix is the square root of the sample probability of the i-th word belonging to the j-th document. The TSVD technique, with K = 150, has been applied to **A** in order to obtain its best approximation according to the Hellinger distance. This process leads to the construction of a K=150 dimensional conceptual space of emotions S. The axes of S represent the "fundamental" emotional concepts automatically induced by TSVD procedure arising from the data. In the obtained space S, a subset of n_i documents for each emotional state corresponding to one of the six "basic emotion" Ei has been projected in S using the folding-in technique[7]. According to this technique each excerpt is coded as the sum of the vectors representing the terms composing it. As a result, the j-th excerpt belonging to the subset corresponding to the emotional state E_i is coded as a vector em_j and each emotional state E_i is represented in S by the associated subset of n_i vectors.

The Emotional State Inference

The inputs from the five sense channels are coded in natural language words or sentences describing them and projected in the conceptual space using the folding-in technique. At time t, the input from the visual channel is coded as a vector $v(t)$, the input from hearing channel is coded as a vector $h(t)$ and the input from touch channel is coded as a vector $t(t)$. These vectors, representative of the inputs from the channels, are merged together as a weighted sum in a single vector $f(t)$ that synthesizes the *inputs stimuli* from environment at instant t:

$$f(t) = \alpha \cdot vis(t) + \beta \cdot hea(t) + \gamma \cdot tou(t) + \delta \cdot sme(t) + \eta \cdot tas(t) \tag{4}$$

where α, β, γ, δ and η are weights that allow assigning different relevance to the specific inputs coming from each one of the three sense channels.

The emotional semantic similarity between the vector $f(t)$ and the vectors em_1, em_2, ..., em_7, that code the six emotions in S, plus the "neutral" state, can be evaluated using the cosine similarity measure between each em_j and $f(t)$:

$$sim(f(t), em_j) = \frac{f(t) \cdot em_j}{\|f(t)\| \cdot \|em_j\|}; \tag{5}$$

An higher value of sim(f,em_j) corresponds to an higher value of similarity between the emotion evoked from the input $f(t)$ and the emotion Ei associated with the vector em_j.

The semantic similarity measure is calculated between f(t) and each em_j The vector em_j which maximizes the quantity expressed in formula (5) will be the inferred emotional state with an associated weight, or intensity. This emotional state will activate a behavioural stimulus with a given intensity given by $sim(f(t), em_j)$.

3.3   The Behavioural Area

The main functionality of this area is to activate a behaviour, which is coherent with the inferred emotional state E_i induced by the humanoid. Behaviour is described by a sequence of *primitive* actions, sent directly to the robot actuators.

In order to give to the robot a non-monotonous, non-deterministic, and non-boring response, each emotional state E_i is related with a group of possible responses according to current information about the environment (for example the perceived object). One of these behaviours is selected evaluating a score w_{bi} associated to each one of them. The score is calculated as:

$$w_{bi} = \alpha_w \, r + \beta_w \, dt; \qquad (6)$$

where r is a random value ranging from 0 to 1, dt is the time elapsed by the instant at which the behaviour b_i has been executed and the instant at which this valuation is effected; α_w and β_w are respectively the weight assigned to the random *value* and to the time. The response with the highest weight is selected.

Since the stimulus is weighted, also the reaction will be executed with the same intensity. This corresponds to quicker, faster or slower movements of parts of the body.

If the emotional state is classified as "neutral" a standard behaviour (to lie down, to sleep, and so on) is randomly selected.

4 The Simulated Environment

The simulator we used for simulating the emphatic humanoid robot is dInfoBots developed in our lab[17]. dInfoBots does not only provide a simulation environment but it is a complete development suite for robot programming using the Orocos framework.

Orocos library provide many facilities for its modular capabilities, for its real-time features and for the simplified support of distributed computing by CORBA standard[19]. Robots and environments have been simulated on a Linux operative system with a customized Scene Graph Library used as World Modelling Engine tool.

The system uses Qt3 library for windows management, OpenGL library for the 3D rendering and ODE library as physical simulation engine.

We have decided to implement virtual models of two real different robots used in our lab: a small humanoid robot Robovie-M and a four legged Sony Aibo ERS-7 robot. As shown in figure 2, the system is composed by three main components: the simulated world, the robots and the applications.

The simulated world manages entities which represents robots and physical objects in the environment and progress the simulation time for the physics engine. Developers can describe the simulated world as a scene graph which enables to represent entities in terms of aggregation of simple rigid bodies. All objects are described by geometrical, colourmetrical and mechanical properties. Rigid bodies are connected by joints that allow movements via a mechanical constraints.

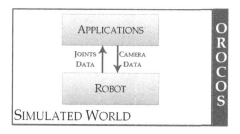

Fig. 2. A snapshot of the overall System *dInfoBots* that includes Simulated Environment and Simulated Humanoid Robot

It is possible to specify different kinds of joints (hinges or universal joints) and each of them is described by a specific freedom mode. Joints can be controlled either by angular velocity or could be free to move affected only by the interaction with other objects of the world. The simulator can provide an egocentric view of the scene by a simulation of the camera mounted on the robot; in this way the robot control loop is closed directly in the simulation. Applications, as shown in figure 2, are considered as a composition of simple Orocos modules. Each module implements a software component of the robot control system.

5   The Simulated Emphatic Humanoid Robot

The Simulated Emphatic Humanoid Robot is modeled using the virtual model of Robovie-M supplied with empathy capability. Emotional robots, as shown in fig. 3, follow the emphatic model that is made up by three main components: The *Perceptual* module as Sub-conceptual area, the *Emogen* module as Emotional Area and the *Controller* as Behavioral Area.

The Basic humanoid behaviours have been developed and implemented in the *RobovieMotion* module. Once this service is connected to *SimJoints*, it is capable to generate a joint data sequence that the robot has to execute in order to accomplish a basic behaviour. Two kinds of behaviours have been implemented: Walk and Action.

Walk uses inverse kinematics to produce sequences of joints that generate stable locomotion. All the Action behaviours are simply skills implemented as interpolation of different robot poses. The poses are represented as vectors of joints and their interpolation is sent to the joint controller.

The main basic behaviours implemented are: walking, greeting, clapping, looking around and kicking. There are also other behaviours used to express the seven emotions: fear, angry, sadness, joy, love and surprise.

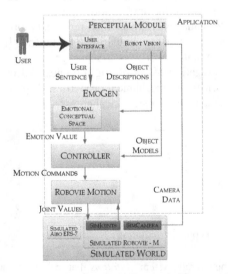

Fig. 3. A snapshot of the Simulated Emphatic Humanoid Robot

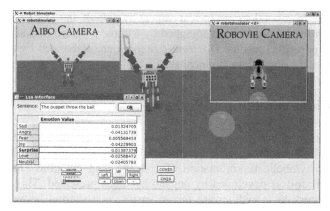

Fig. 4. The Simulated Humanoid Robot Robovie-M executes a "**Surprise**" behavior

A vision system has been implemented. It uses simulated camera data to recognize objects of the world using the colours and geometric features. The objects information are used by the *Controller* module and as verbal description by the *EmoGen* module.

A human user can realize an interaction with the robot through an user-friendly interface. It accepts sentences from user by a computer keyboard and send them to "*EmoGen*" module. The *EmoGen* module elaborates the user sentence and the visual information of the camera and generates according with the Emotional Conceptual Space the correct emotional state. The emotional state and the Objects information are used by the *Controller* in order to generate the motion command. The *RobovieMotion* uses the motion command for the activation of the emotional behavior.

5.1   The Experimental Results on DinfoBots

As shown in figure 4 we have reproduced various emotive situations. In the figure 4 the input phrase of the human is "*The puppet throw the ball*". The dominant emotional state activated in the Emotional Conceptual Space of the robot is "**Surprise**" and the robot executes a "**Joy**" behavior.

Table 1. The input-stimuli results

My SISTER AND MY DOG ARE RUNNING TOGETHER						
SAD	ANGRY	FEAR	JOY	SURPRISE	LOVE	NEUTRAL
-0.0098	-0.2417	-0.1077	0.0842	-0.1219	0.0343	-0.0377
BROTHER AND SISTER PLAY WITH THE DOG						
SAD	ANGRY	FEAR	JOY	SURPRISE	LOVE	NEUTRAL
0.1509	-0.0032	-0.0371	0.1794	0.0624	0.2548	-0.0962
THE CHILD IS SAD WHILE HE LOOK AT THE WINDOW						
SAD	ANGRY	FEAR	JOY	SURPRISE	LOVE	NEUTRAL
0.4566	0.0821	0.2377	-0.2512	0.0481	0.2366	-0.0654
THE PUPPET THROW THE BALL						
SAD	ANGRY	FEAR	JOY	SURPRISE	LOVE	NEUTRAL
0.0132	-0.0413	0.0056	-0.0423	0.0139	-0.0259	-0.0241

The Robovie-M robot does not have a camera by default, in order to achieve visual information, in the robot has been equipped by a camera placed on its head. Table 1 shows four experiments results. Different sentences are elaborated by the system in order to achieve the dominant emotional state.

6   Conclusions and Future Works

The results shown in this paper indicate that it is possible to generate a spontaneous and non trivial behaviour for an Entertainment Humanoid Robot creating a high dimensional sub-symbolic representation of concepts and emotions. The simulation environment dInfoBots developed by our lab has been presented. This tool uses the Orocos framework as a middleware for an easily code sharing between simulated robots and real ones. Orocos used in according with ACE-TAO implementation of CORBA assures a transparent communication of components across a network. In this way knowledge sharing, multi-robot communication and online debugging are allowed. In the future we want to use more advanced humanoid robot equipped with more sensor system that can simulate in a more realistic way the five human senses of the emphatic model. Nowadays we have considered a second commercial simulator, the Microsoft Robotic Studio simulation environment, for building and validating an implementation of our Emphatic Robot[18].

References

1. Ortony, A., Clore, G., Collins, A.: The Cognitive Structure of Emotions. Cambridge University Press, Cambridge (1988)
2. Chella, A., Frixione, M., Gaglio, S.: An Architecture for Autonomous Agents Exploiting Conceptual Representations. Robotics and Autonomous Systems 25, 231–240 (1998)
3. Agostaro, F., Augello, A., Pilato, G., Vassallo, G., Gaglio, S.: A Conversational Agent Based on a Conceptual Interpretation of a Data Driven Semantic Space. In: Bandini, S., Manzoni, S. (eds.) AI*IA 2005. LNCS (LNAI), vol. 3673, pp. 381–392. Springer, Heidelberg (2005)
4. Landauer, T.K., Dumais, S.T.: A solution to Plato's problem:The Latent Semantic Analysis theory of the acquisition, induction, and representation of knowledge. Psychological Review 104, 211–240 (1997)
5. Landauer, T.K., Foltz, P.W., Laham, D.: Introduction to Latent Semantic Analysis. Discourse Processes 25, 259–284 (1998)
6. Thagard, P., Shelley, C.P.: Emotional analogies and analogical inference. In: Gentner, D., Holyoak, K.H., Kokinov, B.K. (eds.) The analogical mind: Perspectives from cognitive science, pp. 335–362. MIT Press, Cambridge (2001)
7. Berry, M.W., Dumais, S.T., Gavin, W.: O'Brien Using Linear Algebra for Intelligent Information Retrieval. SIAM Review 37(4), 573–595 (1995)
8. Peters, S., Widdows, D.: Word vectors and quantum logic experiments with negation and disjunction. In: Mathematics of Language, Bloomington, Indiana, vol. 8 (June 2003)
9. Gardenfors, P.: Conceptual Spaces. MIT Press, Bradford Books, Cambridge (2000)
10. Ultsch, A.: The Integration of Connectionist Models with Knowledge based Systems: Hybrid Systems. In: Proc. of the IEEE SMC 1998 International Conference, San Diego, October 11-14, 1998, pp. 1530–1535 (1998)

11. Zhu, H.: Bayesian geometric theory of learning algorithms. In: Proceedings of the International Conference on Neural Networks (ICNN 1997), vol. 2, pp. 1041–1044 (1997)
12. Landauer, T.K., Laham, D., Foltz, P.W.: Learning human-like knowledge by Singular Value Decomposition: A progress report. In: Jordan, M.I., Kearns, M.J., Solla, S.A. (eds.) Advances in Neural Information Processing Systems, vol. 10, pp. 45–51. MIT Press, Cambridge (1998)
13. Dautenhahn, K., Billard, A.: Bringing up robots or psychology of socially intelligent robots: From theory to implementation. In: Proc. 3rd Int. Conf. on Autonomous Agents, Seattle WA (1999)
14. Fujita, M.: Digital Creatures for Future Entertainment Robotics. In: IEEE International Conference on Robotics and Automation, San Francisco, California, pp. 801–806 (2000)
15. Arkin, R., Fujita, M., Takagi, T., Hasegawa, R.: Ethological Modeling and Architecture for an Entertaiment Robot. In: IEEE Int. Conf. on Robotics & Automation, Seoul, pp. 453–458 (2001)
16. Lakemayer, G.: On Sensing and off-line interpreting in GOLOG. In: Logical Foundations for Cognitive Agents, Contributions in Honor of Ray Reiter, pp. 173–187. Springer, Berlin (1999)
17. Chella, A., Sorbello, R., Anzalone, S.M., Cinquegrani, F., Caccìa, D.: A New Architecture Based on a Simulation Environment for Four Legged and Humanoid Robots. In: 13th IEEE IFAC International Conference on Methods and Models in Automation and Robotics, MMAR 2007 (August 2007)
18. Menegatti, E., Silvestri, G., Pagello, E., Greggio, N., Cisternino, N., Mazzanti, F., Sorbello, R., Chella, A.: 3D models of Humanoid Soccer Robot in USARSim and Robotics Studio simulators. IJHR 2008, International Journal of Humanoid Robotics (2008)
19. Colon, E., Sahli, H., Baudoin, Y.: CoRoBa, a Multi Mobile Robot Control and Simulation Framework. Int. Journal of Advanced Robotic Systems (2006)

Developing Robot Motions by Simulated Touch Sensors

Fabio Dalla Libera[1], Takashi Minato[3], Hiroshi Ishiguro[2,3], Enrico Pagello[1],
and Emanuele Menegatti[1]

[1] Intelligent Autonomous Systems Laboratory, Department of Information
Engineering (DEI), Faculty of Engineering, University of Padua, Via Gradenigo 6/a,
I-35131 Padua, Italy
[2] Department of Adaptive Machine Systems, Osaka University, Suita, Osaka,
565-0871 Japan
[3] ERATO, Japan Science and Technology Agency,
Osaka University, Suita, Osaka, 565-0871, Japan

Abstract. Touch is a very powerful but not much studied communication mean in human-robot interaction. Nonetheless many robots are not equipped with touch sensors, because it is often difficult to place such sensors over the robot surface or simply because the main task of the robot does not require them. We propose an approach that allows developing motions for a real humanoid robot by touching its 3D representation. This simulated counterpart can be equipped with touch sensors not physically available and allows the user to interact with a robot moving in slow-play, which is not possible in real world due to the changes in the dynamics. The developed interface, employing simulated touch sensors, allows inexperienced users to program robot movements in an intuitive way without any modification of the robot's hardware. Thanks to this tool we can also study how humans employ touch for communication. We then report how simulation can be used to study user dependence of touch instructions assuring all the subjects to be in exactly the same conditions.

Keywords: touch, robot teaching, motion development, simulation.

1   Introduction

Observing how dance [1] or sport instructors teach motions, we can note that, with simple touches, the teacher intuitively conveys plenty of information on how to modify the trainee's movement. Touch is particularly appealing as an intuitive method for humans to interact with robots, and has been employed to program robot arms [2] [3] and humanoid robots [4]. It then seems plausible to use touch to develop motions for humanoid robots, and we therefore aim at studying how touch can be employed for human-robot communication. Many humanoid robots are available on the market for an affordable cost, but usually these devices are not equipped with touch sensors. The most straightforward solution would then be to customize the robot by covering it with tactile sensors.

S. Carpin et al. (Eds.): SIMPAR 2008, LNAI 5325, pp. 246–257, 2008.

However several difficulties arise, first of all because the humanoids available on the market are quite small and the wiring becomes complex. If the sensors provide an analog output, (multiplexed) A/D converters must be employed and buses with sufficient bandwidth must be designed. These problems had been tackled in several works, for instance in [5]. If, as in [6] air actuators are employed it is possible to read the error between the target position and the actual position to estimate the force applied by the user. Though air actuators are ideal for the human-robot interaction because of their compliance, their control is very difficult (the response is highly non-linear) and are not usually available on off-the-shelf humanoid robots. One alternative solution would be to use a shadow robot. This technique, [7], consists in having two identical robots, placed in the same position. The user interacts with one of the two robots, and comparing the torques with the ones of the second robot it is possible to distinguish the force applied by the user from the other forces (gravity, friction forces, etc.). Though interacting with a physical robot is probably more intuitive, simulating the touch sensors is a very cost effective solution to allow tactile interaction with a robot. Furthermore, it is possible to simulate sensors not currently available with the current technology in terms of size, bandwidth, signal to noise ratio, etc. Then this technique is general, applicable to any kind of robot. Interacting with a virtual world also allows to view the robot's movement in slow play or stop the motion with no effect on the dynamics, something not feasible in the real world (for instance, slowing down a jump motion in the real world to better observe the motion execution is not possible). In the simulated world additional information can be easily displayed, for example the zero moment point [8]. As a drawback much information measurable by advanced touch sensors, such as the intensity and the direction of the applied force, cannot be obtained by virtual touch sensors which are simulated, for instance, by mouse clicks. We therefore must assume that the user's touch direction is normal to the touched surface. In the case a standard mouse is employed the user cannot either touch multiple sensors simultaneously, as would be possible employing a real robot. We present here results obtained using simulation at different levels. First we will show how it is possible to simulate the touch sensors while employing the real robot to obtain the motion dynamic (therefore preventing any simulation-reality gap). In this case simulation is used to provide a sort of "augmented reality" that enhances the existing robot by providing touch sensors and allows us to study touch interaction. We then show an application of simulation to analyze user dependence of touch instructions in human-robot interaction. The main advantage in using simulation when studying user dependency is that simulation allows all the users to be in exactly the same conditions (same robot, same calibration, same friction of the floor) and to run the experiment in parallel (multiple PCs are more easily available than multiple robots). Obviously simulation also allows a safer interaction, both for the user and the robot. In section 2 we introduce the idea of extending the robot capabilities by creating virtual models equipped with sensors not available on the real robot, and present in detail the simulation of touch sensors. In section 3 we describe a possible algorithm to develop motions using touch. In section 4 we present an example of how simulation was employed to conduct tests on user-dependence of touch instructions. In section 5 we present some preliminary experimental results and in section 6 we conclude summarizing the ideas presented in the paper.

2   Developing Motions with Virtual Sensors

Recently many robots, and in particular small humanoid robots actuated by servomotors, are becoming available on the market for a lower and lower cost. One of the main issues when dealing with these robots is the development of robot movements, which is difficult given the high number of joints (usually around 20). Robot movements are often developed employing slider-based interfaces that require the user to define the robot motion as a set of keyframes, that is, a set of instants in time for which the position of each and every joint is provided.

This approach is very time consuming so many alternatives for automatic motion generation had been proposed in literature [9, 10, 11, 12, 13, 14]. Nonetheless handcrafted motions are still much diffused [15, 16]. It appears then necessary to devise intuitive ways to program robot motions by scratch, and we decided to rely on touch interaction with the robot. Using touch to develop motions has advantages in terms of intuitiveness for unexperienced users, but obviously for tasks for which optimization criteria exist specifically devised algorithms can obtain better performances.

Small humanoid robots available on the market are usually not provided with touch sensors, but as stated in the introduction, these sensors can be simulated, and the user can interact with a simulated robot equipped with such sensors. In detail we can imagine the following development cycle, depicted in figure 1:

1. the robot moves in the real world. Its orientation in the world is captured with a motion capture system and recorded;
2. users watch the recorded motion evolution in a virtual world.
3. users choose an instant in time where the motion should be modified and touch the virtual touch sensors to modify the posture at that time.

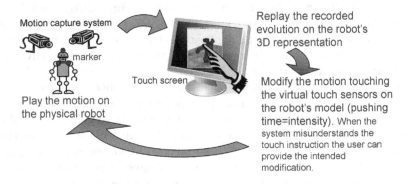

Fig. 1. Phases of the motion development

4. the motion is modified given the user instructions
5. if the obtained motion is not satisfactory, the development cycle is repeated

The trial and error development process of classical slider-based interfaces is therefore maintained, but instead of requiring the user to set each joint by a slider with the proposed approach she/he is able to develop the motion just by touching the robot. Using simulated touch sensors even eases the task with respect to an interaction in the real world, since the movement can be watched in slow-play or stopped. In fact we imagine the user to select an instant in time, stop the execution, touch the robot, eventually choose other instants where the motion should be edited, change the posture by touching the virtual sensors and then play the modified motion on the real robot. In the realized system the virtual sensors can however be touched during motion playback as well.

As previously stated the robot moves in the real world, and we acquire its position and orientation by a motion capture system. To acquire this information three markers placed on the robot's torso revealed to be sufficient. Given the position and orientation of the robot in the world we are able to reconstruct the motion evolution afterwards, since knowing the motion and a model of the servomotors response it is possible to calculate the angle of each joint. If the servomotors support position reading, accurate joint angle information could also be recorded during the motion evolution. However approximated joint angles are sufficient, since their value is only needed to show the user the robot's posture in the virtual world.

Once data are collected they can be used to replay the movement in a virtual world. Using data from execution of the motion in the real world frees us from the necessity of simulating the robot's dynamic. Very approximate robot models can be employed, as long as the simplification does not prevent user-robot interaction. The capabilities of the robot can be extended in the virtual world, providing it with touch sensors, noiseless gyroscopes, virtual cameras and so forth. Additional information can also be displayed, for instance in the developed interface the projection of the (approximated) center of gravity on the floor and the velocity vector of the center of gravity are displayed[1]. Fig. 2(b) depicts a view of the virtual 3D world as rendered by the interface. The robot links are simplified by parallelepipeds, and each face simulates a touch sensor.

These simulated sensors can be clicked with the mouse, allowing the user to "push" the robot links by clicking. Since with conventional devices as mice or touch screens it is not possible to measure the applied force, the output is binary and the interpretation of the intensity in the developed interface is based on the pushing time. Another limitation in employing conventional devices is that just one sensor at time can be clicked. This problem can be solved assuming that if the clicks occur when the robot motion is stopped than all clicked parts are touched together.

---

[1] These visual hints are introduced to allow expert users to improve the motion performance. They are not essential and thus to realize a model for the presented touch interaction interface no information on the mass distribution is actually required.

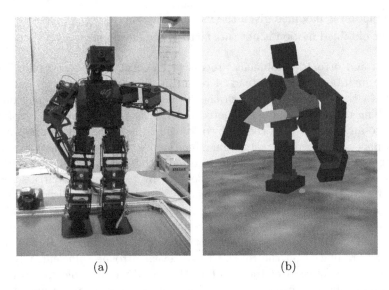

(a)   (b)

Fig. 2. The robot employed in the experiments and its simplified 3D representation. The projection of the center of gravity onto the ground (represented by a sphere on the ground) and its velocity (represented by an arrow) are given as additional information.

To give the user feedback while pushing the robot parts haptic devices could be employed. While this would probably make the interaction more natural, for simplicity we chose to provide visual feedback, i.e. the sensors gradually change color from green to red while being pushed.

3 Interpreting Touch Instructions

Employing touch to develop motions seems straightforward, in particular if we observe human-human interaction. Nonetheless decoding the meaning of touch instructions is not trivial. Often no direct mapping from touched part to modified joint angle is perceived as natural, intuitive by the users. In fact, this one-to-one mapping would be quite similar to the one used in classic slider-based interfaces. Furthermore while with existing methods like teaching playback or compliant joint control the robot moves passively and the user always need to apply forces to the robot, what happens with humans and what we aim to obtain is to have the robot gradually interpret touch meaning and understand how to modify its motion.

One of the issues to be tackled when dealing with touch instructions is the strong context dependence of the touch meaning. For example if the robot is standing, touching the upper part of one leg could mean that the leg should bend further backwards. However if the robot is squatting, the same touch could mean that the robot should move lower to the ground by bending its knees (see Fig. 3).

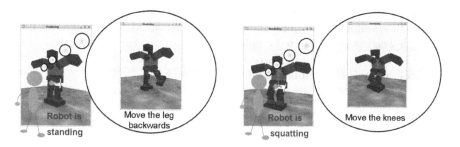

Fig. 3. Context dependence of the meaning of touch instructions. The user touches the robot in the same way, but the desired posture modification (bend the leg and bend the knees, respectively) is different because the robot posture is different.

We can then easily imagine user dependence on the meaning of touch instructions, since if no protocol is fixed different users will tend to touch the robot differently to give the same instructions. Avoiding to force the user to employ a certain protocol can enhance the intuitiveness of the interface. Suppose a user has a desired posture modification she/he would like to apply (for instance, raise the leg). If the protocol is fixed the user must identify which sensors, according to the touch protocol, should be pushed to have the desired modification. On the other hand if the system is capable of adapting to the user and estimate his/her intention, it is sufficient for the human operator to touch the robot spontaneously with no mental effort.

One simple way to have an interface which is able to adapt to the user is to ask the user to provide examples of the mapping between touches and corresponding posture modifications and use a supervised learning technique. The role of the learning algorithm is to realize a mapping between the tuple (*touch information*, *context*) and expected intended modification of joint angles. Currently the context consists of the posture of the robot (represented as the angle of each of the joints) the orientation (roll, pitch and yaw) of the robot's torso, and the velocity of the center of gravity. The posture is needed because the meaning of touches may depend on the posture, as in the provided example in which touching the lap means different things depending on whether the robot is standing or squatting. Likewise, the meaning of the instructions may vary depending on the orientation, for instance the meaning could be different if the robot is standing or is lying down. Finally, touch meaning could also depend on the velocity, especially if the robot is moving fast, for example if it is falling down.

Given the limited number of examples compared to the dimensions of the input space, among the numerous available supervised learning algorithms, like neural networks or Gaussian Mixture Models, we decided to employ k-Nearest Neighbor with a specifically devised metric. While this paper focuses on the simulation aspects the details on the metric and how it was derived are provided in [17]. Briefly each example provided by the user consists of an input I_i and an associated intended joint modification vector M_i (that we assume to be the class to which it belongs). Given an input I_*, the system output vector M_* can be obtained by weighting the joint modifications present in the collected examples M_i, with weights ω_i calculated employing the distance (in the high dimensional space) between the system input I_* and each example coordinates I_i. Concretely, indicating with E the number of collected examples

$$M_* = \sum_{i=1}^{E} \omega_i M_i \qquad (1)$$

Directly employing k-Nearest Neighbor with Euclidean or Mahalanobis distance based weights presents two problems. First of all touch information (pushing time of each of the sensors) should be prioritized over the context. This is to avoid the output being determined mainly by the context instead of by the pushed links, as would happen if touch information is given no priority over the other features of the input (i.e. if the input vector I_i components are all treated equally). As a trivial example, suppose the human operator designed an arm motion and therefore only provided examples involving the arm, then when she/he will push the legs this will cause the arm to move, while in such cases of no available knowledge it would be intuitive not to apply any posture modification.

To solve this problem given an input vector I_* and in particular the touching information T_*, the output M_* is calculated considering only the examples having a set of pressed sensors (i.e., sensor having a pushing duration greater than zero) the same set of sensors pressed in T_* or a subset of them. In other words, indicating with n the number of sensors and with the notation $T_* [s]$ and $T_i [s]$ as the pushing duration of the s-th sensor in the system input T_* and in the i-th example touch information vector respectively, the i-th example is considered if and only if

$$\bigvee_{s=1}^{n} (T_i [s] > 0)) \wedge (T_* [s] = 0) \qquad (2)$$

is false. In other terms $\omega_i = 0$ in equation 1 for the examples in which equation 2 holds.

The second problem arises because every distance function is symmetric. Suppose to have just one training example, where a sensor was pushed for 300 milliseconds, and this corresponded to a desired modification of increasing a certain joint angle by 40 degrees. A user might naturally expect that pushing for less time will cause a smaller change in that joint, while a longer press should produce a larger joint angle change. Nonetheless the system behavior with a distance based weighting is such that any touch on that sensor with duration different from 300ms, either longer or shorter, results in a smaller angle change. For example if $\omega_i = 1/ (1 + \|I_* - I_i\|)$ is used as a weighting function pressing the sensor for 200ms or for 400 ms would give the same modification. To avoid this unnatural behavior the weight ω_i (see Eq. 1) is calculated as $\omega_i = \alpha_i \beta_i$. Given T_*, the touch information components of the input vector, and the various example touch information vectors T_i, α_i is calculated as

$$\alpha_i = \prod_{s:T_i[s]>0} T_*[s]/T_i[s]$$

This value keeps increasing linearly as the pushing time increases. The second factor β_i accounts for all information not used in the calculations of α_i

- the sensor information $T_*[s]$ and $T_i[s]$ for the sensors s such that $T_i[s] = 0$;
- the joint angles of the robot in the system input (P_*) and the angles recorded in the i-th example P_i;
- the orientation present in the system input O_* and the one of the i-th example O_i;
- the center of gravity velocity vectors V_* and V_i, relative to the system input and to the i-th example respectively.

It was chosen to calculate each β_i as

$$\beta_i = \frac{1}{1 + d_i} \tag{3}$$

where d_i provides a measure of the diversity of the current input I_* and the i-th example input I_i. Denoting the Euclidean norm by "$\|\|\|$", d_i is given by

$$d_i = \sqrt{\sum_{s:T_i[s]=0} (T^*[s] - 0)^2 + \|P - p_i\|^2 + \|O - o_i\|^2 + \|V - v_i\|^2}$$

where each vector component is normalized scaling by its variance in the example data set since the units are heterogeneous.

The structure of Eq. 3 emerges from practical experiments: several decreasing functions were tested and the one which appeared to give the most intuitive behavior, $f(x) = 1/(1 + x)$ was chosen. A deeper and more formal analysis will be conducted in future works.

It must then be decided how to acquire the examples of the mapping used by the algorithm. We chose to collect them on-line, during the development of robot motions. This brings two advantages. First of all no special session where the user is required to provide how she/he would touch the robot to express certain pre-defined modifications is required. Secondly the human operator can identify when the system fails to predict her/his intention, and can provide, by the shared protocol, the intended joint modification, so that the mapping between touch instructions and estimated modification intentions can be refined where it needs to be. Ideally the system keeps improving its knowledge base during the motion development and users need to teach the meaning of the touch instructions less and less frequently.

It is therefore required to provide a method for the user to communicate the desired posture modification when the system does not estimate the intention correctly. In the current implementation a classical slider based interface was used.

4   Assuring Identical Conditions

As previously stated we can suppose user dependence of the meaning of touch instructions. In detail the same intended posture modification could be expressed in with different touch instructions and the same touch could have different meanings for different users even within the same context. In order to compare the instruction provided by different users we should put all of them in exactly the same conditions, otherwise differences in the results could derive by those factors. In detail we would need the users to employ identical robots, assure the same servomotor calibration, the same motion capture calibration, the same friction of the ground surface and so forth. These differences can be overcome using a simulator. In this case, the behavior of the robot is identical for any execution and every user. If identical PCs are used the experiment can also be run in parallel with different users assuring them to be in exactly the same condition. Even if a simulator is used to replace the real robot, the development cycle described in section 2 does not need to be altered. In detail, the users keep developing the motion using exactly the same interface employed for the control of the real robot and the simulator can provide a virtual motion capture system that sends the information to the interface simulating an ideal motion capture system that return the exact position of virtual markers.

5   Experiments

Experiments had been conducted using Vision4G, a humanoid robot produced by Vstone[2]. This robot is 445mm high and has 22 degrees of freedom actuated by DC servomotors (Fig. 2(a)). For capturing the robot's position we used the Eagle Digital System developed by Motion Analysis Corp. The robot's 3D representation, used to provide the robot with virtual touch sensors, is presented in figure 2(b). Strong simplifications had been introduced, for instance parallel links, present in the robot legs, had been modeled by a single link actuated by two motors that rotate synchronously. For the reconstruction of the motion the response of the servomotors had been approximated by a simple delay of 200 ms. We'd like to recall that the interface does not provide any dynamics simulation, and the position and orientation of the robot for each time instant is calculated interpolating the motion capture system data.

As a first validation of the feasibility of the developed interface, a stand up motion, a jump motion[3] and a walking motion were successfully realized. In detail the jump motion was realized both with the touching approach and with a classical slider-based interface for comparison. Similar motions were obtained, respectively, in 17 minutes and in over 40 minutes. Though this is just a preliminary results this can provide support to the thesis that motion development time can be reduced introducing touch-based interface. The examples of the mapping

---

[2] http://www.vstone.co.jp/

[3] To ease the task a rubber-band pulling the robot from the top was employed. Details and pictures are reported in [17].

Fig. 4. Screenshot of the rendering provided by the simulator

between touch instructions and posture modification provided by the user were studied. Analysis of the collected data is presented in [17].

User dependence was investigated asking six subjects to develop the same motions (a walking and a kicking motion) using the interface connected to a simulator. All the subjects are all Italian male computer science students, and their age is in the range 23-27 (mean 24.5, standard deviation 1.87). The simulator was developed using ODE, an open source library designed to simulate rigid body dynamics[4]. Figure 5 shows a screenshot of the rendering provided by the simulator. The robot had been modeled by 31 rigid bodies, each of which consists of one or more parallelepipeds(totally 39) linked by 34 joints.The number of joints is higher than the number of DOFs for the presence of parallel links, which in this case has been modeled directly as free hinge joints. The inertia matrix of each rigid body was calculated using the following approximations:

- each parallelepiped has uniform density and weights 35g;
- the real position and weight (63g) of the servomotors was identified and the density inside each servomotor was assumed constant;
- the robot's weight not accounted in the previous terms was assumed to be located in the robot's torso, uniformly distributed.

The main finding is that different users gave different abstraction levels in providing touch instructions:

- a nearly fixed mapping from a small set of sensors to the joints; the context has little or no influence
- a mapping based on physical considerations (the joints are imagined to be "elastic"); in this case, the context, for instance the position of the ground, becomes crucial

---

[4] See http://www.ode.org/ for more information on this library.

- a very high level representation of the motion, where for instance just the limb that should be moved is indicated by touching; at this level of abstraction a single touch corresponds to a motion primitive.

As previously stated since a simulator was employed the differences in the meaning of touch instruction is guaranteed to be due to the user-dependence of the mapping, and not by different environmental conditions during the tests.

6   Discussion and Future Works

Touch is a very intuitive mean of communication, and can be used in human-robot interaction for teaching motions, first of all for tasks like dance or sport movements for which it is difficult to provide a mathematical definition of the performance and for which, therefore, a user evaluation and tuning is very important. However most of the available robots are not provided with touch sensors. One cost effective solution, presented in this paper, consists in interacting with a 3D representation of the robot which extends the robot capabilities simulating sensors not present on the real one. We then presented an application of simulation on studying user dependence of touch instructions. In this case simulating the robot allows us to study the differences in the teaching method of different users when they interact in exactly the same conditions with a (simulated) humanoid robot.

Future works will aim at making the interaction more direct and natural. For instance, we can imagine to employ more advanced virtual reality devices. Another limitation of the current approach is that touch instructions are interpreted just observing the physical context, while we can imagine that knowledge of the task could be exploited to improve the meaning estimation.

Finally while in this work the user defines the target of the robot's motion and the performance of the result is evaluated by the user's subjective criterion, to allow a better comparison with other works definition of a set of measurement other than the development time here employed should be considered.

References

1. Takeda, T., Hirata, Y., Kosuge, K.: Hmm-based error recovery of dance step selection for dance partner robot. In: ICRA, pp. 1768–1773. IEEE, Los Alamitos (2007)
2. Voyles, R., Khosla, P.: Tactile gestures for human/robot interaction. In: IEEE/RSJ Int. Conf. on Intelligent Robots and Systems (August 1995)
3. Grunwald, G., Schreiber, G., Albu-Schäffer, A., Hirzinger, G.: Touch: The direct type of human interaction with a redundand service robot. In: IEEE Int. Workshop on Robot and Human Interactive Communication RO-MAN 2001, Bordeaux/Paris, France (2001)
4. Yoshikai, T., Hayashi, M., Ishizaka, Y., Sagisaka, T., Inaba, M.: Behavior integration for whole-body close interactions by a humanoid with soft sensor flesh. In: IEEE-RAS Int. Conf. on Humanoid Robots (Humanoids 2007), Pittsburg, USA (December 2007)

5. Ohmura, Y., Kuniyoshi, Y., Nagakubo, A.: Conformable and scalable tactile sensor skin for curved surfaces. In: ICRA, pp. 1348–1353. IEEE, Los Alamitos (2006)
6. Minato, T., Yoshikawa, Y., Noda, T., Ikemoto, S., Ishiguro, H., Asada, M.: Cb2: A child robot with biomimetic body for cognitive developmental robotics. In: IEEE-RAS Int. Conf. on Humanoid Robots (Humanoids 2007), Pittsburg, USA (December 2007)
7. Katsura, S., Ohnishi, K., Ohnishi, E.: Transmission of force sensation by environment quarrier based on multilateral control 54(2) (April 2007)
8. Vukobratovic, M., Borovac, B., Potkonjak, V.: Zmp: A review of some basic misunderstandings. Int. J. Human. Robot 3(2), 153–175 (2006)
9. Nakaoka, S., Nakazawa, A., Yokoi, K., Hirukawa, H., Ikeuchi, K.: Generating whole body motions for a biped humanoid robot from captured human dances. In: ICRA, pp. 3905–3910. IEEE, Los Alamitos (2003)
10. Okumura, Y., Tawara, T., Endo, K., Furuta, T., Shimizu, M.: Realtime zmp compensation for biped walking robot using adaptive inertia force control. In: IEEE/RSJ Int. Conf. on Intelligent Robots and Systems (IROS 2003), vol. 1, pp. 335–339 (2003)
11. Furuta, T., Yamato, H., Tomiyama, K.: Biped walking using multiple-link virtual inverted pendulum models. Journal of Robotics and Mechatronics 11(4), 304–309 (1999)
12. Iida, S., Kato, S., Kuwayama, K., Kunitachi, T., Kanoh, M., Itoh, H.: Humanoid robot control based on reinforcement learning. In: Proc. of the 2004 Int. Symposium on Micro-Nanomechatronics and Human Science and The Fourth Symposium Micro-Nanomechatronics for Information-Based Society, pp. 353–358 (2004)
13. Peters, J., Vijayakumar, S., Schaal, S.: Reinforcement learning for humanoid robotics. In: Third IEEE-RAS Int. Conf. on Humanoid Robots (Humanoids 2003), Karlsruhe, Germany (September 2003)
14. Yamasaki, F., Endo, K., Kitano, H., Asada, M.: Acquisition of humanoid walking motion using genetic algorithm - considering characteristics of servo modules. In: ICRA, pp. 3123–3128. IEEE, Los Alamitos (2002)
15. Wama, T., Higuchi, M., Sakamoto, H., Nakatsu, R.: Realization of tai-chi motion using a humanoid robot. In: Jacquart, R. (ed.) IFIP Congress Topical Sessions, pp. 59–64. Kluwer, Dordrecht (2004)
16. Baltes, J., McCann, S., Anderson, J.: Humanoid robots: Abarenbou and daodan. In: RoboCup 2006 - Humanoid League Team Description, Bremen, Germany (June 2006)
17. Dalla Libera, F., Minato, T., Fasel, I., Ishiguro, H., Menegatti, E., Pagello, E.: Teaching by touching: an intuitive method for development of humanoid robot motions. In: IEEE-RAS Int. Conf. on Humanoid Robots (Humanoids 2007), Pittsburg, USA (December 2007)

3D Simulation of a Motorized Operation Microscope

Markus Finke and Achim Schweikard

Institute for Robotics and Cognitive Systems
University of Lübeck
Ratzeburger Allee 160
23539 Lübeck
Germany
{finke,schweikard}@rob.uni-luebeck.de
http://www.rob.uni-luebeck.de

Abstract. We present a 3D-simulation which is used to develop automatic applications for a motorized operation microscope. It is implemented using java and java3d and enables a hardware independent evaluation of the system by the manufacturer as well as the user. An easy switch-over from simulation to the real system is possible because of software interfaces which are used to separate input and output methods. The simulation is also used to specify the parameters of the motorisation so that the microscope can be positioned accurately.

Keywords: 3D-Simulation, Operation-Microscope, Robotic.

1 Introduction

Robotics is a widespread technology and is primarily used to save money (automobile industry) or to act in environments that are inapproachable or too dangerous for people (aerospace, deep sea). In medicine, the robotics is meanwhile used to assist the surgeon doing his work but not to replace him. The experience and the tactile abilities of a surgeon cannot be substituted by a robot yet.

An essential advantage of a robot is based on the ability to position the end-effector with high accuracy. Because of that, the DaVinci telemanipulator (Intuitive Surgical, USA) is used by several surgeons. The surgeon embodies the master and describes the movements of all instruments and the robot acts as the slave and performs these movements. In this manner, 3-4 instrument arms can be served simultaneously. The accuracy of the robot movements is raised by a tremor filter which filters out the shivering of the human hand and also scales the described movements.

In the area of the radiotherapy, the Cyberknife (Accuray Inc, USA) is already used for some years and it enables robotic assisted compensation of the motions caused by breathing [1]. Thereby, the movement of a set of infrared emitters which are right on the skin of the patient is measured in real-time. The displacement of the tumour caused by the respiration can be determined and the

S. Carpin et al. (Eds.): SIMPAR 2008, LNAI 5325, pp. 258–269, 2008.

radiation source is moved by the robot in parallel so that the radiotherapy is limited to the tumour region.

Beyond the real treatment during an operation, the visualisation of the operation area is always also very important for the surgeon. Therefore, microscopes are used for the main part because they are also responsible for the illumination and the enlargement of objects in the operation area.

Although microscopes are very important during operations, they are afflicted with a central deficit. They can only be controlled manually and the surgeon has to interrupt his actual work every time he wants to reposition the microscope. The instruments have to be handed over, the microscope has to be unlocked, aligned anew, fastened again and only after renewed acceptance of the instruments the operation can be continued. This effort will also come up if the viewing area should be shifted only a little bit in order to have a look at an object slightly out of sight.

The motorisation of the microscope supports the surgeon with his actual work by enabling an easy, very exact and automated positioning of the microscope. Beyond, new functions can be provided to the surgeon – the pivotation around a point which maintains the current focus point and moves the microscope on the surface of a virtual sphere around this point is very time consuming or can not be realised manually at all. The adaptation of the optical coherence tomography (OCT) to the camera port of an operation microscope [2] is also a new function which upgrades a current microscope to a surgical assistance systems.

Automatic positioning of the microscope requires defining joint values to reach a defined position. Therefore, the forward and inverse kinematics of the microscope have to be determined. Afterwards, a computer-controlled adjustment can be applied which results in precise positioning of the microscope. The reliability of the kinematics and the explicit determination of all parameters in every joint constellation can simply and economically be checked with a simulation.

Simulations are used in the area of the robotics as well as in the medicine, however, in each case they have another objective. In medicine, they are primarily used for education. Reanimation dolls which are used to train first aid scenarios are already known in this context. The birth simulator [3] which is a combination of a haptic device in a body phantom and a software to simulate biomechanical and physiological functions provides the possibility to practice births and the handling of suddenly appearing complications. An included 3D visualization provides further information about the 3D model.

A training simulator for heart operations is introduced in [4]. Students, anaesthesiologists and perfusionists are prepared for possible incidents during the operation using this simulator. The patient's dummy contains the model of a cardiovascular system with which a complete heart operation can be simulated. Problems like bleeding or edemas are defined by a supervisor via a control PC.

In robotics, simulations are used for development and test of systems as well as to recognise appearing problems early. In [5] the control of a two-legged walking robot is presented which has been developed using a 3D-simulation. It represents a realistic environment to learn and test the synchronous control of the legs. The realization of a suitable interface makes it easy to port the steering to the real robot.

The control concept of a motorised fluoroscopic C-Arm has been developed and tested based on a 3D simulation [6]. This enables a hardware independent evaluation by the manufacturer and the user as well as the conception of new applications using motorisation.

The simulation of a motorised operation microscope connects both areas – medicine and robotics – with each other. The main focus is based on the development of a robotic system. The simulation is used for testing the kinematics and for developing new functions. At the same time, the simulation is used to explain the microscope's handling to surgeons who can test the functions and the new remote control as well as evaluate its suitability in practice.

2   Hardware

The operation microscope HI-R 1000 and the tripod FS4-20 produced by Möller-Wedel GmbH, Germany (Fig. 1) forms the basis of the simulation. It is a microscope with six degrees of freedom (DOF) and the last two axes are already motorised so that the optics can be tilted and shifted to get an overview of the operation area.

A large counterbalance at the lower end of the parallelogram-arm effects a balance to the microscope at the upper end of the arm. This simplifies the positioning of the microscope because the weight does not have to be carried by the user. The motorisation also profits from it because the effort for moving single joints is lower so that the engines can be dimensioned smaller.

For safety reasons, the brakes will be released in the manual mode by pressing a button at the handles and after its positioning they will be fastened immediately. This function will be maintained and it will have a higher priority than the motor mode because the engines are ungeared by pressing this button and can not move the joints anymore. In this manner, a looming collision can be prevented and the microscope can be pushed aside manually.

Every joint is equipped with an additional encoder. Thereby, it is assured that all movements can be registered and the microscope always be positioned exactly. Though, in the manual mode the engines should be ungeared, however, the encoders remain connected with the joints otherwise a wrong start position would be assumed for the next movement.

It is very important that the engines can be moved very slowly because only short distances have to be moved automatically but the defined point must be reached with high accuracy. This has to be taken into consideration dimensioning the engines. Additionally, all engines must reach their final position at the same time in order to make pivotations possible or to move on a previously defined trajectory. Joints that have to move only a short distance have to shift very slowly but joints that have to move a large distance in the same time have to shift fast.

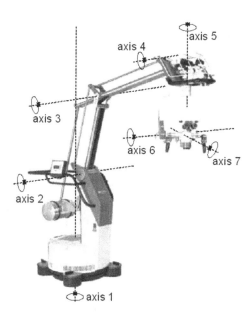

Fig. 1. HI-R 1000 microscope and the tripod FS4-20 with its six motorised axes (1-3 and 5-7) are presented. An additional joint (4) at the end of the parallelogram-arm compensates rotations of axes 2 and 3 and keeps axis 5 parallel to axis 1.

3   Interface

Generally, interfaces are defined to be able to communicate with different kinds of other classes. This enables the easy exchange of these classes. An interface has been developed because the kinematics is identical for the simulated model and the real microscope. The interface translates the calculations in corresponding commands depending on the used output component (microscope or 3D-model). The kinematics is necessary to calculate the position of the end-effector as well as the joints' positions to reach a defined position.

The input of control commands can be done in two different ways, either by a graphical user interface (GUI) or by a remote control which provides only such functions that are used frequently during an operation. The surgeon can make use of these functions easily with the remote control without interrupting his actual work. This includes small motions parallel to the image plane to have a look at objects slightly out of sight or pivotations which are very important to improve diagnose. The interface processes all the information of both input modules and transfers them to the calculation module.

The class *IRobot* defines the interface to communicate with the microscope or the model and it provides methods to control both systems and to read parameters directly from both of them. The model is also used to test the elements of the GUI independently of the microscope.

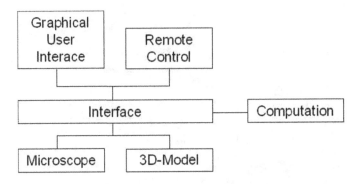

Fig. 2. The interface separates input and output level and it provides all information necessary for the calculation module. This makes the calculation independent of the used input and output components.

The control of the microscope takes place in several steps (Fig. 2). The class *IRobotController* defines the interface to control the motion of the robot. It provides methods to move the microscope parallel to the current image plane or along a trajectory as well as to perform a pivotation around a defined point. Therefore, the kinematics is necessary (*kinematic.RobotController*). This class expands the implementation of *interfaces.IRobot* which is the interface of *simulation.SimulationRobot* and *robot.Robot*.

The class *robot.Robot* supplies methods to move the microscope relatively and absolutely as well as to set and read parameters like velocity, acceleration, working distance and position of the joints. This class uses methods provided by *robot.HardwareControlMW* and *robot.HardwareControlIBG*. These two classes enable the communication with the hardware using a serial interface. The provided methods correspond to the commands of the controller like **getPosition()** or **moveAllAxes()**.

4   Simulation of the Microscope

The class *simulation.SimulationRobot* is responsible for the simulation of the microscope. This class implements the interface *interfaces.IRobot* and reacts just like the real microscope because all axes are restricted by the mechanical range of the microscope, axes 1 and 5 are kept parallel to each other and parameters like velocity, acceleration and step width are identical to the real microscope.

The classes *simulation.SimulationRobotModel* and *simulation.SimulationFrame* have been implemented additionally. They are necessary to display a 3D model of the microscope which is positioned according to the joints' positions that are specified in *interface.IRobot*. Furthermore, this model will also be used to display the position of the real microscope if its joints' positions are available for the simulation.

The package *gui* contains all graphical control panels to move the whole microscope using its kinematics (*kinemaic.RobotController*) or to move a single axis (*gui.AxisPanel*). The elements of *gui* are grouped according to their tasks (pivotation, saving the position of the microscope, etc.) so that a panel is defined for every task and can be added to other panels or frames easily. These panels are shown in Fig. 3.

The control panel is used to move the lens parallel to the current image plane. This is necessary to make an object visible that is slightly out of sight. The Buttons **up** and **down** can be used to increase or decrease the distance between the lens and the image plane. Therefore, the orientation of the microscope is not changed. The tissue stays focussed so that it can be observed while the microscope is moving.

The microscope can be moved around the current focus point using the pivotation panel. Therefore, the working distance is maintained and the lens is moved on the surface of a virtual sphere around the focus point. In this manner, one can easily have a look at an object from different directions.

If the surgeon wants to turn the view around but keep the current image plane, he will move the microscope around the rotational axis defined by the focus point and the middle of the lens by choosing **left** or **right** of the rotation panel.

The exact position and orientation of the microscope can always be calculated using the forward kinematics. The panel "SavedPoints" provides the functions to save these transformation matrices, which can be used to move the microscope later again to one of these positions. It can also be moved along a trajectory which is created combining several saved positions.

All motorised axes of the microscope can also be moved individually as long as the position fits into the mechanical range of the axis. The according control panel is shown on the right side of Fig. 3.

All the functions explained above will later also be available for the real microscope. The surgeon will control these functions during an operation using a remote control which can easily be fixed to one of his instruments.

4.1   The 3D Model

The simulation is implemented using java and java3d. The model is constructed by combining all parts loaded from VRML-files and all joints can be moved in the same way as the real microscope. The effect of movements on parts of the microscope is simulated with the help of the class *simulation.MotionGroup*. This class contains all information about impacts on any part of the microscope caused by the motion of an axis.

Additional elements like *simulation.Table* or *simulation.Patient* can also be presented in the universe of the simulation. These elements must be available as a BranchGroup and have to be implemented directly into the universe. The universe (*simulation.SimulationUniverse*) has a diameter of 20 metres. One camera (*simulation.Cam*) is placed on the z-axis 5 metres apart from the origin and points towards the microscope (Fig. 4a). Another camera is fixed to the last axis of the microscope and simulates its view (Fig. 4b). The scene is illuminated by a directional light which is fixed to the first camera.

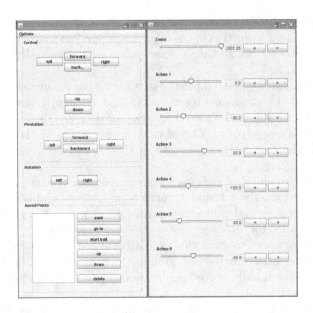

Fig. 3. 3D-Simulation. The control panels of automatic movements are places on the left side and each joint can also be moved individually using the panel on the right side.

4.2   Kinematics

The kinematics of the microscope is very important because it is used to calculate the position of the lens as the microscope's end-effector (forward kinematics) and to calculate the joint's angles which are necessary to reach a defined position (inverse kinematics).

Forward Kinematics: Six of seven joints can be moved independently of each other. The angle θ_4 of joint four depends on the joints two and three: $\theta_4 = -\theta_2 - \theta_3$. If the six independent joints are moved individually, it will result in the following movements of the microscope:

Joint 1:   Rotation of the whole system around z_0.
Joint 2:   Changing the height of the microscope.
Joint 3:   Changing the height of the microscope.
Joint 5:   Rotation of the microscope around z_0.
Joint 6:   Rotation around y_0.
Joint 7:   Rotation around x_0.

Each joint i has its own coordinate system. The transformation from coordinate System i to $i + 1$ is described by homogeneous matrices

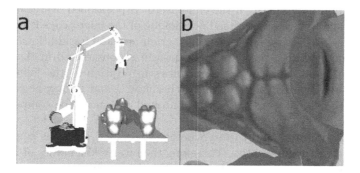

Fig. 4. a) Main camera view into the universe of the simulation, b) View of the microscope onto its environment

$$
{}^{i}A_{i+1} = \begin{pmatrix} \cos\theta_{i+1} & -\cos\alpha_{i+1}\sin\theta_{i+1} & \sin\alpha_{i+1}\sin\theta_{i+1} & a_{i+1}\cos\theta_{i+1} \\ \sin\theta_{i+1} & \cos\alpha_{i+1} & -\sin\alpha_{i+1}\cos\theta_{i+1} & a_{i+1}\sin\theta_{i+1} \\ 0 & \sin\alpha_{i+1} & \cos\alpha_{i+1} & d_{i+1} \\ 0 & 0 & 0 & 1 \end{pmatrix} \quad (1)
$$

The coordinates of the end-effector can be calculated by combining all the homogeneous transform matrices:

$$
{}^{0}A_{8} = \prod_{i=0}^{7} {}^{i}A_{i+1} \quad (2)
$$

The origin of the last coordinate system is located at the lens. ${}^{7}A_{8}$ contains only a displacement along the viewing direction of the microscope.

Inverse Kinematics: The inverse kinematics is responsible for calculating joint positions to reach a desired point and defined orientation. The desired position is determined using e.g. an optical tracking system registered to the microscope and the necessary calculation will be done by the inverse kinematics. The image plane can be placed freely in the 3D space because the microscope has six degrees of freedom. It is only limited by the restrictions of the working space of each joint.

The rotation matrix of ${}^{0}A_{8}$ depends only on the angles θ_{1}, θ_{5}; θ_{6} and θ_{7}. Angles θ_{2} and θ_{3}, which influence the height of the microscope, can be calculated using the geometry of the system. A detailed description of the kinematics of the microscope can be found in [7].

4.3   Test of the Kinematics

When dealing with a motorized (robotic) microscope, a singularity problem must be taken into consideration. The kinematics of some robots (e.g. six-axes robots) will cause singularities easily if the end-effector is positioned overhead and axes one and six align. Such an overhead positioning of the microscope is not possible because of the architecture of the parallelogram-arm and its additional joint four (passive joint). Besides, the parallelogram-arm is constructed in the condition of "elbow up" and, thus, avoids ambiguities in positioning the joints. Even if $\theta_6 = 180°$, there will not be a singularity because z_5 and z_7 may be parallel but they are not identical so that a rotation around z_5 can not be compensated by a rotation around z_7.

The simulation was used to test whether the joints' positions can explicitly be calculated by the kinematics. Therefore, the inverse kinematics of $1.423 \cdot 10^{19}$ joint constellations have been calculated. This large amount of constellations is caused by the limits of the six joints: Axis 1 has no limits and axis 5 can be moved 540°. In both cases, angles between $-180°$ and $180°$ have been used. The motion range of the other axes is 80°, 85°, 170° and 95°. The constellations were calculated with a resolution of 0.1°. The calculation was done with a standard PC (2.4 GHz) and took several days. The calculation of these constellations did not deliver any discrepancies.

Actually, there are ambiguities in calculating θ_5 because this joint can be rotated 540° so that two different joint positions result in one and the same position and orientation of the microscope. This problem is solved by using always that joint position which is closer to the current position of θ_5.

Motion tests with the simulation have shown that the current motorisation of the axes 6 and 7 is far from being satisfactory. Automatic motions like pivotation or positioning with high accuracy can not be provided. The velocity is limited to a range from $1.3°/s$ to $1.7°/s$ so that very slow motions can not be done. This makes it difficult to move the lens along a defined trajectory or to keep it focussed on one point. The time delay between sending the command to stop one of these motors and its actual stopping is relatively large (at least 40ms) and causes inaccuracies while positioning. The working distance of the microscope is between 22.4 and 51.0cm. Assuming a time delay of 40ms, the inaccuracy is between 0.02 and 0.06cm depending on the velocity.

5 Applications

The simulation forms the basis for the development of new functions which are enabled by the motorisation of the microscope. These functions should support the surgeon with his work and improve the diagnosis as well as the treatment of patients. At the same time, the simulation is used to test developed functions and to verify the practise suitability of new control concepts.

1. Defining the target directly in the presented view of this object is the easiest way to navigate. The surgeon can select a point either from a MRI or directly in the operation area and the microscope will move to this point autonomously. An external tracking system is necessary for both variations. The MRI must be registered to the real patient to be able to transfer the

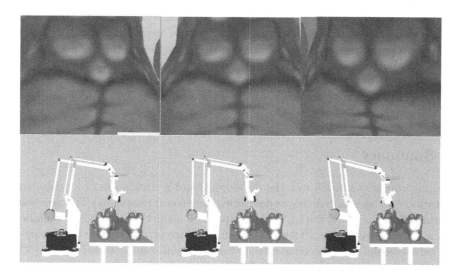

Fig. 5. Pivotation around a point on the chest of the patient. The microscope's view of three different directions is shown in the upper line and the according alignment of the microscope is presented in the lower line.

coordinates from the MRI to the microscope. If the target is defined directly in the operation area using a pointer, the coordinates will be determined tracking the pointer with a stereo camera. The defined points are used to centre the current view of the microscope anew.

2. The knowledge of the exact target is also used to verify the work done during the operation. The position and orientation of the microscope can be calculated using forward kinematics and the transformation matrix can be saved. If one wants to have another look at an object, the corresponding matrix will be selected and the microscope will position itself autonomously. For example, this makes sense after a tumour have been resected. The periphery can be examined again and can also be checked whether other tumour tissue still exists.

3. A diagnosis can usually not be made from one single point of view but it is necessary to judge the relevant place from different directions. If the surgeon does this manually, it will be very difficult and time-consuming. The pivotation around a point will be very simple and fast if the system is motorised. For this purpose, the current focus point is kept as the target and the lens is moved around this point with constant distance (Fig. 5). Therefore, the lens moves on the surface of a virtual sphere whose radius is defined by the working distance of the microscope. The point does not have to be focussed anew for every new orientation.

4. A basic idea of the motorisation is, to support the surgeon with the positioning of the microscope. Therefore, a remote control has been developed which can be fastened to one of the surgeon's instruments. The surgeon

does not have to interrupt the operation any more in order to control the microscope manually but instead he can control the motion directly. The remote control contains 2 switch-buttons to define the motion's direction and 4 push-buttons. These buttons can be used to easily switch from pivotating to moving in the current image plane or to save the current focus point. Thus, movements which are very small but frequently used can be simplified and quickened.

6 Summary

The purpose of this work was the development of a simulation of a customary operation microscope, which was developed for several reasons: 1) The necessary parameters of the motorisation could be specified using this 3D model to enable a very accurate positioning. 2) Automatic motions like pivotation can be developed and tested easily. 3) In the same way, new applications can be added later. 4) The system can be evaluated by the manufacturer as well as by the user independently of the hardware.

First, the kinematics of the microscope has been developed to produce the simulation. The reliability and explicit calculation of all joint positions, which are possible based on the mechanical limits, has proved by the simulation. In addition to the model of the microscope a model of a patient is also integrated to be able to visualise the automatic motion sequences.

Several applications (pivotation, saving target positions and move to them later again) were developed and tested. A remote control which uses the Bluetooth standard has been developed to simplify and to accelerate the handling of the microscope for the surgeon. Its handling and the reliable working have also been tested with the simulation.

Some problems positioning the microscope accurately have already been detected with the simulation while the motorisation was still under construction. Some of these problems could be corrected in the process of construction. The next step will be to integrate Optical Coherence Tomography (OCT). This enables analyses of tissue using an infrared laser. The surgeon can examine the tissue during tumour resection and decide immediately whether it is brain tissue or tumour cells [8]. The combination of OCT and a microscope, which was not motorized, has already been presented in [2]. A method to automate OCT-scans will also be developed and tested with this simulation.

Acknowledgement

This project is part of "e-region Schleswig-Holstein plus", which is a program of the ministry of science, economy and traffic and of "Innovationsstiftung Schleswig-Holstein". The project is sponsored by ISH and European Union from the european stocks of regional development (EFRE).

References

1. Schweikard, A., Glosser, G., Bodduluri, M., Adler, J.R.: Robotic motion compensation for respiratory motion during radiosurgery. Journal of Computer-Aided Surgery 5(4), 263–277 (2000)
2. Lankenau, E., Klinger, D., Winter, C., Malik, A., Müller, H.H., Oelckers, S., Pau, H.W., Just, T., Hüttmann, G.: Combining Optical Coherence Tomography (OCT) with an Operating Microscope. In: Advances in Medical Engineering, pp. 343–348. Springer, Heidelberg (2007)
3. Sielhorst, T., Obst, T., Burgkart, R., Riener, R., Navab, N.: An augmented reality delivery simulator for medical training. In: International Workshop on Augmented Environments for Medical Imaging - MICCAI Satellite Workshop (2004)
4. Dietz, A., Haimerl, G., Moreau, F., Straub, B., Benk, C.: Training simulator for extracorporeal circulation. Applied Cardiopulmonary Pahtophysiology 10 (2006)
5. Geiger, C., Lehrenfeld, G., Müeller, W.: Virtuelles Prototyping einer Robotersteuerung durch interaktive 3D-Simulation. In: Simulation and Visualisierung 1999, Magdeburg, Germany (1999)
6. Gross, R., Binder, N., Schweikard, A.: Flouroscopic C-Arm Simulator. In: CU-RAC 2004, Deutsche Gesellschaft für Computer- und Roboterassistierte Chirurgie, München (2004)
7. Finke, M., Bruder, R., Schweikard, A.: Kinematics of a Robotized Operation Microscope. In: Proc. of the 34th Annual Conference of the IEEE Industrial Electronics Society (IECON), Orland, USA (2008)
8. Giese, A., Böhringer, H.J., Leppert, J., Kantelhardt, S.R., Lankenau, E., Koch, P., Birngruber, R., Hüettmann, G.: Non-invasive intraoperative optical coherence tomography of the resection cavity during surgery of intrinsic brain tumors. In: Proceedings of SPIE, pp. 495–502 (2006)

Real-Time Least-Square Fitting of Ellipses Applied to the RobotCub Platform

Nicola Greggio[1], Luigi Manfredi[1], Cecilia Laschi[2], Paolo Dario[1],
and Maria Chiara Carrozza[1]

[1] ARTS Lab - Scuola Superiore S.Anna, Polo S.Anna Valdera
Viale R. Piaggio, 34 - 56025 Pontedera, Italy
[2] IMT Institute of Advanced Study Via San Micheletto, 3, 55100 Lucca, Italy
nicola.greggio@ieee.org

Abstract. This paper presents the first implementation of a new algorithm for pattern recognition in machine vision developed in our laboratory. This algorithm has been previously presented only theoretically,
without practical use. In this work we applied it to the RobotCub humanoid robotics platform simulator. We used it as a base for a circular
object localization within the 3D surrounding space. The algorithm is a
robust and direct method for the least-square fitting of ellipses to scattered data. RobotCub is an open source platform, born to study the
development of neuro-scientific and cognitive skills in human beings, especially in children. Visual pattern recognition is a basic capability of
many species in nature. The skill of visually recognizing and distinguishing different objects in the surrounding environment gives rise to the
development of sensory-motor maps in the brain, with the consequent
capability of object manipulation. In this work we present an improvement of the RobotCub project in terms of machine vision software, by
implementing the method of the least-square fitting of ellipses of Maini
(EDFE), previous developed in our laboratory, in a robotics context.
Moreover, we compared its performance with the Hough Tranform, and
others least-square ellipse fittings techniques. We used our system to
detect spherical objects by applying it to the simulated RobotCub platform. We performed several tests to prove the robustness of the algorithm
within the overall system. Finally we present our results.

1 Introduction

The impressive advance of research and development in robotics and autonomous
systems over the past few years has led to the development of robotic platforms of
increasing motor, perceptual, and cognitive capabilities. These achievements are
opening the way for new application opportunities that will require these systems
to interact with other robots or nontechnical users during extended periods of
time. The final goal is creating autonomous machines that learn how to execute
complex tasks and improve their performance throughout their lifetime.

Motivated by this objective the RobotCub (ROBotic Open-Architecture Technology for Cognition, Understanding and Behavior) project has been developed.

S. Carpin et al. (Eds.): SIMPAR 2008, LNAI 5325, pp. 270–282, 2008.

This is a research initiative dedicated to the realization of embodied cognitive systems [1], [2].

One of the basic assumptions of this project is that manipulation plays a key role in the development of cognitive capability. A ball is a perfect example of a very common and simple to manipulate toy every children uses. Fitting a ball may be very problematic in image processing because of the light, likely curvatures of the camera's lens, etc. These phenomena cause a deformation on the ball, making it look more like an ellipse. In addition, a ball is a particular case of an ellipse, i.e. when the ellipse has its axes of the same length.

Two main approaches can be considered for circle detection.

The first one is to use the Hough Transform [3], [4]. This approach can be divided into several steps. Since spatial perspective alters the perceived objects, the first step is calibrating the camera (in terms of reconstructing the original image proportions by computing the inverse perspective and the camera's lens distortion). By doing this, a ball previously mapped to an ellipse returns to be drawn as a circle. Subsequently, a pattern recognition algorithm, such as a simple color detection, can be applied and then the Hough circle transform can be applied in order to estimate all the ball's characteristics (e.g. center of gravity position - COG - within the 2D space and dimension). However, this approach can be complex to be implemented, and even elevate resource consumption. First, it requires the camera calibration. Moreover, the Hugh transform needs to be set well, in terms of the accumulator threshold at the center detection stage parameter. We will give a full explanation of our experiments later, in section 5. Finally, all these mathematical procedures require the implementation of complex and therefore error-prone functions, likely also resulting in an excessive computational burden.

The second one is to use ellipse pattern recognition algorithms. We prefer processing a ball thinking of it as it were an ellipse, in order to overcome these distortion problems. Circles in man-made scenes are almost always distorted when projected onto the camera image plane, therefore generating ellipses. The latter provide a useful representation of parts of the image since 1) they are more convenient to manipulate than the corresponding sequences of straight lines needed to represent the curve, and 2) their detection is reasonably simple and reliable. Thus they are often used by computer vision systems for model matching [5], [6]. There are many techniques for ellipse detection. Most of thew work in real-time (even if depending on the image size) [7], [8].

In this paper we implemented for the first time in a real context the *Enhance Direct Fitting of Ellipses* (EDFE) technique [8] for the least-square fitting of ellipses, previously developed by our group. We implemented this as a continuation of a work started as a pure mathematical context in our team by Maini *et Al* [8]. In their first version, the authors implemented and tested their work only with theoretical simulations, in *Matlab*. We implemented and tested these techniques under a robotics context for the first time. We tested our new algorithm and the previous related existing techniques ([4], [7]) under the same experimental conditions. First, we would check the performance differences among these methods, intended as produced error. It is worth note we are not interested in the absolute error of each procedure (yet evaluated for each method in [4], [7], and [8]); nonetheless we are interested in verifying the systems' execution dissimilarities under the same situation. Moreover, we are not interested in analyzing these dissimilarities in terms of mathematical performance, as done by the authors in [4], [7], and [8], but their usage in practical applications and scenarios instead, such as finding the position of a target object within the 3D surrounding space. We used the simulation of a state of art robotics platform, the RobotCub, in order to test it at best before doing this with the real platform. So far, we not only improved a growing open project by adding new capabilities to the robot, but also made our program open-sorce, available to whose need it as tool for their personal research or for improving our work as well. In fact, RobotCub is a completely open project, and by adhering to it we made our work fully available to everybody [9].

This paper is organized as follows. In section 2 we will describe the RobotCub robotics platform, in terms of its mechanics and the simulator we used. Then, in section 3 we will discuss the state of the art problem of the least-square fitting of ellipses. Furthermore, in section 4 we will briefly explore our vision algorithms. In sec. 5 we will describe our experimental set-up. In section 6 we will discuss our results. Finally, in section 7 we will conclude our work and explain our projects as future research.

2   The iCub Robotics Platform

In this section the iCub robotics platforms is described. It is one of the most advanced state of the art robots. It is dimensionally inspired to be a two-year-old human being.

2.1   The iCub Mechanics

The robot is composed of 53 degrees of freedom (DOFs). Most of them are directly actuated, such as the shoulders [10], others are under-actuated, such as the hands [2]. This has been decided according to the placement of the actuators which is heavily constrained by the shape of the body. Of course, the shape is not the only important factor in the robot's realization.

In Fig. 1 is shown the iCub in its final configuration [9].

In vision the head is of particular interests. The iCub's head is completely based on the Faulhaber motors. These are driven by DC micromotors (Faulhaber) with planetary gearheads. The neck consists of a serial chain of rotations and it has three DOF, which have been placed in a configuration that best resembles human movements. The mechanism of the eyes has been developed in order to achieve three degrees of freedom too. Both eyes can tilt (i.e. to move simultaneously up and down), pan (i.e. to move simultaneously left and rigth), and verge (i.e. to converge or diverge, with respect to the vision axes). The pan movement is driven by a belt system, with the motor behind the eye ball. The eyes' tilt movement is actuated by a belt system placed in the middle of the two eyes [10].

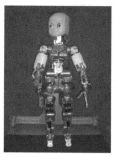  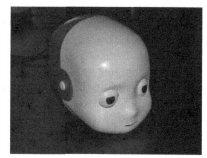

(a) The whole robot (b) The iCub's head (c) The complete iCub's head
without cover

Fig. 1. The RobotCub. On the left image the whole robot is depicted (a); on the central image the head without the cover is shown (b) while in the right image the cover is shown

An exaustive explanation about a kinematic and a dynamic analysis for the upper body structure can be found in [11].

2.2 The ODE iCub Simulator

There are many reasons for which it is important to test new algorithms within a simulator in order to debug them safely [12]. Since there have been build only a few prototypes (less than ten), it is not easy to access the robot. One of these prototype is in the Italian Institute of Technology, in Genoa, Italy (this is the center the robot has been developed in). Clearly, this can be very expensive, especially when more people have to stay abroad for many days in order to perform their experiments. A simulator solves these problems. Scientists can perform their experiments without being close and compare the results finally. Moreover, the iCub platform can be extremely dangerous if not used properly. The motors torque and power can injury a human being seriously.

Tikhanoff *et al.* developed a completely open source simulator for the iCub [13], [14], based entirely on the *ODE* (Open Dynamic Engine).

We use this simulator in order to test our algorithms.

3 Least Square of Ellipses: The State of the Art

A new interesting LS technique, the Enhanced Least-Square Fitting of Ellipses (EDFE), has been developed recently by our work team by Maini *et Al*, and it was proposed in [15], [8]. This is a LS procedure that improves the work described in [7]. In this work, Fitzgibbon *et al.* developed a direct computational method (i.e. B2AC) based on the algebraic distance with a quadratic constrain. Our new approach overcomes the state of the art by solving the problems of numerical instability that can produce completely wrong results, such as infinite or complex solutions, not reported in the original work [7].

Essentially, it is a upgrade of the Fitzgibbon's original work, aimed by the idea of making it *1.* faster (in order to use it in real-timeapplications) and *2.* more precise (it works better on noisy data, loosing precision with better data). The first result has been obtained by using an *affine transformation*, that recenters all the points belonging to the ellipse to be fitted within a square of side length equal to 2 and centered at the origin of the referring cartesian plane. This represents an ellipse similar to the original but normalized within this square. Clearly, the ellipses parameters have to be denormalized after having solved the fitting problem. This overcomes the problem of having huge numbers representing the ellipse's points coordinates, due to the fact the frame grabbers and cameras have ever bigger resolution, therefore making the fitting faster. The second result has been solved by resampling the ellipse data with perturbations. Specifically, if the data points lie exactly on the ellipse the eigenvalue corresponding to the optimal solution is zero thus the original Fitzgibbon's algorithm [7] does not lead to any solution. Moreover, this happens even if the data points are close to the ideal ellipse therefore B2AC performs poorly both when noise is absent and low [15]. The problem has been solved by slightly perturbing the original data by adding a known Gaussian noise. Therefore, the fitting is performed.

For a more precise analysis of the method one can refer to [15], and [8].

However, the author describes his technique only as a mathematical procedure, without inserting it within an actual robotics context. In fact, the authors tested its characteristics only in *Matlab* simulation [15], [8].

We implemented this *state-of-the-art* pattern recognition algorithm and we tested it in a real robotics project for the firs time.

4   ExPerCub: The Robot Controlling Tool

We implemented this algorithm as a tool for our research objective. It is comprehensive of a more complete project. We have to fulfill the deliverable 3.5 of the RobotCub project [9], relative to the implementation of the sensorimotor coordination for reaching and grasping.

4.1   Our Vision Algorithm

The vision module receives the images from the two cameras mounted on the iCub head. It is responsible for processing these images in order to obtain the relevant information about the object to be grasped. These are: shape, dimension, orientation, and position within the 3D surrounding environment (this is accomplished by triangulating the information received from the binocular vision, the head and the neck encoders). In our particular case we made our experiments by using a ball of different colors as test object.

In order to detect the ball, and all its features, we implemented a simple but efficient image processing algorithm. We identify the ball by means of a color filter. The object detection is performed by using of a sample color recognition procedure.

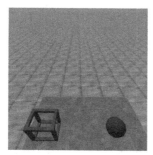 

(a) The left camera output   (b) The object recognized within the left camera

Fig. 2. The input image, as seen by the robot with the egocentric view (a) and the same image with the superimposition of an ellipse, drawn by using the characteristic parameters obtained by computing the EDFE (b)

For the identification of the blob corresponding to the ball, we use a *connected components* labeling algorithm. We assume the largest blob is the ball, so we look for the blob with the largest area. Subsequently, we proceeded by applying our LS technique [8] to the found blob, in order to detect all the parameters of the curve that describes the boundary of the blob. We used the iCub ODE simulator present in the iCub repository. Moreover, we slightly modified the simulator in order to create different scenarios for our experiments (such as by changing the color of the ball, by removing the table, etc.). In Fig. 5 an example of the ball detection algorithm output is shown. In Fig. 2(a) the input to the left camera is presented, i.e. the experimental scenario, while in Fig. 2(b) output of the algorithm is presented. These images are the input image as seen by the robot with the egocentric view (Fig. 2(a)) and the same image with the superimposition of an ellipse, drawn by using the characteristic parameters obtained by computing the EDFE (Fig. 2(b)).

In addition, we implemented a tracking algorithm that directly commands the head of the robot, in order to be able to reconstruct the target object position (in terms of its centroid) by triangulating the information of the neck and head encoders.

In Fig. 3 a screenshot is depicted, that shows an operative situation in which the simulator tracked the ball. The iCub program we implemented is able to localize the position of the ball (which is the target to be grasped in this case), in terms of 3D cartesian position. We adopted the same system reference as the simulator, in order to be fully compatible with the measures and the signs adopted in the virtual environment[1].

Clearly, the simulator information is not exhaustive, but it is a good approximation for the software debug before using it on the real robot.

---

[1] The reference system is centered on the floor plane, at the center of the pole that sustains the robot. The x axis evolves along the front of the robot, the y axis runs along the left of the robot, and the z axis evolves along its height.

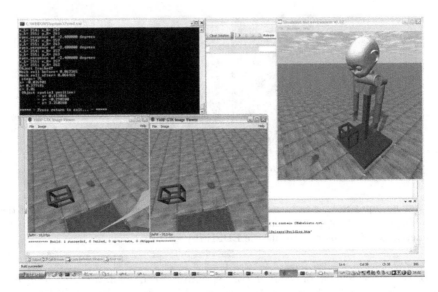

Fig. 3. A screenshot depicting the moment in which the simulated robot tracked the position of the ball in the 3D surrounding environment. Therefore, our program uses the encoders information to triangulate the position of the centroid of the object within the simulated space.

5   Experimental Set-Up

We performed three types of experiments, in order to validate the EDFE pattern recognition algorithm [8] compared with the Hough transform and the least square ellipse fitting algorithm, B2AC [7]. Each of these tests has a well specified scenario, described in the next section. For each scenario we performed the same experiments with the Hough transform, the B2AC, and the EDFE algorithms. We used uncalibrated cameras. We tested these techniques under the same experimental conditions aimed by several reasons. First, we would check the performance differences among these methods, intended as produced error. It is worth noticing we are not interested in the absolute error of each procedure (yet evaluated for each method in [4], [7], and [8]); nonetheless we are interested in verifying the systems' execution dissimilarities under the same situation. Moreover, we are not interested in analyzing these dissimilarities in terms of mathematical performance, as already done by the authors, but their usage in practical applications and scenarios instead. The final error is a combination of all the previous imprecisions. In the next section we will analyze the error propagation process, and we will quantize it in our specific case.

5.1   Scenarios

At each trial the Hough transform, the B2AC, and the EDFE algorithms are used in order to evaluate the ball's center of gravity (COG) within the 2D camera images. Therefore this information is triangulated with the encoders' values in order to determine the ball spatial position. For each scenario we performed at least 30 trials.

Since there is a prospective error, introduced by the spatial perspective, the ball is not seen as a 2D circle by the two camera.

We made the experiment in the scenario no. 1 by using a cylinder considered having a a null depth. (hence reducing the prospective effect). In this way we can test the algorithms by isolating the perspective error, while exploiting them in a real situation at the same time. The experiment in the scenario no. 2 is quite similar, but made using a ball instead of the cylinder, and letting it varying its position not only in the x-axis direction.

1 The robot has to localize a green cylinder in front of it, in terms of 3D cartesian coordinates. The robot stands up and remains in the same position, while the cylinder goes away along the x-axis direction at each trial. The error between the cylinder real coordinates and the evaluated ones is plotted as function of the distance between the middle point of the eyes-axes and the cylinder center. In the next section we will reconsider it for a more complete explanation.

2 The robot has to localize a green ball in front of it, in terms of 3D cartesian coordinates. The robot stands up and remains in the same position, while the ball changes its coordinates at each trial. The error between the ball's real coordinates and the evaluated ones is plotted as function of the distance between the middle point of the eyes-axes and the ball's center. In the next section we will reconsider it for a more complete explanation.

3 The robot has to evaluate the ball's radius while an occlusion hides the object. The robot stands up in front of the ball, which remains in the same position during all the trials. The ball is occluded by a cube placed in front of it more and more at each trial. Both the ball and the cube have been placed over a table, in front of the robot.

6   Results and Discussion

In the scenario *1* and *2* the error between the real and the evaluated cylinder's and ball's position is determined, while in the scenario *3* the error between the real and evaluated ball's radius is calculated. The position error is evaluated as follows:

$$rms_{err} = \sum_{i=1}^{3} \sqrt{(p_{real_i} - p_{eval_i})^2} =$$
$$\sqrt{(x_{real} - x_{eval})^2 + (y_{real} - y_{eval})^2 + (z_{real} - z_{eval})^2} \tag{1}$$

where the $(x_{real}, y_{real}, z_{real})$ and the $(x_{eval}, y_{eval}, z_{eval})$ are the real and evaluated 3D coordinates of the ball's center, respectively. Indeed, this can be considered as the *root-mean square error*. These values are relative to the simulator's reference system, which has the origin in the center of the robot's floor base is located where. The reference system's is orthonormal, and its orientation is as follows:

- the x axis is parallel to the floor plane, and increases with direction orthogonal to the eyes' axis and going away in front of the robot;
- the y axis is parallel to the floor plane, and increases with direction parallel to the eyes' axis and going away to the left of the robot;
- the z axis is orthogonal to the floor plane, and increases going away along the height.

6.1   Error Propagation Evaluation

We evaluated the error propagation for the position detection as follows.

The absolute errors have been evaluated as:

$$err_{i-th-axis} = \sqrt{err^2_{pixel} + err^2_{encoders} + err^2_{misure-iCub}}$$
$$err = \sqrt{err^2_{x-axis} + err^2_{y-axis} + err^2_{z-axis}} \tag{2}$$

each of them measured in *simulator measure unit (we use the abbreviation SMU)*. The err_{pixel} is the absolute error relative to the value of one square pixel. In order to evaluate it we referred to the known ball's radius. By knowing it (as a fixed value, i.e. 0.17 SMU) and by evaluating it at each measure we can estimate the value of a square pixel in SMU (this is the image resolution at the object distance) as the ratio between the known radius and the one estimated with each of the three algorithms considered (i.e. Hough transform, B2AC, and EDFE):

$$err_{pixel-x} = err_{pixel-y} = 0.17/radius_{eval} \tag{3}$$

Therefore, according with the error propagation theory, the error of a square pixel is:

$$err_{pixel} = \sqrt{err^2_{pixel-x} + err^2_{pixel-y}} = \sqrt{2} \cdot err_{pixel-x} \tag{4}$$

The errors of the encoders can be considered negligible within the simulator. Since there is no documentation on the encoders' resolution within the simulator, we considered the accuracy of their information approximated to their last digit, wihch is the forth one (therefore negligible). Finally the errors due robot's lengths need to be considered. Again, there is no information about the error the lengths of the robot's parts have been expressed with. Therefore, in order to fix their accuracy we analyzed the simulator's source code. So far, we found that the lengths of the robot's parts were expressed with the second digit of approximation. Hence, we approximated them as 0.01 SMU.

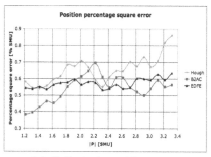
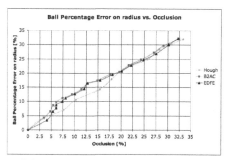

(a) Cylinder's position error   (b) Ball Percentage Error on radius

Fig. 4. The Cylinder's position error as function of the distance while considering the perspective effect null (a) and the Ball Percentage Error on radius, in % of the radius value (b)

6.2 Scenarios' Evaluation

As a first results the object's position error as function of the distance while considering the perspective effect null is presented in Fig. 4(a). Here, it is possible seeing that with exception for the range $[2.15 - 2.35]$ the Hough Transform gives rise to the highest error. The B2AC algorithm is the most precise in terms of quadratic error, within the ranges $[1.2 - 1.9]$, and $[2.7 - 3.4]$. However, it presents several discontinuities, and a total non-linear characteristic emerges, even following the Hough Transform approach's error (but keeping almost lowest). The EDFE seems to be not the lowest error prone, but it has a very regular characteristic of the function of the distance. By increasing the distance it fits the B2AC error curve well, while keeping little bit higher.

The experiment of the scenario no. 3 shows a great linearity between the occlusion of the ball and the error on its radius evaluation. Fig. 4(b) illustrates the results of this experiment.

Here, the Hough Transform gets better results within the range $[5\ \%$ - $20\ \%]$ of occlusion (defined as in equation 5, where P_r is the residual number of pixels, and P_t is the total number of target object pixels, determined with no occlusion), then almost superimposing with the other two approaches after he 20 % of occlusion. The characteristic is quite linear for all the techniques adopted, with the exception of the cited range, in terms of a slight decrease from the linear ideal line for the Hough Transform and a slight increment for both ellipse detection approaches. Fig. 5(a) shows the target object partially hided by the occluding object.

$$occlusion[\%] = (P_t - P_r) \cdot 100/P_t \tag{5}$$

Subsequently, the error introduced by spatial perspective is mapped as a function of the object's distance from the eyes axis midpoint. We isolate the perspective error by comparing the absolute error obtained within the tests in the scenario

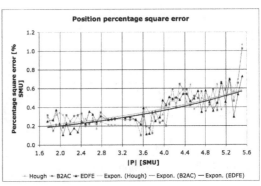

(a) The target object partially hidden by the occluding object

(b) Percentage square error

Fig. 5. The target object partially hidden by the occluding object (a) and the Percentage square error, measured in % of the simulator measure unit (b)

no. 1 and in the scenario no. 2, as absolute errors. It is worth noting that in order to compare these errors, the cylinder and and the ball we used have the same radius (0.17 SMU) within the trials. Therefore the percentage perspective error has been evaluated as the ratio between the absolute perspective error and the module of the distance between the eyes axis midpoint and the object.

Here, it is possible to see that the two ellipse recognition techniques are more sensitive than the Hough Transform to the spatial perspective. This seems quite obvious, due to the fact that the latter looks for circles, and the first two for yet deformed circles, i.e. ellipses. Nevertheless, the Hough Transform smoothes this artifact by bringing it back as a circle, before evaluating the centroid and radius parameters. The B2AC and the EDFE algorithms do not.

Finally, the scenario no. 2 is discussed. We keep this as the last discussion in order to show that, in spite of the fact that the ellipse detection approaches give rise to a bigger spatial perspective error than the Hough Transform, the precision given within the overall system is superior than the one obtained with the Hough Transform. In fact, despite the amount of the perspective error value, the major precision guaranteed by an ellipse detection rather than a circle one brings about to a more exact final result in determining the spatial position of the ball. In Fig. 5(b) this is showed. We did not filter the results, in order to keep them as natural as possible. By acting in this way, the noise affects the trend of the curves most. Therefore, we inserted three trend lines (one for each technique, each of them with exponential characteristic) in order to evidence the most fruiting approach. Here, the B2AC's and the EDFE's trend lines appear superimpose, so that it is not possible distinguishing them from each other. However, the Hough Transform's trend line shows of this technique is the most error prone for balls' spatial position detection in image processing. In fact, it is always higher than the other two.

7 Conclusions

In this work we presented the first implementation of the EDFE ellipse square fitting algorithm, a technique developed by our team by Maini *et Al*, and we applied it to a humanoid robotics platform. The task we planned is the spatial localization of a circular object (i.e. a ball) placed within the surrounding environment. Therefore, we developed a computer vision algorithms in order to implement the EDFE technique for the firs time. Moreover, we implemented a tracking algorithm to localize the object with the Robot's binocular vision, and subsequently we triangulated these information in conjunction with those of the robot's head encoders to determine the position of the object's centroid in the environment, in terms of 3D coordinates with the reference system located at the base of the robot. Therefore, we performed some experiments in order to validate the precision of the overall system in presence of induced artifacts (such as the ball occlusion by another object) and as function of the distance of the target. We made the same experiments by using the Hough Transform, the B2AC, and the EDFE under the same assumption, in order to have the fairest examination as possible. We found that the B2AC and EDFE give rise to a more precise results in terms of the overall system than the Hough Transform.

7.1 Future Work

In the near future we plan to apply our techniques to the real RobotCub robotics platform, in order to compare and validate our results with the real robot, and not only with the ODE simulator.

Acknowledgements

This work has been partially supported by the EU Project RobotCub (European Commission FP6 Project IST-004370).

References

1. Sandini, G., Metta, G., Vernon, D.: Robotcub: An open research initiative in embodied cognition. In: Proceedings of the Third International Conference on Development and Learning (ICDL 2004) (2004)
2. Stellin, G., Cappiello, G., Roccella, S., Carrozza, M.C., Dario, P., Metta, G., Sandini, G., Becchi, F.: Preliminary design of an anthropomorphic dexterous hand for a 2-years-old humanoid: towards cognition. In: IEEE BioRob, Pisa, pp. 20–22 (February 2006)
3. Yuen, H.K., Illingworth, J., Kittler, J.: Detecting partially occluded ellipses using the hough transform. Image Vision and Computing 7(1), 31–37 (1989)
4. Leavers, V.F.: Shape detection in computer vision using the hough transform. Springer, Heidelberg (1992)
5. Dhome, M., Lapreste, J.T., Rives, G., Richetin, M.: Spatial localisation of modelled objects of revolution in monocular perspective vision, pp. 475–485 (1990)

6. Forsyth, D., Mundy, J., Zisserman, A., Coelho, C., Heller, A., Rothwell, C.: Invariant descriptors for 3-d object recognition and pose. IEEE Trans. PAMI 13(10), 971–991 (1991)
7. Fitzgibbon, A., Pilu, M., Fisher, R.: Direct least square fitting of ellipses. IEEE Trans. PAMI 21, 476–480 (1999)
8. Maini, E.S.: Enhanced direct least square fitting of ellipses. IJPRAI 20(6), 939–954 (2006)
9. RobotCub, http://www.robotcub.org/
10. Metta, G., Sandini, G., Vernon, D., Caldwell, D., Tsagarakis, N., Beira, R., Santos-Victor, J., Ijspeert, A., Righetti, L., Cappiello, G., Stellin, G., Becchi, F.: The robotcub project - an open framework for research in embodied cognition. In: Humanoids Workshop, IEEE –RAS International Conference on Humanoid Robots (December 2005)
11. Nava, N., Tikhanoff, V., Metta, G., Sandini, G.: Kinematic and dynamic simulations for the design of robocub upper-body structure. ESDA (2008)
12. Greggio, N., Silvestri, G., Antonello, S., Menegatti, E., Pagello, E.: A 3d model of a humanoid robot for the usarsim simulator. In: First Workshop on Humanoid Soccer Robots, pp. 17–24 (December 2006) ISBN 88-900426-2-1
13. Tikhanoff, V., Fitzpatrick, P., Metta, G., Nori, F., Natale, L., Cangelosi, A.: An open-source simulator for cognitive robotics research: The prototype of the icub humanoid robot simulator. In: Performance Metrics for Intelligent Systems Workshop, PerMIS 2008, National Institute of Standards and Technology (NIST), Gaithersburg, MD, 20899, August 19-21 (2008)
14. Tikhanoff, V., Fitzpatrick, P., Nori, F., Natale, L., Metta, G., Cangelosi, A.: The icub humanoid robot simulator. In: International Conference on Intelligent RObots and Systems IROS, Nice, France (2008)
15. Maini, E.S.: Robust ellipse-specific fitting for real-time machine vision. In: De Gregorio, M., Di Maio, V., Frucci, M., Musio, C. (eds.) BVAI 2005. LNCS, vol. 3704, pp. 318–327. Springer, Heidelberg (2005)

An Introduction to a New Commentator for RoboCup 3D Soccer Simulation

Amin Habibi Shahri

Islamic Azad University (Young Researchers Club), Tehran, Iran
habibiamin@gmail.com

Abstract. This paper describes the concept and the implementation of *Team Assistant 2006 commentary system* for 3d soccer simulation. The idea is to provide a tool that is able to take simulator data as input and generate appropriate, expressive, spoken commentary in real time. the publicity that the RoboCup events get from the media provides an ideal opportunity to show the state of art of these systems during RoboCup World Cup. Soccer simulation commentary system is a suitable test bed for exploring *real time systems*. The *rapidly changing* simulation environment requires that the system generates real time comments based on the information received from the *Soccer Server*. This commentator together with other TeamAssistsant 2006 presentation and analysis tools won the second award in *RoboCup 2006 3D Development* competition for making a significant and innovative contribution to RoboCup 3D Soccer-related research.

Keywords: Soccer Simulation, Commentator, Live Commentary.

1 Introduction

Soccer is an interesting test domain because it provides a dynamic, real-time environment in which it is still relatively easy for tasks to be classified, monitored, and assessed. Moreover, a commentary system has severe time restrictions imposed by the flow of the game and is thus a good test bed for research into real-time systems. Also, using simulated soccer games, makes it possible to take advantage of high-quality simulator's logs and allow us to abstract from the intrinsically difficult task of low-level image analysis. [8]

One advantage of using a live commentator can be observed from organizers' vision. The running of simulation league in comparison to other RoboCup fields, is so quiet and therefore it doesn't have enough visitors. I believe that showing a better illustration of games and real-time commentating of games makes this league more attractive to watch for spectators.

In general, once the commentator recognizes the game situation, he has to report it in a small time interval. This is because of the fast rate of situation change in such environments. In order to have an influence on the audience, the artificial commentator should speak through the language used by a human commentator using his common jargon. In addition the more natural voice it has the more acceptance it will receive from the audience. To achieve this, it has been decided to use

S. Carpin et al. (Eds.): SIMPAR 2008, LNAI 5325, pp. 283–292, 2008.

prerecorded human report statements. It is clear that using natural human voice has a great impact on the quality of communication with the audience, but the excitement of the game cannot be experienced without the existence of the special sound effects like chants, applause and referee whistle. Therefore it is important to generate appropriate *sound effects* according to the game trend.

In this article TeamAssistant2006 commentary system is presented, including its subsystems and their functionality.[4] The remainder of this paper is organized as follows. In the next section a brief review of the related work has been presented. In section 3, the global architecture of the system is briefly described and each component is discussed more deeply in later sections, with emphasis on the *Game Analyzer* and the *Content Selector*. In section 7, I present the other features of the implementation of my commentary system. Finally, in Section 8 conclusions are drawn and future work is discussed.

2   Related Work

For the past 10 years the RoboCup simulation league was two dimensional, all players and even the ball moved on the ground. During this time numerous tools and commentary systems were created such as:

1. Rocco from DFKI[11]
2. Byrne from Sony CSL[2]
3. MIKE from ETL[9][10]
4. Caspian Commentary System[7]

The functionality of the these systems is that, after receiving data from the Soccer Server in each cycle, generate comments to describe the game situation.[1][7] Generally, the transformation process from the Soccer Server data to an appropriate report statement is done through the following steps:

1. Game analysis
2. Topic control and content selection
3. Natural language generation

Although MIKE and Rocco produce disembodied speech, Byrne uses a face as an additional means of communication. Because it is rather tedious to specify soccer slang expressions in existing grammar formalisms, Rocco uses a *template-based generator* instead of fully fledged natural language generation components. That is, the language is generated by selecting templates consisting of strings and variables that will be instantiated with natural reference to object delivered by nominal-phrase generator. To obtain a rich repertoire of templates, 13.5 hours of television soccer reports in English have been transcribed and annotated. Templates are selected considering parameters such as available time, bias, and report style. For the synthesis of spoken utterances, ROCCO relies on the TRUETALK text-to-speech software. Figure 1 illustrates an instance of the text commentary, generated by Rocco.

```
"kasuga" 9 kick off,
"andhill" 5, well done,
we are life from an exciting game, team "andhill" in red versus "kasuga" in yellow, he finds "andhill" 9,
yellow 6 intercepts the pass from "andhill" 9, forward from red 7,
yellow 4 intercepts,
still number 4,
number 9 is arriving,
ball played forward by "kasuga" 11,
failed, good luck for "andhill",
the keeper kicks off the goal,
number 2 does well there,
```

Fig. 1. An instance of the Rocco's textual commentary

Byrne uses a content selection module and an emotion generation module in parallel to animate the face as well as synthesis of speech. Text generation is also done simply through a set of templates.

MIKE (Multi-agent Interaction Knowledgably Explained) is an automatic real-time commentary system capable of producing output in English, Japanese, and French. MIKE uses six SOCCER ANALYZER modules. These modules demonstrate the general applicability of analyzing the focus of a multiagent system and examining the territories established by individual agents.

All the first three systems generate natural-language utterances using a speech synthesizer. As the generated verbal comments have a noticeable difference from the human natural voice, these systems could not effectively catch the attention of the audience.

Caspian commentator uses *prerecorded human report* statements instead of generating text and then converting it to speech. It only provides information about detected actions like passes or shots.

Since its beginning Simulation League is confined to two dimensions in order to reduce complexity. All of mentioned systems were for 2D soccer where ball has no height at all. But in 2003, the 3D simulation was introduced including basic tools to view and replay the simulated game.[5] The tools used in 2D can not be used in 3D simulations because of the lack of one dimension and a different format of the logfiles and none of the mentioned tools were extensible enough for new requirements.

Our vision is to develop a live soccer commentary system for 3D soccer by using prerecorded human report statements, so that one can hardly recognize an artificial commentator is reporting the game. Note that a soccer game consists of many similar situations that can be grouped together. For example many situations in a game can be described as "A definite chance!" Therefore it is possible to have some prerecorded report statements for each group of situations. Not only does it limit the commentator functionality, but it also has an *effective influence* on the audience.

3   System Architecture

The automated generation of live reports on the basis of visual data constitutes a multistage transformation process. In the following subsections, I describe how the maintainable subtasks transform the input into the final output.

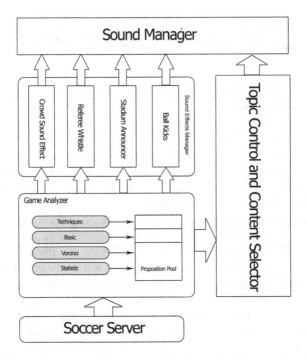

Fig. 2. System architecture and its interrelated components

A three-layer architecture has been used for the my commentary system. The Game Analyzer, form the bottom layer of my architecture. Above this layer, there is Content Selector and Special Sound Effects Manager. Sound Manager comprises the third layer of the proposed architecture as shown in figure 2.

The Game Analyzer receives information from the Soccer Server and determines the game status. The Content Selector subsystem takes the game states from the Game Analyzer and selects an appropriate statement to report the current situation of the game. Then, it sends a request to the Sound Manager to play the selected statement. The Special Sound Effects Manager works in parallel with the Content Selector and decides on the suitable environmental sounds for the current situation, and sends a request to the Sound Manager. Finally the Sound Manager organizes the submitted requests and plays the sounds in a consistent way.

4   Game Analyzer

The TA2006 Commentary system is designed to report both live and replayed games. In order to report a live game, the commentary system connects to the Soccer Server and receives the same information that the monitor program gets for updating its visualization. The system uses the log file of the rcssserver3d to report on a replayed game. The monitor log file is a text file generated by the

Soccer Server during the time that the game is running and contains the data related to each cycle of the game. As a result, two different sources of data input have been considered for the Game Analyzer:

1. Soccer Server: to report on a live match.
2. Log File: to report on a replayed match.

No matter which of these two input streams are used, the received information consists of:

1. players' locations and orientations
2. ball position and velocity
3. play modes such as goal, throw-in, free kick, and so on

This tool uses four SUB ANALYZER modules, two of which carry out high-level tasks. Notably, these modules demonstrate the general applicability of analyzing the focus of a multiagent system and examining the territories established by individual agents. These analyzers are implemented using a *decision tree*.

Soccer is a multiagent game in which various events happen simultaneously in the field. To weave a consistent and informative commentary on such a subject, an importance score is put on each fragment of commentary that intuitively captures the amount of information communicated to the audience. The content-selection module is controlled by such importance scores. From the input sent by the SOCCER SERVER, this system creates a commentary that can consist of any combination of the possible repertoire of remarks. The commentary generation is coordinated by the architecture shown in figure 2, where the gray ovals represent processes, and the rectangles represent data.

There are four SUB ANALYZER modules, of which two analyze basic events (shown in the figure as the basic and techniques), and the other two carry out more high-level analysis (shown as the Voronoi, and statistic processes). These four processes analyze the information from Soccer Server, and also post propositions to the proposition pool.

The Voronoi module calculates Voronoi diagrams for each team every 100 milliseconds. Using these partitions, one can determine the defensive areas covered by players and also assess overall positioning. Figure 3 shows an example of such a Voronoi diagram (+ and diamond indicate players of each team; box shows the ball.)

Furthermore, detecting events and the number of their occurrence may be interesting for the audience. The Statistic module retrieves the statistical information based on the current game state. Here are some instances of the statistical information: successful pass rate, number of shots, number of offsides, ball possession, lost balls, goal shots, etc. By detecting event sequences more information can be extracted such as lost balls after dribbling. The results show that, the audience is really interested in hearing of such statistical information, especially those that cannot be easily retrieved by them. Also it can be used as a reliable metric to judge about the efficiency of the players skills. For example, an increase in the successful pass rate shows that the agents pass skill has been improved.

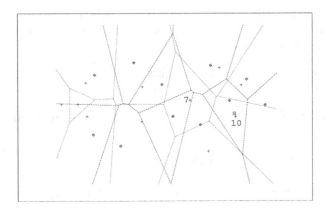

Fig. 3. An example of a Voronoi diagram

Some of the statistical information like number of offsides can be retrieved by keeping track of play mode changes (announced by the referee). On the other hand, there are some items like successful pass rate that should be extracted by analyzing the game.

5   Content Selector

The Content Selector receives the propositions as an input, and decides on the statement to be reported. Each proposition has a *birthday* (the time when it was entered into the pool), a *deadline* (a time beyond which it is "old news"), and a priority. This module selects the appropriate utterance from a set of prerecorded report statements. Only those statements that satisfy the following criteria are picked.

1. **Concise and Meaningful:** Since the commentary system has to keep up with a rapidly changing environment, it is important to use concise statements to describe the current situation. In fact, the current situation may change in every simulation cycle and using long statements may lead to inconsistent commentary.

2. **Various and Exciting:** A commentator, who always expresses a specific situation by identical statements, is boring to the audience. For example it is not pleasing to announce "It is a corner now!" on every corner kick situation. For this purpose, various statements are considered in the set of prerecorded statements to report each situation. In addition, each statement is designed to be exciting so that the audience will experience the fun and excitement of the game.

3. **Impartial:** In fact, the commentator should not report biased statements. Consequently, a set of impartial prerecorded statements have been picked to achieve this goal.

To establish the relative significance of events, importance scores are put on propositions. After being initialized in the ANALYZER MODULE, the score decreases over time while it remains in the pool waiting to be uttered. When the importance score of a proposition reaches zero, it is deleted from the pool. Having an integrated set of prerecorded statements, the commentary system should decide which one is appropriate for the current situation. The selection procedure is a combination of the *Proposition Score Selection* and *Scheduling* and *Interruption mechanisms* which are described below.

5.1 Scheduling Mechanism

This mechanism is designed to set a suitable time interval between two successive report statements. This means that, the commentator may refuse to report a new state in order to meet time restrictions. But, there are some exceptions for important events, such as scoring, that should be considered in the design of this mechanism.

5.2 Interruption Mechanism

As it is mentioned in scheduling mechanism, there are some game states that are really important (e.g. scoring the goal). Therefore it is worth interrupting the current reporting statement and announcing the critical event. In other word, it is required to introduce the Interruption mechanism. Although the interruption mechanism is necessary for the commentary system, but having several interruptions during the game, makes the audience feel confused! For this reason, the interruption rate during the game should be in an acceptable range. Therefore, the interruption mechanism is considered only for critical events like scoring the goal.

Applying the described algorithm in the TeamAssistant2006 Commentary system results in a consistent report of the game, but it still has some shortcomings that will be described in Conclusion and Future Work section.

6 Special Sound Effects Manager

Having implemented the commentator, I found out albeit the commentator was doing well at reporting the game, it couldn't bring excitement to the audience. To address these problems, a new module named Special Sound Effects Manager was introduced which itself is made up of four sub modules.

This module receives the current game state as an input and picks up the appropriate environmental sounds including cheering of spectators, referee whistle, stadium announcer and ball kicks. Then it submits the sound requests to the Sound Manager.

This module plays a key role in conveying fun and excitement to the people who are watching the game.

6.1 Crowd Sound Effect

This is the most effective sound effect among the other ones. In the current implementation spectators are the soccer fans. They wisely keep track of the flow of the game, and make critical situations stand out by the sound effects associated to them. There are three sound effects implemented into this module, namely chant, applause, and scream.

6.2   Referee Whistle, Stadium Announcer and Ball Kicks

According to the FIFA rules, there are several kinds of whistle blows for different events during a game. For example kick off, half time, corner kicks and offside; each has its own style of blowing. The implemented referee whistle module, fully complies with the official FIFA rules. The Stadium Announcer announces the beginning and the end of a match. It also makes an announcement each time a goal is scored. Ball kicks are also an effective sound for spectators.

7   Additional Features

TeamAssistant2006's main power lies in its ability to be extended using *AngelScript* plug-ins.[3] To get a glimpse of what can be done within a plug-in, it's good to mention that in current release the Commentator itself is a plug-in, all sound effects are provided by a plug-in, some training/test sessions are written using plug-ins, the game statistics are both calculated and rendered on screen by a plug-in. In general, plug-ins can obtain:

- Locations of all objects
- State of the match (play mode, time,...)
- Player actions (requires new server to monitor protocol)
- Some processed values (ball and agents' speed)

And Can Perform:

- Move agents and ball
- Change play mode of the match
- Control the log player (change playback speed, jump to a specific cycle,...)
- Draw shapes in the field

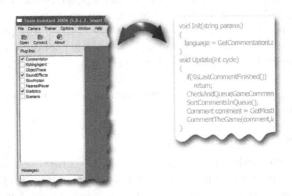

Fig. 4. Plugins and commentator pseudo code

- Draw markers on the field
- Write/Draw on the screen
- Control the camera
- Play audio file

One of the main features of my commentator is its flexibility. It can be easily customized, because its a plugin with common scripts. It is also possible to provide it with different languages. Currently I have provide it with *Persian* and *English* commentations.

8   Conclusion and Future Work

Watching simulated soccer games with a live commentator is far more motivating. The success of commentary systems shows that RoboCup is not just a robot competition. It is a challenging domain for a wide range of research areas, including those related to realtime natural language commentary generation.

Team Assistant 2006 Commentator is designed to be an effective means of communication with the audience, by providing real-time, expressive commentary and reporting the game facts at the right time and in a realistic way. It has been observed that my commentator has a great impact on conveying the excitement to the people who are watching the game. More specifically, successful implementation of the SUB ANALYZER modules in the Game Analyzer Module, leads to correct recognition and tracking of the game states. In addition, utilizing effective scheduling and interruption mechanisms prevents the commentary system to overwhelm the audience with its comments. But it has still some shortcomings and needs to be improved. One is that the audience is interested in receiving the meta-information while being informed about the general flow of the game. Some instances of the meta-information are history of the teams, how many times they play in front of each other, and what the results of previous matches were.

Furthermore, the audience is concerned about receiving technical information such as formation, player skills, and the commonly used strategies in a specific team. To meet this requirement, the Game Analyzer of the commentary system should be improved, so that it can retrieve the required information. Considering that "Team Modeling" is one of the major challenges in the Soccer Simulation Coach Competitions, it is possible to utilize the research studies in this domain, to improve the Commentary system's performance.

Even though my focus has been on the general description of soccer matches, I am currently working on a three-dimensional visualization component to enable situated reports from the perspective of a particular player. Also simulation league goes toward humanoid robots[6], so a more real commentation is necessary. I hope that improved versions will be shown at future RoboCup events.

Finally Team Assistant 2006 is intended to be a general-purpose, highly customizable package. This design required a tremendous amount of flexibility on the implementation side. I think it has the potential to be used as the primary analyzer, visualizer, and logviewer for anyone interested in developing agents for the RoboCup 3D Soccer Simulator. The presented commentary system along with the other Team Assistant 2006 presentation tools, won the second place in RoboCup 3D development competition 2006 in Bremen, Germany.

References

1. Andre, E., Binsted, K., Tanaka-Ishii, K., Luke, S., Rist, T.: Three RoboCup Simulation League Commentator Systems. AI Magazine, 57–66 (Spring 2000)
2. Binsted, K.: Character Design for Soccer Commentary. In: Asada, M., Kitano, H. (eds.) RoboCup 1998. LNCS (LNAI), vol. 1604, pp. 22–33. Springer, Heidelberg (1999)
3. Habibi Shahri, A., Almasi Monfared, A., Elahi, M.: A deeper look at 3D soccer simulations. In: RoboCup 2007. LNCS (LNAI), vol. 5001, pp. 294–301. Springer, Heidelberg (2008)
4. Kazemi, V., Habibi Shahri, A., Hosseingholizadehm, A., Nooraei Beidokht, B.: Team Assistant (2006), http://team-assistant.sourceforge.net
5. Kogler, M., Obst, O.: Simulation League: The Next Generation. In: Polani, D., Browning, B., Bonarini, A., Yoshida, K. (eds.) RoboCup 2003. LNCS (LNAI), vol. 3020, pp. 458–469. Springer, Heidelberg (2004)
6. Mayer, N., Boedecker, J., Silva Guerra, R., Obst, O., Asada, M.: 3D2Real: Simulation League Finals in Real Robots. In: Lakemeyer, G., Sklar, E., Sorrenti, D.G., Takahashi, T. (eds.) RoboCup 2006: Robot Soccer World Cup X. LNCS (LNAI), vol. 4434, pp. 25–34. Springer, Heidelberg (2007)
7. Nejad Sedaghat, M., Gholami, N., Iravanian, S., Kangavari, M.: Design and Implementation of Live Commentary System in Soccer Simulation Environment. In: Nardi, D., Riedmiller, M., Sammut, C., Santos-Victor, J. (eds.) RoboCup 2004. LNCS (LNAI), vol. 3276, pp. 602–610. Springer, Heidelberg (2005)
8. Noda, I., Matsubara, H.: Soccer Server and Researchers on Multi-Agent Systems. In: Proceedings of IROS 1996 Workshop on RoboCup, pp. 1–7 (1996)
9. Tanaka-Ishii, K., Hasida, K., Noda, I.: Reactive Content Selection in the Generation of Real Time Soccer Commentary. In: COLING 1998, Montreal, Canada (1998)
10. Tanaka-Ishii, K., Noda, I., Frank, I., Nakashima, H., Hasida, K., Matsubara, H.: MIKE: An Automatic Commentary System for Soccer. In: The 1998 international Conference on Multi-agent Systems, Paris, France (1998)
11. Voelz, D., André, E., Herzog, G., Rist, T.: Rocco: A RoboCup Soccer Commentator System. In: Asada, M., Kitano, H. (eds.) RoboCup 1998. LNCS (LNAI), vol. 1604, pp. 50–60. Springer, Heidelberg (1999)

Authority Sharing in a Swarm of UAVs: Simulation and Experiments with Operators

François Legras[1], Arnaud Glad[2], Olivier Simonin[2], and François Charpillet[2]

[1] Institut TELECOM / TELECOM Bretagne, Département LUSSI, France
LabSTICC, UMR 3192, CNRS, France
[2] LORIA Laboratoire Lorrain de Recherche en Informatique et ses Applications
UMR 7503, Université Henri Poincaré, CNRS, INRIA, Nancy 2, INPL, France
INRIA Nancy Grand Est, Equipe-projet MAIA, France

Abstract. It is emphasized in numerous prospective studies that the development of swarms of Unmanned Aerial Vehicles (UAV) should be important in the next years. However, the design of these new multi-agent systems involves to take up many challenges. In particular, reducing the number of operators requires to define new interfaces in order to interact with such autonomous multirobot systems. We present an approach that allows one operator to control a swarm of UAVs in the context of simulated patrolling and pursuit tasks. Self-organized control relying on digital pheromones, as well as authority sharing based on several operating modes are defined. Experiments with human operators on the simulated system show that the combination of the two approaches is effective.

1 Introduction

Nowadays several operators (usually one for the platform and another for the payload, not counting support) are required to supervise the mission of a single UAV (Unmanned Air Vehicle). Future systems for surveillance are envisioned using many vehicles that cooperate to perform their mission. In this context the current ratio between the number of operators and the number of vehicles will not be sustainable [9]. The existing approaches for monitoring (close to teleoperation) must be changed to augment autonomy of the system [5] in order to share the authority on various aspects of the mission.

This paper tackles the problem of the operation of a swarm of UAVs. This work was carried out within the SMAART project. This project aims at the surveillance of a military airbase. To perform such a task we consider a system composed of a set of UAVs, *i.e.* of automonous rotary-wing aircrafts (helicopters). This system is simulated through a continuous environment where all UAVs fly at the same altitude. Each of them can perform some simple actions such as take off, landing or reaching a particular location on the base. They carry a camera that allows them to perceive their vicinity and to detect some possible intruders. We also study the coupling of the swarm of UAVs with a sensor network augmenting the surveillance system.

S. Carpin et al. (Eds.): SIMPAR 2008, LNAI 5325, pp. 293–304, 2008.
© Springer-Verlag Berlin Heidelberg 2008

Providing autonomy to UAVs is a problem that can be addressed following two approaches. The first one, the most classical, consists in planning paths and then setting the UAVs to execute them [11, 14]. On the contrary, the second approach relies on the self-organization of the UAVs in function of their interaction with the environment, leading to the emergence of patroling paths [3, 17].

The main disadvantage of the first approach is that it builds a fixed solution, that makes difficult to adapt online to changes such as the addition or removal of agents, or to respond to operator commands. Each of these changes implies to re-plan, which is subject to combinatory explosion when the number of agents or the environment size grows. At the opposite, the swarm intelligence approach relies on the autonomy of agents and their indirect cooperation via environment interactions. In this paper we aim at studying how operators can interact with such a swarm of UAVs. On the one hand, this approach allows to envision indirect interactions with the system. On the other hand, such a self-organized system naturaly adapts to online changes. We also choose this approach as it is impossible for an external observer to predict the UAV trajectories. We show in this paper how an operator can, for instance, control a sub-part of the swarm without reconsideration of the whole system organization.

The reminder of the paper is organized as follows: section 2 mentions works relative to multiple UAVs control and supervision. Sections 3 and 4 present swarm algorithms to deal with patroling and pursuit tasks as well as the associated operating modes. In section 5 we present and analyze experiments performed with human operators on a real time simulation of the proposed system. Finally we conclude in Section 6 by discussing results and proposing some perspectives.

2   Approaches for Multi-UAVs Control

On the one hand, there exists a very large amount of literature in the field of multi-agent systems devoted to enable a group of artificial agents to accomplish one or several tasks in cooperation. On the other hand, most of the research on interaction between human and semi-autonomous system focus on "single instance" systems like intelligent cockpits, industrial process control system, etc. But there is few work conducted on the human control of a multi-agent system. We present here some work related to the domain of multi-UAVs control.

Cummnigs *et al.* work on human supervisory control of multiple unmanned vehicles (tomahawk tactical missiles and UAVs [4]). Their work focuses more on the human factor aspects of this task (workload, number of vehicles, *etc.*) rather than on the control aspects proper. In addition, although several vehicles are involved, they are not interacting, so one cannot speak of a multi-agent system.

A widespread approach to multi-robot control is to endow them with elementary behaviors (follow a target, go to a point, patrol, *etc.*) and to allow the operator to assign behaviors to robots on an individual or group basis. The operator supervises the system of vehicles and assign new behaviors according to the context. Though, behavior-based approaches are useful only if the number of available behaviors remains small and if the operator can anticipate their effects [18].

Control by policy can be used in conjunction with other approaches in order to allow an human operator to restrict the activity of the system through formal constraints [6]. This can be used for example for security reasons (*e.g.* avoid certain zones) or in order to help the artificial reasoning by giving partial solutions.

The *playbook* metaphor refers to a library of plans of action that are available for the operator to instantiate at various levels of detail, hence allowing various levels of autonomy for the agents. This is inspired by football teams' coaches tactics and was studied for the control of tactical ground robots [16] or heterogeneous UAVs [8].

The *Machinetta* framework [15] takes an original stance by assigning a proxy agent to each operator and each vehicle and include these proxy agents in an artificial team. Work is being conducted to apply this approach to the control of large UAV system (dozens of vehicles). But considering a human operator as "just another agent" raises important human factor issues.

3   Multi-agent Patrolling

3.1   Autonomous Patrolling

Patrolling consists in deploying several agents in order to visit at regular time intervals some defined places of an area [11]. In this way, we propose a model relying on digital phermones. They are the computationnal model of chemical substances (pheromones) dropped by ants which allows them to interact. Even if ants individual behaviors are very simple, this indirect mean of communication allows them to self-organize in order to accomplish complex tasks (pathfinding, sorting, *etc.* [1, 2, 13]).

Pheromones are bound to two distincts mechanisms. On the one hand, the evaporation process which realizes a progressive fade of the information. On the other hand, the diffusion process which propagates the information across the environment. This process also exhibits the property of building a pheromone gradient usable by the agents.

In order to realize the patrolling task, we adapt to the UAVs specificities the EVAP model [3] which only exploits the evaporation process (*cf.* algorithm 1). This algorithm is initialy defined for theoretical discrete environments (grid of cells covering the environment). EVAP relies on the environments marking: an agent drops a fixed pheromone quantity Q_{max} when it visits a cell. The evaporation process makes this value decrease so that the remaining pheromone quantity represents the elapsed time since the last visit of the cell (called *idleness* of the cell). So, on the cells set, local gradients appear giving the direction of the highest idleness cells (*i.e.* with the lowest pheromone quantity). As a consequence, the behavior of the agents is defined as a descent of the pheromone gradient. Therefore, it ensures locally the patrolling of the cells which have not been visited for the longest time (*cf.* Fig. 1).

Unlike EVAP agents, SMAART UAVs move in real coordinates according to a given azimuth and a given speed. So, we keep the cells matrix in overlay of the

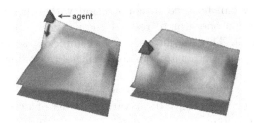

Fig. 1. 3D illustration of the EVAP algorithm (with only one agent). Pheromone field altitude represents elapsed time.

Algorithm 1. EVAP Algorithm

EVAP AGENT
A) Find a cell y in $Neighbors(x)$ such that $q(y) = min_{w \in Neighbors(x)} q(w)$
in case of multiple choices do a random choice
B) Move to cell y
C) Set $q(y) \leftarrow Q_{max}$ (drop the Max quantity of pheromone)

EVAP ENVIRONMENT
For every cell x of the environment
If $q(x) \neq 0$ then $q(x) \leftarrow \rho.q(x)$
$(\rho \in]0,1[)$

---

real environment only for the pheromones deposit and perception. Agents can now perceive the environment through a r radius disk. They are thus able to choose their destination among the cells that belong to this disk (which defines $Neighbor(x)$). The pheromone is dropped on all the cells of $Neighbor(x)$.

Moreover, at the environment level, we add to each cell its own evaporation rate ρ_x. It allows us to modify evaporation speed of some cells dynamically, therefore creating priority zones.

Figure 2 shows how SMAART UAVs patrol over the environment (the simulator was developped in java using Madkit/Turtlekit framework [12]). Agents first start an exploration phase of the environment. When all the cells has been

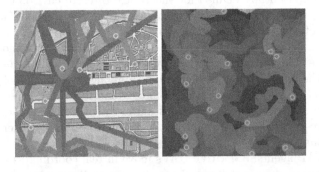

Fig. 2. Base patrolled by a set of UAVs dropping a visit pheromone: initial exploration phase (left) and stabilized phase (right). Brighter color means more pheromone.

visited once, the system tends to stabilize towards an average performance where agents are homogenously distributed inside the environment (see EVAP algorithm performances study in [3]). Moreover it was shown in [7] that the system self-organizes in (sub)optimal cycles of same length. UAVs individual behavior although remains unpredictable, which is desirable in the frame of the surveillance of a military area.

3.2   Operating Modes for Patrolling

The main task of the operator in his/her day-to-day activity is to supervise the surveillance of the airbase by the patrol of the UAVs. The objective is to make sure that every point of the airbase is regularly scanned by an UAV. This can be done homogeneously or with some emphasis on certain zones of the airbase according to the operational context. In this activity, the operator has to evaluate the state and evolution of the coverage of the airbase (potentially neglected zones, *etc.*) and act accordingly on the UAV system. He/she has several operating modes for this observation task:

- observation of the position of the UAVs across the area;
- reading on the HCI (Human–Computer Interface) of the computed average and maximum idleness values for particular zones (landing strip, hangars, tower, *etc.*);
- analyzing a color-gradient representation of the idleness grid (it can be configured so that only idleness values above a certain threshold are represented, *e.g.* show points with an idleness above 3 minutes).

According to the operational context, the operator can assign different priorities to certain zones of the airbase (landing strip, hangars, tower, *etc.*). If the operator sets a higher (lower) priority for a zone, the evaporation value is locally raised (lowered) which leads to a quicker (slower) disappearance of the pheromone and incites UAVs to visit the zone more (less) often.

The trajectories of the UAVs for patrolling can be determined according to two operating modes:

- the UAVs can follow the modified EVAP algorithm and decide their direction according to the local patrol pheromone level (this is their default behavior);
- the operator can assign a subset of the UAVs to a set of positions specified by the operator on the airbase. In this case, the UAVs are dealt over the positions and adopt their default behavior once they reach their respective position.

4   Pursuit

4.1   Autonomous Pursuit

Patrolling the environment is not sufficient to ensure the interception of intruders. This task aims at carrying on the search over a limited area in the case

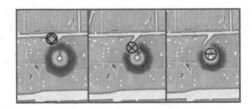

Fig. 3. Illustration of the use of the alarm pheromone by an UAV

that an intruder has been spotted and contact has been lost. When an UAV perceives an intruder, it drops a second type of pheromone (alarm pheromone) which diffuses locally. This diffusion represents a disk of probability of the intruder presence which all the UAVs may use in order to find it again (see Fig. 3). So, as soon as a UAV percieves some alarm pheromone, it climbs its gradient and consumes it. As a consequence, UAVs move towards the signal origin first to consume the isolines of the alarm pheromone field.

The propagation of the information throught the environment allows to attract other nearby UAVs towards the search zone. It aims at improving the interception probability of the intruders before they reach their objective. It is necessary to tune correctly the diffusion coefficient in order to avoid attracting too many UAVs and letting parts of environment without surveillance (the diffusion tuning is conducted empirically for each environment).

The evaporation process determines the duration of the signal. If the signal vanishes before the UAVs have consumed all the pheromone, they revert to the patrolling task without having taken advantage of the pheromone trace. On the contrary, it is useless (and even penalizing) to keep obsolete information that may mobilize some agents to find an already gone intruder. We was able to establish analytically the Q_{max} value and the evaporation rate in order to size up the alarm pheromone propagation.

We define here a second surveillance mode, joint to the UAVs, and based on the use of a sensor network (as proposed in [10]). In fact, the number of required UAVs to ensure a good patrolling rate may be important and therefore too expensive. So, sensors may be placed randomly on the environment or along the border. Each sensor is able to trigger an alert by dropping a given quantity of the same alarm pheromone. UAVs can either use their alarms or the sensor ones for the tracking task.

We do not present here a testbed for the fully autonomous system but rather focus our attention in the next section on the human–UAVs swarm interaction

4.2   Operating Modes for Pursuit

When an alarm is raised in the perimeter of the airbase, the operator switches his/her activity: surveillance/patrolling become secondary, while it becomes crucial to intercept the potential intruders that have triggered the alarm(s). An intruder is considered intercepted if the UAVs manage to detect him/her several

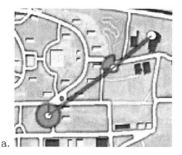 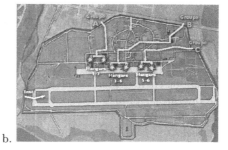

Fig. 4. a. An intrusion illustration: the larger the pie part, the more recent the contact. b. Intrusion scenario.

times in a row (otherwise it gives just another contact and an indication on the position of the intruder). The role of the operator is twofold:

- he/she has to analyze, identify, interpret and classify the contacts (alarms). A contact can be a false alarm (animal, malfunction of a sensor) but also the sign of a well-prepared multiple coordinated intrusion. In such a case, it is vital to correctly interpret the pattern of contact;
- he/she has to supervise the deployment of the UAVs that have to search and intercept intruders.

The SMAART HCI assists the operator in these roles. First, in order to avoid alarm proliferation on the HCI, alarms are aggregated into *contacts* on a temporal and spatial basis (time and distance thresholds) *i.e.* alarms that are raised almost simultaneously at the same location are considered as one contact generated by the same intruder or group of intruder. That way, if a group of three intruders are detected by an UAV and a ground sensor at the same time, only one contact is generated instead of six distinct alarms.

Second, a module in the HCI allows to organize contacts temporally to represent intrusions *i.e.* successive contacts can be linked to represent the hypothesis that they have been generated by the same intruder or group of intruder. Figure 4.a illustrates how this is represented on-screen. Several operating modes are available to the operator for this task:

- the system can classify a new contact automatically by ranking the different hypotheses (create a new intrusion for this contact or affect it to an existing one) and choosing the highest ranked. The ranking is computed by linking the likelihood of an hypothesis to the speed needed by the hypothetical intruder;
- the system gives a time delay to the operator to perform the classification manually before applying the highest ranked hypothesis;
- the operator can perform the classification manually but the system assists him/her by presenting the hypotheses ranked by likelihood.

Third, the trajectories of the UAVs for patrolling can be determined according to three operating modes:

– the UAVs can follow the modified EVAP algorithm and decide their direction according to the local patrol or alarm pheromone level (this is their default behavior);
– the operator can assign a subset of UAVs to a set of positions specified by the operator on the airbase. In this case, the UAVs are dealt over the positions and adopt their default behavior once they reach their respective position.
– the operator can also use contacts or intrusions as intermediary objects to dispatch UAVs rather than to specify positions on the map. UAVs are dealt over selected contacts or along a selected intrusion (privileging more recent contacts).

5   Experiments with Operator

5.1   Protocol

In order to evaluate the interaction between human operator and UAV swarm, that is allowed by the different operating modes of the SMAART HCI, a series of experiments with human operator were conducted on a simulator.

Subjects. The subjects are eight cadets of the French Naval Academy (École Navale de Lanvéoc-Poulmic) aged 20-23. They are anonymized and referred to as X1a, X1b, X2a, X2b, X3a, X3b, X4a, X4b according to the number of their session (1-4) and their console (a or b).

Scenario. The objective of the experiments is to evaluate the quality of the SMAART–operator interaction and the usage of the different operating modes in the context of the two main activities: surveillance and pursuit. The subjects are confronted with a three-parts fifteen minutes scenario: (1) 20' of pure surveillance without intrusion; (2) 5' consisting of a false alarm that allows operators to become familiar with pursuit operations; and finally (3) 25' consisting in a coordinated intrusion by three two-men commandos toward the aircraft hangars, as shwon in fig 4.b. The airbase is equipped with a linear sensor network along the border and 10 UAVs with one hour autonomy.

Qualitative Data. After each fifty minutes experiment, the subject is interviewed by the experimenter along a pre-defined questionnaire. This is the occasion to collect information about the subjects (knowledge of different domains like UAV systems or real-time strategy games) and their evaluation of different characteristics of the system. Answers to specific questions are coded as a number between -1 and $+1$, but all free commentaries and remarks are recorded and transcribed afterwards. These are precious in human-centered design loop, but we will not present them in this paper but rather hint at some of them in section 6.

Quantitative Data. During the operator's activity within the scenario, several types of data are logged by the system:

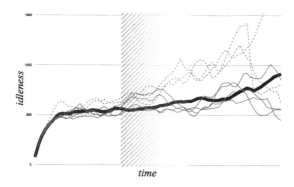

Fig. 5. Surveillance performance with and without operator: thick line was obtained without human operator (lower idleness values are better)

- IMI (Instantaneous Matrix Idleness) at each step in order to evaluate the quality of the surveillance;
- actions of the operator on the HCI;
- intruders progress: reaching waypoints and objectives, being intercepted.

In order to evaluate the performance of the operator on IMI and intruders progress, we averaged the results from 12 runs of the system without operator with the same scenario.

5.2 Surveillance Performance

Figure 5 shows the relative performance (idleness) of the system in autonomous mode (thick line) and of the operators (continuous and dotted thin lines).

Two phases appear: (1) during the first 20' there is no intrusion on the airbase and the objective is only to optimize the surveillance (minimize idleness); (2) during the second phase intruders must be intercepted, surveillance becomes secondary.

During the first phase, we observe that the operators' intervention does not improve the surveillance: on the contrary on average operators induce a -3.2% decrease in performance (individuals vary between $+6.5\%$ and -13%). One can make a striking relation with the following facts from the interviews: (1) the subjects judge the autonomous system's performance on surveillance only as "somewhat good" ($+0.5$ in a $[-1, +1]$ range); and (2) they are unanimous to affirm that human intervention is critical for the surveillance, even though on average it was measured that it had an adverse effect!

In the second phase of the scenario, the intrusions and subsequent alarms disturb the surveillance, which worsens the idleness. This phenomenon is visible with or without operator (see Fig. 5). One can note that the deterioration is much worse for three of the operators (X3a, X4a, X4b, with dotted thin lines on Fig. 5). These operators have massively dispatched the UAVs for the pursuit. Even though, the log files show us that while X3a is the best interceptor (he caught all 6 intruders), X4a and X4b are among the worst despite their intense activity (number of actions on the HCI). It seems that massive intervention by the operator is not a positive factor, neither for the surveillance nor for the pursuit of intruders.

5.3 Pursuit Performance

During the sessions with human operators, 2.1 intruders out of 6 (on average, with a mean deviation of 0.7) reached their objectives. During the 12 runs without operator (autonomous mode) 3.4 intruders out of 6 (on average, with a mean deviation of 1.1) did the same. This corresponds to a 20% increase in pursuit performance.

We observe here a very positive effect of the actions of the operator on the system. The global analysis capabilities of the human make a good combination with the local processing of the UAVs. The operator is able to act on a strategic level (affecting UAVs between the intrusions and the patrol task, anticipating the intruder's next move, *etc.*) while the UAVs perform the actual interception once they are on-site. As a side-note, only two out of the eight operators used contacts or intrusion objects to dispatch UAVs (see Sec. 4.2), the others specified positions manually (using the mouse on the map).

6 Analysis and Perspectives

This paper presents only a part of the experimental results obtained in the SMAART project. Most notably, it lacks a thorough analysis of the individual interviews. Those gave insight in the human–system interaction and spurred recommendations and ideas for future systems. Hereafter, we address two broad topics that arose during these experiments.

6.1 Interpretative Complexity for the Operator

Human operators experience difficulties to judge the performance of the pheromone-based patrol algorithm. This is clearly shown by the discrepancy between the performance measured and evaluated by the subjects themselves. However human operators are needed as they have a very positive impact on pursuit, and the algorithm can face some problems *e.g.* temporary pheromone islets can appear that could be ignored by the UAVs if the system is not supervised.

These difficulties can likely be lessened by instruction and training of the operators, but the representation gap between a human operator and a pheromone-based swarm seems to call for new interaction and representation tools for the HCI, beyond the thresholded view implemented in SMAART.

6.2 Towards an Extension of Control Modes

The human subjects were able to significantly increase interception rates by positioning UAVs across the airbase, notably on the predicted path of intruders.

But operators experienced frustration due to the default behavior of the UAVs *i.e.* upon reaching their designated position, they revert to patrol in the absence of alarm pheromone. The operators had to resort to repeating the same orders to keep UAVs on position.

It would be interesting to add the possibility of confining subsets of the UAVs to specific zones. This would allow a kind of control by policy (see Sec. 2) combined with the current modes. These zones could be manually defined by the operator, computed based on a contact and on an estimation of an intruder's speed, or by a combination of these two modes.

7   Conclusion

This paper dealt with authority sharing between human operator and an UAVs swarm for patrol and pursuit tasks. The swarm algorithm was based on the environment marking by digital pheromones (i.e. the EVAP algorithm [3]) and perceptions were augmented with a sensor network. The EVAP model was extended (i) to allow an operator to influence the swarm behavior and (ii) to simulate UAVs in continuous space. Then a number of different operating modes at various levels of autonomy were implemented as an approach to authority sharing *via* adjustable autonomy. Experiments with human operators have shown that although the human has a positive role to play in the control and supervision of the automation, the representation gap between human and swarm intelligence calls for more advanced HCI tools.

This work was conducted in the context of a Exploratory Research and Innovation contract (*Recherche Exploratoire et Innovation*: REI) of the French Defense Procurement Agency (*Délégation Générale pour l'Armement*: DGA, *Mission pour la Recherche et l'Innovation Scientifique*: MRIS).

References

1. Beckers, R., Holland, O.E., Deneubourg, J.-L.: From local actions to global tasks: stigmergy and collective robotics. In: Artificial Life IV: Proc. of the 4th Int. Workshop on the synthesis and the simulation of living systems, 3rd edn. MIT Press, Cambridge (1994)
2. Bonabeau, E., Dorigo, M., Theraulaz, G.: Swarm Intelligence: From Natural to Artificial Systems. Oxford University Press, New York (1999)
3. Chu, H., Glad, A., Simonin, O., Sempe, F., Drogoul, A., Charpillet, F.: Swarm approaches for the patrolling problem, information propagation vs. pheromone evaporation. In: ICTAI 2007 IEEE International Conference on Tools with Artificial Intelligence, pp. 442–449 (2007)
4. Cummings, M.L., Mitchell, P.J.: Operator scheduling strategies in supervisory control of multiple UAVs. Aerospace Science and Technology (2006)
5. Dixon, S., Wickens, C.: Control of multiple-UAVs: A workload analysis. In: Proceedings of the 12th International Symposium on Aviation Psychology (2003)
6. Dorneich, M.C., Whitlow, S.D., Miller, C.A., Allen, J.A.: A superior tool for airline operations. Ergonomics in Design 12(2), 18–23 (2004)

7. Glad, A., Simonin, O., Buffet, O., Charpillet, F.: Theoretical study of ant-based algorithms for multi-agent patrolling. In: Proceedings of the 18th European Conference on Artificial Intelligence ECAI, pp. 626–630 (2008)
8. Goldman, R., Miller, C., Wu, P., Funk, H., Meisner, J.: Optimizing to satisfice: Using optimization to guide users. In: Proceedings of the American Helicopter Society's International Specialists Meeting on Unmanned Aerial Vehicles, Chandler, AZ, January 18-20, 2005 (2005)
9. Johnson, C.: Inverting the control ratio: Human control of large, autonomous teams. In: Proceedings of AAMAS 2003 Workshop on Humans and Multi-Agent Systems (2003)
10. Kahn, J.M., Katz, R.H., Pister, K.S.J.: Next century challenges: Mobile networking for "smart dust". In: International Conference on Mobile Computing and Networking (MOBICOM), pp. 271–278 (1999)
11. Lauri, F., Charpillet, F.: Ant colony optimization applied to the multi-agent patrolling problem. In: IEEE Swarm Intelligence Symposium (2006)
12. Michel, F., Beurier, G., Gouaïch, A., Ferber, J.: The turtlekit platform: application to multi-level emergence. In: ABS 4 Agent-Based Simulation 4 (2003)
13. Panait, L., Luke, S.: A pheromone-based utility model for collaborative foraging. In: Proc. AAMAS 2004, pp. 36–43. ACM, New York (2004)
14. Santana, H., Ramalho, G., Bohndana, R., Corruble, V.: Multi-agent patrolling with reinforcement learning. In: The 3th international Joint Conference on autonomous Agents and Multi-Agent Systems, pp. 1122–1129 (2004)
15. Scerri, P., Sycara, K., Tambe, M.: Adjustable autonomy in the context of coordination. In: AIAA 3rd "Unmanned Unlimited" Technical Conference, Workshop and Exhibit (2004)
16. Simmons, R., Apfelbaum, D., Fox, D., Goldman, R., Haigh, K., Musliner, D., Pelican, M., Thrun, S.: Coordinated deployment of multiple heterogeneous robots. In: Conference on Intelligent Robotics and Systems, Takamatsu Japan (2000)
17. Wagner, I., Lindenbaum, M., Bruckstein, A.: Cooperative covering by ant-robots using evaporating traces. Technical report CIS-9610, Center for Intelligent Systems, Technion, Haifa (1996)
18. Wilson, M.S., Neal, M.J.: Diminishing returns of engineering effort in telerobotic systems. IEEE Transactions on Systems, Man and Cybernetics - Part A:Systems and Humans 31(5), 459–465 (2001); Special Issue on Socially Intelligent Agents - The Human in the Loop

Rescue Robot Navigation: Static Stability Estimation in Random Step Environment

Evgeni Magid, Kentaro Ozawa, Takashi Tsubouchi[1],
Eiji Koyanagi, and Tomoaki Yoshida[2]

[1] ROBOKEN - Intelligent Robot Laboratory
University of Tsukuba, Japan
{evgeni,ozw,tsubo}@roboken.esys.tsukuba.ac.jp
[2] Future Robotics Technology Center
Chiba Institute of Technology, Japan

Abstract. Rescue robotics is the application of robotics to the search and rescue domain. The goal of rescue robotics is to extend the capabilities of human rescuers while also increasing their safety. During the rescue mission the mobile robot is deployed on the site, while the human operator is monitoring the robot's activities and giving the orders from a safe place. Thus the operator can not see the robot and the environment and a decision on the robot's path selection becomes very hard. Our goal is to provide a kind of automatic "pilot system" to propose an operator a good direction or several options to traverse the environment, taking into account the robot's static and dynamic properties. In this paper we present an algorithm for estimating the posture of the robot in a specific configuration from the static equilibrium point of view. The results obtained by the simulator agree with our prior expectations and were successfully confirmed by the set of experiments with a real robot.

1 Introduction

A long standing goal of mobile robotics has been to allow robots to work in environments unreachable or too hazardous to risk human lives. Urban search and rescue is one of the most hazardous environments imaginable with victims often buried in unreachable locations. Rescue robotics is the application of robotics to the search and rescue domain. The goal of rescue robotics is to extend the capabilities of human rescuers while also increasing their safety. In particular, the inside of severe earthquake stricken buildings or underground area should be investigated in advance of manned rescue operation in order to avoid risk of suffering from secondary disaster. During the rescue mission the mobile robot is deployed on the rescue site, while the human tele-operator is monitoring the robot's activities and giving the orders from a safe place outside of the site (fig.1(a)). The system consists of two subsystems: robot control system and remote operation station. They are connected with a wireless LAN.

Currently rescue robots are operated manually by human operators. An operator can not see the robot and the environment. He/she can only use the data obtained by the robot's sensors. With that information only, having no grasp of the

S. Carpin et al. (Eds.): SIMPAR 2008, LNAI 5325, pp. 305–316, 2008.

Fig. 1. (a)Standard framework (b) Random Step Environment (RSE) example

environment, it is very difficult for the human to operate the robot. In the case of an on-site operator, which stays inside a crawler-type rescue vehicle, the human can feel the inclination of the vehicle. Using the previous experience, the operator naturally "feels on sight" the steepness of the environment. Then the decision on the traversability and path selection becomes more easy. Unfortunately, the off-site operator can not use any of those natural biological sensors and has to judge on the next move on the base of the partial available information, taking subjective and time consuming decisions. Transferring the function of taking such decisions from a human operator to a computer will decrease the burden on the operator. Our final goal is to provide a kind of automatic "pilot system" to propose an operator a good direction or several options to traverse the environment, taking into account the robot's static and dynamic properties.

To deal with this complicated problem, we must first solve a number of more simple tasks. The first step toward autonomous navigation is the ability to treat the information, provided by the robot's sensors, followed by feature extraction, environment decomposition and further simplification in order to create an internal world model. As soon as the internal world model is available, the robot should take a decision on the path within the internal model and then to apply this path in the real world scenario. Usually there exist more then just a single path, so the path search algorithm needs a good instrument to evaluate the quality of each path.

This paper deals with the quality estimation of the path. The simulator generates a discretized path between the via points proposed by a human operator, predicts the posture of the robot in the discrete points of the path and decides on the quality of each posture with regard to static equilibrium, which is a minimal necessary condition for the equilibrium. The results obtained by the simulator were confirmed with a number of experiments with a real robot in the environments identical to the simulated ones.

2   The System Framework

The National Institute of Standards and Technology (NIST) has created a set of reference test arenas for evaluating the performance of mobile autonomous robots performing urban search and rescue tasks. The arenas are intended to help accelerate the robotic research community's advancement of mobile robot capabilities [5,6]. One of the examples, simulating cluttered environment with debris is a so-called Random Step Environment(RSE) or Stepfield, which is widely used in the RoboCup Rescue competitions and rescue related research[11]. RSEs are designed to be easily reproduced, and yet behave in a similar way to real rubble and could be extended to other environments[10]. RSE consists of a final number of random steps of some minimal size simulating a heavily damaged environment of the buildings after the earthquake(fig.1(b)).

In our RSE each cell of is a wooden block of size around 100mm × 100mm and different in height, which may vary from one scene type to another. For our simulations and experiments we used the two sets of heights: {0,100,200,300}mm and {0,100,300}mm, where 0mm height corresponds to the ground level around the RSE-patch.

We assume a simple tractor-like crawler non-reconfigurable robot, corresponding to the main body of "KENAF" robot(fig.2(b)). The main body of "KENAF" consists of two large tracks with a small gap in between; the main specifications of "KENAF" without sensors, front and the back pairs of arms, used in experiments and by the simulation "pilot system", are given in table 1. Further we plan to extend our work to the full-powered "KENAF" with two pairs of service arms(fig.2(a)).As an input for our "pilot system" we use a RSE-map of the environment and a set of via points.

Table 1. Specifications of "KENAF" in basic configuration

Parameter	Measurement
Maximal inclination	
dynamic	60 deg
static	80 deg
Main body length	584 mm
Main body width	336 mm
Track width	150 mm
Height	270 mm
Weight	17.8 kg

3   Stability Analysis

Probably, the most important question which the path search algorithm should be able to answer is if a specific robot configuration is possible or not. This includes not only collisions with the obstacles of the environment case, but also the capability of the robot to keep the current configuration.The robot should be able to stay in the specific configuration without slippering or turning upside-down. In other words, a safe and reliable motion of an autonomous vehicle requires continuous satisfaction of static and dynamic constraints. A vehicle in a stable state can become unstable for several reasons [12]:

Fig. 2. (a)Full KENAF configuration without sensors (b) Main body without service arms and sensors

1. Large inertial forces arising from rapid acceleration or deceleration, or tight turns;
2. Gravitational and reaction forces due to complex terrain geometries;
3. Surface conditions;
4. Unexpected external disturbances;

Assuming conditions 1, 3 and 4 are satisfied we deal with the second case.

3.1   Static Stability

Static stability is a minimal necessary condition for the general vehicle stability. In most papers dealing with the stability and balance issues the authors deal with a legged robot walking on uneven terrain[1,4,7,8]. Such a robot can avoid falling only by applying contact forces with its feet on the ground that compensate for gravity without causing slip (so-called **static equilibrium**). Assuming robot's motion is slow enough to neglect inertia, the robot must always be able to achieve static equilibrium. While for a flat terrain some simple heuristic tests could be done for checking the stability, irregular and steep terrain requires to check that the robot is in equilibrium at every posture.

Existing approaches for a static stability are linear programming and linear projection. A basic interaction model assumes that the terrain is rigid and that contact occurs at frictional points. Under this assumption, "no slip" means that each contact force is restricted to a second-order friction cone, the shape of which is often approximated by a set of linear inequalities. Likewise, "compensate for gravity" means that the contact forces and center of mass(CM) positions satisfy linear force and moment balance equations. So for specific set of contact points, subject to the above approximation, the set of jointly feasible contact forces and CM positions is a polyhedron. The support polygon is the projection of this polyhedron onto CM-space. Using linear programming, we can search explicitly for a set of contact forces that place a particular CM position in equilibrium without computing the support polygon. Similarly, using linear projection, we can precompute the support polygon and thus determine whether it is possible to place a particular CM position in equilibrium without computing contact forces.

Gravity acts at the robot's center of mass (CM), the position of which may vary as the robot moves. While the change is significant for a legged robot, the CM position is constant for a tracked non-reconfigurable vehicle (tank or tractor) and has slight changes for a reconfigurable[1]. The properties of each contact point determine the range of contact forces possible without slip. So, for specific contact points, static equilibrium jointly constrains both the contact forces and the CM position. On flat terrain with point contacts, we have an intuitive notion of what this constraint means. Simply, the robot's CM must lie above the **support polygon** - a polygon with vertices at the contact points. The vertical prism having this polygon as cross-section is the set of all CM positions at which static equilibrium is possible. If the robot's posture places its CM over the support polygon, then we know contact forces exist that achieve equilibrium without actually having to compute them.

3.2   Modeling the Constraint of Static Equilibrium

The number of contacts with the ground and their position relative to the center of mass is well defined for wheeled vehicles or mobile mechanisms with distinct foot pads. However, in a tracked vehicle there is an uncertainty about the number of contacts and their location along the track. Theoretically, the weight of the vehicle is dispersed evenly over the entire contact area of the track with the ground. Interaction between a track and the ground can vary significantly due to surface geometry, ground texture, track tension etc. There might be only few contacts along each track, affecting the vehicle's response to driving commands and balance.

In our case, RSE results mainly in the number of contact points, rather then the entire track contact. The specific features of RSE constrains all contact points to lie on the edges and at the vertices of the environment cells and on the perimeter of the robot crawlers. If a cell is completely under the crawler, it means or that there is no contact between the crawler and this cell at all, or 3 options of the contact: a single point contact at a vertex of RSE cell, a line contact at an edge of RSE cell or a full-plane contact of the crawler with a cell in the case that the main body of the robot is parallel to the ground[2].

We define the appropriate posture of the robot, based on the literature survey and our mobility experiments. The requirements on the appropriate posture are:

1. The surface is rigid enough to provide the support to the robot;
2. The contact surface between the robot and the terrain provides the friction which is enough to prevent sliding forward, backward or aside;

---

[1] CM position relatively to local coordinate frame fixed within the robot's body.

[2] If a cell is partially under the crawler, additional options are a single point contact at one of the 4 endpoints of the crawler or a line contact at a part of crawler's perimeter.

3. The robot has contacts with the terrain with both crawlers and no contact with its main body, thus escaping the situations of getting stuck;
4. The robot has at least three contact points with the terrain;
5. The surface inclination does not result in slippery or turning upside-down;
6. The location of robot's center of mass prevents the robot from tip over due to the center of mass displacement;

While we assume the satisfaction of requirements 1 and 2, the satisfaction of other requirements is checked explicitly within our algorithm.

3.3   Coarse Posture Estimation

The output of our algorithm is an actual evaluation of the robot's posture in a specified configuration. Coarse estimation distinguishes three posture types:

Red State: Presents the posture which is impossible or statically unstable. Fig.3(a) demonstrates an impossible posture, where the robot collides with the environment. Fig. 3(b) demonstrates a case when the robot is trying to climb to an impossible steepness, which will result in turning upside down.

Green State: Stands for the statically stable posture, which satisfies all requirements stated in section (3.2). Fig.4(a) demonstrates a green state example.

Orange State: Is something between red and green states. This posture is possible, but not stable. It does not result in robot's turning upside down, but does not guarantee a single stable posture since there exist two options and the real one will depend on the previous posture, moving direction and other parameters. Fig.4(b) demonstrates a side view of an orange state with two possible postures. The orange state is very important, since it affords the robot to lose the balance on purpose, when for example the robot must traverse the barrier(fig.2(a)). Traversing the barrier includes climbing up and going down with loosing balance twice on top of the barrier.

4   The Algorithm

The location of the robot is described with (x,y) coordinates of the robot's CM in the horizontal plane of the global coordinate frame. In our model we assume that CM is located at the physical center of the robot. Orientation θ of the robot is described by the angle between the robot moving direction and X-axis of the global coordinate frame X_G. Four other parameters (z,ω,φ,ψ) describing the posture of the robot, could be derived from the triple (x,y,θ) and the RSE-map with our posture search algorithm. Angles (ω,φ,ψ) are formed by the normal to the support plane with global coordinate system axes X_G, Y_G and Z_G respectively and fixed at the robot's CM.

Given (x,y,θ) at a current configuration, we assume initial posture of the robot as an input for the contact points search algorithm. As an initial guess,

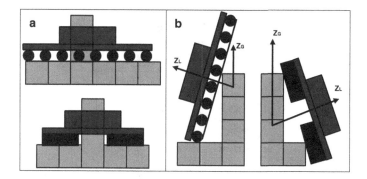

Fig. 3. Red state examples a) Pikes appear under the main body of the robot side view (up) and front/back view (down) b) The robot is trying to climb to an impossible steepness

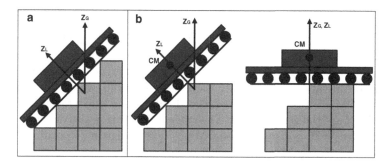

Fig. 4. Acceptable states examples a) Green state b) Orange state - two possible postures

the triple $(\omega_0,\varphi_0,\psi_0)$ is passed from the previous posture, assuming initially that there is no change in the orientation of the support plane in the case of successful posture. In the case of starting point or unbalanced previous posture $(\omega_0,\varphi_0,\psi_0) = (\frac{\pi}{2},0,\frac{\pi}{2})$. Next we build a list of all candidate points, found under the projection of the robot's posture $(x,y,\theta,\omega_0,\varphi_0,\psi_0)$ on the RSE with respect to the requirements, described in section (3.2). Four service points are added for creating a 3D convex hull, based on that list. All points, which can not be contact points are enclosed inside the convex hull. Service facets containing as a vertex at least one service point and facets, which has all three vertices within the same crawler, are dropped. In physical world they will refer to impossible postures(fig.5). Each triangle is marked with the plane equation and then the facets with the same mark are recursively joined into a single facet in the case they have two common vertices, forming a set of candidate planes. Among those candidates only one facet contains a projection of CM and thus provides the recommended triple (ω,φ,ψ) for the next iteration. Since the change in (ω,φ,ψ) may be drastic, the obtained triple provides only the direction for the next

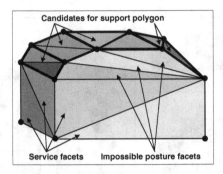

Fig. 5. Service and impossible facets are dropped. Thick black lines show the boundaries of the facets, which may serve as a support polygon.

iteration in (ω, φ, ψ). The iterations stop when the recommended values converge to the previous iteration value.

The obtained facet is checked for its final color. Orange color means that the CM's projection belongs to two distinct adjacent facets, both of which are acceptable postures. A red color facet stands for an impossible posture, while green means a success. An additional color, which was not explained previously is magenta; it appears when we can not obtain convergence during the posture search procedure and means the situation, when between two successive postures the robot's CM position changes its Z-coordinate with a leap while it has to climb a vertical slope of the environment. The magenta posture is also detected between two successive green postures, when CM position change in Z-coordinate exceeds the predefined threshold.

4.1   Qualitative Classification of Green State

Since the basic algorithm checks only static stability, the results show that almost every posture is green - i.e. statically stable. For this reason we provided a more precise qualitative classification of green posture with regard to static stability.

Throughout the history of walking robots several static and dynamic stability criteria have been defined. In [2] authors presented a comparative analysis of the existing stability criteria. Six case studies were considered and a classification of stability criteria showed that no optimum criterion for static and dynamic stability exists. Yet all of them showed to be valid and as for static stability margins only criterion NESM [3] provided the optimal measurements. We applied this criterion for estimating the quality of the green state posture, substituting the foot contact points of the walking robot with the distinct contact points of the robot's crawlers.

NESM stability measurement criterion originates from the Energy Stability Margin (ESM) proposed by Messuri in [9], where ESM is defined as the minimum potential energy required to tumble the robot around the edges of the support polygon, that is:

$$S_{ESM} = \min_{i=1}^{N} mgh_i \tag{1}$$

where i denotes the segment of the support polygon considered as rotation axis, N is the number of distinct contact points of the posture, m is the robot's weight and h_i is the variation of CM height during the tumble, coming from

$$h = R_i(1 - \cos \gamma_i) \cos \tau_i \qquad (2)$$

where R_i is the distance from the CM to the rotation axis, γ_i is the angle that R_i forms with the vertical axis and τ_i is the inclination angle of the rotation axis relative to the horizontal plane. The ESM gives a qualitative idea of the amount of impact energy supported by the vehicle. Then in [3] the authors normalized the ESM to the robot weight and propose the Normalized Energy Stability Margin, NESM , defined as:

$$S_{NESM} = \frac{S_{ESM}}{mg} = \min_{i=1}^{N} h_i \qquad (3)$$

With the help of eq.(3) we define a new state - yellow; green state turns into yellow if the S_{NESM} does not exceed a predefined minimum established in the process of experiment trials with a real robot. As an additional and less important criterion for static stability estimation we employ the square of the support polygon.

5   Simulation and Experiments

The analysis of the proposed algorithm has been performed throughout simulation, constructed in Matlab environment. The goal of the analysis was to estimate the path proposed by the human operator in the given environment with respect to the static stability and to compare with the expected results.

The original map of the RSE is presented with a 2D square grid. While the final output images are scaled to the real RSE map cell of 100mm×100mm size, the calculations are conducted within 10mm×10mm cell discretization. A number of maps were created for the experiments in the real environment and then stored for simulation use. The operator chooses the map and marks start and target points of the robot's CM or a number of via points. The simulator discretises the path, so that we obtain all locations of the CM on the borders of the 10mm×10mm cells of the path and in the middle of each cell; the discretisation of rotation is 1 degree. Then the path, estimated within the simulator as "possible" was repeated in our experiments by the operator in a set of environments identical to the simulated ones.

From our previous experiments and experience of our operator we concluded that in the cases of straight and diagonal barriers the robot should choose the course perpendicular to the barrier. In the case of the pike, if the robot will try to traverse the pike straightly, trying to race through the pike on the high speed, it may tip over or get stuck on the pike; to prevent such situation, the robot should traverse the pike-type of the terrain going a roundabout way.

Next we present a short discussion of the simulation and experimental results and their correspondence for the case of the straight barrier traversing. The

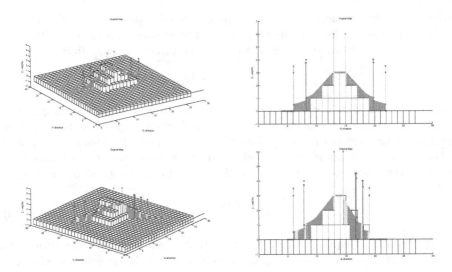

Fig. 6. Straight barrier traversing, map resolution 100×100mm, solution resolution 10×10mm. First row pictures show the straight traversing, second row - diagonal traversing.

height of the bar at each point presents the location of the robot's CM. For magenta case there appear two locations, since at that point the robot have to climb up or down a vertical patch of the RSE cell. For red case there is no real meaning of the height location, since such posture is impossible in general. Thus, for the convenience of the reader, in the red case the simulator shows the previous non-red height and for orange and magenta cases there are additional signs for paying attention. The reader should keep in mind that our final goal is to provide an assistant "pilot system" for an operator of a rescue robot which will search for the good path/paths in the given environment, display it and warn the operator about possible dangerous segments of the path. In other words, the output of the simulator, presented here, is an intermediate result, which will not be completely displayed to the operator.

Fig.6(up) presents the simulation results of the path estimation when the robot traverses the straight barrier with a course at right angle to the barrier. Fig.6(down) presents the results of traversing the straight barrier on the diagonal course. Left figures correspond to 3D view of the barrier and the path, while right figures show the XZ-view. Figures 7(a) and 7(b) show the scenes from the corresponding real robot experiments.

In both cases the robot had to loose the balance twice on the top of the barrier - once when it had to switch from climbing up the barrier to moving parallel to the ground level on the top of the barrier and second time when it started moving down the barrier. In both paths there were detected a number of magenta cases when the robot had to climb up or down a vertical patch of the RSE cell and a number of yellow cases when the static equilibrium was not satisfactory. Even though both paths did not contain any red cases with impossible postures

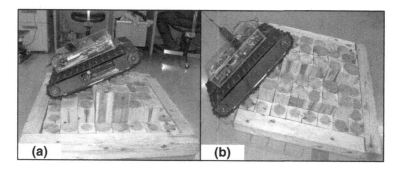

Fig. 7. Scenes from the experiments: (a) straight barrier, straight traversing (b) straight barrier, diagonal traversing

and thus were valid, the quality of the paths was significantly different. While the straight traversal path contained only a small number of yellow points (9 points, 2.45% of the path), the quantity of yellow points gradually increased as the path deviated from the perpendicular to the barrier. Finally, for the diagonal traversal the path contained a significant number of yellow points (91 points, 13.85% of the path). Thus we conclude that the straight traversal path's quality is better then of the diagonal traversal, which agree with our prior expectations.

This quality difference was well-detected during the experiments with the real robot. While to traverse the barrier in the straight manner did not take any serious effort from our operator, the diagonal traversal turned to be tricky. In the yellow points of the path the speed of the vehicle had to be reduced to minimal and required maximal concentration from the operator. In magenta points, when the Z-coordinate was changing from lower to higher level, the climbing ability was not guaranteed and strongly depended on the level change; after some critical level change the vertical climbing became impossible[3]. When the Z-coordinate was changing from higher to lower level, the robot experienced pushes and hammering with a strength depending on the level change. Such hammering may damage the vulnerable sensors and should be avoided as well.

6 Conclusions and Future Work

The final target of our research is to provide an assistant "pilot system" for an operator of a rescue robot, decreasing the burden on the human operator. As soon as a robot obtains data from the environment and creates an internal world model, a selection on the path within the internal model should be done, followed by applying this path in the real world scenario. Since usually there exist more then just a single path, the path search algorithm needs a good instrument to evaluate the quality of each path.

---

[3] Experiments with a high straight barrier set of {0,100,300}mm cell heights showed that the robot would climb it only in a full configuration using service arms (fig.2(a)).

In this paper we presented the algorithm for estimating the posture of the robot in a specific configuration from the static equilibrium point of view. The results obtained by the simulator agree with our prior expectations and were successfully confirmed by the set of experiments with a real robot. Our future work will concentrate on the path planing algorithm, which will utilize the proposed quality estimation of the posture's static equilibrium as a part of configuration evaluation function.

References

1. Bretl, T., Lall, S.: A Fast and Adaptive Test of Static Equilibrium for Legged Robots. In: ICRA 2006, pp. 1109–1116 (2006)
2. Garcia, E., Estremera, J., Gonzalez de Santos, P.: A classification of stability margins for walking robots. In: Proc. of 5th Int.Conf. on Climbing and Walking Robots and the Support Technologies for Mobile Machines, Paris, France, pp. 799–808 (2002)
3. Hirose, S., Tsukagoshi, H., Yoneda, K.: Normalized energy stability margin: generalized stability criterion for walking vehicles. In: Proc. of 1st Int. Conf. On Climbing and Walking Robots, Brussels, pp. 71–76 (1998)
4. Hong, D.W., Cipra, R.J.: Optimal contact force distribution for multi-limbed robots. Journal of mechanical design 128, 566–573 (2006)
5. Jacoff, A., Messina, E., Evans, J.: A standard test course for urban search and rescue robots. Arch. In: Proc. of the 2000 PerMIS Workshop, Gaithersburg, MD (2000)
6. Jacoff, A., Messina, E., Evans, J.: Experiences in Deploying Test Arenas for Autonomous Mobile Robots. In: Proc. of the 2001 PerMIS Workshop, in association with IEEE CCA and ISIC, Mexico City, Mexico (2001)
7. Klein, C.A., Kittivatcharapong, S.: Optimal force distribution for the legs of a walking machine with friction cone constraints. IEEE Trans. on Robotics and Automation 6(1), 73–83 (1990)
8. Mason, R., Rimon, E., Burdick, J.: Stable poses of 3-dimensional objects. In: IEEE ICRA 1997, vol. 1, pp. 391–398 (1997)
9. Messuri, D.A.: Optimization of the locomotion of a legged vehicle with respect to maneuverability. Ph. D. Thesis, The Ohio State University (1985)
10. Poppinga, J., Birk, A., Pathak, K.: Hough based Terrain Classification for Realtime Detection of Drivable Ground. Journal of Field Robotics 25, 67–88 (2008)
11. Sheh, R., Kadous, M.W., Sammut, C., Hengst, B.: Extracting Terrain Features from Range Images for Autonomous Random Stepfield Traversal. In: IEEE Int. Workshop on Safety, Security and Rescue Robotics, Rome, September 2007, pp. 1–6 (2007)
12. Shoval, S.: Stability of a Multi Tracked Robot Traveling Over Steep Slopes. In: IEEE ICRA 2004, vol. 5, pp. 4701–4706 (2004)

Performance Evaluation of Repeated Auctions
for Robust Task Execution

Maitreyi Nanjanath and Maria Gini

Department of Computer Science and Engineering, University of Minnesota,
Minneapolis, MN 55455
nanjan@cs.umn.edu, gini@cs.umn.edu

Abstract. We present empirical results of an auction-based algorithm for dynamic allocation of tasks to robots. The results have been obtained both in simulation and using real robots. A distinctive feature of our algorithm is its robustness to uncertainties and to robot malfunctions that happen during task execution, when unexpected obstacles, loss of communication, and other delays may prevent a robot from completing its allocated tasks. Therefore tasks not yet achieved are resubmitted for bids every time a task has been completed. This provides an opportunity to improve the allocation of the remaining tasks, enabling the robots to recover from failures and reducing the overall time for task completion.

1 Introduction

We study the problem of distributing tasks among a group of cooperating robots. We are interested in situations where each task can be done by a single robot, but sharing tasks with other robots will reduce the time to complete the tasks and has the potential to increase the success rate in case a robot becomes disabled. Search and retrieval tasks as well as pickup and deliveries are examples of the types of tasks we are interested in.

Robots have to physically move to reach the locations of their assigned tasks, hence the cost of accomplishing a task depends not only on the location of the task itself but also on the current location of the robot. If a robot bids for the tasks one at a time, this requires the robot to compute its costs according to the order in which tasks are to be executed, which can be different from the order in which tasks have been submitted for bids.

In this paper we present empirical results obtained both in simulation and with real robots using the algorithm originally presented in [15]. The algorithm, which is based on auctions, does not guarantee an optimal allocation, but is specially suited to dynamic environments, where execution time might deviate significantly from estimates, and where it is important to be able to adapt dynamically to changing conditions.

The algorithm is totally distributed, assuming that robots can communicate with each other. There is no central controller and no central auctioneer, each robot auctions its own tasks and clears its own auctions. This increases the robustness and scalability of the approach.

S. Carpin et al. (Eds.): SIMPAR 2008, LNAI 5325, pp. 317–327, 2008.

The auction mechanism we propose attempts to minimize the total time to complete all the tasks and, at the same time, the total path length for all the robots. It tries to minimize the total completion time by minimizing the length of the longest path, and to minimize the total path length for all the robots by assigning tasks to the nearest robot. With the simplifying assumption of constant and equal speed of travel for all the robots, the first objective. i.e. minimize the total time, is equivalent to minimizing the maximum path cost over all the robots (called miniMAX objective in [17]). The second objective, i.e. minimize the total path length, is equivalent to minimizing the sum of path costs over all the robots (called miniSUM objective in [17]).

The algorithm is simple but robust to failures during execution. If a robot finds an unexpected obstacle, or experiences any other delay, or loses communication, or is otherwise disabled, the system continues to operate.

In this paper we briefly describe the algorithm, and we report empirical results obtained both in simulation and with real robots.

2   Related Work

A recent survey [6] covers in detail the state of the art in using auctions to co-ordinate robots for accomplishing tasks such as exploration [4,11], navigation to different locations [17], or box pushing [8]. Auction-based methods for allocation of tasks are becoming popular in robotics [4,9,17] as an alternative to other allocation methods, such as centralized scheduling [3], blackboard system [7], or application-specific methods, which do not easily generalize [1] to other domains.

Combinatorial auctions have been tried as a method to allocate navigation tasks to robots [2] but are slow and do not scale well. Sequential single-item auctions [12,14,17] can instead be computed in polynomial time and produce solutions that, when the objective is to minimize the sum of the path costs for all the robots, are a constant factor away from the optimum.

We also use single item auctions, but we repeat auctions multiple times while tasks are being executed, so allowing for a better allocation in case of unexpected problems and increasing robustness in case of robot or communication failures.

Our approach aims at finding a tradeoff between computational complexity, quality of allocations, and ability to adapt. The major features of our approach are: (1) the auction can continue even when one or more robots fail to communicate. (2) robots estimate their path costs using Rapidly-exploring Random Trees [13]. RRTs are fast to compute and so are particularly appropriate for dynamic situations where computing the optimal path to achieve all the tasks allocated to a robot, as in [14], might not pay off, because tasks are likely to be reallocated. (3) to deal with cases where completion times had been estimated incorrectly or a failure occurred, tasks are reallocated during execution. The specific method we chose for reallocation is to rebid tasks each time a task has been completed. Compared to continuous auctions, our approach reduces the need for communication and the time spent in clearing auctions. while still providing the ability to react to changes in the environment or in robot functioning.

Our approach is similar to the method presented in [5] where a group of robots is given a set of tasks and robots are selectively disabled in different manners, in order to examine their performance under different conditions. Performance is measured in terms of percentage of tasks completed. Our approach differs also in that we assume a time limit for task completion. Additionally the robots we use are simpler and more prone to errors, hence the ability to change task allocation is critical.

3   Auction Algorithm

In this work we assume that each robot is given a map that shows its own location and the positions of walls and rooms in the environment. No information is given about where the other robots are located and about other moving objects present in the environment. The map is used by each robot to estimate its cost of traveling to the task locations, and to compute the path to reach them from its original location. Each robot is also given a list of all the robots in the team, that is used for task exchange. However, robots do not know all the tasks, they are aware only of the ones they have been assigned and discover the other tasks when they are auctioned. Let's call R the set of m robots $R = \{r_1, r_2, ...r_m\}$, and T the set of n tasks $T = \{t_1, t_2, ...t_n\}$, where each task is a location a robot has to visit. We partition the tasks into m disjoint subsets, such that

$$T_1 \cup T_2 \cup ... \cup T_m = T \text{ and } T_i \cap T_j = \phi \;\; \forall i \neq j \;\; 1 \leq i, j \leq m,$$

and allocate each subset to a robot. Note that a subset can be empty.

The initial task distribution might not be optimal. For instance, some robots might have no task at all assigned to them while others might have too many tasks, the tasks assigned to a robot might be spread all over the environment, or might be within easy reach of other robots, some tasks may be unreachable by some of the robots.

A robot must complete all its tasks unless it can pass its commitments to other robots. Since the robots are cooperative, they will pass their commitments only if this reduces the estimated task completion time. The ability to pass tasks to other robots is specially useful when robots become disabled since it allows the group as a whole to increase the chances of completing all the tasks. This process is accomplished via single-item reverse auctions, in which the lowest bid wins, that are run independently by each robot for its own tasks.

Each bid submitted by a robot is an estimate of the time it would take for that robot to reach that task location (assuming for simplicity a constant speed) from its current location. To generate paths efficiently, robots use Rapidly-exploring Random Trees (RRTs) [13]. Generation of RRTs is very fast, and scales well with large environments. Examples of RRTs for our experimental setup are shown in Figure 2 and Figure 3.

Auctions are parallel, i.e. many auctioneers may put up their auctions at once, but since each bidder generates bids in each auction independently of the other auctions, the effect is the same as having each auction done as a single-item auction that the bidder either wins or loses. Robots compute their bids for all

Repeat for each robot $r_i \in R$:

1. Activate r_i with a set of tasks T_i and a list of the other robots $R_{-i} = R$ - $\{r_i\}$.
2. Create an RRT using r_i's start position as root.
3. Find paths in the RRT to each task location in T_i.
4. Assign cost estimate c_j to each task $t_j \in T_i$ based on the path found.
5. Order task list T_i by ascending order of c_j.
6. Establish communication channels with the other robots and build a list of all the tasks in the system (system task list) for reference.
7. r_i does in parallel:
    (a) Auction its assigned tasks:
        i. Create a Request For Quotes (RFQ) with tasks in T_i.
        ii. Broadcast the RFQ to R_{-i} and wait for a fixed time limit for bids.
        iii. Determine the lowest bid b_{jk} among all the bids received for task t_j. The robot that submitted the winning bid is r_k.
        iv. If $b_{jk} < c_j$ then send t_j to robot r_k, else keep t_j. If r_k does not acknowledge receipt, return t_j to r_i. Mark t_j as assigned.
        v. Ask r_k to update its bids, if any, for the remaining tasks in T_i (r_k has now new tasks). If r_k does not acknowledge receipt of the message, return t_j to r_i.
        vi. Repeat from 7(a)iii until all tasks are assigned. Robots that do not bid on tasks are ignored in the auction.
    (b) Bid on RFQs received from other robots:
        i. Find a RRT path for each task t_r in the RFQ.
        ii. Create a cost estimate c_r for each t_r to which the robot found a path.
        iii. Send the list of costs to the auctioneer that sent the RFQ.
    (c) Begin execution of the first assigned task:
        i. Start executing the first task t_j by finding a path in the RRT and following it as closely as possible.
        ii. If new tasks are added as result of winning new auctions, insert them in T_i keeping it sorted in ascending order of cost, and repeat from 7(c)i.
        iii. If r_i is stuck, or does not complete its tasks within a set time limit, start a new auction to reassign r_i's tasks.
        iv. If t_j is completed successfully, notify all robots of task completion, update the system task list, and restart from 4.

until timeout or all tasks are completed.

Fig. 1. Task allocation algorithm

the parallel auctions assuming they start at their current location. This can results in bids that over- (or under-)estimate the true cost.

The algorithm that each robot follows is outlined in Figure 1. We assume the robots can communicate with each other, for the purpose of notifying potential bidders about auctioned tasks, for submitting their own bids, and for receiving notification when they won a bid. A robot can choose not to bid on a particular task, based on its distance from and accessibility to that task.

Once the auctioned tasks are assigned, the robots begin to move, attempting the nearest task first (i.e. the task with the lowest cost).

When a robot completes its first task, it starts an auction again for its remaining tasks in an attempt to improve the task allocation. If one or more robots can do one or more of its tasks at a lower cost the overall task allocation improves. This is specially useful if the robot got delayed, because this redistribution of tasks enables it to change its commitments and to adapt more rapidly.

If a robot is unable to complete a task it has committed to, it can also auction that task. Any task that cannot be completed by any of the robots, for instance because it is not accessible by any of the robots, is abandoned. We assume that there is value in accomplishing the remaining tasks even if not all of them can be completed.

The robots are given a time limit to complete the tasks, so that they do not keep trying indefinitely. When all the achievable tasks (determined by whether at least one robot was able to find a path to that task) are completed, the robots idle until the remainder of the time given to them is over.

The algorithm allows for dynamic addition of new tasks during the execution, but for simplicity, in the experiments described in Section 4, the set of tasks and of robots is known at start and does not change during the execution.

4 Experimental Setup

We evaluated our algorithm through experiments done both in simulation and with real robots. Due to space and equipment constraints, we were limited to two robots for the real robot experiments, but were able to perform different and more complex experiments in simulation. Both the simulation and the real robots used an identical setup and the same environment.

Simulation experiments were performed in the Player/Stage [10] simulator. Player/Stage has the advantage that implementation details do not change significantly when shifting from simulation to real robots, thus making comparison easier. The experiments performed in our robotics lab used two Pioneer I robots, each mounted with a laptop and equipped with wireless cards for communication with each other. Communication was done through Java Sockets, as they provide features nearest to what the simulated system had.

The main purpose of the experiments we report in this paper was to judge the differences between simulation and real robots and to evaluate the performance of different aspects of the algorithm, such as the auction time and the communication overhead during execution.

Many separate simulation experiments done earlier have been reported in [15,16]. Their purpose was to evaluate the effectiveness of our repeated auction algorithm in comparison to a single initial auction, to measure the impact of loss of communication and changes in the environment, and to measure the robustness of the algorithm. The earlier experiments used robots with 5 sonar sensors and differential drives, scattered in the hospital world environment provided by Player/Stage.

For the real robot experiments, the robots were given a map of the lab which did not include chairs but included table positions, and also a description of the

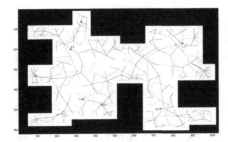

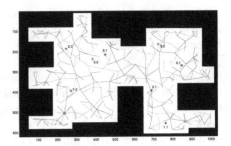

Fig. 2. Experiment I map: robots are circles and tasks are asterisks. RRTs for run 4 are shown by the lines.

Fig. 3. Experiment II map: robots are circles and tasks are asterisks. RRTs for run 3 are shown by the lines.

team, including wireless ids of the other robots. The robots started at different locations, and the tasks were scattered randomly in the lab. Tasks were initially divided equally between the robots. They were given their own approximate positions in the map.

When one robot had completed all its assigned tasks, the idle robot would wait a fixed amount of time (usually the amount of time the other robot had provided as its lowest task bid) waiting for the other robot to start a new auction, otherwise it would start a new auction on its own.

The two experimental setups are illustrated respectively in Figure 2 and Figure 3. The figures also show the RRTs formed by each robot for each experiment.

In Experiment I there were six tasks scattered randomly such that an optimal task allocation would result in an uneven distribution of the tasks between the robots. In Experiment II there were eight tasks distributed such that the majority of the tasks given to Robot 0 was closer to Robot 1 and vice versa. This was done to examine if the robots exchanged tasks successfully and completed them correctly.

We performed 5 runs of each experiment type individually in both simulation and with the real robots. Results are presented in Section 6.

5   Adaptations for Real Robots

There were some non trivial differences we had to deal with between the simulation and the real robot experiments.

1. Player 2.0 has some significant difference in the way motion is dealt with in the real robot in comparison to the simulation. The same command in simulation produced a differing range of motion from when given to the real robot. Thus, motion commands had to be reconfigured to suit the robots.
2. data for ranges of goals, sonar ranges, and collision ranges had to be modified to suit the real robots, as the form factor of the real robots was considerably different from that of the simulation.

3. In the simulations, all obstacles were detectable through sonars. In the real robot experiments however, robots occasionally could not detect obstacles, such as table legs, because the sonar sensors were too far apart and missed the obstacle. This resulted in several collisions and near collisions in the real robot experiments, and far more variability in task completion times than what we had seen in the simulations.

4. Odometry in the real robots was significantly worse than that accounted for in the simulations. However, it was better than we had feared: in most cases, unless there was a tight fit, the robots managed to complete all tasks without collision. Tasks were considered to be complete when the robots arrived within 30 cm of the task (i.e. an approximate robot-length away from the task). Additionally, collisions were tolerated in the simulations; in the real runs, robots that had collided with obstacles were given one chance to recover and then shut down, to avoid damage to the robots.

6   Results

The results for the two groups of experiments are summarized in Table 1 and Table 3. In each case, the robots completed the assigned tasks within 2 minutes, staying well within the 10 minute time limit provided.

The performance of the real robots in each experiment is shown in Figure 4 and Figure 6. The auctions took a very small percentage of the total time (as shown by the light grey bands in the figures, and summarized in Table 2 and Table 4), and caused small delays between one task and the next. This accounted for less than 1% of the time spent in performing the tasks.

The RRTs for run number 4 in Experiment I are shown in Figure 2. In this run, since task 0.0 was auctioned first, due to the way the RRT curved, the estimate for task 2.1 for Robot 0 was very high (it added the cost of going to

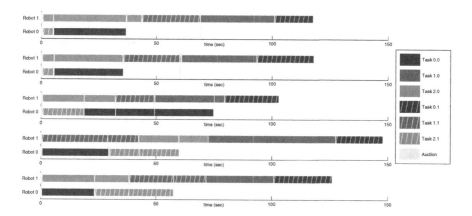

Fig. 4. Experiment I real-robot timeline. Runs 1 through 5 (top to bottom). The task IDs show the task number followed by the number of the robot the task is assigned to.

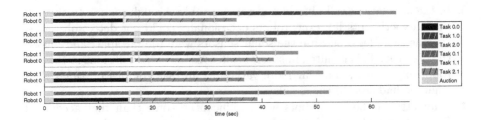

Fig. 5. Experiment I simulation timeline. Runs 1 through 5 (top to bottom).

Table 1. Task Completion Times for Experiment I

Task ID	Robot	Real Robots		Simulation	
		Avg. Comp. time	Std. Dev.	Avg. Comp. time	Std. Dev.
0.0	0	33.478	12.78	13.796	0.75
0.1	1	21.707	3.56	18.755	6.06
1.0	1	35.443	10.82	14.180	2.67
1.1	1	28.041	9.48	7.135	0.62
2.0	1	35.018	5.12	11.828	2.21
2.1	0	17.872	12.28	22.910	2.27

Table 2. Auction Times for Experiment I

Expt Num	Real Robots		Simulation	
	Mean (ms)	Std. Dev.	Mean (ms)	Std. Dev.
1	450.2	185.5	514.0	594.4
2	450.3	164.6	507.4	603.7
3	382.6	218.2	522.4	564.9
4	379.8	193.5	657.3	634.7
5	369.7	153.3	566.8	615.6

and returning from task 0.0 to its cost estimate). Robot 1 initially won this task with a lower cost estimate but Robot 0 won it back after task 0.0 was completed.

In run number 3 in Experiment II (Figure 3), Robot 0 initially got stuck trying to get to task 2.1, and then completed the remaining tasks, but was much slower than usual in completing the first two tasks, probably because of low battery.

The simulation experiments in comparison did not show robots getting stuck as often. The simulation results are shown in Figure 5 and Figure 7.

A significant difference in auction results was a long initial auction time in simulation as compared to the real robot system - this was likely caused by the fact that the computers used in the simulation shared a network and hence took longer to initially establish connections than the robots which had a dedicated network. This resulted in initial auction times being on the order of 1.6 seconds in the first auction, dropping to 0.3 seconds subsequently. While the real robots also had a longer initial auction, such a large drop was not seen in the auction times.

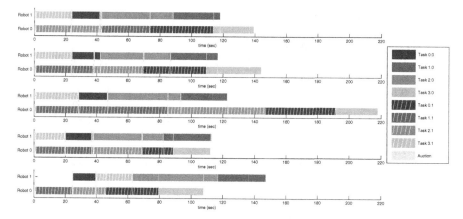

Fig. 6. Experiment II real-robot timeline. Runs 1 through 5 (top to bottom).

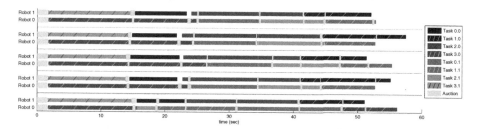

Fig. 7. Experiment II simulation timeline. Runs 1 through 5 (top to bottom).

Task completion times in the simulation were significantly shorter than the corresponding times in the real robot experiments, as shown in Table 2 and Table 4.

The comparative performance between simulation and real robot performance was as follows:

- Algorithm performance: In simulation, the task allocation found was identical to that found by the real robot experiments, thus the simulation results were acceptable. However, the impact of the time taken to perform the auctions was significantly less with the real robots compared to simulation.
- Time: the simulated robots moved faster than the real robots, despite the fact that we tried to find an equivalent velocity setting; thus, the auctions took a more significant portion of simulation time than they did in the real robot experiments. This speed difference also required modifications to the range parameter settings to get the equivalent settings for the real robots as compared to simulation.
- Robot performance: The simulation was much more optimistic about the ability of the robots to detect obstacles and recover from errors; in the real robots, there was a tendency to get stuck that was not seen as frequently in simulation.

Table 3. Task Completion Times for Experiment II

Task ID	Robot	Real Robots		Simulation	
		Avg. Comp. time	Std. Dev.	Avg. Comp. time	Std. Dev.
0.0	1	16.771	1.51	7.495	0.39
0.1	1	35.404	9.76	11.004	2.79
1.0	1	29.678	0.47	11.528	1.79
1.1	0	42.060	23.96	8.773	1.81
2.0	0	46.727	3.90	18.478	1.75
2.1	0	36.862	15.44	8.593	3.18
3.0	0	27.470	4.31	29.268	14.08
3.1	1	22.719	3.39	12.610	0.40

Table 4. Auction Times for Experiment II

Expt Num	Real Robots		Simulation	
	Mean (ms)	Std. Dev.	Mean (ms)	Std. Dev.
1	419.5	213.1	493.4	478.8
2	402.2	232.6	481.9	502.1
3	473.0	259.3	460.6	506.5
4	445.9	247.2	514.4	543.3
5	425.4	231.2	485.6	518.2

In conclusion, the simulation experiments were good indicators of real world performance, though some of the problems faced by actual robots were not perfectly mirrored in simulation.

7   Conclusions and Future Work

We have presented an algorithm based on auctions for allocation of tasks to robots. It is robust to robot failure and environmental uncertainty.

The experiments with real robots showed similar performance to the simulation experiments, even if the real robots were slower than the simulated ones and more prone to delays. In particular, the experiments showed that the task allocations found did not suffer significantly from the change in speed in the robots. As a side effect, the time for the auctions compared to the time to execute the tasks improved when experiments were done with real robots.

The robots proved adaptable, tasks were exchanged during execution, and the final task assignment was close to optimal. The comparison of performance between simulation and real robots showed that simulation results may be relied on.

Acknowledgements. Work supported in part by the National Science Foundation under grants EIA-0324864 and IIS-0414466, and by the Industry/University Cooperative Research Center for Safety, Security, and Rescue at the University of Minnesota.

References

1. Agassounon, W., Martinoli, A.: Efficiency and robustness of threshold-based distributed allocation algorithms in multi-agent systems. In: Proc. of the 1st Int'l Conf. on Autonomous Agents and Multi-Agent Systems, pp. 1090–1097 (July 2002)
2. Berhault, M., Huang, H., Keskinocak, P., Koenig, S., Elmaghraby, W., Griffin, P., Kleywegt, A.: Robot exploration with combinatorial auctions. In: Proc. IEEE/RSJ Int'l Conf. on Intelligent Robots and Systems (2003)
3. Chien, S., Barrett, A., Estlin, T., Rabideau, G.: A comparison of coordinated planning methods for cooperating rovers. In: Proc. of the Int'l Conf. on Autonomous Agents, pp. 100–101. ACM Press, New York (2000)
4. Dias, M.B., Stentz, A.: A free market architecture for distributed control of a multirobot system. In: Proc. of the Int'l Conf. on Intelligent Autonomous Systems, Venice, Italy, pp. 115–122 (July 2000)
5. Dias, M.B., Zinck, M.B., Zlot, R.M., Stentz, A.T.: Robust multirobot coordination in dynamic environments. In: Proc. Int'l Conf. on Robotics and Automation (April 2004)
6. Dias, B., Zlot, R.M., Kalra, N., Stentz, A.T.: Market-based multirobot coordination: A survey and analysis. Technical Report CMU-RI-TR-05-13, Robotics Institute, Carnegie Mellon University, Pittsburgh, PA (April 2005)
7. Engelmore, R.S., Morgan, A. (eds.): Blackboard Systems. Addison-Wesley, Reading (1988)
8. Gerkey, B.P., Matarić, M.J.: Sold!: Auction methods for multi-robot coordination. IEEE Trans. on Robotics and Automation 18(5) (October 2002)
9. Gerkey, B.P., Matarić, M.J.: Multi-robot task allocation: Analyzing the complexity and optimality of key architectures. In: Proc. Int'l Conf. on Robotics and Automation (September 2003)
10. Gerkey, B.P., Vaughan, R.T., Howard, A.: The Player/Stage project: Tools for multi-robot and distributed sensor systems. In: Proc Int'l Conf on Advanced Robotics, pp. 317–323 (June 2003)
11. Kalra, N., Ferguson, D., Stentz, A.: Hoplites: A market-based framework for planned tight coordination in multirobot teams. In: Proc. Int'l Conf. on Robotics and Automation (2005)
12. Koenig, S., Tovey, C., Lagoudakis, M., Markakis, V., Kempe, D., Keskinocak, P., Kleywegt, A., Meyerson, A., Jain, S.: The power of sequential single-item auctions for agent coordination. In: Proc. of the National Conf. on Artificial Intelligence, pp. 1625–1629 (2006)
13. Kuffner, J.J., LaValle, S.M.: RRT-connect: An efficient approach to single-query path planning. In: Proc. Int'l Conf. on Robotics and Automation, pp. 995–1001 (2000)
14. Lagoudakis, M.G., Markakis, E., Kempe, D., Keskinocak, P., Kleywegt, A., Koenig, S., Tovey, C., Meyerson, A., Jain, S.: Auction-based multi-robot routing. In: Robotics: Science and Systems, Cambridge, USA (June 2005)
15. Nanjanath, M., Gini, M.: Auctions for task allocation to robots. In: Proc. of the Int'l Conf. on Intelligent Autonomous Systems, Tokyo, Japan, pp. 550–557 (March 2006)
16. Nanjanath, M., Gini, M.: Dynamic task allocation in robots via auctions. In: Proc. Int'l Conf. on Robotics and Automation (2006)
17. Tovey, C., Lagoudakis, M., Jain, S., Koenig, S.: The generation of bidding rules for auction-based robot coordination. In: Multi-Robot Systems Workshop (March 2005)

Conceptual Framework to Maintain Multiple and Floating Relationship among Coordinate Reference Systems for Robotics

Itsuki Noda[1,2], Hiroki Shimora[1], and Hidehisa Akiyama[1]

[1] Information Technology Research Institute, AIST, Japan
{i.noda,h.shimora,hidehisa.akiyama}@aist.go.jp
[2] Department of Systems Innovation, The University of Tokyo, Japan

Abstract. A new conceptual framework of management of coordinate reference systems (CRS) for robotics is proposed. Management of CRS should be more flexible in robotics than one for traditional GIS (geographical information systems). In general, all CRS used in GIS (geographical information systems) is grounded to a certain global CRS. On the other hand, there are several cases where it is difficult to ground and fix the CRS in robotics area. Therefore, the robot need to have its own CRS, which may not be grounded to another stable CRS. In order to provide a solution to the issue, In the proposal, we propose a new framework of CRS and transformations. we handle a (user-defined) CRS as an atomic concept, which can be defined independently with other CRS. Then relations between two CRS are defined afterword. Therefore, it is possible to have a CRS that has no relation to the global CRS. Moreover, it is also possible to define multiple relation between two CRS. These flexibility enables to bridge GIS and robotic systems for real applications.

1   Introduction

In the field of geographical information systems (GIS), in general, a coordinate reference system (CRS) is considered to be well-known, well-defined and fixed. The most of CRSs used in GIS are grounded to the earth. It means that any position value belong to any CRS can be transformed another position to another CRS one-by-one uniquely. It is a reasonable assumption for traditional GIS usages [1,2,3] because origins of each CRSs can be surely maintained by a certain public organization or system like GPS (Global Positioning System).

On the other hand, in the case of application of location information services related to robotics [4], the above assumptions of the CRSs for GIS can not be hold. Because robots and their environment have a limited resource to measure locations of robots themselves and other objects. their location informations include significant errors. In addition, the fact that robots are movable objects

S. Carpin et al. (Eds.): SIMPAR 2008, LNAI 5325, pp. 328–339, 2008.

brings a further issue on the location information: Locomotion of robots is generally so inaccurate that it it difficult to determine the origin of measurements by sensors on the robots in a global CRS. And, the robots need to make a plan of move based on such ambiguous location information.

The difficulty of this issue is clearly illustrated when a robot is switched-on in an unknown room. Immediately after switching-on, the robot has no knowledge about geographical relation between the robot itself and the environment. Even in such case, the robot may need to move to perform a certain task (like escaping from danger). At the same time, the robot may continuously sense the environment and get partial location information with a certain error. This means that the robot is sensing with moving. In order to integrate the sensing data, the robot need to have its location information in each time position. This means that the robot need at least a CRS to determine its location. However, as a supposed condition of this case, the robot does not know the relation between the environment and the robot itself. This means that the robot must use a CRS that has no relation to the environment in the beginning. Of course the relation may become clear after enough sensing done. But, until then, the robot need to measure its location under the ambiguous CRS.

Such situations are quite common in robotics, especially in researches on SLAM (Simultaneous Localization and Mapping). Several works on SLAM, especially for multi-robots [5,6,7], have already been attacking the issue on ambiguous CRS. These works solve the problem by representing and operating ambiguity on the CRS in internal structures and procedures of robots.

On the other hand, because application field of robotics becomes wider and wider, robots need to share location information on such ambiguous CRS with other systems like sensor-networks. In such cases, the robots should have a way to interact GIS, which are generally used to exchange location information among various systems.

Our purpose of this article is to bridge a gap of concepts of CRS between GIS and robotics by proposing a new concepts of flexible management framework for ambiguous CRSs and transformations between them. In the rest of this article, we figure out requirements to management of CRSs for robotic application in section 2, and propose a formal framework for it in section 3. Also, we show some examples of usages of the framework in section 4.

2   Requirements to Management of Coordinate Reference Systems

2.1   Coordinate Reference System for Traditional GIS

In order to refer a spatial point in a space, we are using a *coordinate value* (CV)that consists of a tuple of scalar values like (x, y, z) or (r, ϕ, θ). Usually, the *coordinate value* denotes a relative relation from a certain origin point by using a certain tuple of axes. Generally, the pair of origin point and the tuple of axes is

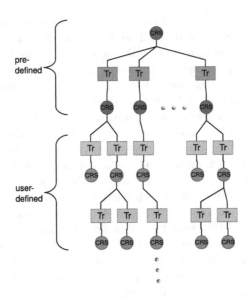

Fig. 1. Traditional Coordinate Systems used in GISs

called a *coordinate reference system* (CRS).[1] Therefore, strictly saying, a certain spatial point can be determined by a pair of the *coordinate value* and a CRS. We call the pair as a *location data* (LD).

We can have a multiple CRSs. In such case, we need information about relationships among the CRSs. In the case of GIS field like OGC's definitions (ISO/TC211 and ISO 191xx series), a new CRS can be defined by a declaration with a pair of CS and a *datum* in another existing CRS. This means that whole relations of CRSs form a tree structure like figure 1. 'Tr' in this figure stands for *transformation*, and denotes a relationship between two CRSs. By definition, a declaration of a new CRS (a CS and a *datum*) implicitly includes a transformation between the new CRS and a existing CRS.

The tree-structured set of CRS is reasonable and useful because a GIS generally handle relatively stable objects, whose location can be precisely measured by global CRS.

2.2   Requirements for Robotic Application

Compared with a case of GIS, a situation of location information processing for robotic applications is more complicated and includes more uncertainty. As described in section 1, a robot switched-on at an unknown place needs to define its

---

[1] In GIS field, *coordinate system* (CS) means a class of CRS, like Cartesian coordinate system (general (x, y, z)-style), polar coordinate system ((r, ϕ, θ)-style), geodetic coordinate system (($latitude, longitude, altitude$)-style), and so on. In other words, a CS is defined as a tuple of types of axes. A CRS can be defined by a pair of a CS and a *datum* that consists of information about an origin point and orientation of axes in the CS.

own local CRS without any relations to known CRSs in order to handle location information of the robot itself and other objects detected by its own sensors. The relations between the local CRS and other CRSs may found afterward by detecting some landmarks whose locations are known in the other CRSs.

Consider another situation in which multiple robots investigate an unknown land like Mars. In such case, no existing CRS are given. Each robot may develop its own map by surrounding on the land, and exchange the map when it meets another robot. In the exchange, the robots need to define a transformation between its own and other's local CRSs. Unlike the definition of a transformation (implied a given datum) for GIS, the relation between two CRSs is not hierarchal but mutual. Especially, if there are three or more robots ($robot_A$, $robot_B$, and $robot_C$) on the land, They may define three transformations between CRS_A–CRS_B, CRS_B–CRS_C and CRS_C–CRS_A. This means that a relation network of CRSs by the transformations forms a general network instead of a tree.

The network of CRS may cause further problem. Consider again the above case of $robot_A$, $robot_B$, $robot_C$ and CRS_A, CRS_B, CRS_C. In this case, there are two paths to transform a location data belongs CRS_A into CRS_B, that is, to apply transformation CRS_A–CRS_B, or to apply transformation CRS_A–CRS_C and transformation CRS_C–CRS_B successively. The two transformation may answer different coordinate values for CRS_B. Such situations can occurs because of sensing noise and uncertainty of robot locomotion. Even between two CRSs, there may be multiple transformations because map-matching used to define the transformation can have various criteria to measure goodness of the matching.

It is easy to implement a management mechanism of CRS and LD just inside of a robot or among tightly-coupled robots in order to satisfy the above requirements. And, many works [5,6,7] have already realized such mechanisms. But, as described in section 1, robots will be applied to widely varied services with various kinds of other information systems like sensor networks. In such case, robots needs to co-operate with GIS to share location information with these systems. Unfortunately, GIS's hierarchical structure of CRSs shown in figure 1 is not suitable to handles the cases of robotic applications discussed above. We need a new framework of CRS that is compatible to GIS's formalizations and also can cover the requirements for robotics. In the next section, we will propose such a framework CRSs that can handle the above cases flexibly.

3   Robotic Coordinate Reference System

3.1   Coordinate Systems

First of all, we define a concept of coordinate systems in the same way as the definitions of the GIS field.

A *coordinate system* (CS) is defined with the following parameters:

- the number of dimensions.
- domain, units and meaning of each dimensions.

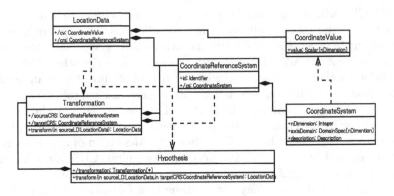

Fig. 2. UML Class Diagram of Robotic Coordinate Systems

- relationship between dimensions.
- (optional) relationship to other CSs.

Typical examples of CS will be:

- Cartesian CS (1D: (x), 2D: (x, y), 3D: (x, y, z), and so on)
- 2D polar CS: (r, ϕ, θ)
- spherical polar CS: (ρ, θ, z)
- geodetic CS: (lat, lon, alt)
- dateTime CS: (t)

3.2   Coordinate Reference Systems

A *coordinate reference system* (CRS) is defined as an instance of a CS. Multiple CRSs can be instances of a certain CS. In order to make it possible to identify a certain CRS, a CRS can have an id that is unique in the world. In other words, A CRS can be defined as follow:

$$\text{CRS} = \langle id, \text{CS} \rangle$$

It is important that no relations to other CRSs are included in the primary definition of a CRS. This makes a structure of the set of CRSs flexible and dynamic as described below.

3.3   Coordinate Value

A *coordinate value* (CV) is a tuple of scalars that indicates relative spatial relation from the origin defined by CRS. Formally, a CV can be denoted as follows:

$$\text{CV} = (scalar, scalar, ...).$$

The number of scalars in a CV is equal to the number of dimensions of the CS of a corresponding CRS. Correspondence between a CV and a CRS is specified by a location data as follows.

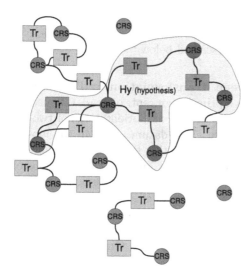

Fig. 3. Example of Networked Relationship of CRS and Tr of the Proposed Framework

3.4   Location Data

A *location data* (LD) denote a certain spatial point in a space by a pair of a CV and a CRS.

$$LD = \langle CV, CRS \rangle$$

We say "an LD belongs to a CRS (LD $\in$ CRS)" when the LD has the CRS as a part.

An LD is the atomic location information in this framework. This means that all location information should be constructed by LDs. For example, a line strings consists of a list of LDs, and, a polygon consists of a exterior linear ring and a set of inner linear rings, where each ring consists of a closed line strings.

3.5   Transformation

A *transformation* (Tr) defines a relation between two CRSs. Here, the 'relation' means how to form an LD that belongs to a target CRS and indicates the same spatial point of a given LD that belong to a source CRS. In other words, a transformation is a mapping function from a source CRS to a target CRS.

$$Tr : CRS_{source} \rightarrow CRS_{target}$$
$$LD_{target} = Tr(LD_{source})$$

where LD_{target} and LD_{source} are supposed to indicate an identical spatial point.

A Trcan be uni-directional or bi-directional transformation between two CRS.

We can define multiple Trs between a certain pair of CRSs. In this case, a source LD can be transformed to a target LD using one of them specified by a hypothesis framework described below.[2]

Relationship Between Transformation and Datum. Tr does not appear in GIS's definitions as a primary concept. Instead, GIS uses *datum*, which defines relative spatial relation of origins and orientations of two CRSs, as a primitive. We can derive a Tr from a given datum. Also, in the most case, we can derive a datum from a given Tr. But, the Tr notation is more flexible than datum notation, because Tr can represent analytic continuations of multiple mapping functions, which is difficult to handle by datum. Also, Tr concepts can be extended into symbolic representation of location information. In this case, Tr can be represented as an association function.

Another difference between Tr and datum is in relation to CRS. In GIS's concept, CRS is defined using a datum. On the other hand, in our framework, a definition of a CRS is independent from Tr. Therefore, we can have a CRS that has no relation to other CRSs, and also can have a CRS that has multiple relation to another CRS.

3.6   Hypothesis

As described above, two CRSs can have multiple Tr paths between them, where Tr path means a ordered list of Tr that connect two CRSs. In this case, we can get multiple transformed LDs in a target CRS from a source LD. And, there are no way to determine which one is the suitable target one.

In order to avoid such case, we introduce a concept of a *hypothesis* (Hy). A Hy consists of a set of Trs that forms multiple tree of CRS and Tr, each of which never intersects with each other.

$$Hy = \{Tr_i\}$$

Because the set of Trs forms trees in a network of whole CRS (as a node) and whole Tr (as a link), there are at most one path between a given pair of CRSs. Because of this feature, we can guarantee that a transformation under a Hy generate one or zero target LD from a given LD.

An Hy is a kind of *belief* of a robot or an application that utilize this framework. 'Belief' means that the robot or application suppose the set of Tr provides suitable transformation for their task. The Hy can be generated, copied, and modified freely by robots or applications. Also, they can share the same Hy to exchange location information.

---

[2] We may be possible to utilize multiple Trs to transform an LD. In order to handle such cases, we need to introduce a mechanism to represent error information into the proposed framework. If we permit to include the error information, multiple LDs calculated by multiple Trs can be considered particle set used in particle filters.

3.7   Illustrated Description of CRS Structure

Figure 2 shows an UML class diagram of the proposed framework. As described above, the main difference to the CRS definitions in GIS is dependency among these concepts. Because of this difference, we can realize a flexible manipulation and maintenance of CRSs for robotic applications. Note that we can convert the definitions of CRS in GIS to the new CRS automatically using the relation between *datum* and Tr.

Figure 3 shows an example of conceptual network of CRSs describe above. As shown in this figure, the relationship among CRSs according to Trs forms a complex network, in which, there are multiple path of Trs to reach from a CRS to another CRS. Also, some subset of CRSs may form a separated sub-network as shown in the bottom of the figure. This means LDs belong to these CRSs can be transformed into another CRS in the sub-network, but can not be transformed into other CRSs in the main network in the middle of the figure. It is also possible to have standalone CRSs that do not connect to another CRSs by Trs. This means that LDs belongs to the CRS is closed to the CRS unless a newly generated Tr connect the CRS to another CRS.

4   Example Operations of Robotic CRS

Figure 4 shows an example of CRS operations for sensing robot behaviors. In the first frame, a robot is switched-on at unknown places. The robot create its local CRS and a LD to indicate the initial position of the robot. Because the robot has no knowledge about this place, the origin of the local CRS may be the initial position. In such case, the initial LD's coordinate value consists of zero (origin) in a Cartesian CS.

In the second frame, the robot move for a while, and estimate the new position by a certain way like sensing or odometers. Then a new LD for the new position is registered using the local CRS.

In the third frame, the robot detect an box object, and register a new LD is created to represent the position of the box under the local CRS.

In the fourth frame, the robot detect a cylinder pillar, which is a well-known landmark that is registered a database of the robot. The robot register a new LD for the pillar under the local CRS. In the same time, it also retrieves a LD of the pillar under a globally well-known CRS.

After then, in the fifth frame. the robot consider the both LDs of pillar's position under the local CRS and the global CRS can be unifiable. Then, it define a new Tr that links the two CRSs. After then, locally-detected position information like the box's location can be transformed into the global CRS. In the same time, other LDs under the global CRS can be transformed to the local CRS. Therefore, the robot can continue to use the local CRS to navigate itself.

Figure 5 shows another example in the case a robot try to merge location informations that belong to different CRSs that are declared according to its movement. In the first frame of the figure, the robot detect three objects by a sensor and determine their positions (LD_1, LD_2, and LD_3) that belong to CRS_a.

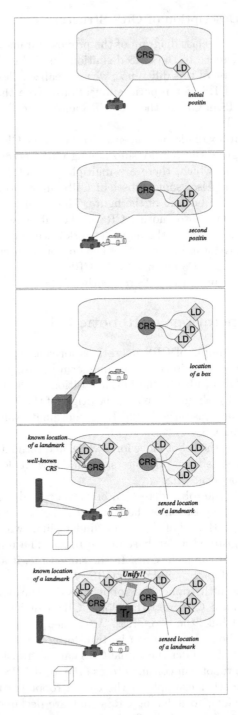

Fig. 4. Example of Operation of Robotic CRS: "A robot is switched on in unknown environment"

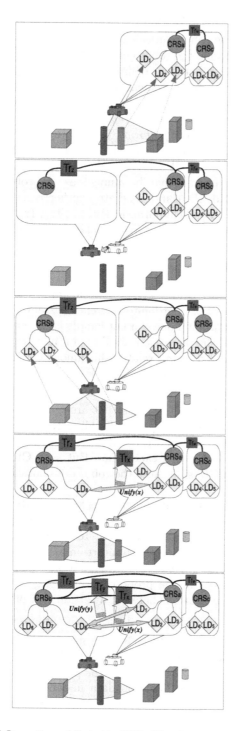

Fig. 5. Example of Operation of Robotic CRS: "A robot merges maps after move"

CRS_a already has a transformation Tr_w to CRS_c that has two location data (LD_4, LD_5), so that the robot can calculate spatial relations among $LD_1 \sim LD_5$. Then, in the second frame, the robot changes its position and declare CRS_b for the new position. The robot may define a transition Tr_z between CRS_a and CRS_b using odometer of the movement. Using Tr_z, the robot can calculate the relation between new location data (LD_6, LD_7, LD_8) detected from the new position and the previous location data $(LD_1 \sim LD_5)$ (in the third frame). On the other hand, the robot may perform SLAM using some landmarks to refine Tr_z. The fourth frame shows the case when the robot supposes that LD_8 and LD_2 indicate an identical position. Tr_x is defined to realize to unify LD_8 and LD_2. Because such unification may be ambiguous, the robot may find another unifiable pair (LD_8 and LD_1) and generate another transformation Tr_y. As a result, there are three possible hypothesis, $Hy_x = \{Tr_x, Tr_w\}$, $Hy_y = \{Tr_y, Tr_w\}$, and $Hy_z = \{Tr_z, Tr_w\}$ to determine spatial relation among $LD_1 \sim LD_8$.

5   Concluding Remark

We have investigated the requirement of robotic application and the limitation of traditional framework of coordinate reference systems (CRSs) used in GIS, and found that the traditional one can not handle issues on CRS for the robotic applications. Based on the discussion, we design a new framework of the CRSs that provides flexible and dynamic relationship among CRSs and also can include the original CRS formalization for GIS.

The proposed framework has the following flexible features for robotics:

– We can have multiple sets of CRSs that are independent with each other. When a robot is working only in a building that has multiple floors and rooms, it is useful to have a set of CRSs each of which corresponds to each floor/room and related with each other. But such CRSs need not to have relations to global CRSs, because the robot does not care about the outside of the building.
– We can have ambiguous multiple relations among CRSs. Generally, a mobile robot try to determine its location by sensing landmarks or using information from sensors in its environment. In the determination process, the robot raises several hypothesis with a certain ambiguity about its locations, because sensing data is generally incomplete and noisy. It will be easy to reflect such situations in the proposed framework, because the framework can accept multiple relations between a certain pair of two CRSs.

There also remain the following open issues in the proposed framework.

– How to represent mobile CRS: When a robot continuously moves, its local CRS should be dynamically changing through time. In order to represent such CRS, we need some extension on the proposed framework.
– How to store and retrieve location data under multiple CRSs: Generally, geospatial database implementation suppose that all location data belong to the same CRS. Therefore, it is difficult to handle location data under multiple CRS and multiple hypotheses.

References

1. OGC: OpenGIS Implementation Specification: Coordinate Transformation Services. rev.1.00 edn. OGC 01-009 (January 2001)
2. OGC: OpenGIS Location Services (OpenLS): Core Services. rev.1.1 edn. OGC 05-016 (May 2005)
3. OGC: OpenGIS Geography Markup Language (GML) Encoding Standard. rev.3.2.1 edn. OGC 07-036 (August 2007)
4. Ohno, K., Tsubouchi, T., Shigematsu, B., Maeyama, S., Yuta, S.: Outdoor navigation of a mobile robot between buildings based on dgps and odometry data fusion. In: Proc. of IEEE International Conference on Robotics and Automation (ICRA) 2003, September 2003, vol. 2, pp. 1978–1984. IEEE, Los Alamitos (2003)
5. Thrun, S.: A probabilistic online mapping algorithm for teams of mobile robots. International Journal of Robotics Research 20(5), 335–363 (2001)
6. Thrun, S., Liu, Y., Koller, D., Ng, A., Ghahramani, Z., Durrant-Whyte, H.: Simultaneous localization and mapping with sparse extended information filters. International Journal of Robotics Research 23(7-8) (2004)
7. Howard, A.: Multi-robot simultaneous localization and mapping using particle filters. The International Journal of Robotics Research 25(12), 1243–1256 (2006)

Conceptual Design of a Power Distribution Line Maintenance Robot Using a Developed CG Simulator and Experimental Robot System

Kiyoshi Tsukahara[1], Yorihiko Tanaka[1],
Yingxin He[2], Toshihisa Miyamoto[2], and Kyouichi Tatsuno[2]

[1] Chubu Electric Power Co., Inc. Japan
1, Toushinchou, Higashi-ku, 461-8680 Nagoya, Japan
[2] Department of Electrical and Electronic Engineering, Meijo University,
1-501, Shiogamaguchi, Tenpaku-ku, 468-8502 Nagoya, Japan
tatsuno@ccmfs.meijo-u.ac.jp

Abstract. We have been developing a conceptual design for a power distribution line maintenance robot system using a CG (Computer Graphics) simulator and an experimental robot system. This system is a semi-autonomous robot system which performs - tasks with task level instructions. We developed the design while during construction of the CG simulator. We believe that we demonstrate a possible solution to working up a semi-autonomous robot system.

Keywords: Robot controller, CG simulation, Power distribution line maintenance robot.

1 Introduction

Power distribution line maintenance tasks are presently performed by human workers, as shown in Fig. 1. The workers have to work in locations high above the ground and near high voltage lines. About 15 years ago, power distribution line maintenance robots [1] were developed for maintenance tasks to improve safety and efficiency. Those robot systems were remotely operated systems using master-slave manipulators or joysticks. It is difficult for the workers to manipulate master-slave arms and joysticks, however, because these apparatuses do not move as dexterously as human arms, and visual display systems do not provide wide view ranges.

To ease the operator's burden, we are investigating a semi-autonomous power distribution line maintenance robot system that performs the tasks using task-level directions, for example "Install the switch gear." We developed the CG simulator in making a conceptual design for the semi-autonomous power distribution line maintenance robot [2]. The CG for the robot mechanism is shown in Fig. 2. The software has been developed on the Windows system, and task instructions are written in Microsoft Access. We improved the description format of the task instructions and work objects for the conceptual design and changed the OS (Operating System) from Windows to Linux. The improvements made it easier to write task instructions and work objects.

S. Carpin et al. (Eds.): SIMPAR 2008, LNAI 5325, pp. 340–351, 2008.

The change in the OS enables direct application of the controller software to the experimental robot system.

Fig. 1. Power distribution line maintenance Task performed by human workers

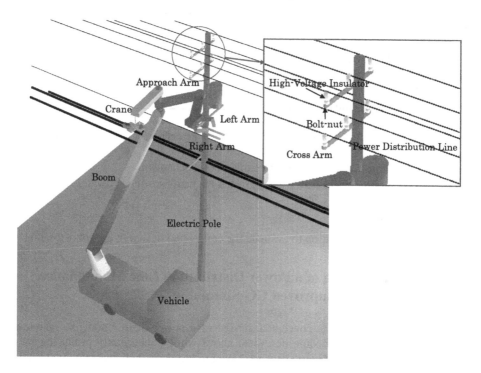

Fig. 2. CG of a power distribution line maintenance robot

In this paper, we will describe a general procedure for the robot systems, the conceptual design of the power distribution maintenance robot using the improved CG simulator, and a task performance experiment using an industrial robot.

2 General Procedure for Conceptual Design of the Robot System

We have been developing the conceptual design according to the procedure shown in Fig. 3.

1) Function design:

The functions of the robot are defined by work environments and motions for the task.
① Definition of work environments: We created 3D-models of the work environments, which comprise an electric pole, a cross arm, high-voltage insulators, electric wire and so on. Work environments define the operating range of the robot.

② Definition of robot motions for the tasks: The motions of the robot arm tip perform the tasks. We describe the motions of the robot arm tip with a task instruction sheet. The motions specify the actuators of the robot arm.

2) System design:

The next step in the design is the system design. We created a CG image of a robot mechanism and a robot controller for execution of the tasks.
① Drawing of a CG image of the robot: Work environments and robot motions specify the operating range of a robot and actuators of arm joints. We constructed 3D-models of the robot mechanism.
② Construction of the controller: We constructed the hardware and software architecture for the controllers.

3) CG Simulation:

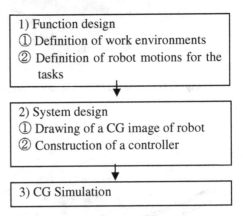

Fig. 3. Procedure for design of tbe robot

We developed a CG simulation to evaluate the conceptual design of the robot system.

3 Conceptual Design of a Power Distribution Line Maintenance Robot Using the Improved CG Simulator

We have been developing a conceptual design of a power distribution line maintenance robot using the procedure described above while concurrently producing the CG simulator. Using the CG simulator we have produced, we will evaluate the design with the robot.

3.1 Functional Design

3.1.1 Definition of Work Environments
We constructed the 3D-model of the work environments. Figure 4 shows examples of these environments. The models are constructed by superimposing the 3D frame

models of the parts in the work environments on two photographs taken from different angles (Fig.4). The 3D frame models of the parts include an electric pole, a cross arm, high-voltage insulators, a transformer, electric wires, and so on. These 3D frame models are drawn using animation software (3ds Studio Max). The data in the 3ds Studio Max file (.3ds) is saved to the "structure." The "Structure" is a word for use in C language. Figure 5 shows the structure format of the part objects. The structure includes vertices, faces, colors, position/attitude of the part object and parent/child relation. The work environment is expressed as a set of the structures named in the Work environment database.

Fig. 4. an example of 3D model of work environments

We determined the boom length by drawing the boom link in the CG of the work environments. We produced the robot database with the same structures.

The part objects are not independent in the former Work environment database. The work environment is expressed as one object. In new system, the work environment is expressed as a set of structures of the part objects. We can easily add and delete parts in the Work environment database.

```
typedefstruct{
    char ObjectName[32];                  //Object name
    vector <SVERTEX_L> svertex_L;   //Local coordinate of vertex
    vector <SVERTEX_W> svertex_W;   //Word coordinate of vertex
    vector <SFACE> sface;                 //Data of face
    int vernum;                                 //Number of vertex
    int facenum;                               //Number of face
    SCOLOR scolor;                          //Data of material
    double TMatrix_L[4][4];            //T matrix of local position
    double TMatrix_W[4][4];           //T matrix of word position
    int drawflag;                           //flag of draw
}SWORKENVIRONMENT;
```

Fig. 5. Structure format of a part object in the work environment sdatabase

3.1.2 Definition of the Robot Motions for the Tasks

The motions of the robot arm tip perform the tasks. We have to describe the motions to specify operating area, velocity, torque and so on. We describe these motions using

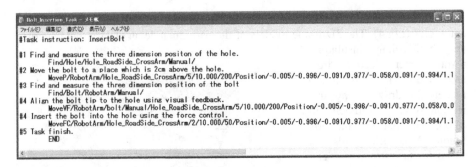

Fig. 6. Knowledge database for "bolt insertion" task

natural language and the move command (in other words, robot language). Figure 6 shows the format of the task instruction, which is a sequence of robot language commands. It is referred to as a task instruction sheet. This sheet is a text file. We can easily write these using a text editor. We named a Task knowledge database, which is a set of the task instruction sheets. Figure 6 shows a task instruction for the "Bolt insertion" task. A motion command is written within a line, and the line is composed of a command name and certain parameters. Parameters include position/attitude, velocity, coordinates for the position/attitude, and so on. Table 1 shows frequently-used move commands. The description in natural language is used in design, and the description in robot language is used in CG simulation (animation).

Table 1. List of move commands

Robot language	Content of instruction
MoveP	simple Movement
MoveJoint	rotate command
MoveFC	movement by a force control
MoveVF	movement by a visual feedback
Attach	connect command
Detach	decouple command

The former Task knowledge database is described using Microsoft Access. We do not need a complex search method in the Task knowledge database. A simple format is better for our Task knowledge database, as shown in Figure 6. We can write the task instructions for various tasks using natural language and the move commands for the power distribution line maintenance robot.

3.2 System Design

3.2.1 Drawing a CG Image of a Robot

We showed the CG image of the designed maintenance robot in Fig. 2. We constructed the CG image by modifying a bucket car [3] for human workers.

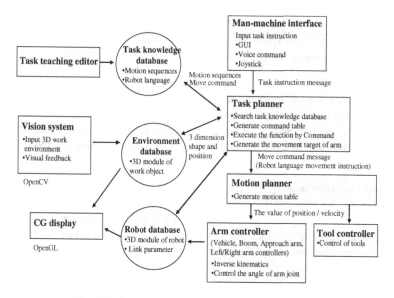

Fig. 7. Robot controller architecture for CG simulator

The vehicle is driven to an electric pole which is to be serviced, the boom is raised near a cross arm 12 meters above the ground, and the approach arm rings the left and right arms close to the work objects. The left arm and right arms are moved with the move commands for the task.

3.2.2 Construction of a Controller
1) Controller architecture

Figure 7 shows the controller architecture of the CG simulator for the power distribution line maintenance robot system. This architecture is based on an "Open Robot Controller Architecture" [4] that we have proposed. The "Open Robot Controller Architecture" has been proposed for easy constructing of a robot controller. The architecture of CG simulator is a multi-agent system composed of eight agents and three databases. The eight agents are the Man-machine interface, Task planner, Motion planner, Arm controller, Tool controller, CG display, Vision and Task teaching editor. The three databases are the Task knowledge database, Work environment database and Robot database. In this system, the instructions and requests among agents are sent with messages in character code. The robot system executes - tasks by exchanging messages among the agents. Each agent is activated by the interruption of socket communications, with agents running the function programs corresponding to the messages.

2) System operations

① Vision system
The function of the Vision system is to input the working environment. The operator takes two pictures of the working environment and superimposes a 3D frame model

of the work object on the pictures (Fig. 4). This operation permits a 3D work environment model to be constructed in the computer. This 3D work environment model is saved in the Work environment database.

② Task teaching editor

Task teaching editor is an agent for editing the Task knowledge database. The operator uses a GUI (Graphical User Interface) for the editor to select the motion commands and input the parameters. When the operator edits the position and attitude of the tip of the robot arm in a task instruction sheet, we indicate theses in the CG with a joystick.

③ Man-machine interface

The function of the Man-machine interface is to input the task instructions. The operator provides instructions for task sin the GUI by clicking a mouse or using a voice input. The man-machine interface recognizes these requests and sends the corresponding task-level instructions to the Task planner as messages in character code.

④ Task planner

After the Task planner receives the task instruction from the man-machine interface, it reads in the task instruction sheet from the Task knowledge database. The contents of a task instruction comprise the sequence of motion commands for the robot arm tip. Then the Task planner transforms the positions from the work object coordinates to the arm base coordinates by referring to the position/attitude of the robot and the work object of the environment database. Finally, the Task planner sends the motion commands to the Motion planner.

⑤ Motion planner

The Motion planner generates an S-shaped position trajectory for the arm tip from the current position to the target position. The generated time-position table is sent to the Arm controller. This table is called the Motion table.

⑥ Arm controllers

Arm controllers include the Vehicle controller, Boom controller, Approach Arm controller, and Right and Left Arm controllers. Each controller converts the positions and attitudes of the arm tip in the Motion table into joint angles by means of inverse kinematics and calculates the T-matrix (Transition matrix). The T-matrix expresses the position and attitude of each arm link. Arm controllers update the present positions and attitudes of the arm links into the Robot database.

⑦ Tool controllers

Tool controllers control tools such as grippers and nut runners used in the power distribution line maintenance tasks. The gripper grasps insulators and the nut runner removes nuts from the high-voltage insulators.

⑧ CG display

The CG display reads the data from Robot database and Work environment database and draws the shapes of the arm links and the work objects in the environments.

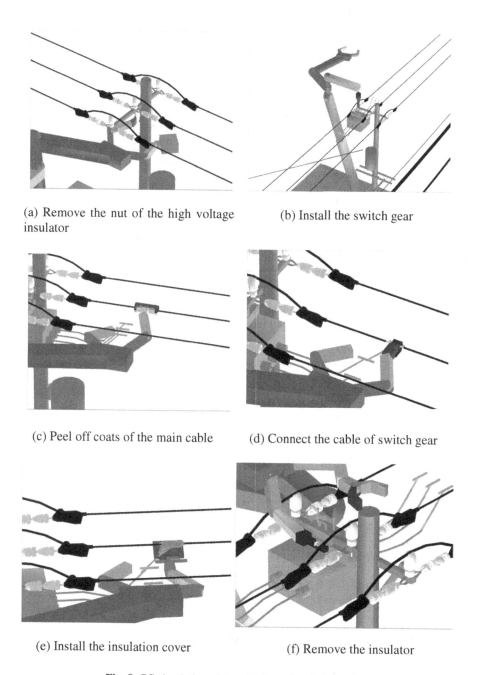

(a) Remove the nut of the high voltage insulator

(b) Install the switch gear

(c) Peel off coats of the main cable

(d) Connect the cable of switch gear

(e) Install the insulation cover

(f) Remove the insulator

Fig. 8. CG simulation of the task "install switch gear"

OpenGL (Open Graphics Library) [5] is used to draw the 3D models of the robot and the work objects in the environments. The CG display is the monitor of the robot system, helping the operator to move the arm. Using the CG display and the pictures, the operator indicates the target position of the arm.

3.3 CG Simulation

Using the CG simulator, we conducted teaching and simulation for a maintenance task, "Install a switch gear," for verification of the conceptual design and task performance evaluation of our proposed semi-autonomous power distribution line maintenance robot. The task, "Install a switch gear," is a major task. It takes about half a day (4 hours) for a human worker to perform this task.

Figure 8 shows the continuous images of the CG simulation of the real maintenance task, "Install a switch gear."

1) Remove the nut of the high voltage insulator. (Fig. 8(a))
The part-recovery box is installed on the right work arm and the nut runner tool is installed on the left work arm. The nut of the insulator is detached with a nut runner tool. The removed nut is deposited in the part-recovery box.

2) Install the switch gear. (Fig. 8(b))
The hook to hang the switch gear is installed on the crane. The switch gear is lifted up between the cables with the crane and fixed to the steel cross arm.

3) Peel off coating of the main cable. (Fig. 8(c))
The paring tool is installed on the right work arm. The coating of the cable is peeled off with this tool.

4) Connect the cable of switch gear. (Fig. 8(d))
The pressure tool for the terminal is installed on the right work arm. The cable of the switch gear is connected to the main line cable with this tool.

5) Install the insulation cover. (Fig. 8(e))
The pressure tool for the insulation cover is installed on the right work arm. The insulation cover is installed with this tool.

6) Remove the insulator. (Fig. 8(f))
The cutter tool is installed on the right work arm and the Gripper tool is installed on the left work arm. The bypass cable of the insulator is cut with the cutter tool, and the insulator is removed with the Gripper tool.

We have determined that the robot system we have designed can perform the task with task-level instructions in an ideal computer world.

4 "Bolt Insertion" Experiment Using Experimental Robot System

4.1 Outline of the Experimental Robot System

We created a CG simulator and investigated the task execution with task-level instructions. The CG simulator conducts the task in the computer environment, where there is no position error. To perform tasks in the real world, we developed an experimental system that performs the tasks in an actual physical environment. This experimental system is using the Vision system (Fig.7) to compensate for the position differences in the computerized world and the actual world. It also uses the Vision system to execute visual feedback to adjust the position of the task objects, using a force control to do contact work.

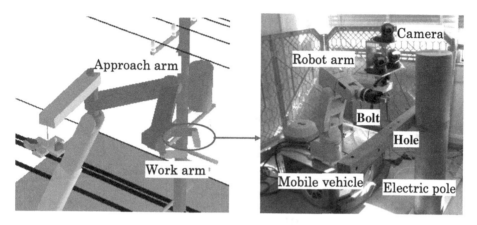

Fig. 9. Relation of CG simulator and the experimental robot

As shown in Fig. 9, the experimental robot system is composed of an industrial robot arm and a vehicle, and it simulates the approach arm and left work arm in the power distribution line maintenance robot. The vehicle is treated as the end of the approach arm, and the industrial robot arm is treated as the left work arm set at the end of the approach arm. Using the experimental robot system, we first tried to perform the basic "bolt insertion" task. This was a simulated "high-voltage insulator insertion" task performed because the high-voltage insulator is too heavy.

We can perform the experiments using almost the same agents for the CG simulator. The computer programs on Linux can execute the task in the experimental system.

4.2 Executing the Task "Bolt Insertion"

The work sequence of task "Bolt insertion" is as follows:

1) Finding the hole (Fig.10(a)).
The operator clicks the hole in the picture.The robot vision then executes measurement of the 3D position of the hole and saves it to the Environment database.

2) Moving the bolt to a position 2 cm above the hole (Fig.10(b)).
The system retrieves the hole position from the environment database, then the robot arm moves the bolt to a position 2 cm above the hole.

(a) Click the hole using the mouse and measure the position of the hole

(b) Move the bolt to a place which is 2 cm above the hole

(c) Click the bolt using the mouse and measure the position of bolt

(d) Align the bolt tip to the hole by visual feedback

(e) Insert the bolt into the hole using the force control

Fig. 10. "Bolt insertion" experiment

3) Finding the bolt (Fig.10(c)).

The operator clicks the marks on the bolt in the picture. Vision then executes measures the 3D position of the bolt and saves it to the Work Environment database.

4) Aligning the bolt tip to the hole using visual feedback (Fig.10(d)).

The system aligns the tip to the hole by visual feedback. The visual feedback method is utilized only to update and track the positions of the hole and the bolt through measurements made using the stereo cameras and to correct the trajectory to the target hole.

5) Inserting the bolt into the hole under force control (Fig.10(e)).

The arm controller measures the contact force between the bolt and the hole using a force sensor provided at the arm tip and controls the arm by means of an impedance control on which the position control is based.

Yasukawa Electric Mfg. Co., Ltd. And Kyushu Electric Power Co., Inc. are also developing a semi-autonomous robot system. They carried the task performance experiments, for example "Band attachment" [6] and "sleeve insertion" [7].

5 Conclusion

We have been developing a conceptual design of a power distribution line maintenance robot system using a CG simulator and an experimental robot system. This system is a semi-autonomous robot system which performs tasks with task level instructions. We developed the design while concurrently constructing the CG simulator. We believe that here we demonstrate a possible solution for the development of a semi-autonomous robot system for a power distribution maintenance tasks.

We will improve the functions of the vision system to provide 3D measurement of positions of the work target and robot arm tip.

References

1. Yasukawa Electric Mfg. Co., Ltd. And Kyushu Electric Power Co., Inc. Development of the Power Distribution Line Maintenance Robot. The Robotics Society of Japan 15(1), 47
2. Sawa, H., He, Y., Tatematsu, H., Kaji, Y., Tatsuno, K.: Computer Graphics Simulator for a power Distribution Line Maintenance Robot. In: IEEE/RSJ International Conference on Intelligent Robots and Systems, p. 194 (October 2006)
3. http://www.aichi-corp.co.jp/syohin/index_sagyou_01denki.html
4. Tatsuno, K.: An Example of Open Robot Controller Architecture. Micro-NanoMechatronics and Human Science (MHS 2005), pp. 35–40 (2005)
5. http://www.opengl.org
6. Mikawa, M., Yoshida, K., Tanno, M., Yoshizawa, N., Matsumoto, M.: Development of Vision - based Teleoperation System with Application to Band Attachment. Journal of the Robotics Society of Japan 18(4), 529–534 (in Japanese)
7. Murakami, S., Yano, K., Takaoka, K., Hashiguchi, Y., Irie, T., Goto, J., Wakizako, H., Hasegawa, T.: Automatic Insertion Work Based on Visual Measurement and State Transition Analysis with Contact Force Estimation. The Transactions of the Institute of Electrical Engineers of Japan. C 122(1), 124–132 (in Japanese)

Author Index

Lecture Notes in Artificial Intelligence (LNAI)